Speaking the Unpleasant

SUNY Series,
The Social Context of Education

Christine E. Sleeter, editor

Edited by
RUDOLFO CHÁVEZ CHÁVEZ
JAMES O'DONNELL

Speaking the Unpleasant

*The Politics of
(non)Engagement in the
Multicultural Education Terrain*

STATE UNIVERSITY OF NEW YORK PRESS

Published by
State University of New York Press, Albany

For information, address the State University of New York Press,
State University Plaza, Albany, NY 12246

Production design by David Ford
Marketing by Anne M. Valentine

Library of Congress Cataloging-in-Publication Data
Speaking the unpleasant : the politics of (non)engagement in the
    multicultural education terrain / edited by Rudolfo Chávez Chávez,
    James O'Donnell.
        p.   cm. — (SUNY series, the social context of education)
    Includes bibliographical references and index.
    ISBN 0-7914-3757-4 (hardcover : alk. paper). — ISBN 0-7914-3758-2
    (pbk. : alk. paper)
        1. Multicultural education—United States.   2. Multiculturalism—
    Study and teaching (Higher)—United States.   3. Educational
    anthropology—United States.   I. Chávez, Rudolfo Chávez, 1951–.
    II. O'Donnell, James, 1951–.   III. Series: SUNY series, social
    context of education.
    LC1099.3.S64   1998
    370.117—dc21   97-45208
                                                                                        CIP

10 9 8 7 6 5 4 3 2 1

To Carrie, Ruth, Carolyn, and Shelley—
four strong engaging women from whom
I continually learn

James O'Donnell

To Graciela

Rudolfo Chávez Chávez, c/s

En memoria
To Our Teacher Paulo
May 2, 1997

You have always been a teacher
In so many ways
In so many dreams
On so many days
In so many of life's streams,
Your healing waters of justice, of giving,
of humility, of hope, of patience,
Of struggle, of passion,
Of Unconditional love, of vision.
You have moistened our parched souls,
Healed our spirits, sharpened our minds,
Helped us to make ourselves whole again.
You have and always will be our teacher,
Even those who do not know you—
Have been touched.
How can we thank you teacher?
How can we ever thank you?
We will miss you.

Rudolfo Chávez Chávez
James O'Donnell

Contents

Acknowledgments

Many people have contributed to the success of this volume. In particular, we wish to acknowledge the reviewers who read the manuscript and provided invaluable critique. For her support of this project we acknowledge the contribution and invaluable assistance of the series editor, Christine Sleeter. Our colleague in the struggle, Donaldo Macedo, for his critique and contribution to this volume. We gratefully acknowledge the contributors whose courage and commitment to a multicultural education not only bring hope and possibility to the multicultural terrain but continue to stretch the envelope of praxis in that terrain. Because the book's initial beginnings were in the NAME Conference presentation in 1993, we acknowledge those participants who provided the initial "push." Professor Roberto Leví Gallegos is *con cariño* acknowledged for his consistent engagement with both of us. We sincerely and gratefully acknowledge his commitment to children big and small, his extraordinary wisdom, his sense of social justice, and his spirit. Notwithstanding, the support of our colleagues here in our terrain of engagement, the Department of Curriculum and Instruction—critical, multicultural, postmodern, a department that is in the throes of living the border by making the border the center at a border university, New Mexico State University—we humbly offer our genuine thanks. We sincerely and graciously acknowledge all our students whom we've learned so much from—respect and admiration.

And as acknowledgments go, many times, because we're in the midst of it, we forget about the richness of the collaborative effort and all the hours conversing, discussing, editing, arguing the finer points, reading and reveling in the epistemological and ontological insights committed teacher scholars have placed to keyboard from their passions of experience—crafting a vision from and for a community that is always bigger than any one of us. *Para* Rudolfo, *gracias Vato por nuestra hermandad y amistad. Para* Jim O', *gracias Vato por lo mismo en la lucha eterna.*

Christine E. Sleeter

Preface

Recently while teaching I experienced a flashback. My culturally pluralistic class of university sophomores were discussing, in small groups, an article by Cherrie Moraga (1991), in which she examines her own identity struggles as a light-skinned Chicana who is lesbian and from an economically poor family. One group was having a particularly raucus discussion. I imagined that group—consisting of about four white students, three Latinos, and one African American—to be relating Moraga's discussion to their own experiences, so I stayed with another predominantly white group that was having difficulty identifying anything to say. When I joined the noisy group, I was aghast to discover that, rather than digging into the issues she raised, they were laughing at what they viewed as her proclivity to whine about her own personal problems! Neither group was able to engage with her arguments, although their nonengagement took different forms.

I recalled my own experiences with similar discussion groups during the late 1960s and early 1970s, when the discussion would have at least attempted to probe the social context of Moraga's personal struggle. While these earlier analyses of the social context of oppression may have been predicated on simplistic and naive conceptions of racism, capitalism, and heterosexism, at least there would have been some engagement with the issues Moraga raised. In my own experience twenty-five years ago, even individuals who may not quite see the social context as problematic would at least have recognized such an analysis as being within the bounds of legitimate discussion. In so doing, they would have tried to engage with Moraga rather than dismissing her arguments as mere whining. In the 1990s, one cannot assume students will automatically try to engage in social critique.

Multicultural education can be viewed as a process of constructing engagement across boundaries of difference and power, for the purpose of constructing a social world that supports and affirms all of us. What does such engagement look like and what kind of politics supports it? Why is nonengagement so prevalent? Whose interests does nonengagement serve? What happens when educators attempt to construct engagement with issues of power, culture, and difference? What happens when they don't?

No doubt readers have experienced class discussions like the one noted above, and like many presented throughout this wonderful volume. As a teacher and a scholar, I found this volume to be highly engaging because it addresses tensions, frustrations, and bursts of success that are all inherent in my own work. Readers will find this volume extremely helpful for its naming of the problem of nonengagement, its discussions of how nonengagement manifests itself in various educational contexts and why, and the varied strategies colleagues use to attempt to engage students, preservice teachers, and inservice teachers with social issues. For example, I fully identified with Sonia Nieto's personal struggle to create community in her courses (chapter 2), and with Nancy Lesko's frustration as students reframed social structure problems into psychological characteristics (chapter 16). I resonated with Mark Dressman's "confessions" of his own gradual and circuitous process of working through complex issues involved in multicultural teaching (chapter 7). I applauded DeLeón, Medina, and Ortiz as they confronted the deficit paradigm embedded in special education (chapter 9). I was inspired by Bahruth's and Steiner's story about their own pedagogy, which transforms nonengagement into engagement (chapter 8).

For progressive educators, work in the 1990s can be highly frustrating. Many of us recall the social texture of three decades ago, in which we came of age in a *milieu* of open critique, activism, and engagement. By contrast, our university students today seem unengaged, and the contexts of their lives seem to support passivity and conservatism. This important book connects the nonengagement we see and experience with its cousin, engagement. It brings into focus a highly important truth: that nonengagement is the other side of engagement, and historically both have existed.

It is easy to oversimplify one's characterization of any historical moment. When considering the concept of engagement, it is easy to fall into the pattern of characterizing some eras with nonengagement and others with engagement. Given that characterization, one might view the 1960s as "engaged," and decades prior to and following the 1960s as "unengaged." But I find it more useful to examine any historical moment for strands of both, recognizing that activism and passivity coexist with uneasy tension, and that that very tension produces shifts in the balance between them.

The 1930s, 1940s, and 1950s are not usually remembered as activist times within the United States. Rather, common images of these decades include surviving the Great Depression, fighting a world war, and then enjoying peace and prosperity with Ozzie and Harriet. But these are very flat and selective images, leaving out a good deal of social critique and activism. During that time period, roots of poverty and exclusion had names and faces: Jim Crow legislation held in place by the Supreme Court's Plessy vs. Ferguson decision of 1898; laws at all levels of government that legalized sex discrimination; federal laws mediated to tribal people through the Bureau of Indian Affairs; and a national power-structure that was clearly white and male. Strategies for dealing with that power structure ranged from hunkering down to survive, to open agitation and organized action (Omi & Winant, 1986). Through agitation and engagement, labor unions gained momentum and voice, the African American community organized for what became a successful struggle to overturn Jim Crow, post–World War II, Mexican American/ Chicano miners led a successful mine strike, middle-class white women entered the work force and refused to leave when World War II ended, Indian tribal goverments were instituted and the very arduous process of cultural and tribal rebuilding began. While engagement in issues of difference, culture, and power did not characterize the dominant society, plenty of engagement was going on in many communities.

The late 1960s and early 1970s were vibrant with discourse of social change, and many visible, activists did not emerge from nothing, but rather from currents of work stretching back decades; and that the momentum it generated engaged thousands more young people who otherwise may have remained politically unengaged. I am one of many examples of those who became engaged because of a context of visible and vibrant activism. My own personal biography situates me in a way that might generate a critique of gender relations, but not of race and class relations (Sleeter,

1996). While many of my friends in the late 1960s and 1970s became engaged in social change issues only temporarily, some of us were so changed by our engagements that we did not return to complacency.

The 1980s and 1990s have witnessed a collapse of activist movements. Proponents of capitalism have declared that leftist alternatives do not work, following the dissolution of Soviet communism, and have driven discourse about social class and the economy to the right. Young women, although many take for granted the goals of the feminist movement of the 1960s, reject the name "feminism" and activist strategies as "unfeminine." Youth of color can no longer identify the legalized racism of Jim Crow as a target for struggle; the experience of exclusion and racism is no less powerful than it was three decades ago, but the causes are not as clear. In addition, many people today experience a tension between challenging "the system" and trying to survive in it. As economic security appears uncertain, good jobs appear scarce, the gap between rich and poor widens, and a conservative political and cultural discourse predominates in media, many young people worry mainly about their own personal futures and far less about the futures of "the other." As one of my students commented recently, if it comes to a choice between investing his energy trying to build security for his own family, versus trying to make the world better for everyone, as he sees it, there is no choice. His own personal family comes first. Their security is not assured, and he is afraid that focusing on other people's perspectives and needs will deflect him from providing for them. He does not see the two choices as connected, but rather as competing.

But at the same time, in this conservative era, activism and engagement are not dead. The balance is not what it was twenty-five years ago, but the everyday context of one's life is rife with tensions. The United States is experiencing a rapidly growing racial, ethnic, and linguistic pluralism that is exciting and increasingly visible The roots of active movements exist in our cities and in many rural areas. There has been tremendous growth in scholarship in ethnic studies, women's studies, cultural studies, and multicultural and bilingual education: at an intellectual level, the 1980s and 1990s offer a flowering of scholarly work. Even as many white teachers reject engagement with multicultural education intellectually, their own day-to-day classroom realities demand it.

There is a saying that the solution to the problem lies within the problem. Following that saying, engagement lies within the problem of nonengagement. Chávez Chávez and O'Donnell, and the many contributors to this thoughtful and insightful book, have named and opened up the problem on nonengagement. In doing so, they have opened many doors toward building constructive engagements.

Donaldo Macedo

Foreword

Tongue-Tying Multiculturalism

I concluded long ago that they found the color of my skin inhibitory.
This color seems to operate as a almost disagreeable mirror, and a
great deal of one's energy is expended in reassuring white Americans
that they do not see what they see. . . .
This is utterly futile, of course, since they do see what they see.
And what they see is an appallingly oppressive and bloody history
known all over the world. What they see is a disastrous, continuing,
present condition which menaces them, and for which they bear an
inescapable responsibility. But since in the main they seem to lack
the energy to change this condition they would not be reminded of it.
—James Baldwin

In order not to be reminded of the "appallingly oppressive and bloody history" of racism and cultural oppression, many white Americans, including some liberals, often engage in the construction of not naming it so as not to "speak the unpleasant." In their book *Speaking the Unpleasant: The Politics of (non)Engagement in the Multicultural Education Terrain*, Rudolfo Chávez Chávez, James O'-Donnell, and contributors provide an illuminating discussion that not only interrogates the dominant ideology but also bares the veiled reality in order to name it.

Speaking the Unpleasant makes it clear that "an act of nonengagement" is part and parcel of cultural reproduction designed to maintain the status quo. In truth, "an act of nonengagement" constitutes a form of engagement to the extent that those who choose not to be engaged are, in fact, complicit with the dominant ideology. It is for this reason that a discourse that names the oppressor becomes, in their view, theoretical and abstract, and wholesale euphemisms such as "disadvantaged," "disenfranchised," "educational mortality," "ethnic cleansing," remain unchallenged since they are part of the dominant social construction of images that are treated as unproblematic and clear.

The discomfort with a language that names it became abundantly clear during a meeting in a major urban university. During discussions concerning the urban mission of the university, the following became obvious: (1) most people felt uncomfortable with the urban mission report that called for direct articulation of the university mission. Many professors and some administrators felt that the language used was too prescriptive; (2) in order to entice white faculty members to endorse the plan, incentives and rewards should be created; (3) many of the white professors needed space and time to be educated about urban issues before they could embrace the urban mission. What became also clear is that in order to discuss issues of race and social injustice, one cannot use a discourse that reminds the white professors of both their inherited privileges and the responsibility they bear for the "appallingly oppressive and bloody history" of racism. Not only we are denied a scientifically acceptable discourse to discuss oppression but we are also encouraged to use a euphemistic language that obfuscates and distorts reality.

Central to this culture of euphemism is the creation of an ideologically coded language that serves, at least, two fundamental functions: on the one hand, it veils the racism that characterizes our society and, on the other hand, it insidiously perpetuates the functioning and devaluing of ethnic and racial identities. I want to argue that although the present culture of euphemism is characterized by a form of racism at the level of language, it is important to differentiate between language as racism and the experience of racism. For example, Pat Buchanan's call for the end of illegal immigration "even it means putting the National Guard all along the Southern frontier"[1] constitutes a form of racism at the level of language that has had the effect of licensing institutional discrimination whereby both documented and undocumented immigrants materially experience the loss of their dignity, the denial of human citizenship, and in many cases, outright violence as witnessed by the cruel beatings of a Mexican man and woman by the border patrol not too long ago. I also believe that even though racism at the level of language is no less insidious, it hides the institutional racism that bears on the lived experiences of those who are victimized by institutionalized racism.

Language as racism constitutes what Bourdieu refers to as "the hegemony of symbolic violence."[2] As educators, we need to fully understand the interrelationship between symbolic violence produced through language and the essence of experienced racism. While the two are not mutually exclusive, "language also constitutes and mediates the multiple experiences of identity by both historicizing it and revealing its partiality and incompleteness, its limits are realized in the material nature of experience as it names the body through the specificity of place, space, and history."[3] This is very much in line with John Fiske's notion that "there is a material experience of homelessness . . . but the boundary between the two cannot be drawn sharply. Material conditions are inescapably saturated with culture and, equally, cultural conditions are inescapably experienced as material."[4]

By deconstructing the cultural conditions that give rise to the present violent assault on undocumented immigrants, affirmative action, African Americans, and other racial and ethnic groups, I attempt to single out those ideological factors that enable even highly educated individuals to blindly embrace, for example, Rush Limbaugh's sexist and racist tirades designed to demonize and dehumanize other ethnic and cultural identities. I also discuss the psychological and political ramifications of fracturing cultural identities by pointing out that the racism and high level of xenophobia we are witnessing in our society today are not isolated acts of individuals such as Rush Limbaugh or David Duke. Rather, these individuals are representatives of an orchestrated effort by all segments of the dominant society to wage a war on the poor and on people, who, by virtue of their race, ethnicity, language, and class are reduced, at best, to half-citizens, and at worse, to a national enemy who is responsible for all the ills afflicting our society. We need to understand the cultural and historical context that gives rise to over twenty million Limbaugh ditto heads who weekly tune in to his radio and television programs. Only through a critical analysis of how racism and sexism have penetrated the deepest level of our cultural psyche can we

begin to understand those ideological factors that enable seemingly educated individuals to blindly embrace Rush Limbaugh's sexist and racist
tirades designed to demonize and dehumanize other cultural identities,
as evidenced below:[5]

1. "Now I got something for you that's true-1992, Tufts University,
   Boston. This is 24 years ago or 22 years ago. Three-year study of
   5,000 coeds, and they used a benchmark of a bra size of 34 C. They
   forward that—now wait! It's true. The larger the bra size, the smaller
   the IQ."

2. "Feminism was established so that unattractive women could have
   easier access to mainstream society."

3. "There are more American Indians alive today that there were when
   Columbus arrived or at any other time in history. Does that sound
   like a record of genocide?"

4. "Taxpaying citizens are not being given access to these welfare and
   health services that they deserve and desire. But if you're an illegal
   immigrant and cross the border, you get everything you want."

In addition to deconstructing the cultural conditions that foster
Limbaugh's sexist and racist tirades, we need also to understand those
ideological elements that inform our policy makers and those individuals who shape public opinion by supporting and rewarding Limbaugh's
unapologetic demonizing of other cultural subjects. For example, Ted
Koppel considers him "very smart. He does his homework. He is well informed." George Will considers him the "fourth branch of government"
and former Secretary of Education, William Bennett—the virtue man—
describes Limbaugh as "possibly our greatest living American."[6] What
remains incomprehensible is why highly educated individuals like Ted
Koppel, George Will, and William Bennett cannot see through Limbaugh's obvious distortions of history and falsification of reality. I posit
that the inability to perceive distinctions and falsifications of reality is
partly but not totally due to the hegemonic forces that promote an acritical education via the fragmentation of bodies of knowledge that makes
it very difficult for students to link historical events so as to gain a more
critical understanding of reality.

Against cruel and racist cultural conditions, we can begin to understand that it is not a coincidence that Patrick Buchanan reiterated in his
first presidential campaign platform that his fellow Americans should
"wage a cultural revolution in the nineties as sweeping as the political
revolution of the eighties."[7] In fact, this cultural revolution is indeed moving forward with rapid speed, from the onslaught on cultural diversity

and multicultural education to Patrick Buchanan's call to our national and patriotic sense to build a large wall to keep the "illegals" in Mexico. It is the same national and patriotic sense that allowed President Clinton not to be outdone by the extreme right forcing him to announce in his state of the union address that:

> All Americans, not only in the states most heavily affected, but in every place in this country, are rightly disturbed by the large numbers of illegal aliens entering our country. The jobs they hold might otherwise be held by citizens or legal immigrants. The public services they use impose burdens on our taxpayers. That's why our administration has moved aggressively to secure our borders more by hiring a record number of new border guards, by deporting twice as many criminal aliens as ever before, by cracking down on illegal hiring by barring welfare benefits to illegal aliens.
>
> In the budget I will present to you, we will try to do more to speed the deportation of illegal aliens who are arrested for crimes, to better identify illegal aliens in the workplace as recommended by the commission headed by former Congresswoman Barbara Jordan.[8]

An analysis of the far-right Republican attack on immigrants and cultural groups and our liberal democratic president's remarks during his state of the union address confirm what has been for decades the United States's best kept secret: that there is no critical ideological difference between the Republican and Democratic parties. Ideologically speaking, in the United States we have a one-party system of government represented by two branches with only cosmetic differences cloaked under the umbrellas of Republicans and Democrats.

If Patrick Buchanan's vicious attack on immigrants were to be interpreted in ways other than racism, how could we explain his unfortunate testament: "I think God made all people good, but if we had to take a million immigrants in—say Zulus next year or Englishmen [why not Englishwomen?]—and put them in Virginia, what group would be easier to assimilate and would cause less problems for the people of Virginia?"[9]

I believe that it is the same racist sentiment that enabled President Clinton to abandon the nomination of Lani Guinier to head the Justice Department's Civil Rights Division just because she accurately demonstrated in her writings that the working-class poor, African Americans, and members of other minority cultural groups do not have representation in the present two-party system where the white-male-dominated capitalist ideology works aggressively against the interests of these groups. Historically, it is the same racist ideology that has forced local, state, and national elected officials to join the chorus calling for an end to affirmative action policies, even though the benefactors of the real affirmative action since the birth of this country have been white males who continue to dominate all sectors of institutional and economic life in this society. For example, according to employment data on Boston Banks from the Equal Employment Opportunity Commission from 1990–1993, the industry added 4,116 jobs. While the percentage of white male officers and managers rose by 10 percent, the percentage of African American officers and managers dropped by 25 percent. While the percentage of white female clerical workers went up 10 percent, the percentage of African American clerical workers dropped 15 percent.[10]

Like multicultural education, affirmative action is also a code word that licenses a new form of racism that assuages the white working- and middle-classes' fear as they steadily lose ground to the real affirmative action programs designed to further enrich the upper class and big business:

> When the Fed raises the interest rates, it helps big business at the expense of individual home owners. When politicians resist raising the minimum wage, it helps big business send off the working poor. When politicians want liability caps, they defend Big Oil, Ma Bell and her offspring and Detroit gas guzzlers over potential victims of defective products and pollution. As the Gingrich revolution slashes school lunches for the poor, corporations get $111 billion in tax breaks, according to Labor secretary Robert Reich.[11]

The contributors to *Speaking the Unpleasant* not only provide us with the critical tools to deconstruct the shackles of oppression but they also reject the facile pedagogy of tolerance where the white teachers learn how to "handle" the "other." While even some liberals call for a pedagogy of tolerance, they remain nonengaged with the wholesale dehumanization of "illegals."

This is not entirely surprising given the liberals' paradoxical posture with respect to race issues. On the one hand, liberals progressively idealize "principles of liberty, equality, and fraternity [while insisting] upon the moral irrelevance of race. Race is irrelevant, but all is race."[12] On the other hand, some liberals accept the notion of difference and call for ways in which difference is tolerated. For example, there is a rapid growth of textbooks designed to teach racial and multicultural tolerance. What these texts do is hide the asymmetrical distribution of power and cultural capital through a form of paternalism that promises to the 'other' a dose of tolerance. In other words, since we co-exist and must find ways to get along, I tolerate you. Missing from this posture, is the ethical posture that calls for mutual respect and even racial and cultural solidarity. As Susan Mendus succinctly argues, tolerance "presupposes that its object is morally repugnant, that it really needs to be reformed, that is, altered."[13] Accordingly, racial and cultural tolerance may be viewed as a process through which the different other is permitted to be with the idea or, at least the hope, that through tolerance the intolerant features that characterize the "other" will be eliminated or repressed. Thus, David Goldberg is correct when he points out that:

> Liberals are moved to overcome the racial differences they tolerate and have been so instrumental in fabricating by diluting them, by bleaching them out through assimilation or integration. The liberal would assume away the difference in otherness, maintaining thereby the dominance of a presumed sameness, the universally imposed similarity in identity. The paradox is perpetrated: the commitment to tolerance turns only on modernity's "natural inclination" to intolerance, acceptance of otherness presupposes as it at once necessitates "delegitimization of the other."[14]

Tolerance for different racial and ethnic groups as proposed by some white liberals not only constitutes a veil behind which they hide a new form of racism, it also puts them in a very compromising racial position readily understood by the victims of racism as observed by Carol Swain, an African American professor at Princeton University: "white liberals are among the most racist people I know; they're so patronizing towards blacks."[15]

Instead of embracing a facile pedagogy of tolerance, the contributors to *Speaking the Unpleasant* courageously propose a humanizing pedagogy that rejects the temptation to "offer formula or one size fit all solutions . . . [as] appropriately characterized" by Lilia Bartolome as "methods fetish."

While rejecting a facile pedagogy of tolerance, the contributors to *Speaking the Unpleasant* call for a pedagogy of hope that is informed by tolerance, respect, and solidarity. A pedagogy that rejects the social construction of images that dehumanize the "other"; a pedagogy of hope that points out that in our construction of the "other" we become intimately tied with the "other"; a pedagogy that teaches us that by dehumanizing the "other" we become dehumanized ourselves. In short, we need a pedagogy of hope that guides us toward the critical road of truth—not myths, not lies—toward the reappropriation of our endangered dignity, toward the reclaiming of our humanity. A pedagogy of hope will point us toward a world that is more harmonious, less discriminatory, more just, less dehumanizing, and more humane. A pedagogy of hope will reject Patrick Buchanan and John Silber's policy of hatred, bigotry, and division while celebrating diversity within unity.

A pedagogy of hope will teach us that the social construction of otherness, in its ideological makeup, constitutes the raison d'être for aggression or the rationalization of aggression. In creating social and cultural separateness so as to demonize the "illegals," for example, the dominant group creates a distance from the "illegals" that engenders the dominant group's own form of ignorance that borders on stupidification. By creating rigid borders, either by building or maintaining walls between people or nations, we inevitably end up with the same reality where things lose their fluidity while generating more tensions and conflicts.[16]

The creation of otherness not only fosters more ignorance on the part of those in power but it also fails to provide the dominant group with the necessary tools to empathize with the "other" who has been demonized. The dominant group loses its humanity in their inability to feel bad in the process of discrimination against other human beings. The dominant group's ability to demonize and its inability to empathize with the other points to the inherent demon in those who dehumanize.

A pedagogy of hope will also point out to President Clinton and others that they could learn a great deal from those human beings who by virtue of their place of birth, race, and ethnicity have been reduced to nonstatus of "aliens" as evidenced by Carlos Fuentes's words of wisdom:

> We will be able to embrace the other, enlarging our human possibility. People and their cultures perish in isolation, but they are born or reborn in contact with other men and women, with men and women of another culture, another creed, another race. If we do not recognize our humanity in others, we shall not recognize it in ourselves.[17]

In order to fully embrace a humanizing pedagogy, we must go beyond technicism of classroom instruction and engage other fundamental knowledges that are seldom taught to us in our preparation as teachers. These knowledges include, according to Paulo Freire,[18]

> The courage to dare, in the full sense of the term, to speak about love without fear of being call ascientific, if not anti-scientific. It is necessary to say, scientifically and not in a pure bla-bla-bla, that we study, we learn, we teach, we know with our entire body. With feelings, with emotions, with desire, with fear, with doubts, with passion and also with critical reasoning. However, critical reasoning alone is not sufficient. It is necessary to dare so that we never dichotomize cognition from the emotional self. It is necessary to dare so we can remain teaching for a long time under conditions that we all know too well, low pay, lack of respect and resisting the risk of falling into cynicism.

It is necessary to dare to learn to dare, to say no to the bureaucratization of the mind to which we are exposed daily. It is necessary to dare to say that racism is a curable disease. It is necessary to dare to speak of difference as a value and that it is possible to find unity in diversity.

Notes

1. Rezendez, M. "Declaring 'cultural war': Buchanan opens '96 run," *Boston Globe*, March 21, 1995, p. 1.
2. Cited in Henry Giroux, *Border crossings: Cultural workers and the politics of education* (New York: Routledge, 1992), p. 20.
3. Giroux, Henry A. "Transgression of difference," Series introduction to culture and difference. *Critical perspectives on bicultural experiences* (Granby, Mass.: Bergin & Garvey). In press.
4. Fiske, John, *Power plays, power works* (London: Verso, 1994), p. 13.
5. Randall, S. Naureckus, J., & Cohen, J., *The way things ought to be: Rush Limbaugh's reign of error* (New York: New York Press, 1995), pp. 47–54.
6. Ibid., p. 10.
7. Cited in Henry Giroux, *Border crossings: Cultural workers and the politics of education* (New York: Routledge, 1992), p. 230.
8. Clinton, W., The state of the union, "Clinton speech envisions local empowerment," For the record. *Congressional Quarterly*, January 28, 1995, p. 303.
9. Pertman, Adam, "Buchanan announces presidential candidacy." *The Boston Globe*, December 15, 1991, p. 13.
10. Jackson, Derrick, *The Boston Globe*, April 22, 1995, p. 13.
11. The Boston Globe, April 22, 1995, p. 13.
12. Goldberg, David T., *Racist culture* (Oxford, U.K., and & Cambridge, Mass.: Blackwell, 1993), p. 6.
13. Ibid., p. 7.
14. Ibid., p. 7.
15. Swain, Carol, *New York Times*, September 19, 1993, p. 158.
16. Rodrigues, Vitor J., *A Nova Ondem Estupidologica*. Lisboa: Livros Horizonte, LDA. 1995.
17. Fuentes, Carlos, "The mirror of the other," *The Nation*, March 30, 1992, p. 411.
18. Freire, Paulo, *Teachers as cultural workers: letters to those who dare teach*. Boulder, Colo.: Westview, 1997.

Rudolfo Chávez Chávez
James O'Donnell

Introduction

Speaking the Unpleasant

S ome years ago at a conference on multicultural education, we presented a workshop on strategies for challenging students' nonengagement with multicultural education issues. Our workshop was scheduled for the final day and near the final hour of the conference. We anticipated that only ourselves and a few kind friends would attend. Instead, a group of more than twenty attended. We discussed with teachers and administrators from the high school, community college, and university levels their frustrations and concerns about issues related to students and staff who remain unfazed by multicultural education issues. These teachers and administrators were European American, African American, Latinas and Latinos, male and female working in private and public institutions. From each of the teachers, frustrations were expressed related to the work that they planned for their students

1

and how these students performed their work but attitudinally re-mained uncommitted to engaging multicultural education issues and practices. What the workshop participants were seeking were ways to challenge their students and to push, cajole, or entice their students to begin to take steps toward acts of resistance to the status quo. An over-shadowing concern that many of the participants voiced was the real-ization that these students would be out into classrooms teaching our future learners. In many ways this book developed from this encounter with these teachers. Some of the stories shared herein are from some of these teachers.

The purpose of this book is to address the clashing, contradictory, and always controversial ideological and ontological postures that em-anate when multicultural education issues are the sum and substance for engagement by learners in various educational settings. Engagement and nonengagement are processes where one presumably ends and the other speculatively begins from the other is indeterminable as noted by the various authors in this volume. We argue that they are so bound to one another that both can be going on simultaneously—thus, the word *nonengagement*. Classroom nonengagement embraces a process by stu-dents and teachers that can simultaneously be unconsciously conscious and/or consciously unconscious when entangled within the temporal and spatial dynamics of the pedagogical process. The term "*non*engage-ment" suggests a single/dual/multiple process. The word's simple iden-tity that presupposes the ontogenetic desire to engage or not engage with the Other within a multicultural education terrain is apparent. A simple duality that is linear and deterministic in construction. On the other hand, by its very nature, "non*engagement*" also depends on the si-multaneous affirmation to an indeterminate complexity that embraces a liberatory hermeneutics—critical, dialogic, and multiperspectival. Hence, engagement organically manifests within and between students and teachers within the temporal and spatial context; simultaneously one can reject, challenge, and/or confront the existent forms of socially constructed oppression and inequities that can be found and trans-formed within locations of contestation—engagement; or temporal and spatial contexts can be denied and/or considered neutral and nonis-sues—nonengagement.

The process of engagement refers to those who do not accept the status quo and begin to unconsciously conscious and/or consciously unconscious transform themselves to understand the status quo and place themselves into a location for liberatory action based on a praxis of social justice. The process of nonengagement refers to those who ac-cept the status quo and reject and resist challenges to the status quo. Again this process can be unconsciously conscious and/or consciously unconscious. Most often, students and others within society either actively accept the dominant ideology that oppresses or they passively accept (Jackson & Hardiman, 1986) therefore, are unconsciously conscious of the systemic acts of oppression. We would argue that students have moved beyond a passive state of acceptance to this active state of acceptance. Students are active in that they need to be conscious of arguments and perspectives that permit them to maintain the hegemony that they feel has been challenged—consciously unconscious. We also understand that the complexity of learning cannot be underscored enough nor can the clenching grip that tacit knowledge coupled with historical knowledge play into everyday learning be fully understood. Attitudinally and otherwise, students and teachers consciously or unconsciously map or remap their ideological and ontological postures about and for a multicultural education.

Previously, we used the term *resistance* to characterize those students who "resisted" hegemonic determinism. But the word has a more instructional, informative, social, and political connotation. For example, in the political and educational writings of bell hooks (1989), Henry Giroux (1983) and several racial identity theorists (e.g., Jackson, 1976; Jackson & Hardiman, 1986) the term *resistance* describes actions taken against the status quo. Thus, resistance refers to a conscious or unconscious act that works in opposition to the dominant ideology of prescribed oppressive behavior. In addition, this act of resistance is transformative in that it allows for self or social emancipation (Giroux, 1983).

The research literature is filled with studies of how students reject and deny the existence of a systemic oppressive state. Whether we are speaking about undergraduate and graduate teacher education students (Ross & Smith, 1992; Grant & Secada, 1990; Roman, 1993); experienced teachers (Sleeter, 1993) or students in arts and science (Davis, 1992; Tatum, 1992), rejection, denial, or nonengagement manifests itself among students. Our research (Chávez, O'Donnell, & Gallegos, 1995) suggests that these students are not just European American but also African American, Mexican American, Native American, and Asian American. Furthermore, they are not only members of generation X in their early twenties but students from the sixties and the fifties who live in the United States and abroad. Moreover, these students have had varied life experiences and will soon embark into our schools as elementary and secondary teachers.

The authors of this book have been asked to describe their encounters with such students, to describe their praxis and how these students manifest nonengagement. In addition, the authors detail how they challenge and engage their students and, as good teaching entails reflection, how they have redefined their praxis to work with these students—

engagement. In the pages that follow we will encounter their praxis, their students, and how each author theorizes about nonengagement and engagement.

This book creates a conversation with its readers around the question, How will we construct a liberatory practice in the multicultural terrain that is proactive, participatory, and coupled with a practice of everyday courage that embraces the necessity and importance of multicultural education within the teacher education enterprise? The authors in the chapters to follow capture the reader with their ability to tell a story by using narrative, primary and secondary research, personal experience, and insights that theory build and continue to map, remap, discover, and broaden the multicultural education terrain. Each chapter is an original piece of scholarship with sound interpretation and synthesis of relevant material that places knowledge in an historical context of ideas and the impact of social and political forces on the material in discussion.

In essence, this book provides opportunities for its readers to construct ontological, axiological, and epistemological constructs that are multicultural in resonance. The array of narratives by the authors construct a montage (see chapter 1) that is embroiled in the deconstruction and reconstruction of how our everyday ontologies are interpreted. The various authors brilliantly show the dimness of what occurs when nonengagement by students becomes the practice. Furthermore, the research the authors put forth illustrates the imperative for engaging students and divulges the subsequent costs of nonengagement that too often results. Finally, the authors offer to the reader how engagement is crucial in the enterprise of teaching and learning. The authors discuss how they address in their praxis nonengagement and explore the myriad ways that the crisis of nonengagement be resolved. Conversely, engagement is crucial in the enterprise of teaching and learning within a multicultural context. "Engagement" as praxis is admitting to the serious crises now apparent in the teaching and learning enterprise. A crises that bell hooks (1994) has soberly described as one where "students often do not want to learn and teachers do not want to teach. More than ever before in the recent history of this diverse nation, educators are compelled to confront the biases that have shaped teaching practices in our society and to create new ways of knowing, different strategies for the sharing of knowledge" (p. 12).

Do not expect to find formulas or one-size-fits-all solutions (de la luz Reyes, 1992) or what has so appropriately been characterized as the "methods fetish" (Bartolomé, 1994) that are status quo to the hegemonic skill-based discourse still prevalent throughout schooling institutions today. This book's imperative is to create a multicultural education dialog for personal and institutional reflection for and about the teacher education enterprise that will continuously probe into pre- and inservice students' tacit knowledge and mystified historicity that ideologically shapes understandings of culture, ethnicity, race, class, gender, and sexual orientation, as well as other socially constructed and hegemonically ridden realities like oppression and the "isms." Implicit throughout this book is the constant realization that entrenched perspectives of everyday experiences are held by students and teachers alike to greater or lesser extents that mirror internalized ideologies that justify the racial, cultural, and/or economic status quo and the devaluing of ethnic, cultural, and linguistic diversity, to name a few, as part of their lived experience in the everyday (King, 1991; Rodríguez, 1993; Sleeter, 1993; Tatum, 1992; West, 1994). The authors herein show undaunting commitment to teaching and learning in the multicultural education terrain. They illustrate by story, by example, and by sound scholarship the intensity within the teacher education enterprise and the political risks involved in yearning to engage learners in what must be.

1

Rudolfo Chávez Chávez

Engaging the Multicultural Education Terrain

A Holographic Montage for Engagers

Multicultural education's history has been tumultuous, dynamic, polarized, embracing of diversity, controversial, explosive, nurturing and, vehemently, nonneutral. The authentic teacher in the multicultural education (MCE) terrain is a hero, a risk taker, a poet of pedagogical nuance who is willing to traverse the topography of the MCE terrain; to learn along with her students; to not understand along with her students; to deconstruct and reconstruct along with her students; to "be" in a learning dynamic that can be as explosive or as mundane as our individual and collective everydays. *Speaking the Unpleasant: The Politics of (non)Engagement in the Multicultural Education Terrain* is our endeavor to address the multidimensional pedagogical polemics of this terrain. The authors in this volume address several discrete and many times disparate issues all located within a context of understanding the complexity of pedagogy in a terrain of nonneutrality with a diversity of learners, many of whom have no desire to "engage" an education that is multicultural.

The purpose of this chapter is to provide a holographic montage for the reader for journeying within the MCE terrain as it is mapped within this volume. Lincoln and Guba (1985) speak to the holographic concept: "Images of systems and organisms [that] are created by a dynamic process of interaction that is (metaphorically) similar to the holograph, the three-dimensional images of which are stored and recreated by the interference patterns of laser beams" (p. 56). Lincoln and Guba capture the essence of this metaphor by quoting Schwartz and Oglivy's (1979) work:

> *With the holographic metaphor come several important attributes. We find that the image in the holograms is created by a dynamic process of interaction and differentiation. We find that the information is distributed throughout—that at each point information about the whole is contained in the part. In this sense, everything is interconnected like a vast network of interference patterns, having been generated by the same dynamic process and containing the whole in the part.* (pp. 13–14) (Emphasis mine)

The parallel of "holographic," in my mind, is the mastery of a multicultural education, of multiculturalism as a *way of life*, and its interconnected and dynamic processes as manifested in the everyday. This also implicates the term *engagement* and how teacher educators working alongside and with preservice teachers come to shed pedagogical light on the complexity of engagement *and* nonengagement within teaching and learning. The issues raised, discussed, and sometimes partially resolved are within the narrative of the personal. Each author or set of authors, with their unique and challenging understanding of the terrain, struggle to reveal to the reader how they, as transformative pedagogists, "speak the unpleasant" in a political milieu that automatically ensures controversy. The various chapters document several contesting issues raised within foundations, multicultural education, and/or varied methods courses with the diversity of preservice teacher education students and teacher educator colleagues that sometimes "get it," while others naively embrace, still others, misinformed or "stuck" within their individual systems of privilege or oppression crudely attack, many times disregard, or consciously minimize concepts, practices, and the diverse and embracing pedagogy of an multicultural education. As the various authors struggle along with the bevy of students and colleagues, they generate and recreate multicultural education's ideological core that further enriches the multidirectional continuum of hope and possibility; extend our knowledge base for comprehending the educational despair that has so plagued our diverse communities; and provide intellectual stardust to the educational universe that will engender a liberatory and democratic education struggling for social justice (see Estrada & McLaren, 1993).

The exponential growth of the MCE literature is well represented in this volume. More telling are the collective passions of experience illustrated herein, witness to the immensely complex *and* growing pockets of hope found within teacher education sites across the country (see also the collected works of Larkin & Sleeter, 1995; Sleeter & McLaren, 1995)—renaissance of an education that both liberates and embraces the practice of diversity and promotes pluralism in a democratic context for social justice. As well, pedagogical authenticity is evidenced in these authors' narratives. Knowing the teacher education community is composed of a rainbow coalition of an ideological magnitude that is hard to imagine, I would like to share with the reader a holographic montage, generative notes, if you will, that will hopefully challenge and further our thinking of how we, as teacher educators, go about embracing a multicultural education and its practices within the context of a teacher education that authenticates democracy, legitimizes social justice, and delegitimizes the hegemonic subtleties of educational discrimination and injustice, while simultaneously celebrating cultural, ethnic, and linguistic renewal and affirmation.

To Conceptualize a Holographic Montage

In the literature as well as in the popular culture, politically correct symbols have anesthetized how we come to think of conclusive concepts pivotal to an MCE. A critical vigilance is paramount. How these authors symbolize, deconstruct, and reconstruct the language of an MCE is central to this volume, to curriculum discourse, and to the teaching and learning enterprise. The holographic montage has several interrelated understandings. We know that language, culture, race, ethnicity, class, gender and orientation, and exceptionality backgrounds, to name a few, matter as we work with students in schools nationwide every day. We know that students interact with and engage one another in a variety of ways. We know that students engage school personnel, especially teachers, for academic purposes, talk to them at times socially and, many times, create significant and consequential one-on-one conversations. Characteristic to schooling is the knowledge that learners bring with them an array of experiences that many times authenticate their daily experiences and provide contextual safety nets for their learning. Moreover, we know schools and the environments fostered within are agencies of socialization that do much more than engage learners academically. Besides academic learning, the schools advance an array of sociocultural interactions that are implicit, explicit, tacit, and overt (Giroux & Purpel, 1983). The multiple learning matrices that unfold create the contextual learning environments within schools that are simultaneously academic, social, personal, interpersonal, and more.

As education must be linked to the lifeforms of self and social empowerment in order for schooling itself to be a force in the continuous struggle for democratic action as a way of life (Giroux, 1988a), so too must be our collective actions as teacher educators. As a teacher educator, I have best realized multicultural education's chaotic calmness by not falling prey to the linearity of teaching and learning and/or to the lure of "control" (see Foucault, 1979) but rather to its morphogenetic qualities (see Lincoln and Guba, 1985). Qualities that depend on the various contextual perspectives that inform and ground a multicultural education (i.e., cultural, ethnic, racial, gender and sexual orientation, class, disabilities, geographic region, etc.). Each learner brings into the learning terrain a holographic montage for democratic action and liberatory pedagogy that is socially constructed. Rather than having the teaching and learning enterprise serve as a function of the state that maintains and reproduces the existing social order (Bourdieu & Passeron, 1992; Freire, 1970; Macedo, 1993), a holographic teaching and learning montage depends on the engagement of all learners, teachers and students alike, and their contextual perspectives. Rosaldo (1993) identifies this succinctly as "space between order and chaos." The pedagogical consciousness revealed throughout this volume is one where the authors, the creators of a multicultural education "space," voice their desires, plans, whims, strategies, moods, goals, fantasies, intentions, impulses, purposes, visions, or gut feelings relative to their pedagogical subjectivities (see Rosaldo, 1993). The overlays of this holographic montage are culturally shaped and influenced by the authors' biographies, their social situations, their historicities, their political location. In essence, the authors' location transpires within a temporal structure that ensures that everyday life will "retain its accent on reality" (Berger & Luckmann, 1966, p. 28; see also Rosaldo, 1993). Thus, the MCE terrain is authenticated in tacitly personal ways where the practice of democracy and social justice for and with learners occurs in "serendipity with the moment."

The "serendipity with the moment" is by no means a relativist's whim (see Guba, 1990, 1993). The "moment" is enmeshed in a demographic and socially dynamic overlay, an overlay that all of us know too well. Culturally, ethnically, and linguistically distinct students now constitute over 30 percent of the K–12 population nationwide. Latinos and Latinas represent well over 40 percent of this growth while Asians and Pacific Islanders show an increase of over 100 percent. In the early nineties the population of those eighteen years old and younger was almost 40 percent Latino and 33 percent African American in contrast to 25 percent for white European Americans. The serendipity with the moment also constitutes who will be teaching and learning *with* the next generation, a population more diverse and of color—45 percent by the year 2000. More striking is the teaching population (both preservice and inservice), over 85 to 90 percent (depending on the region) of teachers remain white and female. Better said is the realization that only twelve to fifteen percent of our present teaching professionals are composed of ethnically distinct minorities (Chávez Chávez, 1995). The writers in this volume such as Cross's "Mediating Curriculum: Problems of Nonengagement and Practices of Engagement"; De León, Medina, and Ortiz's "Engaging Special Education Practitioners with Language and Culture: Pitfalls and Challenges; Goodman's "Lowering the Shields: Reducing Defensiveness in Multicultural Education"; and Lesko's insightful "(E)strange(d) Relations: Psychological Concepts in Multicultural Education" all too well understand the urgency of a multicultural education and provide spectrographic color to the rainbow of hope, provide beacons for methodological direction, and serve, almost too quietly, as pedagogical examples of courage.

Along with the demographic realities mentioned above, the making of a holographic montage is consciously and unconsciously splashed and, many times, saturated with entrenched perspectives about race, ethnicity and culture, gender, and class that to this day permeate the teacher education curriculum (see Banks and Banks, 1996; Chávez Chávez 1995; Giroux, 1993). The serendipity of the moment includes countless examples in the literature that illustrate the contradictions and myths held by preservice students and teacher educators alike (Fernández-Balboa and Marshall, 1994; Fuller, 1994; Goodwin, 1994; King, 1991; Pang, 1994; Sleeter, 1992). Preservice students and teacher educators who "live" and "experience" the everyday justify racial, cultural, and economic status by negating and/or marginalizing the sociocultural and economic disparities that exist and, in turn, place little value on the contextual importance of diversity and difference in a multicultural society. Smith's "Challenging Privilege: White Male Middle-Class Opposition in the Multicultural Education Terrain" and Rumann's "The Struggle for Cultural Self: 'From Numb to Dumb'" address this realization—one that should compel us as teacher educators to responsibly examine society in its multicultural contexts and how and whom we educate and why.

Framing a Holographic Montage in Postmodern Terms

One point becomes remarkably clear, the liberating knowledge construction of a multicultural education pedagogical discourse must be impacted by ontological, epistemological, and axiological presuppositions that *mirror* and *value* the diverse and pluralistic communities that schools serve. Said another way, in framing a postmodern holographic montage teacher educators' respect for and embracing of diverse and pluralistic communities must include ideological conceptualizations of "to be," "to know," and "to know how to do the 'right' thing" (Chávez Chávez, 1997). In order to serve our socio-learning communities we must embrace their totality—a multinarrative totality that is juxtaposed with a diverse and pluralistic context and practices social justice. The whole of a multicultural education cannot be understood by dichotomizing its essence into a series of unconnected learning units. It can best be appreciated by its processual nonlinearity that captures a synergistic whole (Kincheloe & Steinberg, 1993). A multicultural education is also steeped in a teacher education that deconstructs and reconstructs the personal-social (ontological), the "to be" constructs that simultaneously—consciously or unconsciously—*engages* what all learners bring into the teaching and learning enterprise. A social reconstructionist's multicultural education presupposes a critical constructivist perspective (see Guba, 1993; Lincoln & Guba, 1985; Kincheloe & Steinberg, 1993; O'Loughlin, 1992). O'Grady's "Moving Off Center: Engaging White Education Students in Multicultural Field Experiences," Bahruth and Steiner's "Upstream in the Mainstream: Pedagogy against the Current," Díaz-Rico's "Toward a *Just Society*: Recalibrating Multicultural Teachers," O'Donnell's "Engaging Student's Re-Cognition of Racial Identity," and Cahill and Adam's "Identity and Engagement in a Multicultural Education," all in this volume, have declared this perspective crucial in order to engage preservice teachers to struggle with their modernist's/positivist's selves, an identity that is deeply embedded into the "act" of schooling.

Earlier in the decade, Guba (1993) noted that the postpositivist paradigm enjoyed hegemony. In dispute of this claim Hidalgo, Chávez Chávez, and Ramage (1996) argue that one simply needs to inspect many of our fragmented school structures around the country and to observe how teachers and students think about and participate in the factory school metaphor yoked with mediocre "compromises"—compromises tolerated by large bureaucratic structures (Sizer, 1984, 1992). Notwithstanding, there are educational oases that exude goodness, responsibility, and caring as well as academic standards for all students that far exceed the norm of everyday schooling (see Chávez Chávez,

1997; Larkin & Sleeter, 1995; Lightfoot, 1983; Meier, 1987; Romo & Falbo, 1996; Sleeter & McLaren, 1995). Historically, however, the modernist, positivist's paradigm has effectively perpetuated its hegemony (see Cuban, 1993; Kliebard, 1995). In response to the reproductive and segmented and hegemonic constructs of modernism (see Apple, 1982; 1989; 1992), we find educators as those in this volume who are rethinking and reconstructing their teaching realities by demanding of themselves an unprecedented language and practice embracing diversity in its everyday context—human form (see Berger & Luckmann, 1966)—language that requires democratic and liberating metaphors and that appropriates a critical, constructivist stance. Many times, however, we find it difficult to wean ourselves from our own modernist schooling; others have made a decisive leap that has brought hope and possibility (Giroux, 1988a, 1988b) to the educational enterprise (see Nieto's "From Changing Hegemony to Sharing Space: Creating Community in Multicultural Courses"; Téllez and O'Malley's "Exploring the Use of History in Multicultural/Multilingual Teacher Education"; and Anderson, Bently, Gallegos, Herr, and Saavedra's "Teaching within/against the Backlash: A Group Dialogue about Power and Pedagogy in the 1990s" as examples in this volume). Rejecting the modernist's perspective *en toto* would be a mistake, its roots do contain progressive and democratic features (see Giroux, 1991; Kincheloe & Steinberg, 1993; Hidalgo, Chávez Chávez, & Ramage, 1996) on which postmodernity continues to build. Mark Dressman's "Confessions of a Methods Fetishist" (in this volume) honestly addresses how he and his pre- and inservice students have been caught up in the mire of positivist's righteousness that blinds rather than informs. In his poignant story, Dressman, in his struggle to break from a savage unreflective hermeneutic, demystifies his own pedagogical ignorance as a monomyth by making sense of his modernist's schooling. Multicultural education, we believe and as Kincheloe and Steinberg (1993) have so eloquently described, draws upon the progressive and democratic features of modernity as well as the postmodern insights into "the failure of reason, the tyranny of grand narratives, the limitations of science, and the repositioning of relationships between dominant and subordinate cultural groups" (p. 296).

Communication for Engagement

Within this volume we also struggle with the location of truth and its communication. Truth is a descriptive term that describes a quality and that is also descriptive. Schwartz and Ogilvy (1979) argue "how do you describe blue or big when the meaningful referents are themselves changing?" (in Lincoln & Guba, 1985, p. 56). McLaren (1989) insightfully argues that "truth," be it educational, scientific, religious, or legal, can be described not as a set of "discovered laws" but that which must be understood within the realms of power and knowledge relations and which somehow correspond with the "real." Truth cannot be known except through its effects. Truth, argued McLaren (1989), is relational and dependent on history, cultural context, and relations of power operative in a given society, discipline, or institution. Pedagogical truth exemplified in this volume communicates truth and knowledge within a multicultural learning and teaching context that is inextricably bonded with socially constructed epistemological, ontological, and axiological constructs—constructs that should be analyzed as whether they are oppressive or exploiting and not on the basis of whether "true" or "false" (Maxcy, 1992). A compelling perspective is best described in this volume by Gaile Cannella who addresses the notion of truth as deciphered by teacher educators as fear barriers. In "Fostering Engagement: Barriers in Teacher Education" she describes the "fear barriers" that teacher educators must resolve—barriers that "can result in the elimination of critical multicultural education without ever giving [preservice] students opportunity for engagement." Important here is what Rosaldo has contested as the monopoly for truth. In his decentering of the dominant anthropological discourse, Rosaldo (1993) emphasized that culture must be studied "from a number of perspectives, and that these perspectives cannot necessarily be added together into a unified summation" (p. 93). Thus, in my view, the practice and communication of a multicultural education is one with an array of pedagogical perspectives that are idiosyncratic to the contextual *and* processual experiences the teacher and the learner brings *at that moment of engagement*. A holographic montage for engagers, I believe begins with this realization.

My desire is to leave the reader with a sense of the galactic magnitude that multicultural education embraces. Multicultural education's inherent complexity demands that pedagogists *apprehend* and *value* the personal-social knowledge complexity that fountains from diverse and pluralistic contexts. Placing MCE within the location of a postpositivist/naturalist paradigm (see Lincoln & Guba, 1985) can serve as a relevant and preeminent springboard to the teacher educator responsible for the supply and quality of future teachers who, without a doubt, *will* teach in diverse and pluralistic environments. The naturalist axioms as construed by Lincoln and Guba address the communication of reality, truth, and the relation to the knower. This epistemological construction—that is, "to know"—helps teacher educators to *communicate* pedagogical perspectives that demystify dominant structures that rationalize and perpetuate hegemonic subjectivities and accommodate the existing regimes of truth (Sleeter & McLaren, 1995). This informs educators to responsibly envision the complexity of engagement, that is, "to know how to do the right thing" as they struggle for pedagogical authenticity, that is, "to be" within a transformative paradigm (Chávez Chávez, 1997). Moreover, as we nurture our transformative selves we formulate informed and viable options and alternatives with all students that realistically capture the ontological and sociocultural diversity that populates classrooms. In turn, an intrinsic and undying respect for the histories, perceptions, cultural, and linguistic life practices of learners will take root (See Hidalgo, Chávez Chávez, & Ramage, 1996, for an indepth discussion.). Lincoln and Guba's (1985) insightful understanding of what I consider a "transformative paradigm" may serve as a metaphorical tool to soulfully and intellectually personalize our epistemologies; in other words, to ethically understand and communicate our tacit subjectivities. Furthermore, as we reflexively practice a pedagogy that embraces the holographic qualities of differences and the subjectivity of the everyday, we then become unselfishly *engaged* with our perspectival epistemologies; hence *we can see our engagement in the context of our own concerns when engaged with the Other.* In turn, "knowing how to do the 'right thing'" is a result of having multiple perspectives so needed in order to not be "blinded by our own biases" (see Chávez Chávez, 1997; Lincoln & Guba, 1985).

Conclusion

The historicity of a multicultural education is relevant to our struggle and to our holographic montage. Since multicultural education's early, raw, turbulent beginnings, human agency's natural development has transformed multicultural education into a polished integrated whole because it has consistently questioned (in diverse ways) the established educational order. This volume is a convergence of liberatory pedagogical practices for teacher educators by teacher educators, who by their actions and inherent passion for teaching and learning see pedagogy as a dignified enterprise and see the politics of education essential to dreaming for and acting toward social justice. The pedagogical discussions within this volume are constructed by dreamers, dreamers with political and social analysis, with sociocontextual ideologies that promote intellectual pursuit for the betterment of liberatory education and a classroom pedagogy grounded in social justice. We are most cognizant of the technocratic teacher (Giroux, 1988b) who is looking for "the" method, "the way," in order to develop instrumental ideologies that emphasize an technocratic approach that further stifles dreams not only in the teacher but also imprisons students' intellectual horizons. This volume's consistent text is that a multicultural education is the marriage of thought with deed; it is the demystification of standardized epistemologies that delegitimate dominant authority and hegemonic control of learners and that authentically respects the intellectual and contextual matter learners hold and bring to the learning process (Chávez Chávez, 1995).

The cultural workers (see Giroux, 1993) in this volume serve as the principal agents in the educational enterprise who never lose sight of their students and thoughtfully examine and address a variety of underlying and sometimes confounding insights within the multicultural education terrain. The language these teacher educators use to *image* a multicultural education will enhance the discourse and practice in the multicultural education terrain. This volume illustrates the complexity of a multicultural teacher education, while at the same time putting to rest the reductionist clichés that minimize already normative practices. The holographic montage created in this multicultural education "space" encompasses and undergirds an education that is multifaceted and inherently dynamic. Our vision of teaching and learning for the years 2000 and beyond must be transfixed on what has been—a diverse and pluralistic historicity with what is to come. The writers in this volume are committed to a multicultural education and have illustrated their commitment by their pedagogical practice.

Speaking the Unpleasant: The Politics of (non)Engagement in the Multicultural Education Terrain is an investment by its many writers who implicitly practice a multicultural education as a way of life. Although important for teacher educators to understand and internalize aspects of an multicultural education as addressed in this volume, adding activities that are multicultural to an established syllabus will not be enough. What is needed is a resolve to life ways that will consciously/ unconscious and unconsciously/conscious (see Introduction) inform and ground practices that contextualize and value teaching and learning in a diverse and pluralistic context that in "serendipity with the moment" authentically values the Other. The various authors in this volume provide pedagogical images and overlays to the holographic montage critically revealing the entrenchment of the status quo. By their practice, these authors recast educators' personal responsibilities and commitment to the democratic challenges teacher educators have in a diverse and pluralistic context. Hence the authors in this volume exude a commitment to the values of a diverse and pluralistic society. *Speaking the Unpleasant: The Politics of (non)Engagement in the Multicultural Education Terrain* is a poignant reminder to the everyday struggles that are ever so prevalent in teacher education enterprises within agencies of higher education and at local sites. "Speaking the unpleasant" can only be actualized when we as teacher educators *show* how we practice a multicultural education pedagogy rather than *tell* how to practice a multicultural education. The authors herein *show*.

2

Sonia Nieto

From Claiming Hegemony to Sharing Space

Creating Community in Multicultural Courses

What makes teaching courses in multicultural education so difficult? I have been teaching these courses since 1980, and every semester I am reminded of how challenging an endeavor it is. Although the course that is the subject of this chapter, the introductory course, is not a requirement in any program, it is taken by a broad variety of graduate students, ranging from those with no knowledge of multicultural education to those with a great deal of personal and professional experience with diversity. It is a popular course, so that every semester I turn away many interested students. Yet in spite of the tremendously positive feedback I get about this particular course, it is an emotionally draining experience because it brings up a vast array of feelings, from anger and exasperation to satisfaction and jubilation.

One particular class stands out in my mind as being the most problematic but in the end most exhilarating section of this course that I have ever taught. In this chapter, I will tell the story of that course in order to illustrate how some of the many conflicting and contradictory perspectives of students were expressed, negotiated, and, finally, used to create a community. First, I explain how the course challenges the general perception of multicultural teacher education as primarily or only necessary for students of European American backgrounds. After the description of the course, I discuss what I learned from this particular class and how my teaching changed as a result.

Multicultural Teacher Education
For Whom Is It Intended?

Given the changing demographics of the students in our public schools and of those responsible for teaching them, it is no surprise that most discussions of multicultural teacher education have emphasized the need for practicing and prospective teachers of European American backgrounds to be better prepared for the challenges of diversity they face in their classrooms. It has been documented, for example, that there are currently about 2.3 million public school teachers; of these, fewer than 10 percent are members of what are traditionally called "minority groups," that is, African American, Latino, Asian, and American Indian communities (U.S. Bureau of the Census, 1993). In general, most teachers and prospective teachers are white, middle-class females and most have had little personal experience or professional training in cross-cultural issues. Because it is expected that the percentage of students of color in our nation's schools will grow from some 30 percent in 1990 to 38 percent in 2010 (Hodgkinson, 1991), teacher preparation programs need to address this issue in their curriculum.

A growing number of studies in multicultural teacher education have generally documented the futility of superficial or "one-shot" treatments in educating white teachers about diversity (McDiarmid, 1990). The short-term effects of even more sustained and indepth treatments have also been revealed (Sleeter, 1992). Because most teachers, but especially those from European American backgrounds, have been subjected to a monocultural education themselves and because they have had few personal experiences with diversity, it takes more than a series of workshops or even more long-range activities to prepare them to teach students who may be very different from themselves in backgrounds, values, and experiences.

Another key lesson from studies with prospective or practicing teachers of European American backgrounds is the negative attitudes and expectations they often have concerning students who are racially, ethnically, and socioeconomically different from them. Aaronsohn, Carter, and Howell (1995) investigated the attitudes of the participants in three teacher education courses and found that their initial perceptions tended to be incredibly negative. For example, all but one of the practicing and prospective teachers assumed that their students' parents did not really care about their children's education. Even more distressing, although most of them would probably end up teaching in cities and towns with culturally heterogeneous student populations, at first only 10 percent said they would be interested in teaching in such settings. Even this study, which is more optimistic than most, found that only about half of the teachers felt more comfortable around children of color after taking the class (Aaronsohn, Carter, & Howell, 1995).

The very way that most whites perceive of their own identity—either as "just American" without a critical analysis of what this might mean, or as not having any ethnicity at all compared to others who they perceive as being more easily ethnically and racially identified—has also been highlighted as a fundamental problem among many students (McIntosh, 1988; Tatum, 1992). This kind of negation is especially troubling among preservice and practicing teachers because it allows them to deny or downplay the privileges they enjoy solely on the basis of their skin color (Howard, 1993; Sleeter, 1994; Pang, 1994; Bollin & Finkel, 1995). It is a perspective that also allows them to buy into a view of the United States as a meritocracy where success is due solely to hard work and perseverance rather than as intimately connected to and influenced by deep-seated structural inequality based on racial, class, and gender differences. By accepting the meritocratic view of success in our society, teachers and prospective teachers can conveniently sidestep uncomfortable discussions about institutionalized barriers to mobility and achievement and they can proclaim that they are "color blind."

The problem, of course, is that teachers are not color blind. Racial differences and attitudes about them figure prominently in teachers' attitudes and beliefs about why some students succeed and others do not, about their notions of intelligence, and about definitions of students from culturally and politically subordinated backgrounds primarily in terms of deficits. These teachers and prospective teachers, who have had precious little experience with people different from themselves, often display what King (1991) has called "dysconscious racism," that is, a limited and distorted view of racism that fails to take into account how inequality is created and perpetuated by the very structures of schools and society that these teachers generally believe promote equality.

It comes as no surprise, then, that one of the major problems in multicultural teacher education has been the lack of preparation of teachers of

European American backgrounds to teach ethnically and racially diverse populations. Another major concern has been how to recruit a more diverse student body into teacher education programs to better reflect the growing diversity in the schools. Suggestions include restructuring teacher education programs (Brown, 1992; Garibaldi, 1992); making teacher education culturally responsive (Irvine, 1992; Ladson-Billings, 1994); engaging prospective teachers in ethnographic and other field work in the kinds of schools and communities in which they will teach (Trueba & Wright, 1992); multiculturalizing the entire higher education curriculum (Schoem et al., 1993); and, in an effort to diversify the profile of the nation's teachers, aggressively recruiting and retaining teachers from underrepresented groups (Arends, Clemson, & Henkelman, 1992; James, 1993).

All of these suggestions are logical responses to the fundamental problem of the great number of teachers who may be neither prepared nor particularly interested in addressing the challenges of teaching students from culturally and socially dominated communities. However, in this chapter I will suggest that focusing only on white teachers fails to recognize that students of backgrounds other than European American are also largely unprepared to teach students from groups other than their own. While it is true that the unique experiences and perspectives of African Americans, Latinos, Asian Americans, and American Indians as members of culturally subordinated groups may indeed help them to understand marginality per se, it does not necessarily give them an added advantage in confronting actual differences in the classroom and helping them address these differences effectively.

I am not suggesting that teachers of backgrounds other than European American are to blame for this lack of preparation. The situation needs to be understood in the larger sociopolitical context of how difference is perceived, constructed, and played out in our society, with the characteristics and conditions of some groups having far greater status than those of others. All of us, regardless of our backgrounds, learn to internalize these status symbols and to ascribe higher value to some people than to others. In addition, the mere ignorance of otherness needs to be mentioned. Thus, being Mexican American does not necessarily mean knowing about Cambodians, just as being African American does not mean one knows about Puerto Ricans. Because most of us are products of a monocultural education, there are few ways to learn about others different from ourselves other than through direct experience, determined effort, and hard work, or through self-initiated experiences such as immersion in a particular community or a stint in the Peace Corps.

The feeling that multicultural education is primarily necessary for white teachers but not for others is based on the faulty reasoning that all ethnic and racial groups different from the majority are in fact *not very different from one another*. Nothing could be further from the truth. All ethnic and racial groups differ from one another on many dimensions, and within the more general groupings of Latinos, Asians, and American Indians there are often dramatic differences. Even within specific ethnic groups, say Japanese Americans, there are differences of social class, language(s) spoken, geographic location, and the number of generations ones family has lived in the United States.

Just as multicultural education at the elementary and high school levels is not just for African American students—an all-too-common assumption—but for all students (Nieto, 1996), multicultural teacher education too is not simply for whites, but for all preservice and practicing teachers. Because they enter teacher education programs with different perspectives and experiences, teachers of all backgrounds may learn different lessons from teacher education with a multicultural perspective, but they can all benefit from it. An effective program of multicultural teacher education helps all participants shed their cultural blinders, develop an awareness and respect for differences with which they may be unfamiliar, and prepare them for teaching students of all backgrounds with knowledge and care.

In what follows I will describe a course in which there was tremendous student diversity of all kinds, unlike most courses in multicultural education, which generally include mostly white students with a smattering of students of color. Although this degree of diversity is rare, I have been privileged to teach many such classes over the years. All my classes tend to be quite diverse, but this particular course was unusual in the extent of diversity. I was looking forward to it with great anticipation.

However, far from the model of consensus I thought we would develop, the course was mired in conflict and competition and this was in part due to the very diversity that I thought would lead to its coalescence. Why this occurred, the kinds of tensions that resulted, and how they were eventually resolved is the subject of the narrative that follows.

The Course
Introduction to
Multicultural Education

The graduate course "Introduction to Multicultural Education" was developed and first taught by Professor Bob Suzuki in the fall 1975 semester in the School of Education at the University of Massachusetts, Amherst. In fact, this was the very first course I took as a new doctoral student and it was memorable for me not only because of this but also because it spoke profoundly to many of my own personal and professional concerns and questions. Professor Suzuki became one of my mentors and a great influence in how I think about multicultural education. A renowned scholar in the field, he gave the course its soul. In spite of all the changes I have made in the course over the years, it has retained his imprint: a particularly critical way of looking at what was then a nascent field of inquiry. It was a powerful course that first semester, and it has continued to be so every semester since then.

The extensive course syllabus includes a description, outline, format, and grading information. It also provides an indepth description of the course requirements: a reflective journal, a research paper preceded by an oral presentation about the topic in class, and a book critique. Given the nature of its content, the course often brings up strong emotions such as anger, resentment, and alienation. One of the primary reasons for asking students to keep a journal is that it can serve as a sounding board for those who may be reluctant to express themselves in class. The syllabus includes an extensive list of topics along with relevant resources from which students can select to write a research paper. The topics for the research paper and oral presentation are often controversial in nature. I have made an attempt to include issues that will get students to reflect critically and, in their classrooms, to "teach against the grain" (Cochran-Smith, 1991). That particular semester, the topics selected by students included the "English-Only" movement, the pros and cons of I.Q. testing, bias and stereotyping in children's literature, multicultural education and social change, cultural differences in learning styles, and the myth of the "model minority," among many others.

The syllabus ends with an extensive bibliography, organized according to each of the four themes, which are:

1. Analysis of pluralism in the United States;
2. Reinterpretation of United States history and culture, including the study of Nativism and perspectives of people of color, women, and the immigrant experience;
3. Sociocultural and sociopolitical influences on learning, including racism and other biases in schools, and teacher expectations; and
4. The philosophy and pedagogy of multicultural education, with particular attention to developing a sound conceptual framework and connecting multicultural education to social change.

The Course Participants

I was very excited about the great diversity of the course this time, although with an enrollment of twenty-seven, it was a bit too large for the kinds of activities I had in mind and the environment of trust and comfort I wanted to establish. The classroom itself was too small for the number of course participants, especially for how I usually teach my classes (circle for large-group discussions, semicircle for viewing videos and films, and lots of small-group work in different sections of the room). The small size of the classroom made the circle look lop-sided, with rings around the edges. Invariably there were some students who could not fit in the main circle and needed to sit in a second row.

Although they were all graduate students, the course participants represented a broad range of differences in race, ethnicity, national origin, language, age, sexual orientation, teaching experience, knowledge of multiculturalism, socioeconomic status, and political perspective. Among the students were two African American males, one who worked in a professional position at the university and another who had recently been released from prison; an American Indian male whose goal was to study history or perhaps law, but who had decided to first get a masters in education; a Tibetan who as a child had escaped by foot from his country to India and who had been educated in a Tibetan school there; a South African man who had been educated under the oppressive system of apartheid and for whom questioning or disagreeing with a teacher was at first unthinkable; a young woman from Taiwan who was genuinely perplexed by the power of the emotions expressed in class; three island-born, middle-class Puerto Ricans, one an administrator for bilingual education in a nearby school system, another a recent graduate of the University of Puerto Rico who had attended private schools until she went on to postsecondary education, and a third who had recently returned from studying for a masters degree in political theory in Latin America; an Israeli who had emigrated to the United States and wanted to teach ESL (English as a second language) to innercity youths; a Cape Verdean woman with many years of teaching experience in her native country beginning her first semester in a doctoral program; a young Japanese woman who was fluent both in the English language and in U.S. mainstream culture; a white lesbian who was working in a battered women's shelter and whose dream it was to become a classroom teacher; a number of students self-identified as "ethnic" (Italian, Jewish, Irish) and others who considered themselves "just Americans"; three young white women who had recently completed an undergraduate degree in education and who were intimidated by some of the more experienced students and by the level of discourse, which was not only quite complex but also at times deeply troubling.

In terms of teaching and other work experiences, there was a college professor of sociology, a day-care center teacher, a number of elementary school teachers, several full-time doctoral students, a chairman of an English department at a nearby high school, and various post-b.a. candidates for ESL teaching certificates. The students came not only from every corner of the globe but from every corner of the United States. Some had grown up in poverty, others with relative wealth. Their ages ranged from early twenties to midfifties, and their teaching experience from zero to over twenty years.

This group of students was a multiculturalist's dream. The dream, however, would soon turn into a nightmare

Conflict and Hegemony

There was conflict almost from the beginning. The conflict was due not just to the resistance and anger of several white students, but also to the feeling on the part of some students from culturally subordinated backgrounds that their particular difference should have precedence in our discussions of diversity. It was as if these students had finally found a place in the university where they belonged, a place where their difference could be discussed, researched, made public. After what for some had been years of trying to hide their diversity, here was a place where differences were accepted and affirmed.

The problem was that some students, having found a place where they could feel comfortable, wanted to make it their exclusive niche. This was, of course, a logical reaction to having been made invisible in all their other educational experiences. Here was a place where they would finally have a voice, and I welcomed their voices. However, the course frequently became a cacophony of disparate voices claiming hegemony. It was permeated by rage, and this rage sometimes was translated into clamors for dominance. For example, an African American student insisted that race should be our dominant theme; one of the Puerto Rican students contended that colonialism was at the core of U.S. history; and a number of the women focused on patriarchy as the primary social problem in all societies. Many of the white students squirmed uneasily in their seats or exploded with exasperation whenever the topics of racism and institutional oppression came up, while the international students were by and large lost in discussions that focused so heavily on U.S.-based experiences and perspectives.

A number of students stand out in my mind as giving this class its special character. There was Ron, an African American man in his late twenties who had just been released from prison after a conviction for robbery motivated by the need for money to support his drug addiction.* Ron had just graduated cum laude from a prison education program

---

*To protect their confidentiality, all the names of course participants are fictitious.

while on daytime release to attend classes, and after serving his sentence, he applied to and was accepted in the graduate program. The multicultural education class was his first graduate course. Ron was the first convicted felon from the program to complete an undergraduate degree at the university, often having had to return to his prison cell after attending class all day, and the result had been a bifurcated experience. He was an angry man, and he had every reason to be: growing up in a working-class family in an innercity neighborhood, Ron's father died when he was ten and, by the time he was a teenager, Ron's life was characterized by criminal charges and time in jail. He was convinced that life for African American males in America's inner cities was worse than for any other group in society, and it was sometimes difficult for him to hide his anger in class. During one of the first confrontations in class, he turned to Peter, a white student, and said angrily, "You don't wear the face, man!"

Peter, a young man in his midtwenties, was sincere in his search for meaning in our discussions of pluralism and the need for multicultural education. He was studying to be an ESL teacher and he had experience tutoring African American youngsters as well as advising undergraduate students in a school-based tutoring program that focused on working with a culturally diverse high school student body. Originally from the South, on the first day of class he had introduced himself as the great-grandson of slave owners. During the course of the semester, Peter had a number of clashes with Ron and with other students of color in the class. Although he was interested in and committed to issues of cultural and linguistic diversity, some members of the class felt that his level of awareness of racism was minimal. His girlfriend, also in the class, was Yoshiko, a young Japanese woman who was pursuing a graduate degree in sociology.

Yoshiko had spent several years in the United States. She found our class a refreshing respite from the overly theoretical and abstract courses in sociology that she was taking. The level of sophistication with which she understood pluralism in our society was in direct contrast to most of the international students who often seemed baffled by the animosity and anger demonstrated by some of the course participants. Yoshiko, however, also was impatient with the amount of time and attention given to racism and the heavy emphasis on issues of oppression.

Dianne was a lesbian who "came out" to the class several sessions into the semester much to the chagrin and embarrassment of some class participants who felt this was an issue best left untouched. She lived with her partner and taught children at a shelter for battered women. Wanting to become a classroom teacher, she had returned to get her masters degree as a way to get back in the educational field. She felt she had a lot to learn about the kinds of issues she had not herself experienced. Consequently, Dianne was very serious about the multicultural quest on which she was embarking, and she took every opportunity to read and learn about children of various backgrounds.

The conflicts among the students in the course was palpable as soon as one set foot in the classroom. Facilitating the discussions was no easy matter either inside the classroom or out. I practiced the skills of negotiation and affirmation that I had tried to hone over the years; sometimes they worked, and sometimes they did not. I remember one day when Ron chafed at the suggestion that the oppression faced by African Americans could be compared to that faced by lesbians and gays (an issue he still feels strongly about, as evident in his feedback to me, at the end of this chapter). Another day, Peter and James, an African American staff member at the university, almost came to blows over their differing opinions about what stood in the way of the advancement of blacks.

Outside the classroom there was tension as well, and this usually manifested itself in my office. I do not know how many times that semester I sat with crying, angry, hurt, or guilt-ridden students, but it was far more than is usual in a semester. On one occasion, a young white woman wrung her hands in agony as she cried, feeling the weight of the entire burden for racism on her shoulders. Needless to say, this was not an objective of the class, and I tried to convince her of this. Although guilt can be a spur to action, a steady diet of guilt can do little to change the way things are. Another day, Ron came to apologize for letting his anger get the best of him in class and I suggested he speak with other students about it. However, it seemed to me that as long as anger did not directly humiliate or hurt others, there was no need for anybody to apologize. About a third into the semester, Peter came in to see me because he was losing patience with the class. We had a long talk about white guilt, about his exasperation with others in the course, and about his feelings about himself. One of his comments on that day was especially compelling: "I'm a nice guy," he said. In spite of my caution to students about separating institutional racism from individual prejudice and from "being a nice guy," he seemed overwhelmed by what was happening in class. He had decided, he said, to drop the course.

However, Peter came back the following day and he remained in the class for the duration of the semester. In fact, I do not believe anybody dropped out of that class, as difficult as it was. Every week, I braced myself as I walked in, waiting for the next controversy to erupt as a result of students' oral presentations. What would it be? Another critique of Eurocentrism? (I could almost hear some students groan.) An attack on children's book classics as racist and sexist? An insistence on romanticizing the history of oppressed groups? And so it went, from week to week, with one unrelenting issue after another. Many of these issues were absolutely essential to confront, but the way in which they were sometimes discussed resulted in silencing some of the more reticent students.

In spite of the conflict in the class, I could tell as the semester wore on that some unusual friendships were beginning to form. Other changes were also apparent: Ron decided to do his research paper on women in prison, a slight but significant departure from his consuming attention to his own experience; Yoshiko delved into the myth of the "model minority," a myth she had heard for the first time when she came to this country; and Dianne shifted her topic from the history of lesbians to the perspectives of some American Indian Nations concerning lesbianism. The class began to coalesce, uneasy alliances at first, but gradually stronger connections began to be made.

Sharing Space

The turning point in this class began on the day that Dianne presented the results of her investigation into Native American views of lesbians. It was not so much her topic itself that captured the students' attention but the fact that she had brought her mother to class. When she finished her presentation, she introduced her mother and asked her to say a few words about why she had come to class.

Mrs. Butterfield, a homemaker and retired teacher in her early seventies, said that she wanted to meet the students that Dianne had talked so much about. Everyone became silent, watching her attentively as she talked about her experiences as a mother and, specifically, what it was like being the mother of a lesbian. She spoke of her initial rejection when Dianne first told her and of her tremendous disappointment at not being able to look forward to having grandchildren. Although a devout churchgoer, she said she could not speak openly about Dianne's lesbianism in her church, or for that matter, in any other setting outside of this class. In the midst of this very personal and private story she injected unexpected humor into her monologue by saying, "You know, I wouldn't mind so much that they're lesbians. I just wish they weren't Democrats!" This welcome moment of comic relief resulted in thunderous laughter. Finally, Mrs. Butterfield described how much she had grown to love Dianne's partner and how she now embraced and cherished her as a member of the family. At the end of her fifteen-minute talk, you could hear the proverbial pin drop; everyone, it seemed, was at a loss for words. Everyone, that is, except for Ron. He turned to her and said with a deepfelt respect, "You must be very proud of your daughter, Mrs. Butterfield."

That was the moment in which the class changed. Ron had said exactly what was needed at that moment, and it was an especially moving comment coming from him. Until then, Ron had had a fierce devotion to his own experience, and that experience had been a great teacher for him and for many others in the class. But it was when he extended his experience to embrace Dianne's that he was able to create solidarity. Some of the students in the class wept openly, and all were moved by what we recognized as a moment of transcendence. Nothing further could be said, and we took a needed break.

The object of this story is not to create a sentimental or romantic view of the power of multicultural education courses. They can be powerful, to be sure, because courses in diversity can promote empathy and caring that go beyond one's particular experiences. In this case, Dianne's mother was the catalyst that brought conflicting ideologies, anger, and guilt to the fore to create a true community. Furthermore, Ron's modeling of a respectful and compassionate reaction to Dianne's mother was a reminder that we can sometimes get "stuck" in self- or group-centeredness. Something happened in the course after that. There seemed to be more listening, less rage, more introspection, less self-centeredness. There seemed to be a shared understanding that the process of learning about oneself, an absolutely essential process in multicultural education, needs to lead to learning about and with others.

For some students of European American backgrounds, what they had perceived as the onslaught of finger pointing and blame led to a far greater understanding of their own responsibility for creating change. For the students from marginalized cultural groups, there was also an awakening and it had to do with recognizing that, although their experiences were hidden from and denied in the mainstream discourse, they too were limited. After this incident, there seemed to be a genuine interest on the part of most of the course participants to learn about others. On a concrete level, other changes took place: Ron and Dianne met for coffee before class on a number of occasions; Peter went to visit James in his office on campus and they had a long talk about some of their disagreements, and in the end they became friends.

The last day of class was a sad one in many ways. Many people felt as if they were saying goodbye to old friends. It can probably be compared to the solidarity that develops when people experience a common disaster, an airplane crash or a fire. Having experienced the crisis, they could now trust one another. For me, "sharing space" in that class became a metaphor for learning to share the ideological space that students inhabit.

Learning from Conflict

The story of this class, however, is not a fairytale. It did not end with everyone "living happily ever after." On the contrary, some conflicts and dilemmas were never resolved. Anger remained constant for a small number of course participants. Perspectives that differed dramatically continued to differ, and I am certain that some of the teachers and administrators who took the course did not change their thinking, curriculum, or pedagogy in any substantive way. There were some profound changes, however, and a number of people walked away from the course with new insights that helped them transform their teaching and how they think about education in general. I am one of them, and I want to focus briefly on some of the lessons I learned from teaching this course.

First, *the course taught me about the folly of believing that understanding one kind of bias will automatically prepare students to understand others*. The transfer is far easier, to be certain, but it is not automatic. This means that instructors need to be aware that all of us, students and professors alike, bring into our education a particular life experience that, although important and worthy of attention, is also limited. Yet there are tendencies within multicultural education itself that discourage cross-group empathy and connection to others of different backgrounds. Consequently, we need to build into our courses experiences that will foster both knowledge and empathy about the variety of differences that teachers of young people will encounter in their classrooms.

Second, *no matter how we may resist it, teaching courses in diversity carries with it a moral responsibility to help students work through conflicting and powerful emotions*. Of course, we should see ourselves first as academics and as such we need to promote critical and thoughtful analyses of the many issues and concerns that are at the core of multicultural education. But because these issues and concerns also challenge deeply held views and feelings, to leave these unattended is to abrogate part of our responsibility as educators. I am not advocating that these courses become what have been derisively called "touchy-feely" courses, or that they engage in group therapy. But sometimes professors forget that learning is multidimensional, affecting our hearts *and* our minds.

Third, *teaching this course taught me to be patient with the process of change*. Change, if it is to go beyond superficiality, needs time to simmer. I could no more expect the students to apply overnight what they had learned in this course than I could expect a dramatic change in reading scores a month after beginning a new reading program. Over the years since I taught this particular section, I have come across a number of the former participants who have told me of changes they made in their curriculum or pedagogy, of how their views of students had changed, or about how their dissertations had benefited as a result of the course.

The fourth lesson I took from this course is *the need to reform higher education in general, and teacher education in particular.* This cannot be managed by simply adding a course or two in diversity to the curriculum. Reform of higher education in general would help alleviate what occurred in this particular graduate course: because it was the only course where they could discuss perplexing but often silenced issues of oppression and privilege, it became almost a battleground of competing interests. *All* students need more courses that they can call their own. Just as students in the majority have a curriculum that more closely represents them, their history and legacy, and their values, all of our students need the same opportunity. At the same time, all students need more courses where they become a "minority." I often advise male students to take courses in women's studies, and non-African Americans to take African American studies. These are often eye-opening experiences in which they become, for one brief semester, the "other," with all the discomfort and alienation that it may imply.

The reasons for multiculturalizing the entire teacher education program are also clear. A course or two in multicultural education, while important and even necessary, can get lost in the curriculum. It can give preservice and practicing teachers the impression that they only "do" multicultural education in those courses, while they "do" reading in reading courses and social studies in social studies courses. All courses benefit from a multicultural perspective, especially a perspective that goes beyond the superficial "food and festivals" approach to consider issues of privilege and structural inequality. Unless diversity includes an examination of the sociopolitical context of school policies and practices and becomes a central concern of the entire teacher education program, it will continue to be marginalized and isolated from the mainstream of professional development. As such, it can be easily dismissed.

Fifth, *the course reinforced for me the importance of having all of us, students, teachers, and professors, learn to challenge hegemonic policies and practices in our own teaching.* Developing, in the words of Cummins, "collaborative versus coercive relations of power" (1994) with students and with our students' communities is one important way to achieve this. Rather than the authoritarian wielding of power on the part of professors or students, collaborative relations of power means working together to create learning experiences that can both challenge and support all learners. Using a critical eye to analyze our own taken-for-granted viewpoints and practices is crucial for all of us, no matter what our backgrounds may be. For instance, some students felt silenced in the course, as sometimes happens in courses of this kind. Thus, it seemed to me that one of the primary objectives of the course— to provide a safe place to consider and speak openly and critically about difficult issues—was not being met. This is an issue I have faced repeatedly over the years, and I believe this course helped me formulate a response to "silencing" more than any other that I have taught. Although speaking freely cannot take the form of personal vendettas, or cannot be used to cause pain or disrespect of others, or used as a soapbox to malign or disparage any group of people, I also make it clear to students that there can be no "politically correct" or unchallenged perspectives. This sounds much easier in theory than it is in practice. It often proves to be a complex balancing act between providing equal access to all, or hurting personal feelings by making statements that are outright racist, heterosexist, and so on.

Another case in point in this course was the discussion we had of racism as a system of "privilege and penalty" (Weinberg, 1990; McIntosh, 1988). This is an approach that I find particularly appropriate because it helps people see that status and resources are often doled out according to attributes such as race and gender, even though such privileges may be unwarranted. In addition, those who receive such privileges are often unaware of how they benefit from their white skin, maleness, or other high-status attributes. In contrast, racism can be described in ways that are overly contentious and destructive. In relation to this discussion, a statement that generated a great deal of conflict was that all whites are racist if they benefit from a society that is racist. The reactions were swift and angry, and this idea still strikes a chord of dissent. I have found that this approach is generally ineffective. That is, people who are in fact racist or biased may simply dismiss the entire topic of racism, while those who are sincerely working against racism may feel disheartened and disempowered by it. The important point is not that discussions of racism should be suppressed, but in fact just the opposite: they need to be broached directly and honestly, but in a way that creates a sense of community rather than pointing fingers and closing down communication.

Every class I teach brings with it unexpected challenges and surprises. No course, however, has touched me as deeply as this one because it reflected so clearly many of the dilemmas and joys of multicultural education itself, including resistance, transformation, and community. I had wanted to create consensus in this class, and it never happened. Far more important, I learned that consensus need not, and probably should not, be the result of courses such as these. Rather, creating community, with all the messiness this term implies and with continued struggle and conflict, is probably the most we can hope for.

If a community is created in which all voices are respected, it seems to me that this is itself a noble first step. What I mean by "community" here, however, is not only that all voices are respected but that a deeper sense of bonding and caring can develop despite the very real differences that exist. That is, the course participants seemed to recognize their differences and the tensions that they caused, but they were able to form a caring loyalty to one another in spite of this. Creating a community also means that deep ideological and philosophical differences do not disappear. For example, Ron never accepted the idea that sexual orientation is as oppressive as racism, although he demonstrated profound respect and admiration for Dianne's mother in her role as a mother. I would have wanted Ron to make more of a theoretical connection here, but that did not happen. Needless to say, there were probably numerous other examples of the lack of change among the participants. But this does not mean that the course was a failure. On the contrary, I believe it was successful precisely because it promoted a sense of community that had not existed before. In fact, Ron's comment to Mrs. Butterfield remains a compelling example of creating the kinds of communities we all deserve.

Note

I am deeply appreciative of the feedback, critical reflections, and comments that I received from Ron, Yoshiko, Peter, and Dianne. Their insights taught me new and important lessons once again, years after I first taught this class. I also wish to thank Irv Seidman, Larry Blum, and Paula Elliott for critical responses and helpful suggestions on an earlier draft of this chapter.

3

Mediating Curriculum

Problems of Nonengagement and Practices of Engagement

S ince my teaching career began in 1980, I have constantly struggled with how to connect my experiences as a child in segregated schools in the South with my teaching practices. I recall
the foremost mission of the teachers who taught me in segregated
schools in Alabama to be preparation of the black boys and girls in their
classrooms to continue the struggle for freedom for all people. That was
the overarching purpose driving their work. For sure, they dedicated
their work to our academic achievement, but that goal operated along
with a critique of social reality as experienced by different individuals
and groups. My teachers in Alabama held some strong political beliefs
that informed their educational practices. They did not wave a banner of
liberalism or shout a mantra of teaching for social transformation. Their
work seemed to be simple and unpretentious. Yet it was very powerful.

Their power lay in the quiet way they set high expectations. It was in the look they gave us that said we are a better people than that. They communicated in their own way that what we were engaged in was not just a struggle for our own freedom but for the freedom of all people.

The following example is illustrative of how my childhood teachers worked. Recall the question often asked by students, "Why do we have to learn this?" Many teachers in today's classrooms are left responseless when children ask this question and react with quips such as "you will need it in the future," "because it is in the book," or "because I am supposed to teach it." Conversely, my teachers in Alabama responded to the same question by explaining that our educational achievement meant advancement of freedom and equality in America. They told us that our educational achievement was a major determinant of what our lives, experiences, and freedom would be like. We were taught to think of the development of our minds as essential to the development of a more humane America where we would not be judged by our skin color but by how we lived our lives. As teachers, they used their educational practice to inform us about how we should live our lives and what is expected of us. They recognized an oppressive state. They used curriculum to change it and expected us to use our knowledge to do the same. There was also a collective, communal, and cooperative underpinning to what they expected from us. An implicit partnership existed: for the students to achieve academically meant all of our people achieved, for us to achieve freedom meant we all achieved freedom, for us to change the world meant they, too, changed the world. They saw their educational practice as creating free people—freedom for us, them, and all people.

From these childhood experiences, I grew to believe preparing students to continue the struggle for freedom for all people is what education is all about. I learned several key lessons from my teachers that I assumed to be essential for education in any context and time. The following is a summary of what I recall learning from my teachers.

1. Educators should be professionally, personally, and morally committed to the education, development, and future of free people through their work with children and youth.

2. Educators' lives and professional practice should not be merely examples of what they believe but also embodiments of the personal meanings they give to curriculum.

3. Educators should prepare children and youth to serve humanity through the development of their minds and commitment.

4. Students should learn about the human experiences of various people in America.

5. Students should use what they learn in school collectively and individually in the struggle for freedom for all people and to improve the human condition.
6. The gift of education is a spiritual one that should be dedicated to life—our own and others'.

Following these experiences and powerful lessons, a formidable announcement came. The summer before I entered high school, the schools were desegregated. Even with the impending desegregation, I entered high school ready to build upon my education, skills, and passion to advance freedom. I recall a stark difference in what the teachers were like, what they did, how they interacted with us and our families, and what their mission was. The mission of my new teachers in desegregated schools was to teach discrete, seemingly objective academic facts. What was now taught was disconnected from the lives of me and the children I went to school with, from our world, and from the larger mission of critiquing social reality to transform society. For example, I was unaccustomed to a focus on exclusively disciplines, memorization, and recapitulation of information in decontextualized forms from a greater goal regarding the lives of people. We no longer talked about freedom, the diversity of human experiences, and social advancement. The academic no longer coexisted along with the struggle for freedom. It was being replaced with competition, individualism, objective knowledge, and meritocracy. I recall often feeling confused, lost, and disappointed that the teachers who ignited the practice of freedom in me and my fellow childhood peers were no longer teaching us and that their mission was being slowly lost.

As if my high school experience were not a powerful message by itself, I came to a swift, harsh, and certain realization while teaching in public schools, and now at the university, that the mission of my teachers in Alabama was not recognized. The disciplines took on ever higher meaning, standardization of curriculum and assessment guided learning, students competed against one another, and the community was no longer included in the learning process. The struggle for freedom was invisible. I wondered why the mission was different. Was schooling about different things for different people? Was desegregation of schools the end of the schools' role in the struggle for freedom of all people? My questions today are: Is that mission lost forever, can it be regained? Do we want that mission and do we have the common will as educators to stand for that mission?

This chapter describes my struggle to maintain my teachers' mission as a guide for all of my teaching. As a teacher of curriculum theory, design, and development, I see a match between the questions I pose above and the nature of what I teach. It seems clear to me that curriculum courses require that educators clarify, elucidate, and articulate to themselves and to others the purpose of their work. First, I will describe my teaching context and the courses I teach in more detail. I will describe my students' nonengagement in the struggle for freedom (for those who were nonengaged, not all were) related to their curricular visions, practices, and decisions. Finally, I will offer some thinking in progress about my own pedagogical and curricular practices, which are developing as an attempt to challenge, confront, and engage students' understandings and to push them forward as multicultural thinkers. I will describe my efforts to build a framework for my own curricular practices to keep the vision of my childhood teachers alive.

Background and Context

The university graduate such courses that become the means for me to explore how teachers think about the curriculum of schools and its relationship to an oppressive state. Three such courses are (1) curriculum planning, (2) curriculum theory, and (3) curriculum design for urban schools. Each course offers a distinct learning experience but is linked by a curriculum focus and my purposeful engagement of students in thinking about an oppressive state and the relationship of curriculum to its continuation or change. The courses are not sequenced, and students may not enroll with me for all three courses. Generally the students in my graduate courses teach in public schools, mostly suburban. A few teach in urban, parochial, or private schools and even fewer in universities.

The curriculum planning course is the first curriculum course students take. Its primary objective is to engage students (primarily masters-level students) in understanding various conceptions of curriculum development and design and their own conceptions of curriculum. The curriculum theory course exposes students (primarily doctoral students) to different curriculum theoretical perspectives and forms of inquiry. The urban curriculum design course (primarily doctoral students) focuses on urban schools and their curriculum within a larger political, social, economic, and cultural context. Each course operates independently. Therefore, I must rely on a semester to engage students in confronting their understanding of a multicultural education and the struggle for freedom and its relationship to curriculum. I must integrate, as my childhood teachers did, the academic content of the courses with the broader goal in a way that does not fragment or distort the courses. The integrity of the distinct purpose of each course is assured.

Because of the theoretical influences on my beliefs about curriculum, several questions frame each course, although somewhat differently based on the course goals and content: (1) what experiences could lead teachers to a different set of assumptions about curriculum and how it explicates the purpose, content, and organization of schools; (2) how can teachers begin to see curriculum as politically derived from decisions, compromises, and negotiations, and rooted in power; and (3) how can they come to realize how curriculum plays a role in the politics of oppression and domination that include racism, sexism, classism, and cultural supremacy. For example, we discuss where curriculum comes from, who influences it, whose interests it serves, and what ideologies guide it. We analyze their schools' missions, philosophies, goals, and written curriculum documents to determine the conceptions, ideologies, epistemologies, moral orientations, view of reality, and images of teachers and students that frame it. We analyze curriculum documents to determine its relationship to the human experience. Students are often surprised to find a statement in their school's curriculum documents that relates to social justice, equality, and improving society. For example, some statements reference social responsibility, developing peaceful relationships with other people around the world, and caring for the less fortunate. Several teachers from the same school district were unaware that printed on the back side of their district's mission statement was this quote from Joel Barker: "Vision without action is merely a dream, action without vision just passes the time, vision with action can change the world." Teachers began to wonder whether Barker's quote was the district's attempt at changing an oppressive society, or if it was an academic goal.

As I plan for the courses, three questions guide my decision making. First, what impact do I want the course to have on my students (referred to as teachers)? I question how the course can leave the teachers as different thinkers, believers, or perceivers. How can the course influence teachers' thinking about themselves and themselves in the world. Second, I ask what form of assessment will I use that allows the teachers to exhibit what is different about them. I ask how can students integrate and exhibit what they have learned. How can they display how this learning informs their thinking and actions. Third, I fill in the gap between question one and two by asking what should occur through the course to influence teachers to the extent they can exhibit their growth, development, and change. Essentially, I ask what should occur in the course to challenge and support teachers as learners. Here I question whose work should the teachers read, what experiences should they have, and how do I support and extend their learning and practices. My commitment to these questions and to connecting thinking and action was deepened when I heard an expert on large-scale political/cultural conflicts state on National Public Radio in reference to America's response to such conflicts that "intelligent people can reason themselves out of action." He affirmed for me that the thinking and action of teachers should be at the center of course design if the practice of freedom is to inform their work. To connect their practice to action, an implicit element of inquiry is built into each course to help teachers understand curriculum as the embodiment of the purpose of school. While doing this, I learned that many of my students are nonengaged in understanding the oppressive states in society. In the next section, I describe the nature of students' nonengagement through their beliefs about schools and their curriculum.

Curriculum Is . . . Voices of Nonengagement

My teachers in Alabama recognized an oppressive state. Of course, the oppressive state was publicly visible and challenged during the late sixties and early seventies when I was a student in desegregated schools. The public's acknowledgment of oppression and dominance did not automatically mean that teachers would use curriculum to combat the continuance of social injustice. Yet, my teachers recognized and had the courage to use the curriculum as a means to change that oppressive state. They did so implicitly through the curriculum and through living their personal and professional lives as an example of the curriculum and its broader purpose. Another example of what my teachers did will elucidate how they used curriculum to engage our minds in understanding social reality. They used their own lives as a model of what they expected us to do with our own lives. They studied the life experiences of people in America and they taught us about their diverse lives. They taught that knowledge has a moral purpose related to the lived experiences of people and that the knowledge we gain through education should guide us as thinkers and knowers who should not reason ourselves out of action. The curriculum was not separate from my teachers lives. They lived the way they wanted us to live, they used knowledge the way they wanted us to use knowledge. Their beliefs about what schooling was all about and how their lives and curriculum practices connected were unknowingly passed on to me. As a child, I never thought my teachers were engaged in anything but teaching me what was considered school knowledge. They were. But what constituted school knowledge existed within a context of the struggle for freedom. They seemed to view themselves and the curriculum as political and social agents.

I began to consider how I could find out what teachers thought their greater role in schools to be in terms of the purpose they see for what they do. In each course teachers are asked to identify and explain what they see the purpose of schools to be and how their own curricular practices relate to advancing this purpose. At the beginning of each course, most teachers state that their initial expectations from a curriculum course are that they will write or develop curriculum units or guides. They hold the traditional conceptions of curriculum as the written district curriculum document containing a philosophy statement, goals, objectives, and so on. This view is divergent from the curriculum as lived experience perspective that seemed to guide my teachers. To encourage teachers in thinking about curriculum in a manner similar to how I perceive my teachers to have thought about it, I engage them in thinking about curriculum as a constant activity they engage in. I want them to think about curriculum as involving choices, priorities, intentional and unintentional elements, interests, and assumptions and that these frame what children have an opportunity to learn and experience. This aim requires redefining curriculum around thinking, inquiry, decision making, uncertainty, and nonrationality rather than technical-rational theories of curriculum that hold it as linear, mechanistic, static, singular, prescriptive, and preset.

I begin courses by asking teachers to write what they believe to be the purpose of schools. I read what they write and pose questions to which they respond. Certainly to have teachers write what they perceive the purpose of school to be is problematic. First, it is not necessarily a perfect question although it is often considered one quintessential curriculum question. Second, teachers often have not had experiences to engage them in thinking about how their classroom practices relate to the overall direction and purpose of their school other than to the written curriculum. Third, paradoxically one statement often given in response to the purpose of schools, to educate children, is not one with a unity of purpose. What "to educate" means holds quite diverse meanings. So I do not suggest this as a question that yields responses that are clear, coherent, and without contradiction. But I do suggest that it initiates teachers' thinking about the broader curriculum in operation in classrooms in America beyond their daily attention to lessons.

Teachers' responses to the question provide a starting point for continued dialogue about the big picture of curriculum, how their work relates to the broader curriculum, and the power of their individual and collective curriculum decisions. Most importantly, it sets the stage for discussion, analysis, and inquiry into what it is they ultimately perceive their work and their schools to do for children. For example, do they see their ultimate objective as an educator to be providing students with as many academic facts as possible? Or do they see their ultimate objective as assuring children and youth feel capable of improving the world for all people as did my teachers in Alabama?

When asked to expound on the most frequent theme, "to educate students," teachers predominantly respond with statements like:

- Schools have an obligation to prepare students to lead a fulfilling life through decent, sustaining employment and meaningful participation in democracy.

- The purpose of schools in America is to prepare young people to be productive, creative, and responsible citizens. They must be able to understand, maintain, and carry on the social and cultural traditions that make America strong.

- Schools prepare students to take a meaningful place in society.

- Schools should develop the attributes within a student to become a productive, interdependent member of society. Students should learn through the academics the skills necessary to attain a job and be successful on the job.

- Schools prepare children for their adult life or the real world so they can function within the rest of society, be independent, and self-supporting.

These statements represent the general tenor of what the teachers include in their writings. The clearest theme that surfaced from the teachers is that schools are designed to prepare students for their future as effective citizens and productive workers who are fit for society. If the dominant view of teachers is to fit students to society, succeed in society, and obtain jobs, it is unlikely that they problematize that society and see it as oppressive, dominating, unjust, and inequitable. In fact, while reporting how they view schools and curriculum, many articulate idealized notions of democracy, meritocracy, and individualism. When they write about democracy, they write about participating in democratic processes through voting, understanding laws that govern how citizens behave, earning your own way in life, and getting along with others. They describe curriculum as important to sustaining democracy and a capitalistic economy that they view as making America a strong nation, a world leader, and admirably sovereign and imperial. This goal does not cause consternation even as they are daily faced with assertions that, in about half of our schools, "students are enrolled in dead-end curricula that prepare them poorly for work, life, or additional learning" (Wingspread Group on Higher Education, 1993, p. 10). Their goal for curriculum remains the same even when it is not, by most reports, achieved.

The teachers are intrigued when they see how their views of curriculum fit within frameworks explicated by curriculum theorists. The dominant view they hold is described by Eisner as "social adaptation" (Eisner, 1985). A few teachers report another conception of curriculum described by Eisner as "cognitive processes." These teachers state the primary purpose of schools and their curriculum is to teach learning skills. Although labeled lifelong learning, they see its value, too, as lying in the future, as preparation for a technological society for which they can predict what is needed by students, and finally, culminating back into fitting students as productive citizens for society. My early teachers were not fitting me for society but rather were equipping me to deconstruct it, challenge it, and change it. Their curriculum was framed around social critique, diverse human experiences, and social activism.

In addition to viewing curriculum as preparation of children to fit into society, either as it is or as something called a "future technological society," many of the teachers in my courses initially see curriculum as tangible, prescribed, singular, universal, absolute, static, and linear. They further see curriculum as value free, neutral, and objective. They see it as something they are expected to manage in terms of controlling the dispensation of knowledge. Their view of curriculum is more like the banking view of education described by Freire (1970) rather than a liberatory education grounded around the practice of freedom. Teachers primarily see their role as reproducing the society they know by preparing children to fit into society. This industrial view of schooling supports their mechanistic, management, and universalizing view of curriculum. The dominant view of curriculum competes against notions of teachers as political and social actors who understand the political oppressive state and who see themselves as having curriculum agency. It competes against teachers thinking of themselves as curriculum decision makers who construct curriculum along with children to see the diverse perspectives of the world and how individuals experience the world differently. It competes against seeing curriculum as socially constructed and prioritized. It denies thinking of curriculum as multiple, contested, politically determined, and oppressive.

To assist teachers in seeing curriculum through other perspectives, they are challenged to determine the interests and assumptions underlying curriculum development and decision making. They analyze curriculum documents in class and critique various ideologies about curriculum. They are initially unable to see curriculum as a means of domination through, for example, a strong European-centered curriculum, externally driven curriculum development, heavy emphasis on what business and industry expects of schools, and inequitable experiences for students based on class, race, or gender. These notions of curriculum seem to interrupt their long-standing, generalized views of what curriculum is about. It is as if to think about curriculum as an accomplice in continuing practices of oppressions is a violation of allegiance to a sovereign America. The teachers are puzzled when attempting to think of curriculum as an effort to question and to seek truth, representation, and voice. Conversely, challenging curriculum as universal, recognizing curriculum as potentially compliticious in oppression, and searching for truth, representation, and voice led my teachers in Alabama in their struggle against dominance and oppression and toward freedom. The challenge for me is to integrate these same ideas in a supportive and educative manner for the teachers I teach through questions, dialogue, and critical reflection with an eye toward action and empowerment. The challenge is to engage them in seeing their own and curriculum's complicity in nonengagement in a multicultural society.

Curriculum as . . . Critical Practice toward Engagement

I have learned a great deal from my work to understand teachers' views of what schools are for and how these relate to their curricular images and practices. As I analyze what I am learning from my students against what I learned from my teachers in Alabama, I am struck by one profound difference. That difference relates to the personal way my teachers viewed curriculum and their practice and how they used curriculum to teach us collective and individual responsibility toward the struggle for freedom—a struggle that continues in the daily lives of many people and needs to continue living through curriculum. This view contrasts with how my students see curriculum as nonpersonal, outside of them, and with little agency. This distinction caused me to become critical and analytical about my own pedagogical practices. I want to frame my curricular practice around constructing personal meanings of curriculum and building capacity through the personal meaning to influence an oppressive state.

The memories of my black teachers in segregated schools, who would now likely be called critical pedagogues, provided me with a liberatory paradigm that continues to shape my curricular and pedagogical practices. The list of what I learned from them provided earlier is evidence of this. The work of others also informs my own conceptualization of curriculum and how I design courses. Paulo Freire's (1970) assertion that our ontological vocation is to act upon and transform the world through liberatory practice support my courage to keep my teachers' mission alive; bell hooks's (1994) work on the power of our pedagogical practices causes me to pay attention to the broader guides that shape my teaching and to work with teachers to do the same; Peter McLaren's

(1989) work on critical pedagogy helps me to think about schools and how oppressive states continue largely through curriculum; William Doll's (1993) elucidation of postmodern thinking and its meaning for curriculum helps me in both designing the courses I teach and the way I engage students in broader conceptualizations of curriculum; and Lisa Delpit's (1995) experiences and ideas on teaching children of color remind me of the mission of my teachers and the need for it to continue living today. The wisdom, insight, and courage of these individuals touch my life and my understanding of social reality. They aid me in connecting my practices as an educator to my experiences as a child learning in desegregated schools. They converge to help me shape a framework for my curriculum and pedagogical practices.

My framework-in-practice (I am still learning, studying, and growing) leads me to a guiding question that weaves throughout the courses I teach: What images of curriculum do teachers hold and how do these images relate to the struggle for freedom? Because of this question, I resist the frequent pattern of designing courses around issues and problems facing the curriculum of America's schools (e.g., outcomes-based education, national standards, religion in schools, school to work). Rather, I frame curriculum courses around big ideas associated with the struggle for freedom—like democracy, power, language, culture, ideology, and domination and their relationship to curriculum decisions and the lives of students and teachers. To achieve this, I design courses around teachers' understanding of self, students, and the powerful, undeniable link among these. The images of curriculum that teachers hold are at the center of the courses. The courses use various means (e.g., personal theories, professional histories and biographies, graphic designs, metaphors, and curriculum analysis) to aid teachers in identifying and elucidating the implicit images they hold of curriculum; describing their own beliefs, values, and priorities about curriculum; determining the implicit theories they hold and how these are evident in practice; and articulating the images they hold of children as learners and themselves as teachers. Through developing and articulating in the various modes, the teachers begin to see themselves as the embodiment of curriculum and to see curriculum as larger than a written document or bound by the textbook but as having a personal and collective meaning. They begin to see that they and their students give life and meaning to curriculum and that this is subsequently personal.

Based on the framework-in-practice formed through my understanding of Freire (1970), McLaren (1989), hooks (1994), Doll (1993), and Delpit (1995), several principles guide my practice. These include: centering students and their understanding in the courses; and, integrating educative perspectives well. These perspectives include curriculum as: (1) constructed and multiple; (2) what children have an opportunity to learn, think, believe, know, perceive, and experience; (3) complex and dynamic; (4) lived experiences; (5) bound by language, culture, time, and context; (6) partially personal; (7) complicitious in maintaining an oppressive state; and (8) potentially powerful for altering the oppressive state. These pedagogical principles and curriculum perspectives mutually inform each other and frame the courses.

The intersection of my experiences as a child, as a classroom and university teacher, and as a learner from other scholars, leads me to four perspectives on curriculum that shape my pedagogical and curriculum practices. These perspectives include (but I am sure are not limited to):

1. Curriculum as personal vision
2. Curriculum as inquiry
3. Curriculum as moral
4. Curriculum as public and dialogic

The four perspectives are at the same time guides to my pedagogical and curriculum practices and guides to how I want my students to think about curriculum. They are framed around my childhood teachers' notions of curriculum as personal and are aimed at an individual and collective responsibility to changing an oppressive state. I want my students to examine curriculum as personal and to understand how they hold some degree of agency related to curriculum and how their students think about what education is about. Each of the four perspectives alone can influence teachers' thinking about curriculum. As they work together, their potential to link thinking and action is expanded. They have the potential to aid teachers in seeing their personal agency in curriculum and viewing curriculum as a determinant in what children see their lives to be about. What I see my life to be about is partially a direct result of how my teachers saw themselves and how they saw curriculum. Through the four perspectives on curriculum, I am hopeful the teachers I work with will be more thoughtful about nonengagement of curriculum in effecting the oppressive state and that they will gain a sense of agency in rethinking curriculum to change this state. In the following sections each perspective on curriculum is described and linked to challenge teachers' relationship to the continuity of society.

Personal Curriculum Vision

I learned from my teachers in the South that their lives and professional practices embodied their personal curriculum image. That image of curriculum was framed around the practice of freedom. Today, curriculum is widely thought of as being collective, while teaching is viewed as more personal. It is not uncommon to hear teachers speak of "the" curriculum from the district central office while they speak of "their" personal teaching style. Therefore, curricular decisions and what they mean for what children have an opportunity to experience, think, know, do, and perceive about the world is considered to be somewhat standardized and universally held. Constructing a personal vision of curriculum in addition to their already widely held universal vision can help teachers to first identify their image of curriculum. It can further help them reflect on, challenge, and confront the universal vision of curriculum. Reflecting on and imagining their curriculum vision is important to expanding teachers' conception of curriculum beyond that of an external written document that tells them what to teach. It helps them to move beyond thinking of curriculum as something others develop and order and they follow and implement in a technical manner to something that starts with and takes life from them and the children they teach. Framing curriculum as technical, externally developed, and standardized essentially absolves teachers from responsibility about what occurs through the curriculum because they did not develop it, it is state and district developed and approved, and it is similar to what all schools do. If it does not work (as the Wingspread Group suggests), how can teachers be held responsible? If it reproduces social injustice, oppression, and domination, it is not their fault since they did not write or develop it.

Constructing a personal vision of curriculum, conversely, removes curriculum from exclusively external to curriculum as personal experience for teachers and students. It creates a vision of curriculum as an embodiment of self. It requires that teachers examine the beliefs, values, and assumptions they use to make sense of the world and to understand themselves as cultural, personal, and professional beings. As Doll (1993) states, teachers and students need to be free, encouraged, and demanded to develop their own curriculum through interaction with one another. He encourages a view of curriculum not as a "set, prior course to run but a passage of personal transformation" (p. 4).

Understanding the personal and the collective vision of curriculum is important to helping teachers connect their curricular thinking, planning, decision making, responsibility, and practice to what they ultimately want for students. It is essential to rethinking the purpose of curriculum and schools beyond fitting children for a society that has been idealized and romanticized as inviolate but rather one nearing civil unrest and maybe civil war. Thinking about curriculum as personal is essential to teachers seeing their individual agency in curriculum decision making. This agency is crucial to thinking about curriculum as the seed for transformation. It is important for thinking about how everyday curriculum decisions and actions are embodiments of what teachers believe schools are all about. Through constructing their personal curriculum vision, teachers can confront assumptions they believe true, sacred, and impervious from challenge and suspect. They can uncover the hidden ideological interests that underlie their practices (McLaren, 1989). This process also allows teachers to determine their own and students' sense of power, influence, and abilities regarding curriculum development, design, and content. They can see it as a lived experience created between them.

For example, teachers in the courses analyze the explicit, implicit, and null curriculum (Eisner, 1985) that are operational in many schools in America. They become aware of these forms of curriculum and how each influences what they do and what children have an opportunity to learn. They identify examples of each form in their schools. They generally develop quite extensive lists of each. They also become aware of their own roles in shaping each. Many of them take notice of how widespread what they determine to constitute each form to be across their schools. At the same time, they see a large degree of personal capacity to have influence on and shape these forms of curriculum.

Discussions about how curriculum either supports social continuity or fosters social change and improvement need to be confronted. No decisions are benign in this sense. Constructing and elucidating a personal curriculum vision is essential to seeing curriculum as political and as inextricably linked to the reproduction of an indecent and unjust society. It is essential to accepting and acknowledging that curriculum is not objective, ahistorical, neutral, and apolitical. It is essential to seeing that curriculum decisions hold consequences, and that those consequences often result in a lack of attention to how curriculum strongly pushes teachers into nonengagement of an oppressive state and eventually does the same to students.

In addition to exploring theoretical conceptions of curriculum, teachers explore their own conceptions of curriculum in the course, the images they hold for curriculum, and the ultimate aims they hold for their practice. They are asked to think about the collective perspective on curriculum through the theories, written curriculum documents, and policies related to curriculum. They are also asked to think about curriculum at the personal level in terms of their own decisions, power, and influence regarding curriculum. Thinking about curriculum at the personal level creates a struggle for the teachers. While many of them feel they have little influence over curriculum, many come to realize the amount of influence they do have regarding curriculum. Some also come to realize they have long-standing visions of what curriculum is that may not have been explicitly taught to them but were rather developed through being students and teachers familiar with and not challenging what constitutes schooling. They also realize that these visions are not quickly changed.

In one course for example, teachers articulate their personal vision of curriculum through personal theories (Ross, Cornett, & McCutcheon, 1992) on curriculum. Teachers complete a three-part process in which they identify what personal theories implicitly and explicitly guide the numerous decisions they make daily. They then look for evidence of these personal theories in their practice through videotaping and analyzing classroom activities. As they analyze and report on the juxtaposition of the theories they initially identified and what they see in the videotapes, they are frequently alarmed by the traditional and parochial nature of what they see occurring. In fact, some state that what they observe could have been taped years ago with teachers at the center, students as somewhat passive, and disciplines, facts, and figures guiding what occurs. The teachers then develop a plan of inquiry about their practice that includes what they want to continue to learn about themselves as curriculum decision makers. In another course teachers develop a graphic image that depicts their image of curriculum. They generally articulate a metaphor they hold of curriculum and transfer this into a graphic image. In other instances the graphic image derives from a visual picture they tacitly hold of what teaching and learning looks like. In still another course, teachers elucidate their personal curriculum vision through a review and critique of educational policy and what image the various policies hold for the purpose of schools. This culminates in constructing their own personal policy for education. This personal policy allows them to express in detail what they see as the broader purpose of curriculum.

It seemed a personal vision of what schools were all about led my teachers in Alabama to a personal commitment to education for the struggle for freedom. Can the curriculum of today's schools be targeted toward building a more decent and just society where the practice of freedom guides the purpose of school? What if the curriculum were designed around social change through understanding the social reality of oppression, injustice, classism, racism, sexism, religious intolerance, and homophobia? What if the curriculum were designed to critique how these persistent patterns in our society make it oppressive and shortchange it from becoming what it could be?

Curriculum as Inquiry

The lived experiences of various peoples in America seemed to guide inquiry for my teachers in Alabama. This caused them to constantly engage in inquiry to understand these experiences so they could help us understand them. I, too, encourage teachers to place curriculum at the center of inquiry. An inquiry focus can support the transition of viewing the curriculum as static, external, to be managed, exclusively driven by academic disciplines, and contained in textbooks to something more dynamic, complex, constructed, lived, and experienced. Curriculum viewed as inquiry can help teachers move from thinking about the curriculum as aimed at preparing students to fit into society as productive workers and citizens to a focus on how the social world is experienced, mediated, and produced. It can lead teachers to view curriculum as multiple, diverse, constructed between them and children, in search of truth and multiple voices, and potentially transformative to change society. Capacity can be built through a lifetime of inquiry. As this capacity is built, teachers begin to see how they should constantly reflect on, question, and inquire about curriculum. Inquiry can allow teachers to surface the curriculum practices and conditions that continue the current oppressive state, which undermines and distorts the purpose of fitting children and youth into society, getting a job, and being a good citizen. Curriculum as inquiry takes teachers and students from outside of curriculum and places them as tantamount to the curriculum. Curriculum is created through their personal interactions. Continuous inquiry shifts curriculum from something that changes every five years to something that changes naturally. Inquiry becomes associated with learning, growth, and development.

Framing curriculum as inquiry helped me dislodge the teachers' certainty surrounding curriculum. The work of Wheatley (1992) and Doll (1993) on chaos theory informed how I cast curriculum as something the teachers and students determine and experience and as something that, when led by children, would naturally result in questions of how the world works and why. Class discussions include how curriculum is not something so ordered just because it appears in notebooks from the central office and in textbooks as ordered. Order develops within children through the learning process. We talk about how the need for information has a powerful drive in organizing the curriculum. We talk about how building relationships with others and with information energizes children and their desire to learn rather than building on unit after unit as controlled by the written curriculum or the textbook. Discussions on curriculum as complex, dynamic, and emergent are offered to replace previous notions of curriculum. This leads to a long discussion and analysis of what types of questions children ask and how that would make the curriculum different. Questions surface like one asked by a third-grade African American male student to his European male teacher, "Why won't I get to be a doctor when I grow up?" The stunned teacher responded, "You will if you want to be." The child responded, "Then why aren't there more African American doctors? Didn't they want to be?" In this example, the teacher was unprepared and uncomfortable with the question. Clearly, children have profound interests in the way the world works and why. The child recognizes social oppression and injustice, the teacher does not.

I suggest to teachers that they consider continuous inquiry into curriculum as related to big ideas rather than discrete facts and figures. I encourage them to think of it as something they participate in constructing in infinite decisions every day. I encourage them to think about the potential power of those decisions in determining what children have an opportunity to learn, think, experience, believe, and do. I encourage them to inquire into whether they want to use curriculum to reproduce their idealistic, romanticized notions of the world or to engage students in understanding its oppressive state for many people and the human responsibility to change that state. For example in one course, teachers grapple with such concepts as justice, domination, ideology, indoctrination, knowledge, and culture. They are expected to study these concepts from different orientations (e.g., education, sociology, anthropology, history, political). To achieve this goal, students read, work with professors from various departments, and analyze curricula used in schools. My aim is for them to see such concepts operationalized at various levels within curriculum and practice and to understand how they connect to nonengagement in recognizing and changing an oppressive state.

Fortunately, a great deal of research, including my own, and work regarding teacher development is focused on teacher learning, reflection, and inquiry. Through this experience and listening to others involved in such work, it becomes clear that initial questions guiding teacher inquiry are often focused on how to fix the children, how to do discipline better, how to get children to value education better, and how to get the parents involved in the school. Until the questions become situated around a broader purpose of schools and how schools, curriculum, and teaching continue a state of oppression, inquiry falls short of what it could be to really foster the development of teachers and changes in classrooms and schools. Inquiry has the potential to cause teachers to see themselves as transformative intellectuals who (1) treat students as critical agents, (2) question how knowledge is produced and distributed, (3) utilize dialogue, and (4) make knowledge meaningful, critical, and emancipatory (McLaren, 1989, p. 239). For example, in one course students are asked to research and explain various perspectives on epistemology (among them empirical, symbolic, phenomenological, critical). They are required to describe the view of reality, the moral orientation, the view of humans and their relationship to knowledge, the purpose of knowledge, and the assumptions and interests that frame each perspective. They first report being unaware of the various perspectives on knowledge and that each relates to different world views. They then are pleased at their ability to determine how the different perspectives are operational in different forms in curriculum and how they have unknowingly been unaware of their influence on them as teachers and on the children they teach. They see the contradiction between what they may report to believe and the evidence of the different forms of epistemology in practice. Many begin to think of how they and their students can become critical agents to surface contradictions and influence more what they learn and experience. This is an important move to recognizing an oppressive state.

The teachers from my childhood seemed to view the written curriculum as a means through which they achieved a greater purpose— that of preparing students for the struggle for freedom. The academic disciplines were not softened, but they were not the ultimate purpose of schooling. Freedom, justice, and equity for all people was the purpose. The disciplines provided multiple lens through which the teachers and students explored the experiences of people, examined social realities, and built the skills, capacities, and will to work toward social justice. How can we direct inquiry toward teacher development of the skills, knowledge, and dispositions for them to become (1) analytical about society, (2) more committed to understanding how their work is inextricably linked to that society either as continuing its oppressive state or in attempting to change it, and (3) social and intellectual activist whose mind, speech, work, and behaviors fit with recognizing the oppressive state, working to change it, and working with students to do the same. How can inquiry authentically engage teachers in curriculum decisions? How can the inquiry focus on teachers and students understanding the political, social, and economic interests underlying curriculum and how they can be part of the struggle for freedom for all people? How can curriculum inquiry engage teachers and students in constructive critique and dialogue to develop intellectual and social powers (Doll, 1993)?

Curriculum as Moral

Moral commitment to me and my childhood peers, the moral commitment to our future lives, and continuing the practice of freedom guided my early teachers. Their lives, teaching, and curriculum were morally formed. Now, however, some teachers view teaching and not curriculum as including a moral dimension. For example, some think of teaching as implicitly teaching right and wrong, conforming to society, and building character. They also think about teaching as caring, altruistic, in service to others, having ethical perspectives, and making a difference in the lives of those they teach. Conversely, curriculum decisions are not viewed in this way because it is viewed as external to them as teachers, developed by others, and implemented by them. Therefore they see themselves as holding little personal agency related to curriculum, having no right to inquire into it, and subsequently seeing no moral aspect to curriculum. This extends to teachers not thinking of curriculum as related to the lived experiences of people but rather as transmission of discrete, objective disciplinary knowledge and facts. It is difficult for them to see the humanization and moral aspect of curriculum. This sets up a diametric tension in teachers' work with teaching being moral work and curriculum not being moral work. Teaching cannot really be moral, however, when curriculum decisions are not considered likewise. I cite Freire's (1970) view that our "ontological vocation is to be a Subject who acts upon and transforms his [sic] world and in so doing moves toward ever new possibilities of fuller richer lives individually and collectively" (p. 14). Clearly teachers, children, and society can benefit from viewing curriculum as moral.

In my work with teachers in courses, I struggle to get them to think about the moral purpose embedded in curricular decisions and practices whether acknowledged or not by them or others. I ask them to consider that curriculum decisions determine what children will get to learn, think, perceive, and do and that these decisions are moral ones. I try to get them to be more directly responsible to that moral purpose by being explicit about it. For example, in one course where teachers are designing integrated curriculum, I require that they develop questions that guide the integrated unit. These questions relate directly to the topic, theme, idea, or concept that frames the unit. They have little difficulty determining the curriculum questions that guide the unit until I ask, Where is the question that will guide you and your students in thinking about how this learning experience relates to their ability to understand the world and how people experience it differently?

Here is an example. A group of teachers were developing a unit on power. Their guiding curriculum questions were: What is power? What can it do for us? How do we get it? How does it change? During feedback to the group on several occasions I asked, Where is the question that tells us that spending time studying power has academic benefit as well as benefit in understanding the world? I ask them, how will this learning experience change the way your students view their world and how they choose to live their lives? Finally, and with much urging, they included questions on how various forms of power impact individual and group lives, how power and domination are related, and who is served by power. They stated to me, "This type of question was a struggle because we do not think of our work as being connected to the way our students view the world and live their lives. We just wanted them to think about the various forms of power like mechanical, mental, physical, and natural. We have never been asked how what we do relates to the social condition and how it can be improved. We think of our work in academic terms only and as unrelated to the social reality of various groups other than in general terms like getting along with each other, respecting others, and fitting in."

Viewing curriculum as moral allows me to engage teachers in thinking about curriculum as bound by language, culture, and history (McLaren, 1989). This perspective, by definition, places curriculum within a moral context. It strips it of objectivity and places it within the realm of choices, decisions, compromise, and negotiation. I find it intriguing that the broadest theme that teachers evolve to describe what schools are for—preparation of the young to be good citizens, fit into society, and be good workers—is not viewed clearly as a moral purpose. Each piece of the theme carries a moral message. Some teachers are able to separate preparation for democracy and for being a good American from a moral activity. At best, they see implicit moral elements to this theme. Some teachers interject the traditional argument that if there are any elements of the curriculum that are moral, it is the social studies curriculum. I struggle to get them to see how all curriculum decisions are moral decisions. I want them to see the moral dimension operating at both the individual and collective levels and that both are essential to understanding the moral dimension of their practice. The moral must be cast within the social and public sphere.

A sample of personal theories from one teacher illustrates how some teachers are able to begin to think about and recognize the role of curriculum in continuing the oppressive state. Examples of his theories include: students are engaged in the practice of freedom, students and teachers are comfortable with a culture of change, and school community members are responsible for one another. These theories were added by the student to his initial theories, which focused largely on his content priorities and discipline. They reflect the expansion of his thinking about curriculum.

I am sure a transformation does not occur that causes these teachers to think about the moral purpose of curriculum during all of curriculum planning, of for example a unit on power. But I am sure they have a chance to think about their work as having a broader purpose and meaning. I am sure that they think about the skills and knowledge they need to do this. The next time they use such slogans as "curriculum should be relevant to students lives, relate to the real world, and prepare them for future citizenship," they will rethink what they really know about their lives, the real world, and the future. They will think about curriculum as moral work and that they can choose this to be explicit or implicit work. They will think about how their curriculum choices and actions really relate to children's lives and how the world is reproduced or changed.

My teachers in Alabama saw a moral purpose overriding their work. They seemed to use that purpose as a guide for making decisions about what and how they taught, how they interacted with us, how they treated the disciplines, what they did in the community, how they related to other teachers, and how they interacted with families. They saw curriculum as a means for them to engage our moral souls. The curriculum and their teaching were both instruments of social justice. They used curriculum to reject and transform social continuity and oppression rather than to preserve it. What dangers exist when idealized understandings of reality translate into curriculum? What experiences can support teachers in viewing the world through diverse perspectives, diverse eyes? How can teachers develop the courage to use curriculum to transform society?

Curriculum as Public and Dialogic

As teachers surface their personal curriculum vision, center curriculum in inquiry, and begin to view it as moral, they also need to center it in their professional lives and activities. My childhood teachers situated curriculum within their individual and collective lives and responsibilities. According to many of today's teachers however, privacy and isolationism surround curriculum to threaten this possibility. This is somewhat paradoxical considering earlier discussion of curriculum as external, developed by others, and as common across schools. These views of curriculum could led to conclusions that it is highly public and widely understood. Yet at the teacher level and classroom level, privacy and isolationism become prominent. General expectations about what is expected from each teacher may be understood by colleagues, but personal curricular practices are hidden, protected, and thought to be negatively challenged, accusatory, and contentious if inquired about. Isolation of curriculum decisions maintains: implicit power; absolution of responsibility; views of curriculum decisions as external; a lack of curriculum moral agency; a stifled context for inquiry; and an absence of venue for personal visions to be explicated, responded to, and situated within a community.

For example, it is interesting to observe how students are initially intimidated and hesitant to share their personal theories with one another publicly in small groups. They become more comfortable as they build relationships with one another. However, when requested to share their personal theories with a colleague in their school the hesitation reappears, and this time with greater intensity. Teachers respond with comments like there is no one I am that close to, there is no appropriate context or time during school for such a conversation like that to occur, no one will care, they will think I am weird, aren't I opening myself up for criticism, or they will not share their personal practices with me. They generally have not had experiences sharing their personal theories or have faced ridicule, teasing, or rejection rather than support, collaboration, or encouragement. Often, however, they are surprised at the response from colleagues. Many state they are pleased their colleagues did not say to them, "Oh you must be taking a university class." They conversely engage with them in thinking about what their curriculum leads them and students to think about and want to do.

Teachers and students are members of a community. They can better grow and develop when they have a responsibility to and feel a common purpose to a community—a purpose they partake in evolving. Some teachers report efforts underway in their schools that pull the staff together to determine their common mission. Sadly, dialogue is often not maintained long enough to determine what that mission means for curriculum and its relationship to the social state. I provide examples from my own research on site-based management that show curriculum is largely invisible in dialogue, conversations, and deliberations. I read excerpts from my interviews and fieldnotes that show curriculum is infrequently mentioned in the site-based management meetings I have observed. I show examples of perceived conversations about curriculum to be conversations about commercial programs or developing a school mission (such as a technology-, inclusion-, or global-education focused school). The broader discussion of curriculum regarding lived experiences and the social condition are invisible.

As curriculum becomes public, dialogue about curriculum can increase, inquiry about curriculum is fostered, a safe milieu can be created for expression of personal visions, and comfort is created for the moral agency of curriculum. A context can be created for teachers and students to critically examine various knowledge forms that shape how the world is experienced and explained. Efforts to place curriculum within the public sphere of professional practice are important to move beyond silencing teachers' curricular practices that have great implications for whether or not they reproduce oppression and domination or work toward building the knowledge, skills, and will to alter oppressive states.

As discussed earlier, curriculum is both individual and collective. McCutcheon (1995) describes solo and group deliberation in curriculum development. This includes solo or individual and group or collective curriculum development processes. I relate her concepts to help teachers make connections between their involvement in individual and collective curriculum deliberations, decisions, and actions. The moral purpose to curriculum, the understanding of the oppressive state, and the development of the will to improve society must occur at the individual and collective level. Greater potential arises when there is both individual and collective commitment to curriculum work especially when it surrounds critique of social reality. When curriculum work is undertaken within a language of public life, emancipatory community, and individual and social commitment (McLaren, 1989), greater possibilities exist for examination of nonengagement, domination, power, and oppression. Teachers can combine their efforts to engage students in understanding the social world and developing the desire to be part of what it will look like rather than fitting them into some unclear technological future that is not easily predicted. They can stimulate and support conversations about curriculum and what their work is all about. As teachers who shared their personal theories with their colleagues learn, dialogue can move teachers from being implementers to building conversations with others regarding curriculum. They begin to think about themselves outside of implementers of others' ideas and decisions and to see their own personal theories, their own agency, and their own ability to use curriculum to change the oppressive state.

As a child, I did not experience public dialogue among my teachers about the larger purpose they held for curriculum. I often heard it, however, in their dialogue with my mother when they explained what they viewed education to mean for the students they taught. There was evidence of the dialogue through the shared mission to prepare us for the struggle for freedom. They all engaged us in this common experience. How can support and time be built into schools to foster dialogue on curriculum? How can dialogue about curriculum be critical of social injustices and inequalities within a framework for change and improvement? How can environments be created wherein individuals and the collective can constructively critique their work and the complicity of curriculum in social oppression and domination?

Conclusion

I still pose the questions that led me to write this chapter. How can teachers think of their curricular practice as evidence of what they believe schools to be about? How can they move to recreate their own professional lives rather than to view them as controlled by various curricular policies (including the written curriculum, textbook adoptions, board policies, and now curriculum standards)? How can curriculum be assessed to make explicit and known its complicity in social oppression and domination? How can educators become responsible to acknowledging this role of curriculum and responding to it in a way that advances the struggle for freedom for all people?

I realize the persistence and insidiousness of nonengagement in maintaining an unjust and inequitable world. I worry that my efforts and the efforts of countless others are still too isolated to have large-scale impact on the images held nationwide about curriculum. Can I continue in a profession that is not committed to the practice of freedom? I have for a long time realized the influence of race, class, gender, and culture on curriculum decisions and practices. I am now even more convinced of the profoundness of how these mediate curriculum. I am convinced that curriculum teaching should be about understanding and being more thoughtful and critical of this mediation. If educators recognize this function of curriculum, then we must start to respond to it in responsible, educative, professional ways. With efforts underway, I am hopeful that the situation described by hooks can be reversed. She states, "We found again and again that almost everyone, especially the old guard, were more disturbed by the overt recognition of the role our political perspectives play in shaping pedagogy [and I add curriculum] than by their passive acceptance of ways of teaching and learning that reflect biases" (1994, p. 37). When the passivism shifts to become activism (teaching practice with an activist intention), when we are disturbed by the overt and implicit political, social, and cultural underpinnings that situate curriculum as continuing social oppression, when we expect teaching colleagues to be clear on how they use curriculum to foster the struggle for freedom, then and only then will the mission of my teachers in Alabama be alive. Only then can we say teachers' struggle against nonengagement is alive. Then we can hope for freedom, justice, and equality.

4

James O'Donnell

Engaging Students' Re-Cognition of Racial Identity

teach at a land grant university in the southwestern part of the United States. My primary position is working as coordinator of secondary student teaching, but I also teach classes in multicultural education, curriculum development, and qualitative research. In each of these courses as well as in my student teaching seminar, issues

The term *re-cognition* illustrates a process of conscious recovery. Growing up in a race-conscious society means having conscious and unconscious experiences of race. Given the dynamics of white racism, the experience of race for many whites may be lost to their conscious understanding. Having students reconstruct those early experiences with race may enable some students to capture the cognitive and affective qualities of those early experiences. By making the unconscious conscious, a re-cognition of one's racial identity and participation in a race-conscious society may emerge.

related to diversity and multiculturalism are addressed. In each of these teaching contexts issues related to students' non-engagement and opposition to dealing with, discussing, and thinking about multiculturalism and, utlimately, making changes to affect positively students' lives are present. In this chapter I want to focus on my work as an instructor in a multicultural education course. It is in this course and context that my pedagogy has been developed and is implemented in each of the above mentioned teaching contexts.

In this chapter I describe who my students are and the importance of knowing the students that we teach as well as their social, cultural, and historical contexts. I have discussed elsewhere the theoretical assumptions that undergird my educational approach to teaching about issues of diversity, multiculturalism, and especially of race and racism (O'Donnell & Gallegos, 1993). I have explained the necessity of creating a classroom climate in which students are expected to listen to each person's perspective and to address the content of the ideas and not the character of the speaker. Further, I emphasize the necessity for each participant, myself included, to speak in the first person, therefore, from our own experience. In this chapter, I explore the tension that comes with teaching about race and racism. How I understand this tension and how I attempt to engage students to engage this tension.

My Students

The students ($N = 1469$) in the college of education with whom I work are approximately 62 percent European American, 33 percent Hispanic American—namely, Mexican—American, 1.2 percent African American, 2.5 percent Native American, 0.3 percent Asian American, and 1 percent Other. The majority of students are female, approximately 75 percent. The average age of the students is twenty-six. Based on this average, the majority of the students' lived history is between the years 1966 and 1992, 1992 being the year of these demographics.

I think that it is important to take note of the historical time period in which most of these students have lived. The Civil Rights movement began to change its thrust; the women's movement, *La Raza*, the American Indian movement, and the growing anti-Vietnam War movement may have been experienced by many of these students' parents, siblings, and relatives. Out of these struggles developed the curriculum, pedagogy, and commitment to multicultural education (Nieto, 1992; Sleeter & McLaren, 1995). In 1973, for example, the American Association of Colleges of Teacher Education's proclamation expressed in the one-page document *No One Model American* signaled the initiative for developing teachers with a multicultural perspective. (It is ironic that many of our present preservice education students appear to have had little, if any, multicultural education.) Not only have many of these students lived through the closing years of the aforementioned "movements," many began their adolescence (fourteen years of age) at the start of the Reagan era, in 1980—an era that ushered in a period of intolerance for dialogue about the United States and its culpability in propagating domestic and international violence as well as rekindling an ethos of individualism, competitiveness, and greed. In addition, our students have been privy to an onslaught of criticism addressed toward multiculturalism, pluralism, and the politics of difference (e.g., Bloom, 1987; D'Souza, 1991; Hirsch, 1987), as well as presently witnessing the dismantling and demonization of hard-won civil rights initiatives such as affirmative action.

Within this climate, the teaching of multicultural education is not easy. And teaching about race and racism is particularly not easy. Students often become defensive, resentful, and angry (Davis, 1992; Roman, 1993; Tatum, 1992).

Race remains a divisive issue in this country and a greatly misunderstood phenomenon. Racial politics, though characteristicly different from 30, 50, 100, or 135 years ago, remains as "business as usual," advantaging one group and disadvantaging another. Part of the need for teaching about race and racism is to inform our students about the dynamics and manifestations of racism and to enable our students to identify, to confront, and to challenge racism and other forms of discrimination. But to teach about race and racism is not easy.

It is not easy because many students, white and students of color, question racism's existence and relevance today (Balenger, Hoffman & Sedlacek, 1992; Chávez Chávez, O'Donnell, & Gallegos, 1995). Many students often recoil at the mention of the topic. They offer responses to what racism is by stating that racism does not occur today because it was dealt a severe blow in the distant past. Some students cry out that the media is creating a problem by focusing on the issue of race in every daily event. Others argue that by talking about "it," division and suspicion grow. Some students reason that racism like affirmative action exists to appease the guilt of white liberals. "And I'm not guilty of anything," a white male student asserts in my class.

"No one is asking you to feel guilty or to accept responsibility for a system that you and I and the rest of us in this class grew up in. But to assume that racism is somehow a moot point today is to deny a large part of our social and cultural reality as well as an historical past that remains part of our present," I, a white male multicultural educator, state.

Such an exchange occurs in classes on multicultural education. The exchange, however, is not always between myself and a white male. Sometimes it has been a white female. The above statements denying the existence of racism or murmurs that talking about "it" creates divisiveness are not always stated by white males or white females but by some students of color who do not wish to engage in a discussion and analysis of the topic of racism. But within my classes, there are white students, male and female, and students of color, male and female, who are eager to address, to analyze, and to understand this thing called "race and racism."

I welcome this range of responses and perspectives. Some students will be angry (at me for bringing the subject up); some students will be upset, will feel guilty, and will be defensive. There are also students who will be angry (at a system and society that perpetuates racism); some students who will feel affirmed, who will feel renewed, and who will be ready to act. It is precisely this range of responses that creates and enables the possibility for transformation. It's the divergence of perspectives and lived experiences encountered within a dialogical framework that permits students the possibility to question themselves and their society.

For the majority of students who are angry and anxious about the topic, I have come to realize that three issues lay at the fountain of this discontent, anger, and guilt that many students present in a multicultural education course. One, most students enter our courses with a long history of educational practice that has asked them to be silent participants in their education. Shor (1992) notes that many college students come from a public education system that is big on transmitting information but reluctant to have students engage critically with the information. Further, the information is usually distant from the students' lived experience. Many of our students are deficient in their abilities to critique and to analyze and, therefore, to engage in a critical discussion and exploration of their lives within this society and culture. (See Dressman, this volume, for a discussion on the paradoxical nature of reflection.)

Two, the curriculum encountered in most of our students' secondary and elementary experience lacks an exposure to a multicultural perspective. Textbooks, for example, still describe a main storyline of white, male achievement (Sleeter & Grant, 1991, cited in Nieto, 1996). Many students are missing history. Many students are missing engagement with characters, stories, plots, and themes that reflect and tell the experience of "other and difference" in our society.

Three, the issues of a pedagogy of transmission and a curriculum dominated by a white, Western, "civilized" rhetoric and perspective creates a racialized (and colonized) identity. This created racialized identity marks the Other but does not mark whiteness as a constructed racial category. I argue that it is to this racialized identity forged within the historical, social, and cultural context of this society that many students, especially white, angrily and desperately cling. In a multicultural classroom in which the question of whiteness as a racial category emerges, the conflict, defensiveness, and denial exhibited, I feel, results from many students' unrealized racial marking and identity. This unrealized racial identity creates the anger, tension, and rejection encountered in a class on race and racism. *But* this identity "crisis" can also provide the key for transformation.

Unrealized Racial Identity

Many students' discontent, anguish, and frustration exhibited in a multicultural education course dealing with race and racism, I feel, emanate from this unrealized racialized identity. In part, many students, but especially white students, are unaware of themselves as racial beings. Because the dominant discourse on race has marked race as a salient feature of the lives of the Other, and has marked white as "normal" (Omi & Winant, 1994), the struggle becomes one of teaching white students about their racialized self. Similarly, some students of color question the significance of race and the prevalence of racism by denying race and racism as pertinent issues worthy of analysis (Chávez Chávez, O'Donnell & Gallegos, 1995). Each perspective, however, emerges from a racial discourse that both groups of students have as part of their understanding about race and racism. For example, many students cling to the notion that racism is an individual pathology and that, to rid the society of racism, "sick" individuals need to be taught healthy nonprejudiced attitudes. This "rotten apple theory" as Henriques suggests (Henriques, 1984 cited in Troyna & Hatcher, 1992) purports that "sick" individuals are at the heart of racism. Therefore, strategies to address racism that only focus on individuals neglect the systemic nature of racism.

The overarching reality I address is that racism is an ideological issue that affects the entire system, that is, all individuals as well as the society's policy-making and enforcing institutions (Hall, 1986; Jones, 1972). Students need to re-cognize how they are participants, even reluctant participants, living in a race-conscious society (Omi & Winant, 1994).

To realize the self as a racial being is not simply to self-identify and acknowledge one's raceness. What is important is to enable students to re-cognize their historical selves as racial beings and to deconstruct the racial discourse informing this racialized identity.

Racialized Identity

Within my courses, we talk about a racialized identity as well as discuss and describe a gender identity or class identity or sexual identity. Each of these categorical identities can be analyzed and discussed. And separating out and focusing on one particular aspect of identity is to make the task manageable. Identity is a complex product process. "Product" in that I can define myself presently and "process," in that I am becoming (see Brown, 1994; Bruner, 1990, especially chapter 4). To single out one aspect of that identity for analysis is not to intentionally discard the complexity of identity formation. Each aspect of our social identity such as gender, ethnicity, class, race, religion, or sexuality impacts and informs our identity. The reason to address one aspect of our social identity, that is, race, is for analytical purposes.

Within the United States, there are historical, social, and cultural discourses on race that inform the composition of one's racial identity. Many whites, for example, may dismiss the idea that they are racial members. But this idea itself is part of a race discourse that informs the social and cultural experience of whites with race. Frankenberg (1993) explains how "whiteness" is historically, socially, and culturally constructed within a race discourse of dominance and that naming "whiteness [as a race category] . . . assign[s] *everyone* a place in the relations of racism" (p. 6, author's emphasis).

To assert that students have a racialized identity is to state that race as an historical (past-present), social, and cultural phenomenon impacts and informs their understanding of race and racism. This informed perspective of race and racism may well be hidden, but the nature of their understanding of race and racism reveals their comprehension of race and defines their racial identity. This racialized identity, however, does not imply a conscious understanding. Some students may be acutely aware of their racial identity while others may not.

> At the micro-social level, racial projects also link signification and structure, not so much as efforts to shape policy or define large-scale meaning, but as the applications of "common sense." To see racial projects operating at the level of everyday life, we have only to examine the many ways in which, often unconsciously, we "notice" race.
>
> One of the first things we notice about people when we meet them (along with their sex) is their race. We utilize race to provide clues about who a person is.
>
> Our ability to interpret racial meanings depends on preconceived notions of a racialized social structure. (Omi & Winant, 1994, p. 59)

Students' racialized identity is formed within the "racialized social structure[s]" that characterize the relations among racial groups within this country. Omi and Winant (1994) explain how the historical drama among racial groups in this country secured for whites the naming of the white self as "normal" and marked racial groups of color as Other and Different. But for many whites the sense of "differentness" in this instance signifies "different from us (white, that is, 'normal')."

The pathology methaphor supports this "differentness." It has provided us with deficit theories and deceitful searches for "g" to explain and to maintain the racial status quo (e.g., Gould, 1981). Said (1993) employs a critical analysis of the white European author's construction of the "other" and demonstrates how this description aptly depicts the race ideology of the author and society. White students must confront this "differentness" and explore the "whiteness" ideology before they are able to move beyond.

Enticing Students to Engage

I have discussed elsewhere (O'Donnell, 1995) how some students' language reflects a racial ideology of assimalationist theory and colorblindness, how the concept of culture is essentialized to mark and to explain racial difference, and how the ideology of individualism and meritocracy blocks many students' structural analysis of racism. These students have learned well the conservative (essentialist) and liberal (individualist) ideological discourses on race and racism. They have learned the racial discourse so well that many have negated their own racial identity. An instructional task related to the teaching of race and racism within a multicultural education course is enabling students to re-cognize their own racial identity.

The purpose of the term *re-cognition* is to indicate process in teaching students about race and racism. As stated above, the society in which we have been brought up is a race-conscious society (Omi & Winant, 1994). The issue of race is present if not in our immediate world, that is the spatiotemporal realm of everyday life, then in the larger macrosociety. For example, both the recent reactions and responses to the O.J. Simpson verdict as well as the Million Man March are part of students' everyday encounter with the issue of race and racism. Similarly, discussions about "reverse discrimination" and affirmative action and editorials and talk shows on the "divisiveness of multiculturalism" become part of our students' conception and comprehension about race and racism. Students may engage or not engage directly in discussions or read newspapers but, as part of the popular culture, residual elements remain (Chávez Chávez, O'Donnell, & Gallegos, 1995).

For the most part students enter into our classes with limited experience in working with such social issues as racism. Many students have had little opportunity to explore and to discuss the dynamics of racism and even to glimpse and to discuss the many manifestations of racism. For the most part discussions around issues of race and racism are absent from public forums and sadly this includes schools. A related issue is that race and racism are seldom talked about in mixed racial groups (Tatum, 1992). Therefore, many of our students enter our classes with a limited language that can provide insight into dealing with the dynamics, manifestations, and contuors of this social issue.

Though these students may enter our classes with a limited and or distorted language to describe and discuss race and racism, I would argue that all students come into our classes with lived experiences of race and racism. I argue that to grow up in this society is to grow up with an awareness of race and, therefore, an awareness of racism. Social experience within the United States implies a tacit knowledge—that is, a commonsense understanding—of the dynamics of race. Further, this tacit knowledge provides a rationale for explaining race and racism. All students, therefore, need the opportunity to speak the unpleasant and to engage in dialogue to map their racial experience. Working with students to re-cognize—that is, reconnect and reconstruct—their prior experiences with issues of race and racism can lead some students to acknowledge and accept their racial identity.

The process of reconstructing students' past experiences is a meaning-making process. Identifying and selecting events are acts that require reflection for making meaning. The act of putting experience into language, written or oral, is a meaning-making process (Vygotsky, 1987, cited in Seidman, 1991). A further, meaning-making process occurs in the sharing of students' texts.

In my work with students, many deny that race is part of their identity, that is, that they are a racialized being. Students need to become aware of how our race-conscious society names and represents the players and the contexts in creating the boundaries and rules of engagement. And students need to be able to acquire the conceptual tools to deconstruct and challenge the ideological hegemony of race.

An activity that I use to encourage students to explore, examine, and re-cognize their history as racialized beings is a paper on the development of their racial identity (O'Donnell & Gallegos, 1993). The paper requests from students an examination of experiences that they identify as pertinent to their realization of themselves as racial beings. (See Diaz-Rico in this volume for description of a similar type of activity.) The racial identity paper asks students to explore the constitutive details of these experiences by describing the situation and the context.

The activity enables students to reconstruct the experiences and explore how the family, relatives, and friends, their neighborhoods, the media, TV, movies, books, music, and especially schooling inform students' understanding and knowledge of race. Within the process of reconstruction and in the sharing of these experiences, the relationships and connections among students' everyday experience and the larger macrostructure of society are developing. An important element at this point is to link students' individual experience to the macro-sociocultural realm.

Some students are less able or ready to engage in the introspective nature of the activity. Opposition to this activity comes in the form of brevity in the assignment and a superficial exploration and discussion of the topic. Students do have a right not to fully engage with an activity. I respect that right. But in using this activity, I have noticed that how and when the activity is introduced plays a part in how some students choose to respond to the activity.

In the past, for example, I have used this activity early in the course, but recently I have introduced the activity much later in the course. I have found that before students can begin to grapple with their own history it is necessary to establish a conceptual framework and provide students with a language to discuss race and racism (e.g., Tatum, 1992; O'Donnell & Gallegos, 1993). Prior to having students explore their own individual experience, students are introduced to the complex nature of racism through various biographical (e.g., Baldwin, 1963; Sáenz, 1992); scientific (e.g., Gould, 1981) and historical (e.g., Zinn, 1980) readings. Each of these readings addresses a particular context necessary for understanding the complex nature of racism. Further, the readings are selected for their discussion of race and racism with an emphasis on schooling and education. I have discovered that most students "take" to the activity of writing about their personal experience with race after the topic has been examined from a "distance" and its pervasion in society established.

Re-Cognizing Race Hegemony and Ideology

A primary task in working with students on issues of race and racism is to enable students to make connections between their individual experience and the macrostructural realm. Initially, many students focus on the primary role of the family in the development of their racial perspectives. But, through discussions, most students are able to perceive how school and their workplaces, for example, inform their understanding on race and impact their racial identity. In some ways students are able to trace the development of their perspectives and many are able to witness how their perspectives have changed and evolved based on their lived experience. Though many students may identify the family as a primary source of their racial perspectives, most students can also articulate how through other social experiences their perspectives have altered. These consensual and contradictory elements revealed in students' stories indicate the cracks in the ideological program. Enabling students to discuss the moments of questions, doubts, and concerns they have regarding race and racism provides most students an avenue for change. To assume that students are not thinking or thoughtful about the issues undermines a pedagogical process in which ethics, respect, and dialogue describe the teaching relationship.

This process of having students reconstruct their racial experience and of sharing these experiences further opens the discourse on race ideology and plants the seed for transformation. As indicated in the description of the activity, students are asked to identify those social elements and contexts in which they have learned about race. Many are still at a loss to see these learnings as having an impact on their racial identity. But the shared stories and the ensuing discussion on their refusal to accept carte blanche the "teachings," their questions of doubt and wonder, and their different lived experiences indicate the contradictions in the ideological wall. And these contradictions can lay the foundation for students' transformation.

The sharing of the stories reveals the idiosyncratic experience as well as the collective. For example, many white students describe their neighborhoods and immediate communities as segregated. Some white students discuss how they lived in a segregated community but they describe how their schools were "integrated." A closer examination and discussion of this "integrated" phenomenon often reveals that, for some white students, students of color occupied physical space but not the white students' social space. Discussing students' experiences with tracking in their secondary schools often exposes the institution's role in segregating groups of students (O'Donnell, 1995). Emerging from these individual stories is a "collective text" (Bigelow, 1990) in which students' experiences with race are written.

It is important as multicultural educators to realize and to understand the politically conservative climate that informs many of our students' experiences. This conservative climate enables us to mark to some degree "where our students are coming from." In knowing our history and our students, we can come to know our students' "commonsense" in a Gramscian manner. In knowing this common sense we can be prepared and, thus, creative in our pedagogical stance to counter this common sense.

In Gramsci's construct of ideological hegemony, the idea of common sense is a product of the hegemonic process. Through a process of socialization, students are born into a particular historical period whose contending ideas, ideology, become part of the everyday of students' individual, institutional, and cultural lives (e.g., Berger & Luckmann, 1967; Boggs, 1984; Golding, 1992). This process "by which people's everyday commonsense understandings are shaped by, and brought into conformity with, the existing social and economic system" represents Gramsci's concept of hegemony (Troyna & Hatcher, 1992, p. 46).

Reading the "Texts"

Though many students can write about and discuss their experiences and make connections among the varied stories shared, it is difficult for many to realize how the "text" is written. One, most students do not have a language to examine race; they lack a definition of what race is and what racism is. Much of the language on their understandings of race reveals an essentialist conceptualization. Though few express a biological determinism, their use and interchange of terms such as *race* and *culture* indicate that a "natural" antipathy exists among different groups. In *essence*, some "thing" causes this aversion within groups.

Two, many students lack an understanding of history. Most students do not perceive themselves as historicized. For many history is a long list of facts that delineate a story of progress. In this story of progress, right overcomes wrong, new advancements replace not displace the old, and this material accounting of "progress" signifies the development of our "civil" society (see Bury, 1932). But all students have lived experience as racial beings and, through the exploration and sharing of this experience, the complex nature of race ideology in our society can be explored. In working with students on this understanding, conceptual tools need to be shared to enable their understanding.

Recent research with children and their perspectives on race and racial interactions indicate that children are actively attempting to understand the meaning of race. Troyna and Hatcher (1992), for example, studied the racial perspectives of ten- and eleven-year-old white children in primarily white primary/elementary schools. The focus of their study was to understand the dynamics of race and issues of racism in children's lives. They wanted to know how race and racism operated in children's interactions and understanding of their social milieu. They found that "racist ideologies are not passively received but are used in ways which help children make sense of their material and cultural circumstances" (1992, p. 196). Children are exposed to a wide and varied social discourse on issues of race and racism both in and out of school. The contradictory messages of domination and racial egalitarianism run through the social, cultural, and institutional world of children's lives. Within this social milieu children are negotiating, selecting, and interpreting their own understanding of issues of race and racism via these "adult" messages as well as their own direct experiences. Their world is marked by parental, cultural, and institutional messages of race and racism.

In a similar study of white Australian school children, Rizvi (1993) explains that children's racial understandings are constructed within their everyday experience. The nature of this everyday experience is related to the larger social and cultural discourse on race and racism within Austrailian society. As with Troyna and Hatcher, Rizvi describes how children negotiate and make sense of a racist ideological discourse emphasizing that "while popular racism is an ideology that organizes children's thinking, it does not determine it" (p. 134).

Frankenberg (1993) in her study of white women and their experiences and understanding of race and racism, shares a story in which one of her participants explains how her uncle rejected her protests of his remarks about an African American whom she and her uncle encountered on an afternoon stroll. The fact that this incident lingers in the woman's memory as a significant event in her understanding of the issue of race and racism indicates the social and historical nature of the social construction of race. Unable to assert her contestations of the adult's world perspective, the child's experience and therefore perspective of the incident becomes sedimented and remains in effect unanswered and misunderstood. As an adult the woman reencounters the incident and confronts the emotional pain and anguish associated with the incident. The loss of personal autonomy and integrity realized in the reconstruction of such racial incidents may provide the potential for change. (See, in this volume, Goodman's discussion of pain and reconciliation.)

To stop at this individual level of inquiry, however, is to partially instruct students about the dynamics of race and racism. Macedo (1994), for example, argues that "the sharing of experiences should not be understood in psychological terms only. [This sharing of experiences] invariably requires a political and ideological analysis as well" (p. 175). Students' stories can reveal the range of racial discourse they have acquired. At the same time, a concerted effort to identify the linkage among students' experiences and articulation of their racial experience to the sociopolitical realm of race discourse in the form of ideologies, policies, and practices can further outline for students how race operates in U.S. society.

Conclusion

In understanding the role of race in children's social construction of reality we can better understand how college students, young and old, respond to the issue of race. Race needs to be understood as an ideology that imbues the social, cultural, and political fabric of society. Understanding race as an ideology also enables us to enact educational interventions to transfrom its ideological and material holdings.

Many of the experiences or events shared in students' racial identity papers deal with themselves as children or young adults. Several describe situations in which they were not in a position to question or to voice dissent. Exploring with students these moments of dissent and examining the details of their experiences enables many students to clarify their understanding of race and racism.

It is important to enable students to see how their perspectives (ideas, beliefs, and attitudes) about race are connected to a larger ideological program and discourse on race. The problem encountered in this task is enabling students to realize how their "social" identity is linked to a "self" identity. Our ideology of individualism often masks our social collective. On the surface, many students accept the idea that they are members of various social groups based on social characteristics such as race, ethnicity, gender, age, and so. What is difficult for many students to appreciate is how the ideological discourse on these various social characteristics inform identity, not only as object, in that certain social labels are ascribed to "me," but as a subject, "I," whose "self" is informed by the ideological discourse, for example, on race. Therefore, I can be described as white, Irish, and male. Each of these labels is imbued with social ideological meanings. These meanings inform not determine how I act white, Irish, and male or how I may describe and define White, Irish and male.

In my work with students around issues of multiculturalism and, especially, with issues of race and racism, students' oppositional stance is understood. I expect it. Students' opposition, however, is not accepted; it is challenged. After nearly ten years of working with students on issues of multiculturalism, I have come to realize the importance of listening to students. Listening to their reasons, listening to their voice for its emotion, its forcefulness, its quiver, and its questions. Listening to what they have to say and how they say it provides me, the instructor, with the material to begin demystifying the concept of race/multiculturalism.

5

Lynne T. Díaz-Rico

Toward a Just Society

Recalibrating Multicultural Teachers

The Need for Antiracism Education in the Preparation of English-as-a-Second-Language (ESL) Teachers
The Context of Education in California and the Nation

The number of language-minority students in California (approximately 1.5 million students in 3.1 million language minority households) and in the United States (estimates vary from 3.5 to 5 million limited-English-proficient students) has created a pressing need for bilingual teachers (Díaz-Rico and Smith, 1994). The severe understaffing of bilingual classrooms in California has ensured a continuing role in the language minority classroom for predominantly Euro-American, middle-class teachers. Moreover, the number of classrooms in which no single home language prevails favors a model in which students are educated in an

English-language instructional environment that is modified to include support for English-language learners.

English-as-a-second-language (ESL) teachers with a strong interest in language acquisition and a sense of compassion for the difficulties faced by culturally diverse students are often successful in promoting the academic success of language-minority students. Specialized preparation in teaching methodology includes a curriculum of multicultural education, in order that ESL teachers develop the skills of advocacy for, and appreciation of, language-minority students. However, multicultural education must go beyond preparing teachers to apply token or additive approaches toward the study of ethnic groups. Banks and McGee (1989) call for an approach to multicultural education that is both transformative and geared toward the promotion of social action. This level of curricular transformation necessitates a comprehensive intervention in the mindset of the mainstream teacher.

Middle-class, Euro-American teachers, however well intentioned, often enter ESL teacher education with racial, ethnic, and class prejudices. David Reid (1992) captures the ubiquity of these prejudices:

> We are all caught up on the continuum of racism. The only viable position is an anti-racist one which acknowledges the ideological influences and recognises that everyone in one way or another is involved in discriminatory structures, and needs to take a stand against racism to dismantle both racist structures and racist attitudes. (p. 16)

For the most part, racist beliefs are unexamined and earnestly denied by the population of prospective teachers, who are often imbued with idealism and liberal values. Endemic to modern American society are stereotypical beliefs about cultural and linguistic disadvantage, cultural mismatch, or lack of positive parental values as a cause of low achievement on the part of minority students. Classrooms and teachers operate within a macroculture in which ethnic slurs and racially motivated hate crimes are on the increase (Hamilton, 1994), especially on school campuses (Bodinger-deUriarte, 1991). The increasing racism in the mainstream culture affects the belief systems of white college students (Balenger, Hoffman and Sedlacek, 1992). Chávez Chávez, O'Donnell, and Gallegos (1995) document that undergraduate teacher education students enter multicultural education with attitudes and beliefs that largely reflect the hegemonic racial status quo. Educated whites usually think of racism in terms of the overt behaviors of individuals that can be readily identified and labeled, and a person who does not behave in these identified ways is not considered a racist. Most white students deny their own racism (Scheurich, 1993).

Research suggests that changes in the belief systems and attitudes of college students can be accomplished by participation in a multicultural course, but that the change has little lasting effect (Grant & Secada, 1990). Research indicates that deliberate attempts to confront students with evidence of the hegemonic nature of racism fails to change the view that racism is the set of isolated acts of prejudiced individuals, rather than a social practice embedded in institutions within the dominant culture (Chávez Chávez, O'Donnell, & Gallegos, 1995).

Classism is as endemic as racism in the belief systems of middle-class, prospective ESL teachers, yet there is no question that ESL teachers will face the responsibility of educating poor students. According to the National Center for the Study of Children in Poverty, one out of four children is now living below the poverty threshold; this includes five million children under the age of six. Another 2.7 million of children under six are in the "near poor" category (Li & Bennett, 1994). These children are an increasing part of the school population. Language minority students comprise a large chunk of this population; 24 percent of Hispanics, for example, are currently living in poverty (Vobejda, 1990). Despite the reality of widespread poverty on the part of language-minority students, a critical discourse about the origin and nature of this poverty (Wright, 1977) is largely absent from teacher training.

Teacher education institutions, for the most part, define themselves as service agencies geared toward providing local school districts with technical experts; largely absent is the image of the teacher as an individual who furthers the exercise of social justice or promotes a more equitable social order (Giroux & McLaren, 1987). Therefore, providing a curriculum of mere additive or celebrative multiculturalism begs the question, "What techniques must be incorporated into a multicultural teacher education program to produce a genuinely transformative teacher, one capable of promoting social action?" Anything less than dedication to the ideal of educational equity for students reduces multicultural education to a "stroll down ethnicity lane." Multicultural education instead must include techniques of transformation whose goal is *to promote engagement in the struggle to achieve a just society*. At best, such a curriculum includes explicit attention to antiracism and promotes a prospective teacher's active entry into a multicultural lifestyle.

The course Teaching in a Multicultural Society is designed to increase ESL teachers' effectiveness in expanding nonmainstream students' access to the core curriculum. This is accomplished by inviting teachers to reexamine their beliefs about genetic inferiority/superiority, cultural deprivation, institutional racism, the personal responsibility of teachers toward equity in the classroom, and the employment of a bias-free curriculum. The course treats such issues as the influence of culture on schooling, the cultural practices of schooling, and the sociopolitical context of schooling. As the instructor of the course, the author tries to actualize a four-fold pedagogy: examination of the core readings of the course with impartiality and critical thinking; participant's ownership of responsibility for personal psychological growth; provision of opportunities to express opinions both confidentially and publicly; and freedom to counter the instructor's passions with apathy or counterpassion. Given the discomfort caused by the examination of issues of race and culture within a mainstream society that discourages such inquiry, participants enter the classroom with some reluctance to disclose their opinions. Participants may have already experienced courses dealing with issues of race, gender, and social class in which their opinions have been excoriated, ridiculed, or held suspect, leaving them inert or scorched by instructors with an incendiary personal or political agenda. Thus, an undertow of self-protection or unwillingness to disclose opinions often characterizes classroom discussions.

Students in the university classroom may resist engagement on issues of social equity and multicultural education and be reluctant to reexamine political beliefs, gender issues, or race/class prejudice. Such resistance may take overt form, such as strident vocal opposition, or covert form, such as lip service or superficial conformity to a superimposed or proposed set of values. Such engagement may not modify subsequent teaching behavior or catalyze transformative change. Worse, external pressure may cause students to rebuff attempts to alter their belief system. A curriculum that introduces pressure to change deeply held beliefs may become an emotional minefield. It is clear that only those participants who take responsibility for their own growth will permit self-change and personal development in ways that lead to mature emotional and cognitive progress. Using what Foucault (1982) calls "techniques of the self," or "technology of the self" ("technology" defined as a set of techniques), a curriculum can be deployed to challenge the belief systems of the prospective ESL teachers in a way that presents an opportunity for growth without engendering a hypocritical or sycophantic response accompanied by pseudoepiphanies of enlightenment but devoid of deeper attitudinal or behavioral change.

The Continuum of Engagement and the Technology of the Self

The range of engagement can be represented as a continuum from overt racism to transformative involvement in the struggle to achieve equity (see figure 5.1). The image of the continuum provides a visible vector, a

1	2	3	4	5	6	7
overt racism	covert racism	political correctness	speaking up	participating in cultures	initiating events	transformative leadership

FIGURE 5.1. The Continuum of Involvement in Transformative Engagement

graphic that contrasts the lukewarm nature of complacency and suggests alternative positions may be available and attainable. Visualizing the growth toward engagement in the form of a continuum is not to suggest that growth in the capacity to become both aware and effective in overcoming racism is a linear process. On the contrary; each person confronts monumental social edifices that invest the status quo with authority and invisibly support acquiescence. The little-understood relationship between belief and actualization, the tension between conviction and cowardice, and the subtle rewards dealt to the privileged too often rend asunder whatever hard-won conversion is gained by work on oneself. The image of a continuum can provide some rough benchmarks that represent students' capacity to respond to transformative exercises.

Unfortunately, prospective teachers are too often content to exemplify the middle position on the continuum of beliefs and practices, a position that leads them to define themselves as "politically correct." The ideal of political correctness seems to have evolved during the 1980s when politically liberal individuals sought verbal labels for minority groups that were noninflammatory and would not be interpreted as racist, discriminatory, or hostile. For many well-meaning individuals, the mastery of noninflammatory terms became synonymous with the externalizing of positive intent toward issues such as equal opportunity for minorities. Thus voicing politically correct labels with the intent of avoiding confrontation came to function as a metonymy for liberal social action.

The work of the multicultural course, then, is to provide the opportunity for prospective teachers to reconceptualize the continuum of engagement so that the neutral position (one's belief that political correctness is, in itself, a satisfactory social position) becomes a starting point, rather than a comfortable abode. Essential to this growth are two key concepts: first, that the individual is responsible for self-assessment and planful self-change using the available technologies of the self; and second, that the measure of engagement be *recalibrated,* so that the continuum is truncated to remove overt and covert racism from the spectrum, and a new continuum is conceptualized which extends from political correctness to transformation (see figure 5.2). This continuum is similar to Bennett and Bennett's (1996) developmental model of intercultural sensitivity (see figure 5.3).

3	4	5	6	7
political correctness	speaking up	participating in cultures	initiating events	transformative leadership

FIGURE 5.2. The Recalibrated Continuum of Involvement in Transformative Engagement

The continuum of engagement in figures 5.1 and 5.2 should not taken as a psychological reality but rather as a set of labels for clusters of techniques grouped together to accomplish similar objectives. As a whole, this set of techniques can be considered a technology of personal change: a toolkit, a syntax of tactics. In Foucault's terms (Martin, Gutman, & Hutton, 1988), a technology of the self comprises "those practices that permit individuals to effect by themselves or with the help of others a certain number of operations on their own bodies and souls, thoughts, conduct, and ways of being, so as to transform themselves in order to attain a certain state."

Foucault's model for the analysis of ethical challenges posed by use of the technology of the self posits four distinct features: descriptions of the "ethical substance," "mode of subjectification," "ethical work," and "telos." "Ethical substance" is defined as "what constitutes the prime material of moral conduct." The "mode of subjectification" is "the means by which the individual establishes a relation to the rules of conduct." The "ethical work" is "the specific transformation of oneself invited by an ethical commitment." Lastly, the telos is the "mode of being for which an ethical being aims" (from Bernauer, 1988, pp. 65–66).

In the context of the multicultural course, the ethical substance is that aspect of the participant's belief system that must be altered to support a lifestyle that actualizes political and/or social action toward achieving equity. The prevailing model of individualism in contemporary American mainstream culture encourages a two-fold notion: that the work of improvement focuses on change within the individual, and that within this improvement no important distinction need be made between the personal and professional self. There is no technology of self is offered by the American mainstream culture that permits a change in belief other than that of the individual's ability to marshal an inner dedication to internalizing a new set of values and behaviors. The ethical substance is comprised of an internalized, individualized self. This creates difficulties; each person carries the weight of the triad of beliefs that: (1) the entire self will be unilaterally changed if one set of beliefs changes; (2) the individual should not acknowledge that external or group values have been influential in creating change in the internalized

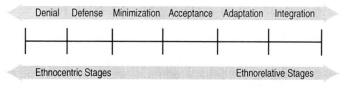

FIGURE 5.3. A Developmental Model of Intercultural Sensitivity
Source: Bennett, 1995.

self; and (3) a change in belief is tantamount to admitting that the old belief set, hence the former self, was flawed.

The means by which the individual is expected to internalize professional rules of conduct (Foucault's "mode of subjectification," or "regimen of change") is to generate a rational and elaborate vision of teaching. However, in reality the pressure of time detracts from the participants' capacity to devote time to mastering a complex system of information organization. Indeed, other evidence suggests that teachers employ a much simpler organizational system, especially under stress, a bare-bones phenomenology consisting of "myself/the students/everything else" (Díaz-Rico, 1992). It is therefore necessary that the regimen of engagement be understandable and straightforward.

The ethical work is the specific transformation of oneself that is invited by the commitment to change. Clearly, ethical work in the classrooms of graduate schools is predicated on the assumption that a class participant is an autonomous professional. This places the burden of responsibility directly on the individual to succeed or fail, to grow or to stagnate, to bond with an instructor or to fend off intervention. When the ethical work must be performed as an individual, class meetings become exercises in what child developmentalists call "parallel play," a situation where individuals are in proximity with one another but do not share interdependent goals. The only alternative to this nature of ethical work is for group members to become team members, with the entire team moving together on issues of engagement. At present, the ethical work remains the individual's personal responsibility.

The nature of the telos, the goal toward which the process of sustaining engagement extends, is consonant with the liberals' vision of educational attainment: success for the individual through personal striving. The telos of the class participants' ethical work is to become an individual superstar graduate student, with academic achievement as the ostensible criterion of success. This telos, in turn, highlights the contradiction of the role of the instructor of a graduate class; one's success is defined as the success of class participants in performing their own,

Level of engagement	Enjoyment of other U. S. cultures	Understanding one's own and other U. S. cultures	Engagement in seeking justice
Maintaining "political correctness"	View video: *Into the Circle* or *La Vida de Maria* + other video interviews	Self-discovery essay; analysis of terminology	Analysis of "political correctness"
Speaking up	Defending multiculturalism	What's in a name? Ethnographic look at culture; reaction papers on required reading from Heath, Hsu, Spindler & Spindler	Examining privilege; confronting racist speech
Participating in cultures	Intercultural contact as cultural capital; readings: Bourdieu, Moll; experiencing an intercultural avocational community activity or hobby	Ethnographic readings specific to culture in target classroom	Confronting the shadow; discussion of stress management
Initiating events	Experiencing then recreating a cultural event	Ethnographic child study	Designing a social action for the classroom; acquiring the technology of knowledge for multicultural curriculum (Bennett, Ch. 7–9)
Transformative leadership	Creating a handicraft item	Critical language study	Adopting a mechanism for parent involvement in the classroom

FIGURE 4. Technology of the Self across Levels of Engagement and Dimensions of the Transformative Work

individual, ethical work. A group telos, admittedly, would be more powerful; the biggest change in implementing engagement in the struggle for equity would be for participants to set a group, shared goal of change.

The important distinguishing focus at this point is on the individual's *use* of the technology of the self, that this set of techniques be represented to participants in the multicultural course as a set of *choices and options* on which individuals must act. The ability of the individual to exert control and choice avoids the domination of professor over student in the name of growth, and remands the course content to the custody of the self, as a technology of the self rather than a technology of power. This orientation avoids the common pitfalls of the college course whose ideological stance encounters resistance. This set of techniques restores the freedom to the self to move along the continuum. The continuum is used here to outline the progression of academic activities in the course Teaching in a Multicultural Society (see figure 5.4).

Three components or dimensions of work comprise the technology of the self. The first is the growth of *a sense of enjoyment* of other cultures; the second is a growth in *understanding* other cultures; and the third is the growth in *engagement in achieving equity*, the willingness to become involved in the struggle for justice. In this chapter, the work is confined to enjoyment, understanding, and engagement in equity for cultures represented by immigrant or indigenous minorities within the United States Intercultural understanding in a global or multinational sense falls outside the purview of this work.

Shoring up the Starting Block
Protection against Backsliding to Levels 1 and 2

An appreciation of the United States of America is a necessary beginning for a multicultural curriculum. The video *Into the Circle*, featuring a Native American powwow, provides a eloquent introduction to the American dream. Another poignant introduction is *La Vida de Maria*, a video that details the academic success of Maria, the daughter of migrant workers, who graduated from the University of California, Santa Cruz. Other sources of insight into minority views are interviews filmed by the author with Native American, African American, and Hispanic leaders (Díaz-Rico, 1996a, 1996b).

The beginning of the actual process of recalibration is the acknowledgment of racism in society. At the beginning, efforts must be made to strengthen the liberal tendencies of the "politically correct" individuals, to try to forestall passive acceptance of racial and cultural intolerance on the part of class participants. Rather than try to invoke a self-confession from class participants to having themselves acquiesced to racist practices in the past, a more neutral yet personal approach is to use a self-discovery paper to introduce the topic of racism in society. The prompts for this five- to seven-page autobiographical essay are: What is your racial and cultural background? What was the racial and ethnic composition of the environment (urban or rural) in which you lived as a child?

What were some incidents in your past that led you to the awareness of racist beliefs and practices in society? What events in your life have provided you with intercultural or interracial experiences? Writing this essay and sharing it privately with another class member can bring out the sense of a common bond: many people observed or experienced racist practices while growing up; many were hurt by these, either personally or vicariously, and are willing and eager to see these practices stopped. Many individuals remember a period in their lives—usually late adolescence—in which they sought out contact with other cultures in order to expand their own intercultural or interracial understanding. In addition to the self-discovery essay, class participants need to be provided with a glossary of terms they will encounter during the course. Careful attention to the definition of terms in multicultural education (see Nieto, 1992) helps to establish a common working vocabulary.

In addition, class participants may have heard the term *political correctness* used in a derogatory manner, as though removing racism, classism, and sexism from language were somehow out of vogue, or the prohibition of ethnically/racially noninflammatory speech was not a worthy social goal. College students know that there are bigots in U.S. society; most prospective ESL teachers have overheard racist comments made by peers, colleagues in the schools, or relatives. Some students are also aware that U.S. institutions are struggling over the issue of prohibition of racist speech. Few Americans, however, are sure of how to react to the issue of political correctness. Judith Martin, under the nom de plume "Miss Manners" (Martin, 1995), provides a useful discussion of political correctness. Martin skewers those who would characterize the emphasis on politically correct speech as the "ridiculous" and "touchy" overreactions of those who cannot "take a joke." Her analysis distinguishes the immoral from the rude and suggests appropriate practice: practicing bigotry is immoral; expressing bigotry is rude. Reacting against the expression of bigotry in a rude manner is also rude; reacting against the expression of bigotry in a civilized manner is not rude. Consideration should be given to motivation, so that well-meaning people who use politically incorrect terms are not inordinately punished; however, those who apologize in advance for bigoted statements are not excused. Objections to bigotry should match the severity of the transgression, ranging from "I beg your pardon?" to "How dare you!" to "You will be hearing from my lawyer." A part of the technology of the self at this level includes techniques for responding to the expression of bigotry. Role playing a conversation in the faculty lounge is a useful simulation for practice in countering racist and classist statements (see Díaz-Rico and Weed, 1995, 285–90, for a sample simulation prompt).

Attaining Level 4
From Political Correctness to "Speaking Up"

Three important issues stand out in the current debate on racial and ethnic equity. The first is whether the multicultural society is a desirable goal for the United States; the second is the definition of ethnic; the third is the issue of first amendment limits on the freedom to use "non-politically correct" speech. The contemporary debate on the use of affirmative action hiring policies touches on the first issue. Many Americans are comfortable with the idea that the ethnically elite and privileged members of society somehow deserve its rewards, and theybelieve that diversifying the composition of the leadership class of society is not particularly desirable. Thus an important part of the early work of the multicultural educator is to have class participants convince themselves that cultural diversity is a worthy social goal. Using an excerpt from Henry's 1994 book, *In Defense of Elitism*, students discuss Henry's propositions, that the number of college admissions be reduced by 50 percent, that the unsuccessful applicants to higher education be given vocational training, and that this determination of college admission be based solely on standardized testing. The use of this prompt seems to focus the issue of polyracial social leadership. An overview of the rationale and utility of multicultural teaching is presented in Díaz-Rico (1993), which provides a case study based on an actual incident in which a teacher was accused of racism by parents after the Los Angeles riots of 1992.

A second important issue is the white middle class's tendency to assign ethnicity to everyone but the white middle class. Using the exercise "What's in a name?" (prompts: What does your name mean to you? Where did it come from? What does it mean to your family? Do you like your name?), students come to understand that every name is the bearer of a personal and cultural identity. In addition, reading and writing a reaction paper to Heath's *Ways with Words*. (1983; Part I. "Ethnographer learning") helps class members to understand that the white community of Roadville has a culture just as does the black community of Trackton. White middle-class readers of this ethnographic study sometimes report increased understanding of their own families. After these activities, students are much more willing to accept the relativism of cultural practices, even the practices of schooling that they unwittingly have absorbed and endorsed as a part of the hegemony of the values of the dominant culture. This examination of their values can then be combined with assigned readings that characterize U.S. mainstream culture (Spindler and Spindler, 1990, pp. 22–41, 56–70, 96–121; Hsu, 1986) and contrasted with descriptions of native American values and lifestyles

(Bennett, 1995, pp. 59–60, 367–71). These readings help to create appreciation of alternative cultural values.

In order for class participants to accept the work of achieving equity in education, they must at some point examine their own complicity in the privileges of being white and middle class in a society predicated on inequity. "Privilege" is defined as the state of benefiting by special advantages, favors, or rights accorded to some to the exclusion of others. In effect, the "politically correct" or neutral position on the original continuum, which requires that the individual assume a politically correct public stance, is in fact a socially privileged position, one that directly or indirectly benefits from the discomfort of others. Many class members have liberal beliefs; they conceive of a world in which minorities can work hard as individuals to achieve middle-class status. However, this belief does not include a reconstructing of the social order so that the current middle class loses its privileges. McIntosh's article "White Privilege and Male Privilege" is a very useful tool for exploring the advantage experienced by those who are white, male, or middle class. Reading McIntosh's article is an uncomfortable experience for most class participants. The course seems to pivot around participants' reactions to this article—those who are willing to examine their own complicity in hegemonic privileges and those whose reaction is characterized by inert discomfort.

Many class members become aware for the first time of the many social advantages they have reaped at the expense of those who are non-white, non-middle class, or female; they often react with fear that they will be asked to forego these privileges, or with guilt that they were so long willing to live with a peripheral recognition of the inequity of their privilege. The overt reaction to this fear and guilt takes several forms. Participants sometimes avoid the subsequent discussion, feigning illness or family duties; they sometimes enter the classroom and seek out those fellow participants who seem to share their race, gender, or social class; they defend their own privilege with arguments citing entitlement due to merit; or they create arguments to defend privilege based on such theories as social symbiosis ("women need men to protect their privilege" or "lower classes need capitalists to create employment opportunities"), or even theories similar to social Darwinism ("there will always be poor people" or "some people have character flaws").

Because reactions to this article seem to be central to the ability of participants to acquire subsequent techniques of engagement, it seems important at this point to make available a technique that moves participants beyond a wholistic or undifferentiated emotional reaction. In order to channel the backlash of anxiety this article produces, it is useful to give class participants a grid derived from McIntosh's article with the forty-two kinds of privilege listed, and ask them to rate on a scale of

1 to 4 how willing they would be to forego each particular privilege. The understanding that some privileges are more vital to them than others permits a more rational and analytical discussion of privilege. This rating is a key technique in helping class members to audit their own investiture in privilege.

The movement from level 3 to level 4 is accomplished when participants are no longer content to be neutral in the struggle to achieve a multicultural society—when the battle becomes their own and not someone else's. Without this commitment, they may intellectually experience the course content and examine the tools of change at more advanced levels, but the work of internal change will not be accomplished. Those who are unwilling to go further may be sanctioned to play a role of "devil's advocate" to other participants, thus providing to others some energy of reverse polarity from their own resistance. This may be more profitable to the class as a whole in the long run, rather than having the class drained of momentum from the inertia of those who are pushed past their capacity for change.

The role of the instructor at this point in the process of engagement is fraught with difficulty. Class participants often seem willing to project hostility on the instructor when they are feeling anger, or to punish a discussion leader with passive withdrawal or absenteeism. The instructor can only be true to the philosophy of encouraging critical thinking, personal responsibility for change, opportunity to express opinions, and freedom to be apathetic or counterpassionate. Having technologies available like the privilege rating exercise to convert emotion into analysis directs and channels emotion toward change.

Level 5
Participating in Cultures

The middle class in a capitalist society is often mesmerized by capital. Massive and pervasive advertising campaigns define "valuable" as that which is new and expensive. A similarly circumscribed value system defines only certain kinds of knowledge as important. Bourdieu (1973) points out that individuals enter school with different cultural capital, which in turn influences school success. Teachers seem to invest energy in students according to the potential payoff for this investment as a function of a child's existing cultural capital. A part of the work in valuing minority cultures in the United States is to convince teachers that "those homes" are a source of knowledge capital (Moll, 1993), rather than a locus of disadvantage. Moreover, teachers must define their own successful intercultural experiences as cultural capital, which in turn will enhance their own investment in students. This accomplishes the work at level 5 in the dimension of enjoying other cultures.

The work at this level on understanding one's own and other cultures can be accomplished by reading enthnographies of cultures specific to the classrooms in which the ESL teacher will be employed, such as Delgado-Gaitan's *Crossing Cultural Borders* for the Chicano culture.

The work at this level on engagement is subtle and challenging. Reading James Baldwin's essay *In Search of a Majority* helps class members to become aware of the psychological concept Carl Jung calls "the shadow." For each person, one's own unacknowledged fears and blind spots can function as gateways to an expanded vision of possibility and understanding of the Self. In a similar fashion, according to Baldwin, American society positions the American Negro as the "shadow," the basement class of a society characterized by vague class distinctions and economic insecurity; a class that can be used to assure oneself that one is still okay ("I may be bad off, but at least I'm not black.")

Concomitantly, an ESL teacher needs to discuss and confront one aspect of the shadow that is very real: the physical dangers of working in urban schools. Techniques of the self must include a set of professional security practices that provide protection yet preclude the need for an exaggerated concern for personal safety. A discussion of stress management (see Gold and Roth, 1993) helps teachers to face the issue of professional "burnout."

Level 6
Initiating Events

In order to sustain professional lives organized toward a commitment to ideals of multicultural equity, and maintain private lives enriched by intercultural participation, individuals must be able to initiate multicultural events. A useful activity at this level in the dimension of enjoyment is for class members to attend an event sponsored by another culture (church service, powwow, theatrical performance) and recreate some aspect of the event for the rest of the class. Class members have sung a gospel song for the class, read excerpts from the play *A Woman Warrior* (based on Maxine Hong Kingston's writings) and shared a collection of artifacts purchased on the Hopi reservation, including a group tasting of *piki* bread. The need to recreate some aspect of the event involves the participant more deeply than would be the case if the assignment were merely to visit and observe.

In the dimension of intercultural understanding at this level, class members complete an ethnographic child case study, focusing on a child from another culture. The rationale for the case study is to help prospective teachers to see schooling from the point of view of the student. This research can lead to an increase in the knowledge base about teaching students of diverse abilities and characteristics. The methodology is considered "qualitative research" because rich, descriptive data is provided about the contexts, activities, and beliefs of diverse students in educational settings. Results are examined within their context (Goetz and Lecompte, 1984), and involve inferences drawn from several different kinds of data from many sources—field notes, school data, elicited texts, demographic information, and unstructured interviews (Erickson, 1977). The research is accomplished by an observer who participates to some extent in the life of the student who is observed. At the conclusion of the study, hypotheses are generated that direct future inquiry. The domains of inquiry included in the case study are cognitive: linguistic, personal, social, and moral development; individual differences in ability; a cultural profile of the family and its values; an assessment of English-language ability; and a look at classroom behavior. The case study is a major research paper of fifteen to twenty pages. Class members are provided with a detailed rubric.

In the dimension of engagement, class members are invited to choose one kind of social activism (writing letters, staging a press conference) from *Kids' Guide to Social Action* (Lewis, 1991) and write a plan for a multicultural education teaching unit featuring this social activism that incorporates all four of Banks and McGee's (1989) levels of integration of ethnic content (contributions, additive, transformative, decision making, and social action). Class members also are assigned Bennett's (1995) chapters 7–9, which contain detailed instructions on implementing an authentic multicultural curriculum.

Transformative Leadership

The extreme resolution of the continuum of commitment is the assumption of a warrant for social and political activism. The tools for enjoyment at this level are physical: each class member is asked to create a handicraft item that originates in a minority American culture. In this way, participants understand with their bodies (power is embodied: Foucault, 1979; Dreyfus and Rabinow, 1982). With this activity, the technology of production becomes a form of knowledge/power within the technology of the self (Foucault, 1988).

An important tool at the transformative level in understanding American culture is critical language study (Fairclough 1988, 1992), which provides a way to analyze the power of language to embody emotionally weighted or biased text, institutionalized racism, or unacknowledged hegemonic cultural practices.

Both critical language study and the study of power (see Gore, 1994; Foucault, 1989) are necessary for ESL teachers to understand the nature of power in the domain of education. ESL teachers often operate in highly politicized social contexts, in which decisions are made daily that influence the climate of acceptance for minority or nonstandard languages, that control the quality and quantity of materials available for instruction of ESL students, or that affect the number of students per class, the ambiance of the classroom, the time of day of class, or other factors that make successful instruction more or less possible. These decisions are the net effects of power. ESL teachers need to be educated directly about power in order that the very idealism that motivates them is not abused when progressive optimism is unwarranted or violated by decisions that disempower ESL students and teachers.

Foucault emphasizes that power is productive as well as repressive. A deduction from this assertion is that ESL teaching will be better—more productive—as a result of the use of these techniques. Part of the research needed within the postmodern paradigm is to document specific power ploys and to use them wittingly to increase the ability of minority students—and their teachers—to speak up, speak out, and master a repertoire of productive practices.

Díaz-Rico and Weed (1995, chap. 11) describe the potential role of ESL teachers in the formation of educational policy from the level of the classroom through the level of the community to the state and national policy formulation process. This chapter is recommended as a tool for leadership development.

The dominant paradigm of progressive idealism is not wrong—it is simply not enough, not strong enough to overcome the restrictive structures and barriers that ESL learners experience when they are confronted with a new culture and language. In the dimension of engagement, practicing or prospective ESL teachers need to see a role for themselves in school-site leadership. Class members are asked at this level to propose, carry out, and critique one activity that impacts school-site policy in a substantive way. These efforts are then shared in the group as a whole. This gives class members experience in leadership within the school and some collective critique for their efforts.

The Response of Class Members to the Course Content

Although every effort is made to treat class members as individuals, it is possible to draw some generalizations about the students who enroll in the multicultural class. The majority of students have as a career goal the profession of English as a second language. The program has drawn participants from several populations: the first is the pool of teachers from a mainstream cultural background who have been assigned to teach minority students and who have chosen to explore this area as a career but are not yet committed to the profession. The second group are experienced ESL teachers who have some identification with the profession and who are returning for career advancement. This group may also contain members who enjoy traveling and teaching abroad. A third group is comprised of individuals from U.S. mainstream cultural backgrounds who have married immigrants to the United States or foreigners. The groups may have overlapping membership. Each group has their distinct reaction to the class activities.

Class members who are not yet committed to the profession are the most difficult to engage, whether because of their unacknowledged negativity toward minorities or immigrants, or because they feel that their own culture or cultural hegemony is threatened and undermined by newcomers. Students in this group may be struggling with maintaining political correctness and acquiring a basic desire and ability to speak up in defense of their students. Those students who are already bicultural, who have some interest and desire in traveling abroad, and/or who have already been engaged in, and enjoy, teaching students from other cultures are those who can be motivated to become even more engaged. These are the students whom I am able to move toward transformation. Overall, in Foucault's terms, those who already have some technology of the self in place are the most likely to acquire the techniques available in the multicultural course.

One example of recommitment to engagement that resulted from a class exercise is the experience of Lourdes, a young woman of Puerto Rican ancestry who enrolled in the M.A. in Education, ESL Option program after spending several years teaching in a local elementary school. She was casually reading the self-exploration paper of a classmate when she ran across a statement to the effect that the classmate's parents had raised their children with the attitude that the Mexican culture were superior to that of other Spanish-speaking immigrants, such as Cubans or Puerto Ricans, partially because the Caribbean Spanish speakers had "lower-class accents." Lourdes was then able to intuit that her students' parents were struggling to respect her as a bilingual teacher because they felt that her Spanish was inferior and she would provide a poor linguistic role model. What she had previously interpreted as lukewarm support for primary language instruction on the part of the parents may have been parents' distrust for her expertise. With this insight, Lourdes was able to code-switch when speaking to Mexican parents, pronounce phonemes such as the final /s/ more carefully, and avoid slang expressions. She was thus able to bond with parents more closely. This, in turn, created in her a sense of support from the parent community, leading to rededication on her part to advocacy for bilingual education, which was an issue of transformative involvement for her. Thus indirect insight into her students' culture via the biographical expression of another class participant provided her with a key impetus that forwarded her own growth.

Conclusion

A caveat: as may be true in other constructivist efforts, growth in this class setting is not even. There is often a period of chaos, uneasiness, and confusion on the part of class participants when their belief systems are shifting and their commitments are solidifying. The role of instructor is complex: to maintain the control of the process in the hands of the participants, and to challenge class participants to grow. Growth varies with individuals across levels. Development may not be immediate, but delayed; the growth of the self may not be noticeable or comfortable or even desirable until years later. For these participants, personal and professional payoffs may be professional lives organized around ideals of equity and access and private lives committed to intercultural contact and affirmation

Teachers who are committed to the ideal of equity and opportunity for all can be a positive influence in schools. A course in multicultural education that offers a repertoire of technologies of the self can help participants to forge from the raw material of the "merely politically correct" the transformative leadership that will be needed to face the monumental tasks that lie ahead.

6

Gaile S. Cannella

Fostering Engagement

Barriers in Teacher Education

Social justice as the moral focus of education has been advocated by philosophers (Dewey, 1959), curriculum theorists
(Kliebard, 1986; Pinar, 1975, 1988), and teacher educators
(Giroux & McLaren, 1986; Greene, 1986; Kessler, 1991; Spodek, 1982,
1989; and Zeichner & Liston, 1990) as well as multiculturalists (Banks,
1994; Oakes, 1985; Ogbu, 1978; Sleeter, 1989; Sleeter & Grant, 1993).
John Dewey proposed that the responsibility of education is to advance
the welfare of society, educating all children for leadership in their own
lives and as leaders in shaping, directing, and changing society. Although education has the greatest potential for removing class barriers
and empowering individuals, current practice inhibits and oppresses
those who do not "best fit" the system (Dewey, 1959; Rawls, 1971;
Zeichner & Liston, 1990). The achievement of social justice requires that

attention be focused on education that empowers all voices in a democracy, a critical multiculturalism in which multiple languages, subjugated knowledges, counterpositions, and critical research are accepted and valued (Estrada & McLaren, 1993; Kincheloe, 1993).

This chapter is one educator's story outlining the complexities of critical multicultural engagement within a social justice teacher education program involving both early childhood and elementary majors. The story begins with a partial description of the program. Barriers to engagement within the development and implementation of such a program are discussed. These barriers include ideologies and power experiences of those who would construct and implement the program, the teacher educators, as well as institutionalized views of knowledge and education. Further, the life experiences and perspectives of the teacher education students themselves emerge as obstacles to critical analysis of dominant ideologies.

Social Justice Teacher Education

Our university of over 40,000 students is located in the southwest in a small culturally diverse community and is generally dominated by whites who comprise over 95 percent of the college population. Although women now make up almost 50 percent of the student body, females were only allowed to enter the university within the past thirty years. White males continue to dominate the faculty, especially in tenure track positions. For over 100 years the educational curriculum focused on the sciences with the creation of the Colleges of Education, Business, and Liberal Arts in the early 1970s. Our students are predominantly white, middle-class individuals, often children of alumni or parents who are uncomfortable with their children attending college in a large city. The university has the reputation for being extremely conservative and is currently dominated by republican students.

Over a two-year period, many of us in the College of Education have worked with public school teachers and community members to outline and begin a teacher education program that focuses on social justice. These collaborative efforts have involved multiple meetings, retreats, readings, discussions, arguments, and soul searching. We have worked together to conduct seminars on the ideas of such scholars as Dewey, Apple, Banks, and Ogbu. A few of us even lead sessions in which the works of Freire, hooks, and other critical multiculturalists were examined. We (university teacher educators and public school personnel) have debated and continue to contrast traditional teacher education field experiences versus social reconstructionist (Zeichner & Liston,

1990), critical experiences. We have even argued the merits of eliminating apprenticeship forms of student teaching.

As one teacher educator, I feel that we have only cracked the surface of most social justice issues (e.g., race, gender, language diversity) and have not been willing to risk our own identities by examining others (e.g., sexual preference, class, white privilege, religious privilege). Nevertheless, we have agreed to focus efforts on a program that attempts to give voice to the diverse family and cultural experiences of our children. We may not have fully examined our constructions of what "respect for diversity" means, but we have agreed that experiences with diverse family and community structures are important for preservice teachers. Before entering courses in which methodology and classroom practices are emphasized, our early childhood and elementary students now spend two semesters working in family and community environments, examining differing cultural perspectives (including their own) and exploring historical, political, and value contexts in which lives have been constructed.

Semester I
Children, Families, and Communities

The focus of the first semester is the examination of one's own cultural perspectives and the exploration of multiple world views. Students are asked to employ critical reflection as they explore the notion of "knowledge" as cultural, gendered, and political construction, created by diverse communities and groups in specific contexts. They write language life autobiographies as oral history and ethnography are explored (e.g., *Maggie's American Dream* by James Comer, 1988; *Ways with Words* by Shirley Brice Heath, 1983; ethnographies from *The Cultural Experience* by James Spradley and David McCurdy, 1988; and life histories from *Affirming Diversity* by Sonia Nieto, 1992). Through family partnership field work, students develop collaborative relationships with children and their families from cultures different than their own. Students also interact with community workers in churches, public housing, and community agencies.

Throughout the semester, the constructs that educators have traditionally posited as universally human are explored as embedded within cultural and political biases and agendas. For example, notions of child development have been constructed by the European American, male-dominated field of psychology. From a social justice, critical perspective, we believe that the concept of child development must be explored as a social construction. The universalist nature of child development has been refuted by cross-cultural research (Heath, 1983; Rogoff, 1990). Children from different cultures exhibit different forms of competence. The interconnections between the child and the values within his/her social world cannot be ignored. Child development is examined as useful only if conceived as multidirectional and multidimensional. The human values, messages, and artifacts within a culture are viewed as creating experiences from which emerge the child's growth. This multidirectional perspective on child development then leads to the examination of multiple views of appropriate parenting and the need to understand and positively value different forms of parent/child interactions within differing cultural contexts.

Students are introduced to notions of cultural power and dominant ideology. They are asked to examine issues such as deterministic family bias, discrimination (e.g, language, gender, race), and middle-class privilege. Finally, the role of language, in various forms and from various perspectives, is continually examined as a tool in constructing equitable or inequitable opportunities for human beings.

Semester II
Children, Schools, and Society

The focus of the second semester is to deconstruct the historical and political context from which schools have emerged and to examine the power relations and oppressive states that result. The history and foundations of education and the social histories of those typically under represented in schools are critiqued. This historical analysis also includes contributions to education by those who have not been given voice, those whose contributions have been disregarded (Weis & Fine, 1993). Equity in schooling is examined using such work as *Savage Inequalities* by Jonathon Kozol (1991). Individual teacher experience is given voice using the work of multiculturalist classroom teachers (e.g., *White Teacher* by Vivian Paley, 1979). Students are asked to continue a dialogue with members of communities that are linguistically and/or culturally different from those who have traditionally constructed and controlled school environments. This discourse is supported using parent and community member panels, observations within schools in which diverse knowledge perspectives and content are displayed, and continued partnerships with family and community members whose life experiences are different than the preservice teacher.

Constructions within society of "appropriate knowledge" and "best practices" are examined. Underlying social and political assumptions and the effects of these value assumptions on children from diverse backgrounds are explored. An example is the notion of Developmentally Appropriate Practice posited by the National Association for the Education of Young Children. Grounded in progressive developmental perspectives that are proposed by the field of psychology, developmentally appropriate practices support the Piagetian focus on logical thought and scientific exploration and foster the notion that a group of experts can determine the learning environment that is appropriate for all children in all contexts (Cannella, 1995; O'Loughlin, 1992). Students are asked to examine the oppressive messages contained in a normative, progressive developmental perspective (e.g., adult privilege over child), the silencing of multiple voices when an appropriate versus inappropriate dichotomy is created (e.g., devaluing of cultures with strengths that are not considered appropriate), and the limitations that are placed on liberatory teaching (Macedo, 1994; Silin, 1995).

As we worked to develop and implement this two-semester, premethodology experience, we explored our own beliefs and biases along with the preservice teachers. At times we agreed; at times we could reach no form of agreement. As ideas were debated, developed, and implemented, barriers to social justice education emerged. These obstacles included institutionalized higher education and the ideologies of teacher educators themselves, as well as preservice teachers.

Engaging in social justice teacher education encompasses not only preservice teachers and schools, but institutionalized power structures and knowledge, university communities, and teacher educators themselves. Barriers to multicultural engagement in teacher education can thus be discussed as embedded within the professional and personal context of higher education as well as within the personal lives of preservice teachers.

Barriers in Higher Education

The political (e.g., promotion, territoriality, administration) and deterministic (e.g., publications, grades, courses, credits) nature of the college/university context influences the individuals whose professional lives are tied to its existence. Institutionalized perspectives and the beliefs, powers, and fears of those teacher educators who function within the institution emerged as barriers to the construction and development of social justice teacher education. These barriers were evidenced in three ways: through university-level structures, in the reproduction of the dominant knowledge base, and in the institutionalized perspectives of teacher educators.

University-Level Structures

Particular structures within our university that were blocks to social justice teacher education included the hierarchical, power-oriented, administrative structure and the narrow, credit-driven, grade-based conception of education that are common to institutions of higher education. The administrative structure appeared oriented toward higher levels of administration (rather than faculty and students) and power responses to those who provide money to the institution. For example, when a new department head was appointed, not only were social justice issues revisited anew, but totally different conceptualizations emerged. Different personnel, with different social justice perspectives were placed in implementation positions. A further example includes complaints by alumni parents when their daughters as preservice teachers were placed in school settings that served diverse groups of children, especially the poor, African American, or urban children.

The structures of daily practice in institutions of higher education were barriers to the flexibility needed in the exploration of social justice education. As examples, work with diverse cultures and communities was not always conducive to the three-credit-class structure established by the university. Work with groups of twenty to thirty preservice teachers was not easily accomplished when credit loads require 120 students for full-time teaching. Methods of crediting students and faculty without placing unrealistic time expectations on them became a major issue.

Content-Based Knowledge

As we worked to reconceptualize teacher education, forms of institutionalized official knowledge repeatedly emerged as obstacles to our creative action. First, content-based knowledge, usually representing the Western canon, dominated views of educators whose graduate degrees were grounded in a particular traditional discipline (e.g. science education). Future teachers were believed to never get enough content, especially related to science, math, and literacy. General education courses that would implicitly explore multiculturalism and social justice were not considered necessary. Women's studies, "developing nation" perspectives (a clearly oppressive terminology), or cultural study would be supported only if a student had elective space.

Institutionalized Views of Teacher Education

Most teacher educators believed that dominant knowledge and methods already address social justice. There was no reason to interrogate teacher education as proposing biased pedagogical strategies (hooks, 1994) either in the direction of skills or child-centeredness. "No one is oppressed by the methods we use. Everyone is given opportunity." "Skills-based or learner-based instruction include all the views of learning and education that are possible." Teacher education is so strongly rooted in the field of psychology that a program without Western child development and learning theory was not even discussed. Multidirectional views of development could be introduced in education courses, but educational psychology must remain as the foundation for understanding children. Teaching methods grounded in disciplinary content were also not questioned. Otherwise, how would students know what and how to teach?

Teacher Educators as Barriers to Engagement

As our teacher educators (and I include myself) have interacted to construct social justice teacher education, personal beliefs and fears have emerged as barriers. These barriers can result in the elimination of critical multicultural education without ever giving students opportunity for engagement.

Fears

Fear is perhaps the easiest barrier to recognize and examine. Teacher educators feared challenging university and state requirements; we did not address the oppression imposed by bureaucratic agencies and the business powers that lobby for control (e.g., technology and textbook companies). Our concerns often represented attempts to satisfy these groups. On the whole, we could not eliminate the fear of research/theory; most of us clung to the practitioner (often called clinician) versus researcher distinction, fearing the time, effort, and intellect necessary for scholarly inquiry. Most importantly, we exhibited fear of alternative knowledges and revolutionary, liberatory pedagogies; we were often unable to face our own cultural biases and assumptions. "I will not call myself a racist. That is too damaging and insulting. I am not a racist." A white, male early childhood educator clearly expressed his bias toward women who do not choose to stay home with their children, "Our children have been damaged by a generation of child care." Another fussed, "These ideas are too radical. They will cause problems in schools. I do not view teachers as change agents." Most importantly, we were afraid of the loss of power if we addressed our fears; we could lose control of our own individual personal and professional worlds.

Power and Philosophical Beliefs

Power issues were embedded within the belief structures exhibited as we deliberated and planned courses of action. Many of us could be placed into a particular (or multiple) teacher educator category dependent on these beliefs. Our teacher educators tended to be either *investigators, centrists, wholists, or criticalists.* The beliefs that dominate any of these categories can be understood as historically and culturally constructed. Further, each perspective can provide a contribution to the achievement of multicultural engagement. Each can also, however, be a barrier.

Investigators

Investigator teacher educators appeared grounded in the research realities of the academic setting. Although they were not the only individuals who valued and conducted research, scholarly productivity appeared to be their major goal. The world was viewed as open for exploration. Research should be conducted from a variety of perspectives. Quality academic programming would be achieved when professors pursue their research interests and share that expertise with students. Because of the time issue, wholistic program development could not be the concern of researchers. Science and culture were viewed as separate. As one professor sarcastically explained, "Multicultural engagement will only be addressed when individual professors value a social justice orientation, whatever that might mean for different individuals."

Similar to the specialist described by Macedo (1994), the investigator perspective served as a barrier to a longitudinal, "whole program" design. The investigator knew his/her specific field, but was ignorant of constructions of knowledge that were more integrative and global in nature such as teacher education, educational foundations, or cultural relations. Investigators were open to the development of their own courses, but seemed to believe that philosophical diversity, academic time requirements, and knowledge boundaries made impossible the development of whole programs in which critical multiculturalism could flourish. These specialist investigators were therefore able to rationalize the denial of responsibility for such programs (Macedo, 1994).

Centrists

Centrist teacher educators appeared to privilege experience over critique or theory, at times even unconsciously denying values as inherent to human action. "That's ideological. We need to be practical." "We need to expose preservice teachers to all kinds of teaching methods from which to choose." Methodological pluralism (Agger, 1989) dominated discourse. The world was treated as objective and whole with human beings who simply explain it differently. Ideological contradiction and confrontation were considered too difficult and "messy" for preservice teachers. Centrists expressed the belief in a "balanced curriculum." McLaren and Tadeu da Silva (1993) have described these beliefs as neopositivist, providing teachers with a "shopping mall" variety of theory and practice.

This simplistic allegiance to openness served as a barrier to programmatic multicultural engagement. When we perceive ourselves to be open to diversity and methodology, no critical analysis is considered necessary. As one educator expressed, "I teach my students a variety of methods so they can be quietly subversive." Further, the privileging of experience over critical thought results in essentialism, the belief that the experience is necessary and represents Truth for all humans. This essentialism is most often used by dominant groups to maintain power (McLaren & Tadeu da Silva, 1993).

Wholists

Wholist teacher educators expressed the belief in process-oriented meaning construction. Child-centeredness and whole language perspectives dominated. Research was used to support these views as leading to democracy, autonomy, and empowerment. These educators referred to themselves as "progressive." Skills-based instruction and other methodologies that appear didactic were considered oppressive and damaging. As Delpit (1993) has explained, wholistic educators function as if explicit expectations are against liberal principles and limit both freedom and autonomy. When the teacher exhibits "expert power," students are disempowered. Power relations must therefore be equal in the classroom. A discourse of "equality" is used that verbally gives the impression that the learner has all the power over his/her own life. "Children should be allowed to use their own language and cultural strengths." Multiculturalism is viewed as assisting children in the expression of their own culturally based language and style.

Although the status quo is not verbally supported, this belief in child-centeredness and process orientation as educational "savior" falsely denies the existence of a "knowledge of power" in our society. A multidimensional obstacle to multicultural engagement that addresses social justice was created. First, in our society, power is held by a variety of white, patriarchical institutions (e.g., legislatures, test constructors, bureaucratic agencies, schools, businesses) in which particular forms of knowledge and product production are privileged. Denying this power with preservice teachers leads to the false assumption that social justice is being addressed through child-centeredness and a process orientation. Secondly, child-centeredness privileges the view that learning is exploration and individual meaning construction. Other forms of human functioning that are also culturally constructed (e.g, memorization found in the four-thousand-year history of oral learning in India; nonindependent, group-centered perspectives) are denied. An unquestioned belief in any one view of human learning (e.g., child-centeredness, process learning, whole language instruction, skills learning) can lead to a lack of engagement. Finally, discourse constructed around notions of "equity" can actually serve to reinforce domination by leading to the belief that multicultural engagement is occurring.

Criticalists

Criticalist teacher educators were those who believed in the examination of themselves and others from a critical, historical perspective as both oppressors and oppressed. Forms of knowledge were seen as politically and historically grounded and constructed within culture, time, and social practice. As McLaren and Tadeu da Silva (1993) have explained, knowledge is not pure or innocent. Knowledge and learning are always located within positions of power. Preservice teachers should be expected to recognize the complexity of social relations and to critically examine their own politically and socially determined positions. The experiences of preservice teachers (and their students) should always be given voice and affirmed. However, these experiences should also be critiqued for underlying oppressive assumptions (e.g., racism, sexism, classism). Within the educational system, goals, content, and practice are understood as related to dominance and power and therefore requiring continual critique. Actions are based on the creation of a more just community.

Social justice and multicultural engagement were the foundations of the criticalists' belief structure, yet barriers to their own purposes also emerged. First, because language is so closely tied to beliefs and action, a new discourse has been constructed that addresses oppression, social justice, and critical multiculturalism. While new forms of discourse are absolutely necessary, this language can be a barrier to those who are just beginning to examine the issues (i.e., preservice teachers or teacher educators). For example, the new vocabulary and critical language often overwhelmed even other teacher educators. "Oppression, hegemony, dominance, culture of power, critical pedagogy . . . I have trouble understanding these ideas (and I often don't agree). Our students will really have problems." Further, and most importantly, not only does criticalist language require expansion of "vocabulary," the ideas are threatening to those who feel that they have been successful in their own world. Whenever the term *liberation* was discussed for inclusion in course work, a number of teacher educators expressed opposition. One individual clearly stated: "Those ideas are too revolutionary. They will cause trouble. We can't go that far."

Secondly, criticalists can overlook the multiple definitions for critique that are employed by human beings who may not be criticalists. Critique is often viewed as negative criticism and contributing to a "right/wrong" dichotomy. A graduate student's interpretation of the work of Patrick Shannon is a good example. "This critique of basal readers supports the notion of whole language instruction," an either/or situation. The critical analysis of any belief structure (including criticalist beliefs) may be lost if used to construct dichotomies.

The beliefs of teacher educators are foundational to multicultural engagement. Critical social justice issues will not be addressed in some teacher education contexts. In our environment, investigator beliefs resulted in the construction of a social justice perspective that focused on individualism. Social justice became an "individual issue," very similar to the American emphasis on independence. Centrists either did not agree with multiculturalism or believed that their open view of education already addressed "diversity." Multiculturalism was simplified and essentialized by this view. Wholist constructions supported the dominant ideology of universal human learning, a person-centered, whole-context perspective. This unidirectional view silenced other views of learning (including those not yet conceived).

This author's allegiance is to the criticalist view, the belief that all human knowledges and activities are first of all social constructions and therefore value laden, contextual, political, and in need of analysis. I believe that this is the most likely perspective from which to achieve social justice. However, criticalists must be cautious that we are not bound by our own discourse and that we do not silence others with our enthusiasm.

Personal Barriers for Preservice Teachers

Ultimately multicultural engagement is dependent on the preservice teachers themselves. The elimination of institutional barriers and the construction/implementation of a program that is grounded in a critical multicultural perspective may or may not result in engagement by undergraduate students. During a recent academic year, thirty students progressed through our Children, Families, and Communities—Children, Schools, and Society sequence. One Hispanic female, one Anglo male, and twenty-eight females were involved. Most grew up in either suburban or middle-income rural communities. When describing themselves, the majority of Anglo females discussed their romantic, family, and religious lives. The romantic life centered around a "boyfriend" who was usually also a university student. The family life emphasized definitions of "good parenting" and expressions of closeness. The religious life was always Christian and most often addressed love and salvation. Throughout experiences, most students supported the status quo and refused to critically examine it. Analysis of student field notes, position papers, critiques, ethnographies, and conversations revealed two themes that tended to dominate thinking and inhibit multicultural engagement: Christian prejudice, and a form of subordinated white privilege.

Christian Prejudice

The Christian religion often dictated the content of discussions, field experiences, and reactions. One student's personal discussion in her family ethnography illustrates the language and perspective that dominated.

> As one of Christ's followers, I have chosen to live according to the way He once lived, as an earthly being here on earth. . . . . When God looks upon His children, he does not see color, race or gender. He sees only our hearts and longs to get inside them. (student-constructed family ethnography 1)

Christianity was used by students to establish a superior moral stance in which beliefs were not to be challenged, and create an immorality of difference in which those who did not "fit" were viewed as immoral or lazy.

Superior morality

The superior moral stance was most often related to the inappropriateness of alternative beliefs. Underlying assumptions regarding "eternal life" was the view that there is one right way for human beings to believe and function.

> It's going to take a lot of patience for me, because I'm a Christian. I don't want to force my beliefs on her, but I do want her to know that Christ is my savior and he's the way to heaven. . . . I still hope and pray that the family would know the love of Jesus Christ and have eternal life. (student-constructed family ethnography 2)

Another student expanded further on the notion that there is one set of appropriate beliefs.

> I was a little bothered to find out that Hindus believe we worship the same God. The God we believe in is so different from the God they

believe in . . . the two are not the same by any means. We believe that there is 1 god. This god created the universe. He is omnipotent. He also gives unconditional love. We do believe that worshipping idols or any other god is a sin. *But,* God loves each of us so much that he sent his son who was holy and perfect (free from sin) to suffer and die on a cross to take on our impurities so we may have eternal life with Him (in heaven). The only way to get to heaven is by proclaiming Jesus as the Savior. Everyone can have this gift, but few receive it. (student-constructed ethnography 3)

This superior stance emerged as students examined beliefs concerning parenting. In reference to a Korean immigrant child's behavior, one student stated, "To me it seems that the old Bible verse that says 'spare the rod and spoil the child' was put in for some reason." Another student described her discussion with Indian parents regarding right and wrong behavior for children. The parents felt that parenting beliefs "depended on whether the parents were liberal or conservative." The student wrote in her journal: "I told them that my beliefs were based on Christian morals."

Immorality of difference

An immorality of difference was applied to all those who did not comply with what students perceived as "Christian behavior." Gays, lesbians, and the poor were those who were most often implicated as immoral, individuals who would have no problems if Christian beliefs were followed. Most students avoided discussions of homosexuality even when their peers attempted to introduce the subject. For example, one student explained how her best friend in high school, a gay male, changed her father's view of homosexuality. Everyone listened, but no one asked questions or commented. Silence prevailed. When comments were made, qualifiers were always included, "I think it is wrong, but what do I do with a child who has a gay or lesbian parent?" One student did discuss her interaction with an African American mother:

We acknowledged that Christ is the single, most important Truth in our lives and discussed the topic of homosexuality and bisexuality. She told me how her sister had "stayed away" from that one Truth (Jesus) and had begun living her life as a homosexual. . . . We were both happy that her sister came around and is now married.

The poor were also viewed as those who did not know the "right values" on which to focus. In reference to living in poverty, one student wrote: "Due to our sinful nature, we as humans tend to focus on the things we don't have and not the things we do have! To make our world a happier place, it is up to us as God's children to focus on the important things" (student-constructed family ethnography 4).

Four or five students were already volunteering to work with families and children as part of Christian organizations when they entered teacher education course work. Overall, students never chose to critique Christian beliefs. However, in one situation the student did express concern over the type of religious activities used with children who were almost all African American living in public housing:

> One method we use to present the gospel to the children is the Power Band. The Power Band is a bracelet that has beads on it and each colored bead represents a different part of the plan of salvation. Black represents sin, red symbolizes Christ's blood, white is the color for forgiveness and cleansing, green is the symbol for growth in Christ, and gold represents our eternal life in heaven. For most of the colors, the kids can understand the relationship with its symbol, but they seem to have trouble with black and white. I struggle with the fact that we use black as the color of sin and we say sin leads to separation from God. I wonder if the kids ever feel like black is separation from God. I wish we didn't use colors to define good and bad and right and wrong. (student-constructed ethnography 5)

The construction of a superior moral stance and the belief that difference is immoral are major barriers to multicultural engagement. Belief in moral superiority always places one in a hierarchical location, a position in which "my beliefs are more advanced/appropriate than your's." The range of diverse perspectives (e.g., languages, subjugated knowledges) that can be understood and respected becomes quite narrow. When difference is viewed as immoral, the foundation is laid for intolerance. Justification is created for refusing to even attempt to understand the perspective of the Other (Halpin, 1989).

Subordinated White Privilege

A form of subordinated white privilege emerged in the conversations and beliefs exhibited by white female students. An increasingly large number of scholars have explored the "privilege" that white women have gained from association with white men (Collins, 1991; Hurtado, 1989; hooks, 1994; Lerner, 1972). On all standard of living measures, Native Americans, African Americans, Latinos, and some Asians fall below whites. Because of their association with white men, white women have been more financially able to stay in school. Even in childhood they have been "protected" from the outside world through racism and classism (Hurtado, 1989). Collins (1991) describes a belief in "specialness" that sexual politics and white male power have instilled in white women. In talking to white women, Fannie Lou Hamer states, "you had this kind of angel feeling that you were untouchable" (Lerner, 1972, p. 610). Our teacher education students exhibited both the internalized oppression found in most white women and a tendency to naively judge the Other (Halpin, 1989) supported by privilege.

Internalized oppression

Clearly internalized oppression emerged as our white female students endorsed the power of the white male. Women were blamed for their own circumstances and expected to yield to their "position." "Women may set themselves up for discrimination." Another student even felt that women should live by the rules that have been established:

> Men are viewed as the sex with power, so they should be the "strong" doctors; and women, being the weaker sex, should be the one to ad- minister love and care, just like a nurse does. The rules that we live by should not be looked on as negative. Not everyone can have their way, and I feel that if there are rules to live by, then we should live by them.

Christianity even played a role in internalized oppression as revealed by this student's belief concerning marriage: "I'm a Christian and am proud to do what my husband and my God tell me to do."

Judgment of others

A naive judgment of others supported by the context of white privilege (Hurtado, 1989) was obvious in very direct communications concerning immigrants, minorities, and simplistic understandings of our democra- tic, capitalist system. One individual clearly stated "I have never been fond of immigrants." Another explained:

> I have very strong convictions about what immigrants to any country should and should not do. One of the things that I feel is very important for an immigrant to do is learning to speak the language correctly and fluently. I do understand that they (the family partnered with the stu- dent) are not making permanent residence in America, but while they are here, I feel that they should teach their child proper English pro- nunciations. (student-constructed family ethnography 6)

Class readings, discussions, and experiences were designed to foster analysis of complex social issues and the value-laden, political context in which we find ourselves. However, minorities were continually blamed for their oppression and whites were held as individuals who set goals, work hard, and have no responsibility for the context in which "Others" find themselves. Whites were considered successful simply because they worked harder. Several students echoed the "this generation does not have slaves" perspective as minorities were blamed for not knowing how to act (like whites).

> I feel that as White people, we are advantaged. However, I do not feel that we are to blame for other people's disadvantages. We are not to blame, as the present generation, for the enslavement of Blacks that occurred hundreds of years ago. I can feel sympathy for those who were enslaved, but they are no longer alive. Although many times the White people are in control of situations, the blame cannot be placed on them for being aggressive. They have worked to become what they are and deserve respect for attaining their goals. (culture paper 1)

Failure was placed on the shoulders of parents and children. One student felt "children will become successful students if they apply themselves." Another wrote "White children succeed because their parents help them to study by establishing a study time and by encouraging them to work with other students for better understanding of a subject. Black children, many times, are allowed to run around and play" (culture paper 2).

One day in class, a normally quiet student expressed the belief that had been expressed by others on many occasions in a variety of ways: "Many blacks want to make us feel guilty about how they have been treated in the past. I do feel sorry for them, but if they would just move on with their lives, I think they could do better for themselves." Rather than understanding, empathy, and support, preservice teachers engaged in mistrust, pity, and condemnation.

Democracy was conceived as "majority rule," with no understanding of even our founders' concern for the "tyranny of the majority" or the complex socioeconomic and political forces influencing our electoral system. Whites were viewed as powerful in our democratic system because they work to achieve: "As adults, many white people apply more often for the better paying jobs. They are in office because they campaign strongly and apply themselves when running in an election" (power paper 1). In a discussion of democratic power through elections, two students summarized the ideas that had been previously expressed by many others: "If minority adults would become involved in elections and run for office, there is no doubt in my mind that they could win if they are the better choice."

The fact of the matter is, the individuals who "run" this country (our government), are voted on by the people. If you are a citizen of the United States, you have the freedom to register and vote. If a white male from the upper class wins an election, then the majority of the people who voted, wanted him to win. This is a democracy. This does not mean however, that this country has a stark white record when it comes to freedom.

Most preservice teachers had no problem with the ideas of a "culture of power" (Delpit, 1993) and that the members of that culture are privileged.

> I do agree that there is a "culture of power." However, I do not feel that it is inappropriate to have such an institution in America. I think that the presence of this "invisible law" helps a society. It allows for a self-evaluation by measuring oneself to others, a self-in-relation view. I feel that it helps the individual to know where they stand and enables them to help better themselves according to these standards. If a person finds that they are lacking in a certain area, according to this "culture of power," they are given an opportunity to improve by adjusting themselves to fit into the "culture of power." (power paper 2)

Further, those who are not in power were also condemned for needing and wanting it: "To say that one race is overbearing and only accepting of one view is immoral. . . . To feel jealousy towards a more powerful person to the extent of anger is uncalled for and unexplainable. . . . This is irrelevant to the advancement of the American society" (power paper 3).

Critical multicultural engagement is most likely to be impossible when preservice teachers have internally accepted their own oppression and have learned to judge the Other through the lens of white privilege. Internal acceptance of oppression blocks the analysis of power. They accept what happens to them as inevitable. Further, the maintenance of their own privilege (however subjugated) is tied to the oppression of others through the use of judgment and blame (Collins, 1991; hooks, 1994). Reconceptualization of self is most likely necessary before multiculturalism can be engaged.

In our setting, the Hispanic female, the Anglo male, one female who had become a teen parent at fifteen years of age, and one other female engaged in critical multiculturalism. These students initiated historical examinations of oppression, used their own time to interview community members, volunteered in a variety of community settings, and attended meetings designed to give voice to traditionally oppressed groups. Fostering social justice appeared to be the goal of their educational experiences and future life's work. However, they were a small minority. Most students engaged the status quo, denying the existence of oppression or even discrimination in today's world. Some learned the jargon well and continually discussed how they would always allow for "individual differences." Others were insulted and even angry that we would spend so much time on these issues.

We recognize that confronting hegemonic forces, challenging dominant ideologies, cannot be completely conceptualized or acted on based on a two-semester experience. This is only a fraction of time in the life of a future teacher. However, time is a comparatively minor barrier. As we have attempted to both construct and implement social justice teacher education, barriers within the context of our own teacher education environment and barriers from within students themselves have emerged.

Discussion and Future Directions

The barriers to multicultural engagement described in this chapter have been limited to the university setting and the students themselves. Although implicitly included, the societal context from which these barriers have emerged and the school context in which future teachers ultimately function have not been addressed. As a teacher educator, I have, however, learned a great deal from the analysis of barriers within our environment. We can now understand that our immediate obstacles include an institutionalized definition of content found in higher education, the beliefs held by teacher educators themselves, religious biases and prejudices that dominate our students, and a form of subordinated white privilege that develops as part of the lives of many white females. What paths can we construct through or around these barriers?

We must come to understand the dominant ideology of our institutions. An extremely conservative, hierarchical, and scientifically oriented context will most likely require a different strategy for the introduction of subjugated knowledges, insurgent languages, and critical research than a liberal arts environment. What forms of knowledge have been silenced in the sciences, mathematics, or literacy? Perhaps professors who consider themselves scholars in a discipline would be open to the interrogation of their own fields. Perhaps some of them have been silenced within their own scholarship. In our environment, we must construct a path in which scholars who have not themselves become multiculturally engaged (very often those who are white males and have not recognized their own privilege), feel that they can become part of our movement. This will be difficult, but we must talk to and communicate with them.

Further, we must critique our perspectives on content that leads us to believe that general college education courses and teacher education content are separate. Women's studies, minority culture investigations, the study of oppressed languages, and other forms of subjugated epistemologies should become part of the course requirements for teacher education. We must question what we consider to be appropriate content. We may need to relinquish some courses in methodology and traditional teacher education.

The institutionalized content of teacher education and the beliefs and fears of teacher educators are possibly the greatest barriers to multicultural engagement. For this reason, attention to the education of future teacher educators may be of more immediate importance than preservice education. Graduate, doctoral level education could provide the ultimate path to multicultural engagement for undergraduates. Currently, graduate students complete their programs and take positions in colleges and universities all over the United States without having historically, much less critically, analyzed views of learning, curriculum, or teaching content. Rarely have they been immersed in feminist, criticalist, phenomenological, or other subjugated forms of thought. They have not addressed social justice or oppression. Although these students plan to educate future teachers, they do not recognize teacher education as a field of study with a history that is politically and socially grounded. As graduate students in a state university like my own, they teach large numbers of undergraduates. They may then enter the professorate to become investigators, centrists, wholists, or (in small numbers) criticalists. In most cases, they have not been multiculturally engaged as part of their graduate program.

Graduate education must be critically analyzed and reconceptualized. Future teacher educators must learn to examine themselves as both oppressor and oppressed. They must become familiar with the histories of those who have dominated education and those who have been silenced by the field. A continued focus on research is essential for two reasons. The dominant ideology of the academic community is grounded in scholarly investigation and publication. Teacher educators must learn not to fear functioning as researchers. More importantly, critical engagement requires research skills that would give voice to multiple perspectives and the construction of new ways of viewing the world.

As we continue to work with undergraduates, in our context the issue of Christian prejudice cannot be ignored. How do we involve students in the analysis of their own moral beliefs and the harm that these beliefs may bring to others without attacking them as spiritual beings with the right to choose whatever morality that might comfort them in their own lives? For the present, three possibilities emerge. Historical and political analysis of notions of morality and ethical behavior could serve to introduce the concept of social construction without focusing on religion. Feminist, psychological, and differing cultural views on morality could be starting points. Second, historical analysis of multiple religions could be part of a requirement for cultural study within teacher education. Finally, we must recognize that one or two courses or semesters is probably not enough time for future teachers to fully appreciate the historical and political embeddedness of their own beliefs. For preservice teachers to ultimately analyze their own Christian prejudices (as well as other biases), a focus on social justice and multicultural engagement must become the goal of the entire college experience. This focus must be the foundation for all content and experiences.

Similar possibilities may be constructed to combat barriers associated with subordinated white privilege. Additionally, young white women will not be able to recognize their own privilege without experiencing the lives of others in a variety of ways, not simply in traditional school settings. Readings and discussions must be enriched and critiqued using actual experiences that are designed to give voice rather than essentialize. I am reminded of the young female graduate student involved with our work with residents of public housing. She read critical ethnography. She understood the notion of subjugated epistemologies and oppressive ideologies. We spoke the language of social justice and critical multiculturalism. Yet, when we began interacting with individuals who lived in poverty, attempting to create an environment that gave voice to all, she no longer wanted to be involved. She could not live daily with "their" forms of communication or the common concerns of "their" lives. Our teacher education students must become involved in the political, socioeconomic, and social contexts of the lives that they have not experienced. The ties of white women to privilege based on race and class must be examined, giving voice to women of color and working-class women.

Analysis of women's histories and the critique of education as a gendered field are necessities. Students should explore the notion that all knowledge is gendered (McLaren & Tadeu Da Silva, 1993) by exposure to both written histories and the oral histories of contemporary women. They should conduct research themselves with the purpose of analyzing gender in the classroom and work place. They should talk with women of all ages, races, and socioeconomic backgrounds.

For multicultural engagement and social justice to be the major goal of longitudinal teacher education, those involved in implementation must admit to their political preference (Kincehloe, 1993). We must be willing to place social justice at the forefront of our goals, decisions, and actions, to infuse critical multiculturalism throughout a teacher education program. Students must be provided with the language and competencies supported by those in power. Further, they must be given multiple opportunities to explore liberatory teaching. Rather than methodology text books, the work of Freire (1985, 1978, 1973, 1970), Shor (1987), hooks (1994), Paley (1995, 1992, 1981, 1979), Kozol (1991, 1989, 1985), and others can be used. Apprenticeship teaching should be either eliminated or minimized. Field experiences must involve children in their lived worlds and continual attempts to tie these worlds to educational environments (Silin, 1995).

I have seen students in teacher education emerge with a critical multicultural perspective that becomes the dominant force in the interpretation of the remainder of their teacher education program. These students choose to examine the categorization and devaluing of teen parents and the silencing of gay and lesbian children within the school context. They recognize the ways that we have attempted to "protect" children from their own world by ignoring AIDS, death, pain, and suffering as if these were not part of their lives. They are aware that we have silenced both children and adults with our focus on English as the appropriate language. They have become advocates for social justice in the construction of their own classroom and have given voice to all who enter. However, these preservice teachers are rare. One, two, or three emerge over a long period of time. The majority remain controlled by dominant ideology and unwilling to engage in critical analysis.

We (as teacher educators, researchers, and students) should become visible through our writing, our speaking, our actions, and our lives. To some of us, social justice is the major issue in our democracy and should be the major focus of education. The barriers to multicultural engagement will only be overcome when others see that we are engaged.

7

Mark Dressman

Confessions of a
Methods Fetishist

Or, the Cultural Politics of
Reflective Nonengagement

A friend who teaches language arts at a Bureau of Indian Affairs school has been studying the newest fashion among her middle school Navajo students: wearing African American "hip-hop" clothes.

"What do you think that means?" I asked.

"Well, it's part of their identity crisis," she concluded, based on her experience with adolescents in general and her years of working with this cultural group. "They want to be anything but Navajo."

During a visit to a first-grade class in an impoverished neighborhood, I admire as Connie, an exceptionally thoughtful whole-language teacher, engages her students in planning a follow-up "creation" to a children's book about a "monster's" house. "Let's make a house of our own," she suggests to her eager students. "What shall we put in our living room?"

108

"A sofa-bed," one child suggests.

"How about a fireplace?" Connie replies. "Every living room should have one of those."

Later she reflects on her great frustration with this year's class, which does not seem to "get" many of the allusions in the literature that she teaches. In one case, her students did not know about face cards. "They had played Twenty-One, or 'Blackjack' as they called it, and that was about as far as they went," she said. "They didn't understand what a jester was or the word royal; they had no idea what it was. Normal kids—my children or my sister's children—have that knowledge."

L ike the teachers above, I, too, have always thought of myself as an observant and reflective professional—as someone who sees his classroom as a potential site for exploring ways that good teaching and a thoughtfully designed classroom environment might change for the better both his students' lives and the society of which we are all a part. And I must admit also that until very recently I always felt intuitively that the greatest—and perhaps the only valid—source of insight at the disposal of any teacher who chose to embark on this quest was honest self-reflection on her or his own unique professional and life experiences. My own experience of teacher education courses, taught by research "experts" ten years out of the classroom whose main expertise, in retrospect, seems to have been in painting idealized views of How It Could Be if only I'd try it their way, has been dismal to mediocre at best. I understand, therefore, and have some sympathy for the claims of undergraduates in the classroom that what they need from "methods" courses is more method and less "theory," and for the claims of teachers in the field that personal experience deliberately reflected upon is the best, and perhaps the only valid, source of practical knowledge.

This chapter, then, constitutes my best attempt to reconsider, in my reading and writing and my own self-reflection, what it takes, what it *really* takes, to begin to see through the assumptions and hegemonic discourses of "good practice" as they are enacted within programs of teacher education. To explain how I've arrived at this point, what conclusions I've drawn, and what their implications may be for both myself, preservice education majors, and for practicing teachers, I will first have to practice what I will preach, by presenting as a case study, and with as much candor as I can muster, the data of my own teaching career. Then I want to analyze that presentation and the experiences of the teachers above in light of perspectives that run against the grain of many commonsense assumptions in, I think, some enlightening ways. And in conclusion, I would like to consider how we might cultivate a more *reflexive* way of thinking and acting than that provided by the traditional focus on instructional strategies, and so begin to make a Real Difference in teaching and learning.

Developing a Reflective Practice

For a long time following my student teaching it seemed as if a combination of common sense, trial and error, and reflection on my own learning processes might be enough to solve any instructional problems I encountered. My first job after graduating from college was as a Peace Corps volunteer in Morocco, where for two years I taught English as a foreign language to Moroccan high school students in a very small town in the interior of the country. I struggled in my first six months with issues that no amount of college instruction or experience in an American classroom could have prepared me for, and in the end, it was only by studying the example of other teachers in my school and by making a careful study of my own problems and strategies in learning Moroccan Arabic that I was able to develop instructional strategies in English that worked for both my students and me. My career as a reflective practitioner was launched when, at the end of two years of very hard work, I was able to distill some principles of English language instruction in the context of Moroccan secondary education from old lesson plans, from sharing ideas with colleagues, and from observing my students' written and verbal performance for a presentation at a spring conference of English teachers that was very well received. For myself and, I believed then, for my fellow volunteers, that conference and presentation became a celebration of my own gift, as college-educated Americans of the Kennedy generation, for drawing on interior strengths and finding ways to succeed, where, it seemed, others merely got by.

These strategies of observation and reflection that seemed to work so well in Morocco were less effective when I returned to the United States and, after a year's graduate study, took a job as a secondary language arts teacher in a bilingual community school on the Navajo Indian Reservation. Trying to reach these students made all my unacknowledged, commonsense assumptions about formal education as an essentially empowering, liberatory force, about the culturally transcendent power of the literary experience, and about the indisputable rightness of my mission as a teacher, stand out in bold relief. I'd always believed that formal education prepared people for Life, and was the ladder to Upward Social Mobility—wasn't that everybody's dream? But here were students who seemed outside "getting ahead," at least as I thought of it. I knew that, historically, schooling had always (and sometimes violently), been imposed on Navajos and that now, even though they elected their own school board and determined their own curriculum, it was understood that going to school, learning English, and reading books was all about accepting Anglo ways. If by going to school you could get a job that would pay enough to buy a pickup truck that would help you do the things that constituted being Navajo, then it was worth it to do so; but to *like* what you studied, particularly those subjects like English or social studies (American history?!), to show too much interest in things outside the Navajo world, was often considered a sort of betrayal of the Navajo Way by many families in the community.

I worked hard to justify and to make the teaching of Anglo literature relevant for my students. As an English major in college, I had always felt that literary texts were artistic expressions of values and perspectives that were timeless and universal. I believed that the literature we read would open new possibilities to my students and explain a world to them which I believed that sooner or later they would have to learn to function in—that is, my world, the world I had come from. But, for the most part, this did not happen; instead, students' written responses and conferences with me mostly revealed their alienation from themes, characters, and plot situations that I considered a basic or essential part of being adolescent, growing up, and dealing with parents, adult authority in general, and peers of the same or opposite sex. It was not that at that moment in their lives my Navajo students were not also dealing with the issues presented in the literature we read, but that the ways those issues played themselves out in protagonists' behavior within the narrative were often at odds with their own cultural views and the commonsense solutions they would have proposed. In short, the more I tried to explain these differences and "fill students in" on the origins of Anglo culture, the more I inadvertently suggested that the Navajo Way and the Anglo Way had little in common, and the more I realized that I was exacerbating what I viewed at the time as the primary problem that my students faced in preparing for their future, at least as I saw it: their sense of difference from the mainstream of American culture and life.

At the end of my third year on the Navajo Reservation I made a personal and career decision that it was time for me to return to "mainstream American" culture. I taught in a suburban Catholic middle school in the midwest, and then taught for five more years in a major urban school district. From the reservation I took a sense of disillusionment—but not of failure—as a teacher. I counted a number of successful projects—introducing the first children's novels to the curriculum, a writing project about all the things that grandmothers do for you (like lend you her pickup or give you some sheep), some great field trips—as well as a substantially enlarged portfolio of methods and teaching ideas among my achievements, and consoled myself with the knowledge that I had stayed longer than many and accomplished more than most.

Then, in the last weeks of the school year, I had a breakthrough. In talking with six of the least "Anglo-cized" students in my senior English class it came up that they really didn't have a very systematic knowledge of the epic narratives that form the core of Navajo traditional belief. We negotiated that they would each read several chapters of some books on Navajo "myths and legends" that were in the library, and then, as a pedagogical experiment, they were to *tell me* the stories before they wrote their reports. A week later we pushed desks into a circle and as they began to tell me about the Twelve Holy People and about Changing Woman, who was impregnated by the sun as she slept and gave birth to Hero Twins who redeemed the world's humanity, I realized that they could be talking about not only the Twelve Olympian Gods, about Leda and the Swan, and about Romulus and Remus, but also about the Twelve Apostles, about the Virgin Mary, and about the Apostles Peter and Paul. And I thought I saw then, and I reconfirmed and developed the insight as I reflected further, that my vision of bringing culture to my students through comparative study of the "eternal truths and verities" of the literary canon had not been ill conceived, but simply had not dug far enough down or been analytically sophisticated enough to penetrate the cultural "deep structure" of the literary narratives we were reading.

Failed Discourses
The Consequence of Reflective Nonengagement

I scoff at this curricular model now, but at the time, and given my own educational and cultural background, to take the position that literary texts were deeply cultural products—albeit, as I had concluded from my own study and reflection, the products of a notion of culture that crammed all of human experience and narrative under the umbrella of one great "monomyth" (Campbell, 1949/1972)—that should be *read* by students as cultural tropes labeled me as a "radical" among my peers. When they bothered to think about these issues at all they usually either justified "the literary experience" as a private, for-its-own-sake "life-enrichment" exercise, or in production-line terms, as the need to "cover material" that students would "need" in the next grade or in college. I, on the other hand, had a "Unified Theory of Literature" to guide me, a noble, self-reflective vision of cultural empowerment to motivate that Theory, and by trial and error and a good deal of reflection, I had acquired what I viewed as a formidable repertoire of instructional strategies—at least one for any occasion or text—that I felt put me ahead of the pack professionally. In my second year off the reservation, when I was asked about my "teaching philosophy" in an interview for the position of reading/language arts teacher in my urban district's new "magnet" Paideia middle school, I could state without guile or hesitation that Paideia, which stressed the reading and discussion of the Great Books of (Western) civilization within three pedagogical modes, could have been my philosophy.

Briefly, "Paideia" is the swan-song project of Mortimer Adler, an octogenarian classicist at the University of Chicago who is better known for his entrepreneurship as editor of the *Encyclopedia Britannica*, a series of "Great Books" of (again, Western) civilization, and a graded series of "Junior Great Books" for schools. In its principal manual (1984), Adler argued that America's educational problems stemmed from the watering down of its school curricula and the inadequacy of its teachers' cultural knowledge and instructional practices. Every child deserved the very best education, by which he meant an education centered around texts which had stood the test of time and had become classics of (Western) civilization. He was fond of the "empty vessel" metaphor, to which he added an egalitarian twist: children's intellects might be empty cups of differing sizes, but that was no cause for filling most with water, some with vinegar, and a few with cream: it stood to reason (an awful lot of Paideia, in retrospect, "stood to reason") that the only just way to educate all children was to fill every cup with as much "cream" as it would hold. The handful of other districts around the country who were trying Paideia—Chicago, Atlanta, Anchorage—used it in their gifted and talented programs, but the school's hope was in its egalitarian promise and its expanded empty-vessel metaphor, and our students, who came from African American, Appalachian, and white middle-class backgrounds, were recruited from throughout the district on those premises.

For a time, hope burned bright. After some initial problems—for example, the texts were too hard for the students to read—I found ways to compensate by slowing down, reading aloud, and focusing on "quality, rather than quantity" (an Adlerian maxim I gleaned from the Paideia newsletter), and so students got through. But once the hoopla of Paideia's promises had passed and the exoticism of reading texts like *Hamlet* and the *Odyssey* in the eighth grade began to wear thin, resistance grew, as did my frustration with my students' refusal, rather than inability, to recognize, in plays like *Antigone* or epics like the *Odyssey*, what I regarded as Our Common Humanity, no matter how "supportive" my instruction was or how "relevant" I strove to make each lesson and assignment. While students might notice the archetypal in a comparative study of creation myths if I pointed it out to them, or even if I "extracted" the information using Socratic questioning techniques, it was also clear that it had little significance to them. All the Venn diagrams and comparative matrices in the world—all my vain attempts to marginalize issues of difference and lionize abstract "collective truths" within a text—could not capture their interest or imagination. What I would now see as "resistance" but what I then labeled as "trouble making" (and the teacher practice literature currently calls "reluctance") and blamed on the parents of some "kids with problems" grew more and more regular, as did the conferences and phone calls I made to homes with little positive effect.

In the midst of building disaster, however, there were also some notable successes. During a comparative study of "trickster" characters, we read some selections from Langston Hughes' "Simple" series, and the students wrote their own stories with Simple as the main character. After school one day I was part of a conversation with two African American colleagues about all the vocabulary they had to describe skin color and texture. I dimly realized that their skin was salient for them in a way that it was not for me or for most whites; in our next writing assignment the students brainstormed all the metaphors and similes they could think of to describe skin, and then wrote some stunning poems entitled, "My Skin." As a last example, I cut out the headlines of supermarket tabloids, glued them on construction paper, and had the students write their own outrageous stories to match them; they immediately grasped the genre format and wrote stories that any supermarket tabloid could have printed with very little editing. It should have been clear to me that it was the opportunity each of these successes allowed for students either to talk back to prescribed views of the world or to work out their own responses to Big Questions using conventions appropriated from genres that spoke to them—to "reinvent" literature, as Dirck Roosevelt (1995) has put it, in local and particular ways—that accounted for their engaged and enthusiastic and creatively literate actions; but instead, on self-reflection I wrote these events off as clever but trivial lessons that killed time between the larger, more culturally "relevant" literary projects of the Paideia curriculum.

Why "Reflection" Is Not Enough

When you are born into a politically, economically, culturally dominant class, race, and sex, there is just no good reason for you to see yourself as classed, ethnic, or gendered. The privilege you enjoy you do not perceive as privilege at all, but as part of the natural order of things. I was raised by my liberal parents to loathe racism, to see poverty as the consequence of social and historical injustices that demanded remediation, and to resist viewing women as subordinate to men. But I was also raised, as Cornel West (1994) has remarked of white liberals, to believe that these and other groups should be "'included' and 'integrated' into 'our' society and culture" (p. 6)—hence my structuralist preoccupation with comparative literature—without ever thinking to ask how "they" felt about becoming one of "us," as well as refusing to see that difference matters, too. In my nuclear family, overtly prejudicial beliefs were untenable; their expression by other relatives and neighbors angered my parents and threatened the peace, and so to avoid trouble, we tended to avoid talking about these matters much. Lacking a discourse to talk honestly about these issues in ways that did not threaten to destroy all communication, I chose not to examine or discuss them at all, and I hoped that my discretion in these matters would be taken as the better part of social consciousness. Later in my career as a teacher I consciously worked to avoid what I viewed as discriminatory behavior of any kind—in grading, in my personal interactions, in the opinions I formed of colleagues and students—figuring that if I just avoided involvement in these problems they would never intrude on my peace. And yet the story I have presented here clearly shows that in all my conscious reflection about my curriculum and my instruction I never saw the unconscious consequences of being a privileged member of the white, male middle class in my work that students and colleagues who were of color, poor, or female often, and obviously, did. Even more spectacularly, I confess, this story shows that whenever I did have considerable success with my students, as when they wrote about their grandmothers or their skin, I consistently failed to read the cultural implications of that success productively, and instead, upon reflection, wrote these successes off as inconsequential distractions to the "real" curriculum, *or as pandering to my students' own parochialism!*

Think, then, of what it means for an entity, whether it be a self or a mirror, to "reflect" what is before it. It means that light, or sensation, reflected from things "out there," strikes its surface and, penetrating no further, glances off to produce an image—an *image*—of its referent. This image is flat, not three dimensional like its referent: it has no depth, and what is more, it is distorted in conformity to the contours of the mirror or the self reflecting it, rather than to its referent's contours. This is why *reflection* is not enough, and why "reflective" practice is not likely to do more than help teachers practice "innovative solutions" to self-defined "problems" whose imagistic parameters do not correct or remediate the politics of their cultural vision, but conform to the cultural lens through which teachers viewed their classroom lifeworld all along.

Cogito, ergo sum: no wonder then that reflection feels so empowering, for detailed self-reflection is always and ultimately an act of self-confirming self-service. And yet anyone who has experienced life in classrooms as a teacher can also understand why self-reflection in and of itself would be reassuring to teachers: because life as a classroom teacher, even in the best of circumstances, is usually hard, lonely, unsupported, and offers little material reward. In 1995, teachers in my state make about twenty-two thousand dollars a year to start; the average teacher salary is around thirty. Although they are required to take a bewildering range of "methods" and "foundational" courses before they are licensed, they usually emerge from teacher education programs with only the barest practical understanding of how to proceed. Their mostly white liberal professors, who, like most of them, lack the discursive means to talk about issues of difference in ways that do not threaten a false and tenuous peace, choose not to examine or discuss difference at all, hoping that their discretion in these matters will be taken as the better part of (a false) social consciousness. Instead, they opt for the progressivist universalism of the latest "one size fits all" (Bartolomé, 1994) method, based on the self-evident premise that if you ignore the political side of difference and "focus on what works" you can neither be convicted of discrimination nor accused of "making trouble" with your practice.

Once out in the schools, elementary teachers are likely to spend six hours a day in near-constant contact with twenty to thirty small children, and secondary teachers may see as many as 180 different students a day—a higher rate of client contact than any lawyer, doctor, or other professional would dream of tolerating. Faced with these numbers and handed "core" curricular materials blanched of any ethnic, gendered, or class-based perspective—ironically, so that no one will notice how white, patriarchal, and middle class they are—to work with, who might not be charmed by the fetishism of methodological, one-size-fits-all ways around the complexities and unfamiliarity of difference? Thrown back constantly on anemic material resources and a truncated view of difference as inherently problematic, who would not embrace, if only as a matter of survival, what Stephen Toulmin (1990) calls the "hidden agenda of modernity": a conservative agenda sustained by the cultic belief that one's own humanity, if not the stability of a volatile social world, depends on the quest for certainty, not the exploration of difference, and that *the only thing certain* is, "I think, therefore I am."

Given this understanding of teachers as conflicted individuals caught in a web of societal and institutional dysfunction, what intervention can be made in the reflections of teachers like the two who opened this chapter? How could teacher education lead the first to interpret her Navajo students' appropriation of the signs of hip-hop as their admiring, positive attempt to appropriate the moves of Black cultural resistance to White cultural domination, rather than as a negative flight from being

Navajo? How might the first-grade teacher, Connie, come to understand that a sofa-bed might be a more familiar, more valued feature of her students' livingrooms than a fireplace?

Perhaps the most direct approach would be to make clear to teachers the extent to which in a multiethnic, classed, and gendered society, no amount of denial or good intentions can mask or evade the fact that in their daily interactions with others, race, class, and sex *do matter.* White, middle-class men and women need to see that to others, *they* are "the other," and that the interpretive frame they impose on social interactions is not self-evidently universal at all, but one laden with their own ethnic, classed, and gendered interests. Once they have this knowledge, the scenario goes, conversion will follow; and if it does not, well, then in the coming Armageddon no one will be able to claim that they weren't informed.

Such an intervention was the first tried on me as a teacher. At an inservice during Black History Month a principal from another school gave a talk to the faculty about how all whites were racist, all men were sexist, and all members of the middle and upper classes were classist; there was no escape from this fact, and if I were anywhere as moral as I hypocritically claimed to be, I would concede this as fact and begin to examine the ways that I oppressed my students. This was my first exposure to what Cornel West (1994) describes as "racial reasoning": the rhetorical construction of rigid categories of subjectivity based on ad hoc consensual markers of racial (or social class or sexual) "authenticity"— categories which then are presumed to act as predictors of individuals' attitudes, beliefs, and actions. Overdetermined and mechanistic to the extreme, this reactionary reflection of the way dominant groups view the subordinate does not clear the air and "set people straight" about the way that race (and class and sex) work within society; instead, as West argues, the gaps and contradictions within the categorical logic of racial reasoning become strategic trump cards in the maintenance of power relations by those dominant groups. To illustrate his point West uses the case of Clarence Thomas, who was clearly "authentically" black, but also an intellectually mediocre, sexist jurist and no friend of equal opportunity, to show how the Bush administration caught the leadership within the black community by the illogic of its own racial politics—because, within the categories of racial reasoning, Clarence Thomas was well qualified to fill the shoes of Thurgood Marshall.

In my own case, being labeled a white male middle-class oppressor out of hand was more confusing and dehumanizing than illuminating for me. What I could have gotten from that inservice—namely that race, class, and gender did matter in my teaching in ways that my own privileged position blinded me from seeing, and that it is through the appreciation of difference, rather than bland, monomythical structuralism that meaning is created—was lost in the moral outrage I felt at having my own humanity and individuality taken away. Perhaps I should have been able to appreciate, for the first time, how it felt for the racially, sexually, and economically marked to be treated like a category, but I did not. Instead, I remember looking over at the African American teacher who smiled and nodded with every point the speaker made, and remembered how, just the week before, she had kept a group of Appalachian girls behind for lunch so that she could lecture them on matters of feminine hygiene, because, she explained, their mothers hadn't. A few weeks later I would be screamed at during a faculty meeting by my principal, an African American woman and a figure in the local Republican Party, because I objected to the plan she announced to place students into "teachable" (read: tracked) groups the following year. The following year, as building rep for the teachers' union, we would tangle again, this time over her discriminatory placement of the five special education classes the district had assigned the school (she claimed "somebody downtown was out to get her") in unremodeled and unsuitable rooms (a voc. ed. workshop that hadn't been used in years; dark basement classrooms, a choir-rehearsal room where the desks had to be balanced on a terraced platform) at far parts of the building that were well removed from the sight of visitors to her model Paideia program. Blatant contradictions of this sort, on reflection, made accusations that my ethnicity, my gender, and my social-class background marked me as an Oppressor seem ridiculously short sighted to me. That inservice and the ones that followed it were meant to mark the start of the deconstruction of my privileged point of view and the reconstruction of a curricular and instructional praxis in which issues of racial, sexual, and class difference were central. But that didn't happen. Instead, I left the Paideia program and spent two more years trying to make my Unified Theory of Literature work at another school, with not much more success. While there Rodney King was beaten, the Los Angeles riots occurred, and the false and tenuous peace within the school district collapsed for lack of a discourse of difference that would move discussions of multiculturalism beyond exercises in either finger pointing or denial.

I entered full-time doctoral study in 1990 expecting my faith in methodological solutions to instructional and curricular problems to be extended and rationalized. The reading and language arts courses I took in my first semesters did, in fact, attempt just that; but the more trite, saccharine testimonials I read to the power of the writing workshop and "quality"—that is, slick and expensive—children's and adolescent literature to seduce reluctant readers and writers into becoming lifelong lovers of books—that is, of novels—the more I noticed how white, how blandly middle class, and how disembodied the "learners" were in these narratives, and how unlike they were to the multiethnic, materialistic, physical, sexual, gendered, politically hip children and adolescents I'd been teaching. It was then that I started to appreciate heterogeneity as the central condition of being human, rather than as the condition that made teaching problematic.

In other courses around the same time I began to read critical ethnographies (*Learning to Labor*, Willis, 1981; *Ain't No Makin' It*, MacLeod, 1987; *Learning Capitalist Culture*, Foley, 1990) and critiques (Brodkey, 1987; Rosen, 1985) of some other ethnographies (*Ways with Words*, Heath, 1983) that weren't so critical. As a teaching assistant I supervised student teachers, and from my position in the back of numerous classrooms I developed a new, ironic appreciation of the dynamics of "resistance" that complemented my reading. As a teacher, students' refusal to "get with the program" had been nothing more than a source of irritation to me, a sign on good days that I had miscalculated in my planning and on bad days that my students needed social intervention. Sitting in the back rows of classrooms now, feeling alternately bored and offended by what was going on up front, I became a little resistant myself at times and had to actively restrain myself from cracking a joke with the kid next to me or otherwise throwing a monkey wrench into the gears of education. Resistance, I came to see, was an utterly sane and reasonable, even creative and resourceful and necessary human response to rationalized teaching and texts that presumed to be their own, self-evident, raisons d'être. Slowly, haltingly, and a little blindly I started to read the books that weren't on any course reading list in the college of education and to acquire an academic discourse of difference centered around some new words, like *hegemony*, *deconstruction*, and *liminality*, and new ways to use old ones like *subjectivity*, *reproduction*, and *reflexivity*.

Interrupting Reflection with Reflexivity

For a while I was quite taken with my new words and program of work, and thought that in my college teaching I might simply exchange the fetishes of methodology for the fetishes of Critical Theory, and then never look back. I held, and still hold, the Althusserian view that schools are the State's primary Ideological Apparatus, or ISA, for reproducing a society divided into managers and workers, haves and have-nots, that teachers are its frontline instruments, and that the patronizing intellectual vacuity of most teacher education programs plays a vital role in reproducing good teacher-workers who know just enough to do their part without ever obtaining the means to effectively question or challenge the whole (Althusser, 1971).

It would seem to follow, then, that the only way to interrupt these processes of social reproduction would be to confront their once and future agents, teachers, with the conditions of their relationship to the Ideological State Apparatus of the school, in terms that rendered their agency and their culpability in this process indisputable to them. Having thought and talked their way through the dynamics of social reproduction as they manifested themselves in curriculum and instruction, teachers would experience such a case of ideological/intellectual disjuncture and psychic distress that they could not continue for long in practices that sustained and supported their own, and their students', dehumanizing oppression.

But this scenario, as noble and well reasoned as it might seem, ignores and contradicts the lessons of this chapter, because it is predicated on the same conceit I've tried to challenge in my confessions here, namely that reflection is enough—that is, that as rational beings our minds control our bodies and that our thoughts control our actions, so that a change of mind must lead to a change of action; ergo, change is an interior, intellectual process. Theories—at least the ones that are homegrown through reflection—do little more than rationalize actions we've taken or would like to take; they are the images of our action, not its source. My Unified Theory of Literature merely codified and legitimated the one-size-fits-all view of cultural action that I hoped would allow me to avoid engaging painful social issues in my work. Likewise, "racial (or gendered or classist) reasoning" allows its users to reflect on acts of discriminatory, racist (or sexist or classist) behavior they have experienced, and empowers them through the codification and legitimation of a separate-categories-for-each view of cultural action that makes them into the categorically oppressed, and white middle-class males into the categorically oppressive, in hope of avoiding engagement with their own discriminatory biases. That there is a very large kernel of truth in either of these points of view does not compensate for what either leaves out, or excuse the culturally myopic action either might legitimate.

If self-reflection cannot be the key to multicultural engagement, then what of theories imported from outside our lived and conscious experience? In my own case, I can only report that theory presented to me "on a platter"—that is, apart from its empirical context—sometimes makes for a challenging intellectual meal, but it is one whose implications I do not digest readily in my work. In 1980 in a graduate course in introductory adult education at Teachers College in New York City (where I had come fresh from the Peace Corps) a professor tried to convert me and about six other students in the class to the pedagogical vision of Paulo Freire. It was an extremely frustrating experience for him; I remember us getting told off and the class ending early soon after I remarked, "But now, this Freire—he's a Marxist, isn't he? You can't deny that." A year later on the Navajo Reservation I picked up *Pedagogy of the Oppressed* (Freire, 1970) again, and this time, I thought I got it. Navajos certainly were oppressed, and this "banking concept" of education that the school (not me, I reflected, but the "system") imposed on them was leading us all down the primrose path of false consciousness; what was needed was some pedagogic action that would liberate students from the false promises that were decimating their own cultural integrity as a people. But that insight had little impact on my teaching then or later.

Sometimes (on reflection) I like to remember that adult education course sowing seeds of doubt in the cracks of my monolithic cultural views, which sprouted years later during my return to serious graduate work. But there is little hard evidence to support such a novelistic turn of events; on the contrary, I entered doctoral study fully expecting to have my ideas about teaching literature and composition extended and reinforced. Whatever radical pedagogy I profess today I hold as a response against the intellectually shallow tenets of what gets promoted as "good practice" in literacy journals, as well as against practices that I witnessed and that shook me deeply as a supervisor of student teachers. However, although those practices have been theorized for me in the critical ethnographies I mentioned above, along with some subsequent reading of poststructuralist and feminist theory, these theoretical resources have contributed little to my own practice as a teacher. Ergo, I admit, I can only *profess* my radicalism; for, were I to return to teaching secondary language arts, even after five years of intensive theoretical work, I'm not so sure that my practices would be all that radically different from before. Certainly I would try; certainly I would abandon my Unified Theory of Literature and include more multicultural texts and perspectives in my work; but would I deal with the school system any better or respond any more constructively to students who sometimes just don't care to act like some theory says they should? Like Courtney Cazden (1988), who returned to teaching kindergarten after a nine-year absence, only to observe herself fall back into the same discursive patterns that she had identified in her research as interfering with children's intellectual growth, might not old (bad) habits reemerge in my teaching, couched in new theoretical skin, if only as my conditioned response to the unchanged contexts of schooling and of students' lives?

So, *sumus, ergo cogitimus*, then? Are we, therefore we think? Well, not exactly; for the activities of the mind and those of the body, that is, those of conscious rationality and conditioned response, are not divided out so neatly. A sizable body of evidence from a variety of fields—anthropology (McLaren, 1993; Turner, 1969), sociology (Bourdieu, 1990), linguistics and psychoanalysis (Kristeva, 1989), semiotics (Peirce, 1931/1958; Fiske, 1989)—suggests that consciousness is not an all-or-nothing state, but instead constitutes a range of liminal states, some just within range of our apprehension and others more distant and less accessible. These states are intimately tied to conditions within both mind and body; it is within them that the subjective self we project to the world—a self which strives for coherence among its words and deeds and to align itself with what is consensually "normal" behavior in a given setting—comes apart and reassembles itself in adaptive response to new situations. Culture works within these states, as do ideology, sexuality, and everything else we know and feel about ourselves and others and the world—everything that we generally take for granted as we negotiate a day.

To make lasting change through engagement of our own and other people's actions then, it is this range of consciousness-mediating words and deeds that needs to be tapped, because such change is not reflective, but *reflexive*: it operates *on* deeds and on words-as-deeds within our liminal consciousness, rather than reflecting superficially on prior acts. The best documentation of "naturally occurring" reflexivity as an adaptive, pre- or quasi-conscious exercise that I am aware of is found in studies of resistance within mass popular culture and, ironically, in studies of students' resistance to schooling. In his accounts of the ways that working-class and other socially subordinated groups produce their own ideologically subversive meanings from mass-produced commodities like TV programs, jeans, and sporting events, John Fiske (1987, 1989) refutes the stereotypical image of the mass consumer as the pawn of Madison Avenue or Hollywood. Instead, Fiske portrays consumers as "semiotic guerrillas," wily appropriators of the signs of late industrial capitalism who, in the micropolitics of a given moment, produce meanings that escape the control of the dominant and so wage a dialectical struggle of attrition, "a constant erosive force upon the macro, weakening the system from within so that it is more amenable to change at a structural level" (1989, p. 11). In a similar vein, a number of studies of student resistance, from Paul Willis's (1981) *Learning to Labor* to Peter McLaren's (1993) *Schooling as a Ritual Performance* to my own recent study of third graders in school libraries (Dressman, in press), portray students less as reactionary victims of the system than as reflexively critical *readers* of its logic, who, from positions of relative powerlessness, are able at times to manipulate the rules of instructional discourse and force a compromise with its reproductive regime in situations where more direct action would certainly play into the hands of the powerful.

In each case, the success of a reflexive act of semiotic resistance turns on its perpetrators' ability to locate key gaps in the flow or logic of a discourse, or find turns of phrase or image that are polysemic and therefore potentially ambiguous, and, with timing and guile, "flip" the interpretation of a situation—and the power relations it enacts—to their own advantage. Such moments of reflexivity are extremely creative and fleeting and really cannot be planned (although they can be looked for), nor can they be planned *for* (although they can be anticipated). They both shock and delight, for they bring into ironic apprehension the conflicts and contradictions at the core of culture and ideology that reflection tries to patch and gloss over. The collective power or reflexive semiotic resistance is seismic; it moves mountains of history inches at a time. On the surface, repairs might be made, structures shored up, foundations reinforced, and things may even seem "back to normal"; but nothing will ever be the same. The production of lasting change takes time and takes timing.

This is why I believe that reflexivity should replace the emphasis on reflection that dominates much of preservice teacher education today. Reflexivity touches most people in liminal moments of consciousness where the "hidden agenda of modernity" holds sway over their sense-making activity; while reflection, as I have argued here, works to cover cracks in that agenda's façade. In the undergraduate and graduate courses I teach, *my* hidden agenda increasingly has been to look for moments of reflexive opportunity, as well as to anticipate and learn to appreciate the reflexive acts of my once and future students.

Following this agenda requires, ironically, that I *cannot* ignore methodology in the "methods" courses I teach on the premise that if I just don't mention methods and "theories" found in standard textbooks my students will remain safe from seduction by their one-size-fits-all charm. Such a practice is doomed to failure because the tendency to fetishize technical procedures is not something that students pick up in education classes, but is part of the ideology they pick up long before they enter a college of education, just by living in the modern world. Finally, as Lilia Bartolomé (1994) makes clear, it is not methodology itself that is dehumanizing but its use as an "antidote" for difference when difference is read as "deficiency" by teachers. Some methods, particularly those that rescript power relations between teacher and students or among the students themselves in more horizontal terms, can serve as important heuristics—as "rules of thumb" that lend themselves to culturally reflexive adaptation—for beginning teachers.

As a more reflexive way of dealing with methodology in preservice courses, I choose to problematize the methods I teach in two ways. First, I make a point of accompanying standard teacher-practice texts with others that repoliticize their "value-free" rhetoric. I use a standard content area reading textbook in the first half of each content area reading class meeting, for example, but in the second half we read *The Politics of the Textbook* (Apple & Christian-Smith, 1991), an edited volume on topics ranging from race, class, gender, and disability bias in content area textbooks to the ways that adolescent romance readers resist the standard curriculum and ideology of "developmental" reading. I follow a similar pattern for the more theoretical and research-oriented courses I've taught; in one that is titled "Theories of Instruction," for example, I've paired empirical studies conducted in positivist frames with excerpts from Foucault (1977) and readings from bourgeois humanists like Mortimer Adler (1984) and Alan Bloom (1987) with Louis Althusser's (1971) "Ideology and Ideological State Apparatuses." The result for some of these students has been a decentering of their long-held assumptions about schooling as an institution and the political neutrality of research methods (or as one doctoral student put it, "I don't know *what* I believe anymore"). Other students have intimated that they've had to learn "how to read" all over again, meaning that they've begun to see the ways that texts lure them as educators into reading "the literature" of the field from a particular ideological position. I view these students' remarks as hopeful signs that they are becoming reflexively more critical of schooling and their roles in it, although I must also admit I have yet to see how transformative this new wariness will be.

My second strategy is wilier, and often turns, as described above, on using a single word or phrase to expose the contradictions and lapses of judgment in what is often recommended as "good practice." For example, I once assigned a methods class to read an article in *Language Arts* entitled, "Don't You Dare Say 'Fart'" (Mamchur, 1994), in which a teacher's censorship of a middle-school student's use of the word *fart* in a writing assignment is repudiated. During class discussion, the students all agreed that *of course* that teacher should not have stifled the poor child's developing "voice," and that they would *never* act that way in *their* classrooms. Just as we were all feeling pretty good knowing how we'd handle such a delicate problem in the writing workshop, I asked, "But what if the kid had written *fuck*? Then a way was opened to take a hard look, not at easily disposed of issues like "censorship," but at the ways that, as agents of the state, teachers' policing of words like *fuck* and *fart* in public discourse forms an outer perimeter of police control over how children might learn to talk about, and use, their bodies. These moments, as I have explained above, are hard to predict or plan for, but their spontaneous quality produces moments of reflexive engagement that would be difficult to achieve otherwise.

My reflexive strategizing, I acknowledge, does not represent anything approaching a "comprehensive" way of razing the hegemonic structure of preservice and inservice teachers' commonsense assumptions and general nonengagement with teaching in a multicultural world. Moreover, as strategies they are far from "sure bets" in the classroom, and when they fail or when they trigger "the wrong" response, I sometimes find my own consciousness engaged in some reflexively decentering ways. For example, during a recent class discussion about a chapter by Christine Sleeter and Carl Grant (1991) on textbook bias, an angry student interrupted the conversation, saying in effect, "So what if textbooks are biased? That's no excuse not to learn from them." This student went on to complain about "all this nonsense about gender and pronouns": he wasn't offended at all if people were always generically referred to as "he." While I struggled to keep my composure, several women and a Chicano student in the class replied to his charges far more diplomatically and effectively than I could have at that moment; it was all I could do to keep from showing the student the door and asking him not to return.

I was left to wonder afterward less at the crass insensitivity of the student than at my own reaction, which was one of fear masked by outrage. For what this student threatened in me was no less than the old fear I had as a secondary English teacher when a cherished method failed to engage students in an "appropriate" manner. And what did my reaction signal about the extent of my own engagement with issues of multiculturalism, whose central tenets must surely include the admonition *not* to rush to judgment but to try to understand the actions of others from their subjective position—that is, from the details of their own life experience? Surely, for all my theorizing about reflexivity, becoming multiculturally engaged cannot mean replacing one's old orthodoxy with new dogmatisms. In the case of this student, I was further chastened several weeks later when I learned that he had personal reasons that did not exactly justify, but certainly explained, his apparent insensitivity at that moment. In a moment of what I am coming to acknowledge as uncommon sensitivity (and true reflexivity) on my part, I was able to use these reasons to engage him with alternative interpretations of his personal situation.

A final confession, then. Although I remain somewhat hopeful about the potential of reflexive pedagogical approaches, if pursued *over a period of time*, to interrupt the reflective view of teaching and learning that helps to perpetuate conditions of social injustice in classrooms, I can offer little evidence at this moment that, when practiced as a "method," reflexivity always works its charms any better than any other fetish. On the other hand, that is not exactly the point of this chapter. Instead, the point I've struggled to make here is that there are no magic rites in education that guarantee engagement that will lead to Real Change. For as Lilia Bartolomé (1994) has suggested, the salient question to ask about any pedagogical approach is not, Does it work (every time)? or Can I make it work for me? but What possibilities does it open for (re)humanizing modern classrooms? and, by extension, How will this pedagogy (re)humanize me? On these counts, I've tried to argue that it is reflexive and not reflective teaching that holds the potential to open spaces at liminal levels of preservice and practicing teachers' apprehension of their classrooms, their students, and their curriculum— enough space to insert and turn a decentering text or word or two that will, in time, rescript the hidden agenda of modernity, and rehumanize us all as the various political, ethnic, classed, gendered, sexual, physical, materialistic beings that we are.

8

Robert E. Bahruth
Stanley F. Steiner

Upstream in the Mainstream

Pedagogy against the Current

I must recognize that students cannot understand their own rights
because they are so ideologized into rejecting their own freedom, their
own critical development, thanks to the traditional curriculum. Then,
I have to learn with them how to go beyond these limits, beyond their
own learned rejection of their rights.
—Paulo Freire (Shor & Freire, 1987, p. 107)

" Just tell me what I need to know to get an A" is a familiar phrase
often retorted from incoming college students, resultant from
years of public schooling. As critical pedagogues, we often in-
herit such students who have been conditioned into a teacher-centered
model of discourse. Students have learned to respond to the expectations of the teacher: parroting, memorizing, and regurgitating from a

series of facts and official bodies of knowledge promoted by the mainstream canon. The resulting "stupidification" (Macedo, 1994) demands a counterhegemonic pedagogy.

In this chapter, we will problematize student nonengagement in response to counterhegemonic pedagogical praxis. According to Leistyna and colleagues (1996), praxis is "the relationship between theoretical understanding and critique of society . . . and action that seeks to transform individuals and their environment" (p. 342). This demands that, "the educationalist lives the instigating dialect between his or her daily life—the *lived school* and the *projected school*—which attempts to inspire a new school" (Gadotti, 1996, p. 7). We also provide our understanding of nonengagement in relation to resistance, a description of our praxis, and organic examples to contextualize the evolving willingness to engage on the part of our students in response to our efforts.

Over the years it has become more and more apparent that learning requires engagement on the part of the learners (Smith, 1981). To engender student engagement, where students are involving their very beings and human conditions in the meaning making of academic subjects, one must recognize that learner backgrounds and life experiences, including their academic experiences, are the only tools they have to engage in current learning. Prepackaged lectures and curriculum or test-driven instruction tend to be oblivious to student-based meaning making, and propelled by an applied scientific notion that learners are "identical empty vessels which, if filled with the same substance, would yield the same, replicable results" (Ada, 1990, p. ix). The basic assumption here is not only erroneous, but punitive to students who have nonmainstream backgrounds. Metaphors or stories teachers use to present lessons are often biased toward learners from dominant cultural backgrounds. This inspires an effort to provide our students with a university experience that would prepare them for the pluralistic classrooms they will be encountering as teachers.

We began by recognizing the shortcomings of more traditional approaches to preservice and inservice preparation where school reform efforts have been consistently superficial and cosmetic at best without the deep structural changes necessary to produce true restructuring. Although the pedestrian perception exists of college as a place where professors are concerned with and students are challenged to explore new ideas, dialogue of a high intellectual ante is rare in most classrooms, and the transmission model of passivity among students prevails (Boyer, 1987; Fox, 1993; Steiner & Bahruth, 1994). Technicist approaches have led to deskilling of teachers (Beyer & Apple, 1988), and the call for the intellectualization of the profession (Giroux, 1988, 1996) requires an end to insulting the intelligence of teachers while forging a pedagogy based in their organic experiences. The need to deconstruct monolithic educational practices must be accompanied by pedagogical recommendations anchored in the experiences of educators who have been willing to experiment with research-based pedagogical shifts where engagement becomes the critical focus (Giroux & McLaren, 1986; Giroux, 1996).

Alternatives need to be made clear for present and future educators, along with respective ramifications. Teachers can flow with the mainstream and subsequently reproduce hegemony, or question the status quo and problematize the system, which has continually failed in its stated intentions of promoting a democratic society, thereby taking steps toward transforming society through teachers as cultural workers. Taking the path of critical pedagogy requires a philosophical shift. The teacher is no longer the only knowledge base. Nor is the current knowledge base sufficient for teaching. Teacher scholars would have to explore and understand social, political, and historical contexts of hegemony (Chomsky, 1995) to be effective in counterhegemonic pedagogy (Giroux, 1983). Teachers, no longer the dominant voice in the classroom, invite students to become active learners and critical thinkers, and their voices are respected. We collectively work to become a community of learners.

In an effort to build such a community, Shor (1990) purports that the initial challenge of the critical educator is to deconstruct authoritarian modes of discourse in traditional classrooms and to establish a democratic "culture circle" (Brown, 1978) where students' lived experiences are invited and encouraged in the construction of meaning: "A progressive position requires democratic practice where authority never becomes authoritarianism, and where authority is never so reduced that it disappears in a climate of irresponsibility and license" (Freire, 1987, p. 212). While there is no simplistic formula for generating a pedagogical space that turns on a culture circle, it is clear that understanding Freire's praxis, coupled with experience and reflection, has fostered our evolving criticity as practioners.

An Evolving Sense of Culture Circles

Introduction to culture circles came through, *Literacy in Thirty Hours: Paulo Freire's Process in North East Brazil* (Brown, 1978). Freire's work was unknown at the time; it was the notion of teaching literacy in thirty hours that captured our attention. The process described seemed incredibly natural and the eloquence and humility of the pedagogy was astounding. It has since taken more than ten years of scholarship to comprehend the subtleties of reading the word-world (an effort deemed worthwhile and driven by a gnawing discontent with traditional approaches to literacy and learning). Our transformation as educators is constantly ongoing. Two major pieces consolidating Freire's pedagogy came in dialogues between Freire and Macedo (1987) and Shor and Freire (1987). Most empowering was how Freire expanded the notion of literacy to include reading and writing the world as cultural agents and subjects rather than objects of history, thus becoming a basis for establishing a culture circle as a pedagogical space.

Orchestrating a culture circle is intellectually demanding and requires constant criticity and professional reflection. The classroom is rearranged in an attempt to provide a space where students can develop their voices in a human environment of respect and affirmation. Arranging students in a circle is a pedagogical move whereby the physical environment of the classroom is transformed from the straight row, front-facing arrangements in traditional classrooms. This change provides opportunity for change in the human environment in the classroom; however, other changes must accompany this rearrangement if a culture circle is to evolve. Eye contact among the learners is important and just this shift can capture the curiosity and imagination of students. To complete the shift the teacher must also consider a change in discourse patterns and views of authority, knowledge, curriculum, and learning. What is apparent is that a culture circle does not evolve simply by having students sit in a circle.

Our challenge is to provide a focus without dismissing the voices of participants in the dialogue. Teachers must recognize both conscious and unconscious attempts to derail the discourse. Focus is often maintained by asking follow-up questions. We are not attempting to lead all students to a singular destination other than the evolution of their own criticity. Knowing absolutely where a circle is headed would be antithetical to critical pedagogy and would exclude the teacher as a participant-learner. It would also be acritical in that it would reify the teacher as authoritative representative of an immutable, static body of knowledge (hooks, 1994) (we may as well have remained seated at the desk in the front of the rows). Further, we would be presenting ourselves as though we have arrived, when we wish to demonstrate the importance of maintaining a disposition toward life-long learning.

The teacher's charge is to oversee the evolution of a human environment where all participants, including the teacher, share their wrestlings to make meaning of their development based on the experiences they bring to the classroom (Freire & Macedo, 1995). The teacher recognizes that students can only make new meanings based on prior understandings anchored in the organic nature of their knowing. The heterogeneous nature of our culture is most widely represented only when all views are heard. We begin by deconstructing prior schooling.

To provide this contrast, we reflect upon García's (1995) account as a Mexican American growing up in a mainstream education. He was consistently asked to give up his "ethnic survival kit" (Trueba, 1991); a disregard of first language and cultural diversity, placement in a more technical track resultant of generalizing intellectual abilities of minorities, low expectations diminishing any hope of higher education, too few minority teachers, and an absence of formally educated role models among the impoverished have all been acts of academic oppression (Chávez-Chávez, Belkin, Hornback, & Adams, 1991).

Anaya (1995), another victim of mainstream education, conceptualized the effects on any students with the slightest bit of diversity: "As a lifelong educator, I have argued for years that education must take into account the culture of the individual child. No one can develop his full potential in an uncomfortable environment; one only learns to escape from an uncomfortable environment as quickly as possible" (p. 400). The importance of student voice and conscious work to provide pedagogical spaces for mutual appreciation is critical. In contrast to male-dominated, teacher-filtered discourse, students require time and safety to find their voices.

Transition toward building such a democratic classroom presents challenges. Students accustomed to the "flattering pedagogy" (Morton, 1992) of mainstream education may initially respond through nonengagement. They may get frustrated in their search for the "right answer." Students have been disabled by traditional, teacher-curriculum-centered pedagogy, which has misled them into believing in the myth of "authoritative right answers." Montessori's (1964) notion of "flexibility of thought" is a feature of the dialogue which often transpires in culture circles. Students eventually discover there are no simplistic, monolithic solutions to the struggle for a democratic society and that democracy lies within the ongoing dialogue; the struggle itself, ever in progress. To clarify, we find it necessary to delineate our current understanding of the ways students respond to differing pedagogical settings.

Resistance, Nonengagement, and Engagement

The terms *resistance* and *nonengagement* can be used to describe two populations of students and their ways of responding to differing pedagogical paradigms. They seem to be in complementary distribution. Students who resist traditional schooling are responding to pedagogical practices that are politically biased against them. *Resistance* then becomes the critical term that replaces *discipline* in that it forces the interrogation of pedagogical practices rather than placing blame on the victim while leaving the pedagogy unchallenged.

Nonengagement refers to student response to critical pedagogy and cultural studies where the pedagogy is not giving them cause to resist but inviting them to discover their own voices. Student nonengagement is most often the conscious or unconscious rejection by learners from the dominant culture to discovering their own voices, to critical thinking, and to the subjectification of their learning. The main source of nonengagement in critical pedagogy often comes from these students who are distressed when the pedagogy is no longer flattering, or from the known delivery system, which emphasizes memorization and test-taking abilities and a hidden curriculum. Suddenly, they are required to think—to analyze, synthesize and wrestle with making meanings for themselves instead of just memorizing and parroting back disjointed or irrelevant facts from fragmented curricula. In culture circles they must discover their own voices—a cognitively demanding responsibility—too often a novel academic experience. These students often discover they have weak voices or no voice at all because they have been living in a materially privileged human condition. Further, they feel threatened when the silenced voices of the dominated minority students come forth loud and clear, toned with anger and accusation against the biased system. However, with engagement, students who have been oppressed by traditional educational experiences tend to thrive in culture circles precisely because the pedagogy addresses their frustrations and provides them with spaces to use voices previously silenced, ignored, or misunderstood. Becoming critically aware of differing students' experiences provided us with the need to critique our own ways of approaching student learning, which has led over time to a dramatic shift in praxis.

Discovering the Water in Which We Swim

Through our readings, years of classroom experimentation, and wrestling with meaningful learning we have come to realize that the shift in pedagogy starts within. Dykstra (1996) speaks to this act as "throwing tradition to the wind and do[ing] what made more sense," which has brought us to teach and learn in an environment that promotes disequilibrium, to question, to experience firsthand, to view through a new lens, and to "discover the water in which students swim."

In our discourse we question the myth of a prescribed curriculum as the mechanism to a learned individual. We question and view teacher-proof packages as mechanisms to devalue critical thought in order to perpetuate oppression. We lament this "deskilling of teachers" (Beyer & Apple, 1988).

The oppressive curriculum is, for teachers, similar to the function of recipes for women in Guatemala. Anthropologists Margarita Estrada and Professor Brenda Penados at San Carlos University, Guatemala City in 1991, related the lengthy preparation and painstaking cooking of Guatemalan traditional dishes as an activity that oppresses and undermines a woman's status in Guatemalan culture. They argue that the ritual of Guatemalan cooking as a prescribed curriculum perpetuates oppression of women and the male-privileged status quo; both need to be questioned. When cultures of college students, teachers, or Guatemalan women are occupied with fragmented details and time-consuming busy work these mechanisms must be recognized as tools of oppression or repression. Critical pedagogy, a pedagogy of liberation, becomes our rebirth into a world of critical consciousness and agency. Teachers become the midwives of critical consciousness.

Culture circles hold the potential to provide the pedagogical spaces necessary for democratization and humanization of the classroom. Through problematization of the status quo, space is provided for counterhegemonic transformation, since it is clear that the current hegemony has created a stacked deck against all but the privileged. Power becomes the focus of analysis in our quest as citizen-learners to comprehend our collective human conditions. Often the teacher's role is to pose questions that provide an intellectual space for problematizing culture itself (Freire, 1970, 1973). Dialogues evolve along generative themes of daily living involving all participants. Some participants may be reproducing and benefiting from undemocratic cultural and social practices while others may be victims. Since this is the water in which they swim, they may not even be aware of the extent of their participation. Victims may not be aware of roles they play as accomplices in their own victimization. The consciousness-raising dimension of Freire's pedagogy of the oppressed becomes a vehicle for empowerment of all participants to transform social and cultural practices and to challenge myths and basic assumptions of the hegemony they have inherited through social reproduction and colonization. Only when students critically discover the water in which they swim can we expect them to view teaching in new ways.

According to Giroux (1996):

Youth signifies in all of its diversity the possibilities and the fears adults must face when they reimagine the future while shaping the present. The degree to which large segments of youth are excluded from the language, rights, and obligations of democracy indicates the degree to which many adults have abandoned the language, practice, and responsibilities of critical citizenship and civic responsibility. (p. 140)

In Farsi there is the saying, "A wolf does not give birth to a lamb." As public intellectuals responsible for the next generation of teachers, we must evolve in our own criticity if we are to provide a space for our students to do the same.

Coming to Know Who We Are

We both came to realize a need to critically look at mainstream education early in our lives and have consciously made efforts along the way to democratize classrooms—every student's inherent right. For Stan, the feeling of nonengagement started in grade school, where the notion of questioning was perceived as a personal attack toward authority and never problematized with students in an attempt to promote critical thinkers. Coming from a working-class family, he and others of the same cut in society were demoralized through lower-tracked classes, discouraged away from higher education, and robbed of intellectual challenge.

Robert, a member of working-class culture, was also discouraged from going to college by his high school guidance counselor, and only attended at the urging of his mother. Thanks to grade school educated fathers and high school educated mothers, who instilled a strong work ethic and a will to dream, both opened the doors for subsequent siblings and their offspring to obtain college degrees.

Early efforts as educators were informed by negative personal experiences whereby we refused to prejudge the innate potential of any student. Robert's transformation and empowerment, however, did not fully occur until his teaching became theoretically and philosophically charged. He began a quest as a transformational intellectual through scholarship and reflective practice, and the effectiveness of his teaching has been documented in the literature (Hayes & Bahruth, 1985; Hayes, Bahruth, & Kessler, 1991).

Both Stan and Robert share Giroux's clear perception of himself as "an historical accident" (McLaren, 1988). In Giroux's (1996) own words, "Lacking the security of a middle-class childhood, my friends and I seem suspended in a working-class culture that neither accorded us a voice nor guaranteed economic independence" (p. 4).

In a similar vein, Macedo (1994) relates his own horror story of victimization at the hands of his high school guidance counselor who attempted to steer him away from college and into TV repair, based upon his proficiency in English. He facetiously comments, "Perhaps my guidance counselor was not really operating from a deficit-orientation model but was, instead, responding to a need for bilingual TV repairmen" (p. 1). Many times, we have found that challenging such educational practices requires us to speak the unpleasant.

As colleagues we came together to work in an experimental teacher education program supported through a three-year grant from Funding for the Improvement of Post Secondary Education (FIPSE). It was clear from the first encounter that we both were dissatisfied with present practice of teacher training and welcomed the opportunity to try something different. Our mission was to bridge content courses, methods classes, and application in an elementary classroom setting over two semesters. Normally, content/core courses and methods courses are taken in isolation and application of course work comes with the culminating practice of student teaching. Connections between content in courses and elementary classrooms are left up to the students. We took on the charge of ensuring the connections. We began by changing the entire structure of scheduling university courses. Critical of the fragmentation model of courses, eighteen hours of college credit were purposely blocked into meeting five days a week for four hours each day. Fridays were reserved for an elementary classroom experience with a two-hour debriefing in the afternoon with students, professors, and practitioners.

Four college professors, the two of us and two from the humanities area, came together to team teach this block of courses. The composition of preservice elementary teachers reflected the largest percentage of diversity among all education courses. We were 26 percent Hispanic, 1 percent African American, 1 percent Native American, 2 percent Basque, 50 percent nontraditional and traditional students, and 20 percent were males, which constituted the majority in our entire college. Students self-selected into this alternative program. Our challenges, insights, and applications of critical pedagogy to the mainstream are outlined in this chapter.

Praxis: Taking Theory into Action

Working with a cohort of preservice elementary teachers, initial attempts at democratic discourse were not without glitches. During the first week of class, a fifty-year-old Anglo male dominated the discourse to the point of frustrating and alienating his peers. At this juncture we had two challenges: to raise the consciousness of both the group and student by problematizing the issue; and bring the problem into the culture circle in a nonconfrontational manner to continue the deconstruction of traditional pedagogy with an organic example from the group's dynamics. Confrontation would have reaffirmed authoritarianism; precisely what we choose to avoid. Had we not problematized or addressed issues of democratic discourse one student would have frustrated the pedagogy and caused nonengagement of the entire group.

If we do not postpone—actually expedite—the syllabus and utilize the organic teachable moments of the evolving culture circle, we merely "cover" the curriculum. The curriculum becomes the antagonist of nonengagement while contributing to the development of false concepts about teaching and learning: "Students, I believe, learn as much from the process of a course, its hidden curriculum, as from the explicit content" (Schniedewind, 1987, p. 170). Critical pedagogues are aware of the "hidden" curriculum and politically motivated to be counterhegemonic.

In order to effectively democratize the classroom we must first develop our own criticity. For example, How do we do this without dehumanizing or demonizing the student or taking away his needed voice? Rather than relying on direct teacher confrontation of the student we chose to pose questions within the culture circle. We asked the students, Who haven't we heard from? and What voices are missing? Further, How are the missing voices essential to democratization of the classroom? In essence, critical pedagogy is a "pedagogy of question" rather than a pedagogy of answer (Freire, 1991). Questions are contextual rather than rhetorical. We were asking the students to engage in the discussion in a nonthreatening manner, unlike a practice in which answers have been predetermined by teachers and curriculum guides in a banking model.

According to Shor (1990), "When we behave in experimental ways in a classroom, we are learning on the job how to become democratic change agents and critical teachers and participatory problem-posers. We are taking responsibility for our own redevelopment as educators" (p. 350). Shor states that this process of recreating our profession can take years. Working in collaboration with creative colleagues can enhance the pedagogy and lower the risk by providing sounding boards. We had daily access to discuss and develop the pedagogy as it emerged, calling each other in the evenings and mornings before class, going for walks between classes, continually wrestling with the emergent content and brainstorming new possibilities to the point that our spouses became frustrated with time we spent together. We had a "din in the head," a constant subconscious rumbling of thoughts and ideas due to our intense investment in creative and intrinsically motivating pedagogy (Krashen, 1983).

The decolonizing aspect of mainstream students through critical pedagogy often raises their consciousness to the extent that they realize no one was truly privileged in schools with so political an agenda as reproduction rather than democratization and transformation. They come to realize their own education was impoverished, not by voices they heard in schools but by the absence of voices uninvited or silenced. Counterhegemonic experience in our culture circles, where voice became an element of the evolving community of learners, provided our students with a deeper appreciation for what was missing in prior educational contexts. Dialogue also included attempts to foster a meta-awareness of community as it was evolving.

Building a Community of Learners

Our collaborative efforts generated critical questions used to provoke discussions with students. In contrast with traditional fragmentation of fifty-minute class periods, discussions required longer blocks of time to blossom. Rather than asking students to participate in learning while playing cognitive hopscotch, we integrated courses and field experiences. Longer gatherings, the organic nature of interactions built on life experiences of all participants and immediate needs of the group, appreciation of individual voices, and democratization of the classroom provided a space for developing criticity and a passion for lifelong learning.

Passion for learning must be kindled and nurtured in subtle ways so as not to drive students further from intended purposes of education. First, we must spend time getting to know the people within our classroom community. One exercise begins with student perceptions as they enter a classroom and immediately begin to size up participants. Physical appearance, clothing, hair style, facial expressions, and body language all emanate a perception in the eyes of the beholder. In a limited way they are "reading the world" (Freire & Macedo, 1987). We must extend this vision of the world into looking for what they do not see through the eyes.

We begin with what we know. A good place to start is by humanizing the instructor (hooks, 1994) by posing questions about ourselves. Students are asked to predict our personality through their initial perceptions and the questions we ask. What words could you attach to my personality? Do I have family? What is my idea of a good time? What is the genre of literature I most enjoy? We ask students to share their perceptions, but we do not confirm or negate their predictions until all share their thoughts. Then we talk about ourselves through their perceptions, confirming and negating when necessary. Students ask additional questions for clarification. They begin to see how a person is more than initial perceptions. The real confirmations for the students' initial perceptions happen throughout the semester as they see us as other players, other humans in the classroom community.

A continued stream of questions is used to stimulate thinking; not necessarily expecting responses, but to enhance how they think about all humans. Can we know everything about a person from perceptions? How does knowing something about a person's background effect perceptions? Would a visit to a person's home help? Our first meeting was in one of our homes. We prepared a meal together. What do we really know about the way a person thinks, feels, and dreams based on perceptions? How do we really get to know someone? What is the meaning of the Native American saying "never judge a man/woman until you have walked two moons in their moccasins"? What does it take for people/teachers to move away from initial perceptions? By modeling, we make connections to our role as teacher.

We talk about how initial perceptions the first day of school can become subliminally implanted through preceding reputation, media, fear, and lack of knowledge. Often, this limited view has a negative effect on our relationship with a child. Someone who comes to school disheveled or of a different skin color may be perceived as having a poor home life, slow learner, illiterate, having a poor attitude, trouble maker, or resistant learner. This negative imbalance is what we call the "Herdman Effect"—a term generated from, *The Best Christmas Pageant Ever* (Robinson, 1972), where all the kids from the Herdman family were socially promoted because teachers feared having two Herdmans in the same room. Their reputations preceded them, based merely on initial perceptions. The teachers never got past preconceived notions. "Those of us who presume to 'teach' must not imagine that we know how each student begins to learn" (Gussin-Paley, 1994, p. 78).

We explore the issue of perceptions and first day of school further. Excerpts from several books describing the first day of school are passed around and discussed (*Roll of Thunder, Hear My Cry* [Taylor, 1976; *Savage Inequalities* [Kozol, 1991]; *Bridge to Terabithia* [Paterson, 1977]; *When the Legends Die* [Borland, 1963]; *New Boy* [Storey, 1993]). We write from the perspective of a character in a story. The realities of this exercise and discussion begin to surface in the form of personal stories as our community rethinks past schooling experiences. Outbursts of tears and suppressed hatred are unloaded into the group. We begin to deconstruct ill effects of past schooling practices. We want to critically revisit the tradition of teachers teaching the way they have been taught, using the same methodology for the past 100 years (Cuban, 1984), and teachers working in isolation (Lortie, 1975). We bring these issues into the classroom community to deal with collectively, not in isolation as tradition would dictate. The pedagogical shift becomes a community effort in the same way we might hope that our students would approach their future students. In fact, we observed as much as they worked with their elementary students in the field experiences.

Promoting a Disposition Toward Lifelong Learning

Our pedagogy has left its mark on these individuals. This transition in praxis from teacher centered to a community of learners allows us to start with personal story as a framework for lifelong learners: "I believe that the ways of telling and the ways of conceptualizing that go with them become so habitual that they finally become recipes for structuring experience itself, for laying down routes into memory, for not only guiding the life narrative up to the present, but for directing it into the future" (Bruner, 1994, p. 36). By allowing personal story we begin to deconstruct schools and education on an individual basis: "When teaching and learning are seen as genuinely interactive behaviors, we discover that we cannot effectively teach *children we don't know*. Getting to know the children in a new group, say at the beginning of a year, is therefore a first priority" (Britton, 1989, p. 217).

Stories from members in the classroom community came in varied media. Some were through dialogue journals, others through reflective writing and/or group debriefings. Participants also presented portfolios to the entire class and more profound stories occurred during these presentations.

Alice, an African American, came to realize the impact the drive-by shooting of her brother had on her schooling. She realized for the first time in the twenty years since her brother's death why her mother was so adamant about an education as a way out of inner-city Chicago. The culture circle provided the safety for her to share, to reconstruct, and to enrich the lives of us all.

Janet, a twenty-year-old Anglo, released the anger caused from an unfair generalization about her character that a teacher allowed to be printed in the school newspaper. It changed the way other students and teachers looked at her for the rest of her high school career and she vowed never to let such an injustice happen again. At the time of this writing, Janet was spearheading a grassroots movement to block the closing of a recreational facility on the poor side of town. A new facility had been built for the affluent with prohibitive membership fees for low-income people. The evolving criticity of the students was effecting the way they looked at their world, fulfilling an application of Freirean pedagogy by becoming agents of history through action.

Arlene, an early college dropout, returned twenty years later. She shared her story of denial to be class valedictorian because she was not of the "right" family. Her self-esteem had been so damaged that it took nearly twenty-five years to get the college degree she justifiably deserved. Through a safe atmosphere Arlene found an opportunity to share her personal story, deconstruct significant events in her life, and reconstructing a future for herself.

Colleen, a single mother and first-generation college attendee, came to the first meeting in one of our homes and isolated herself in a corner. On noticing this behavior we engaged her in dialogue. As we came to understand Colleen we learned there was a reason for her shriveled body posture, nonexistent eye contact, and poor self-esteem. All had been systematically stripped from her through the course of her prior schooling.

In the course of getting to know her we also learned she had no family support and the classroom became her new family. By the end of the class, Colleen had become the group historian, took photos, and organized a class publication.

Rod, married and a father of four children, positioned himself to come to school full time. For the first time in his life he wrestled with meaningful learning in group debriefings, in contrast to his prior schooling. He completed our class and found himself back in the traditional, dehumanizing structure in some college courses and resisted the insult to his intelligence. He nearly got booted out of the university, but was determined to become a critical educator. Rod realized the battles a risk taker must face. The entire pedagogy we had been working through the previous semester got challenged by the system. Rod did not give up. He took the F's, rethought his plan of action, and decided to play the game to prove a point of the ridiculousness of transmission model classes. He retook courses and got As and Bs. Through lessons learned he has determined not to be a colonizer of minds but to educate towards critical literacy.

Juanita, a Mexican-born, first-generation high school graduate and now college student, shared her struggles through a predominately mainstream elementary and secondary education. Despite obstacles, Juanita became empowered in the fifth grade with a teacher who taught through an additive bilingual praxis that reified her home language and culture (Hayes, Bahruth & Kessler, 1991). Affirmation of an inclusive pedagogy was reaffirmed during her portfolio presentation. Juanita related an experience with a high school teacher who gave her a failing grade: "I wrote to my fifth-grade teacher and told him I was getting As in all my classes except science. I told him, 'That's all right Mr. B, because I know it's something wrong with my science teacher and not me'" (Juanita, personal letter). Empowerment belongs to the learner and cannot be taken away. She knew in her heart that it was not her, but a bias of her science teacher. Juanita now felt an obligation to pass on the legacy by becoming a teacher for *all* children.

Another way of generating a posture toward lifelong learning with a lingering effect in the students' minds was through literature shared in the group or directed toward an individual based on a personal story or experience shared: Your story reminds me of a book I read; You might find that story interesting to read. Each story connects us to another story/book/article. We model the benefits of lifelong learning by suggesting a book, further reading, or making copies for the group or for read alouds during class time, and by reciprocal interaction between teacher and students. Students' voices are valued over a parroting of the teacher. At the end of the course we had one student, Sarita, comment that she had read more books for this class, though not required reading, because the format had stimulated her curiosity enough to go to the library and check them out on her own. Another student, Mark, surprised us all during his portfolio presentation when he handed out copies listing the books mentioned or discussed over the course of one semester. The list included four pages of single-spaced titles. Discovering the utility of literature, a lifelong reading posture starts from modeling.

One example of students reflecting personal empowerment occurred while discussing children's reading of faddish literature. Out of curiosity, a student had read a book in *The Babysitters' Club* series and reported that the one she read featured a boy babysitter in the title and cover yet in actuality he never babysits through the entire book. In her opinion the title was misleading and left her dismayed, which in turn led her to problematize this misrepresentation with elementary students. Another student in our group connected her story to his reading of *The Emperor's Old Clothes* (Dorfman, 1983), chastising the subliminal messages portrayed through Disneyfied distortions of folklore (see also Giroux, 1996), which led to Postman's (1985) *Amusing Ourselves to Death* and the mind programming that occurs through television taking us away from oral traditions and reading good literature. Discussion ended with the importance of encouraging children's reading by providing a wide range of literature and allowing for rich discussions while problematizing limitations of television and shallow literature. Our college students became empowered beyond deskilling textbooks and regurgitation of meaningless content.

Through modeling the teaching and learning within a community of learners our students are becoming change agents. We recognize restructuring of classroom protocol will be met with resistance in most school settings, but we problematized this several times in our classes. As in any new situation, we talk about them reading the world they have entered first and then to begin planting seeds among people who are sincere about teaching all children. In some cases there may be only one other person to collaborate with in a building. Most importantly, students, parents, and colleagues will follow if you walk your talk. Those who have developed criticity as community members, readers of the world, and lifelong learners will hardly consider the notion of public education under the traditional model again. Despite challenges they face in the future, these students have tools and dispositions to negotiate the obstacles. We know and they know that the experience they received from a liberating pedagogy has changed them for life. In the highest expression of literacy they have become writers of the world (Freire & Macedo, 1987).

Extending the Pedagogical Shift

Student empowerment at the university also presents a set of challenges. Over the years, we have become more overt in the politics of our pedagogy and more aggressive in our deconstruction of the status quo. Ironically, as we have become more adept at the pedagogy of question and the orchestration of culture circles, we have met with less nonengagement. Several factors seem to be at play here. First, we often have students requesting and attending other courses with us, providing a critical mass (pun intended) of engaged students. As these students dialogue and interact with "newcomers" to our courses we find them generating their own acute critical questions. Second, the general widespread attacks on education from a complete spectrum of ideologies are becoming too loud to ignore. Our early focus on the deconstruction of the myths of neutrality and homogeneity in mainstream schooling helps students to discover sooner the water in which they swim. According to Freire, "The defenders of neutrality of literacy programs do not lie when they say that the clarification of reality at the same time as learning to read and write is a political act. They are wrong, however, when they deny that the way in which they deny reality has no political meaning" (as cited in Gadotti 1994, p. 59). After just a few classes students often react with anger when they realize *what has been missing* in their education. We challenge them to view the political nature of education and to determine early in their careers whether they are going to be "teachers as intellectuals" (Giroux, 1988) or "intellectual dupes" (Crichton, 1993). The following anecdotes reflect more recent experiences with nonengagement and how we have been able to defuse it.

Recently, our teacher education program added a course on diversity and a few students were upset about the additional program requirements. In our first class meeting, a group of eleven Anglo students sat waiting to begin. They were welcomed to the class, asked to arrange their desks in a circle, and given a skeletal syllabus listing the text, literature to be used, and a rough outline of the semester, along with requirements, evaluation procedures and other details usually found on a syllabus. After a brief introduction of the course, students were asked to introduce themselves and to explain what they hoped to get out of the class.

One student complained outright and asked for a justification of the new requirement stating he had no intention of ever teaching in a culturally diverse classroom. When asked, "Would it matter more if you knew you are presently sitting in a culturally diverse classroom?" He surveyed the room, apparently looking for an ethnically/racially diverse classmate. Suspicions were verified when he said this class was a "normal" classroom. We began by mapping the many ways we were diverse as a group to make the familiar unfamiliar.

A female student offered gender as one example of diversity. We formed small groups and discussed other ways diversity can exist in a classroom beyond the obvious, superficial distinctions we have become so conditioned to notice and respond to, often in negative ways. As groups reported their findings, we had a wide range of categories of diversity represented; from obvious factors including rural/urban backgrounds, religion, socioeconomic status, political affiliations, age, and quality of educational experiences to more subtle distinctions including handedness, hobbies and interests, family structures, ideological orientations, strengths and weaknesses, fears and phobias, and those who loved or hated Rush. As Giroux (1996) states:

> Educators must rework the discourse(s) of cultural studies to provide some common ground in which traditional modernist offerings of difference and politics around the binaries capital/labor, self/other, subject/object, colonizer/colonized, white/black, man/woman, majority/minority, and heterosexual/homosexual can be reconstituted through more complex representations of identification, belonging, and community. (p. 135)

In the process we deconstructed two myths: that of homogeneity and, more importantly, the myth of the mainstream yardstick itself. After the first session, students were open for engagement and receptive to a series of activities allowing us to mark the twain of the mainstream. At the end of the course one student wrote:

> Dear Roberto,
> Before class even began, I had a pretty good idea where you stood. The articles and discussions helped solidify in my mind the how and why.
> The most significant experience for me has been watching the class members change their attitudes. I guess I experienced the transformation myself last semester, but watching it was great fun. It really works!
> At the beginning of this semester, some members of the class had doubts about the way you ran the class. Terms like "waste of time," "irresponsible" and "unprofessional" were used to describe their frustration at "trying to live with ambiguity." I first noticed the change begin when one student said they wished they didn't have to do all the busy work for their other classes, so they could spend more time on the "real stuff" for this class. Later, during a discussion on which instructors they would recommend, one of the (formerly) most vocal critics said, "Bahruth, for one." Of course these discussions took place before your

arrival, but I can't help wondering if you would really be surprised at the level of animosity or the depth of the complete turnabout of thinking. You must have seen it before, often. Is that why the . . . warning about living with ambiguity was necessary? . . . Maybe that accounts for the hostility at the beginning of the class—safety is a rare thing in most classes. . . . Of course the content was great, but seeing the actual change in class members was most impressive! (Shelly, final reflective paper)

Fighting the Rapids of Tradition

We would be hiding some truths if we did not talk about resistance we and our students received from other faculty. After a semester or two with us students actively resist traditional teacher-centered classrooms, which previously went uninterrogated. The backlash from colleagues comes in the form of comments such as, "You are ruining our students," and "You incited the students to gang up on me," and "The students are not as respectful; they question my assignments and my tests," or "They question my authority." We have also been requested: Could you put the chairs back in rows? by colleagues sharing classrooms with us. Teaching through critical questions to make the familiar unfamiliar has produced our response, Should I ask the person using the room before me to put the chairs in a circle when he/she is finished?

On the other hand we more often receive praise from colleagues who recognize the important contributions these same students make in their classrooms. Comments like, The FIPSE students stand out, or These students are more articulate than many of my graduate students, and The quality of the students' work stands out among their classmates and they ask questions that reflect deep thought. Once the criticity is awakened they are no longer passive learners absorbing official bodies of knowledge. In their evolving pedagogical understandings the act of reflective practice becomes second nature. Students also turn a more critical eye toward faculty evaluations.

These students may still be obligated to take courses taught traditionally, but now enter these classes knowing they have a choice in what to take away and for the first time they are playing "the game" by their own rules. They have acquired coping strategies in order to get the diploma, but the impact of becoming a critical thinker is set in motion for life. Student resistance to pedagogical structures representative of past educational experience demonstrates our success and their critical thinking.

Attitudes and dispositions toward traditional forms of grading shifted from teacher centered to evaluation requiring responsibility from the individual student with reciprocal responsibility among the community of learners. Dialogue journaling between classmates provided a means to formalize their thinking and to begin the day's discussion. A multitude of activities blending theory, content, and practical applications with elementary students were interjected throughout the semester. In smaller groups, students collaborated with practioners to develop and implement these activities. Results, from reconsiderations to celebrations, were brought to our debriefings with students, faculty, and practitioners, again, providing a voice for all. We approached grading through a pedagogy of question rather than a hierarchical performance standard. From the beginning, students knew the ongoing and culminating exercise would be to create portfolios reflecting questions that evolved from the group as a whole. What do teachers need to know? What actions do teachers take to guarantee learning for all? What is important for others to know about you? What might your classroom look like in the future? In the process of the collective experience and the qualitative measures used, our goal was to intellectually charge their professional development. Activities required analysis, synthesis, and application. Portfolios oblige students to take control of, and reflect on, their learning. In a few cases students self-selected out of teacher education when faced with the challenge of controlling their own destiny and the demands of a deeper sense of teaching.

Students now have a posture to look at life through new lenses. They regain a sense of reading the world that had been stripped through formal schooling. In culture circles students become interdependent, but not dependent on the teacher. We become a community of learners, and students take that belief and practice into their professional world.

Conclusion

In order for this pedagogy to happen in our lives within the university we looked for and initiated a language of possibility. Macedo (1994, p. 152) raises three extremely provocative questions about colleges of education and their ability to provide the pedagogical spaces necessary to educate for transformation rather than social reproduction. Often the rigid structures of bureaucracies impede the very change their leadership would claim they are attempting to provide. Change must be recognizable, understandable, and evaluated by status quo standards. However, certain specific recommendations would be helpful to those who wish to practice critical pedagogy.

First, physical structures such as time and space must be taken into consideration. We opted for longer classes, away from the fifty-minute fragmented structure. The critical mass of discourse necessary for a culture circle to evolve must be at least ninety uninterrupted minutes. In our three-hour-long classes students have commented that discussion was so rich that the class seemed shorter than many fifty-minute lectures.

Second, we request rooms where furniture is movable, with enough space to form a circle, and also where we can set up cooperative groups. Universities still construct buildings based on transmission models and occupancy is determined based on straight rows facing forward. Administrators need to appreciate alternative models for education.

Third, current evaluation procedures are shallow and deter professors from innovations that disrupt student comfort zones. Put another way by Dykstra (1995):

> In essence, measurement against common standards creates strong pressures to conform to implicit, unexamined standards. Regardless of initial statements of purpose of the student surveys or of denials about their present use, it is the case that student surveys and *selected* testimonials are the sole data in the category of teaching upon which tenure, promotion, and salary decisions are made. As a result there is no real innovation in teaching at the university and professors are not really encouraged to even consider such innovation.

Since part of nonengagement may manifest itself when a disgruntled student (often one who is used to "getting the A" without doing much thinking) is suddenly challenged by the pedagogy; we run the risk of receiving a harsh evaluation rather than the mediocre, almost neutral, evaluations of professors who don't stray from tradition. Traditional evaluation instruments are flawed and a poor measure of critical pedagogues; however, administrators can provide leadership to protect professors who are taking the risk to depart from a transmission model of discourse in their classrooms (Morton, 1992). Certainly, for nontenured faculty, support from administrators must be sought and guaranteed.

Finally, in relation to administrative dispositions, encouragement, patience, interest, and understanding would be signs of true leadership and support of attempts to provide a richer educational experience for students, contrary to Eiseley's (1987) assessment of the status quo: "A university is a place where people pay high prices for goods which they then proceed to leave on the counter when they go out of the store" (p. 117). Critical pedagogy is the pedagogy of other, and deans and department chairs must not jump to demonize or marginalize efforts simply because they are not recognizable (Gabbard, 1993). We must find our voice, according to Greene (1994): "I say this because I need to suggest what it was like to learn to pay heed to the silences. I say it because

I realize how it made me attentive to multiplicity, to perspectivism, to the importance of having enough courage to look through my own eyes—and, yes, speak in my own faulty voice" (p. 16). Similarly, Villanueva (1993) problematizes the plight of minority voices in the hegemony of academia. We must engage our administrators in dialogue about critical pedagogy. A disposition of true leadership would be to consider a praxis that departs from and challenges the status quo. Moffett (1989) poses the critical question: "one generation sometimes has to fish or cut bait, has to *mean* it when it posts its noble goals, has to face the fear of actually achieving what it says it wants for its young. Are we that generation, or will we just provide more instances in the pattern of history?" (p. 24). As we see things in our profession we have two choices. We can succumb to the mainstream and become programmed toward deskilling our intellect or we can become critical pedagogues and liberate ourselves and our students.

9

Jozi De León
Catherine Medina
Robert Ortiz

Engaging Special Education Practitioners with Language and Culture

Pitfalls and Challenges

There is an urgency to address minority school failure in the United States. According to the U.S. Department of Commerce (1989), Mexican Americans had the highest rate of persons with fewer than five years of schooling (15.9%), as compared with Puerto Ricans (9.6%), Cubans (5.5%), and people from Central and South America (6.7%). Equally alarming is the low educational attainment by Mexican American youth. Mexican American students had a median educational level of years of schooling at 10.8. High school dropout rates during the 1988 academic year are equally disconcerting, with only 59 percent of Mexican Americans in the 18–21 age range graduating from high school as compared to 82 percent of non-Hispanics in this same age group. In fact, Mexican American students often experience academic school failure that is pervasive, persistent, and disproportionate when compared with the majority population as well as other subordinate populations (Valencia, 1991).

One major contributing factor to minority school failure in the United States is the disturbing frequency by which culturally and linguistically diverse students are referred and placed into contextually inappropriate special education programs (Grossman, 1995; Rueda, 1991). Mexican American students are often relegated to lower status classes in schools where they experience differentiated instructional practices, and remediated curricula presented in a fragmented and drill-and-practice manner. These students often encounter curricula that are both culturally insensitive and not in the students' home language.

As revealing as these data are, it is essential to dovetail descriptive statistics with more theoretical and philosophical explanations for minority school failure. The literature is replete with explanations relative to school failure (Dunn, 1987), while other theories are aimed at cultural ecological arguments (Ogbu, 1987). It is a widely held belief that Mexican American students drop out of school due to characteristics or circumstances these students bring with them to the educational arena. These characteristics often include poverty, distressed family systems, and linguistic differences. School failure, thus, is deemed as a "student" problem with the school sharing little responsibility for that student's failure to achieve.

The purpose of this chapter is to focus on the relationship of special education placement and the academic failure that often ensues from negative experiences encountered in these programs. Through personal interviews, we will show how these students systematically begin to fail early in their educational lives. No matter how well intentioned, when teachers do not engage with language and culture in the classroom, culturally and linguistically diverse students are adversely effected.

Overrepresentation of Culturally and Linguistically Diverse Students in Special Education

In 1973, Jane Mercer was the first individual to bring attention to the overrepresentation of minority students (primarily Hispanic and African American) in special education classes. Her findings created a wave of consciousness raising about the plight of language minority students in the American educational system. What was actually happening to these students? Were more language-minority students actually in need of special education services due to some previously uninvestigated causes or were language-minority students unjustifiably placed in these programs due to a process that was discriminatory? In the final analysis, it was determined that these students were being placed in special education because of a process that did not take into account language and cultural differences. Initially, the exclusive use of intelligence measures that supposedly made a determination about innate ability were largely to blame (De León, 1995). Student ability was measured on the basis of responses to questions intended to reflect cognitive ability, yet were culture specific and reflected a very narrow view of knowledge. Low scores were interpreted as lower cognitive ability rather than more accurately being identified as a mismatch between the test and the culturally and linguistically diverse student taking the test. When the scores of Hispanics and African American students taking the tests placed them in the mentally deficient range, placement into special education was seen as the only solution. One wonders about such thinking when such large segments of the student population from culturally and linguistically diverse backgrounds were qualifying for placement into special education based on test scores. Furthermore, this seems to point to an expectation that students from culturally and linguistically diverse backgrounds would automatically have lower functioning levels. When such large percentages qualified for special education, no one thought to question the outcome.

While we speak historically about a problem with overrepresentation of language-minority children in special education, the irony is that the problem continues to persist today. Issues of overrepresentation, nondiscriminatory assessment, and fair and appropriate placement of culturally and linguistically diverse students continue to be major discussions in the bilingual special education literature (Cummins, 1980, 1984; Figueroa, 1989; Hamayan & Damico, 1991). For example, in a study of school districts in Texas, Ortiz and Yates (1988) found that a disproportionate number of Hispanic students in second through fifth grades were placed in special education classes as learning disabled. At least 53 percent of the culturally and linguistically diverse students had been referred for special education for at least one language-related problem. Many of these students were referred because teachers were not able to distinguish differences from disabilities. The whole process of identification has been addressed from prereferral (Ortiz & Garcia, 1988) to actual assessment practices (De León, 1990) and to placement decisions (Ysseldyke & Algozzine, 1983).

If overrepresentation in placement of cultural and linguistic minorities in special education is addressed from a critical perspective, there are many factors that may contribute to the situation. First and foremost, one needs to examine the power structure in the school system. Schools are set up to be responsive to a mainstream American culture. In a multicultural society, an insistence on a monocultural educational system negates the validity of individuals from diverse backgrounds and ignores many individuals when they are measured against a monocultural model (Nieto, 1992). The monocultural model also establishes features within the system that make it additionally more difficult for culturally and linguistically diverse students to succeed. The curriculum does not incorporate the students' culture, language, or learning styles, or it incorporates them to a very limited degree.

Valuable knowledge is determined and judged from a monocultural perspective, therefore, knowledge that may be relevant and important to different culturally and linguistically diverse groups does not get included. The valuable knowledge is imparted to the student and when the student does not appear to gain said knowledge quickly enough, judgments are made about that student's experiences, home environment, and worse, his/her character and/or ability. Statements such as: "Michael is having difficulty in kindergarten because of his limited experiences"; "It is no wonder Nicolas is having problems with his grades. He comes from a very poor home environment. His parents are also negligent in getting him to do his work"; "Maritza tends to be inattentive and has poor work habits. She is functioning below grade level in all areas requiring written expression and comprehension.

Initially, attempts are made to provide the student with assistance. Often such attempts are disparaging to the children and their families. The student may be provided with more worksheets or the child might receive one-dimensional tutoring after school. The solutions stem from a fundamental belief that it is not the material presented or the child's inability to relate to it or the form in which it is presented, but rather that there is something inherently wrong with the child that must now be corrected by intensifying exposure to the material. When the student continues to fail, another program (often labeled remedial) may be offered as an intervention. Assumptions that the child's ability is in question are being built. Remedial programs now offer content at a slower pace so that the student will "get it." The student may go through a series of these remedial programs. While content may be offered in a different form in these programs, or it may incorporate more one-on-one instructional sessions, often the nature of the content has remained the same. The student still cannot relate to it and has little from his/her experience that he/she can use to make sense of it. When the student continues to fail, "gatekeepers" within the system feel justified in making the referral to special education. Finally, they are certain that the student's ability is the problem. They turn over the case of the student to someone who will give them "scientific" and precise information about the student's ability—the school psychologist. The scores will tell the truth. Again, the student from a culturally and linguistically diverse background is assessed using an ethnocentric yardstick. If he/she has not been assessed accurately by the previously used ethnocentric yard-stick, the belief that the present measurement is different is indeed an il-lusion. Incorporating a statistical validation of the test does not make the scores valid where culturally and linguistically diverse students are concerned. It only reaffirms preconceived notions that the student is "the problem." As long as the focus is on the student and does not in-clude an examination of teaching practices, curricula, or the school sys-tem, society continues to be myopic and ill informed where culturally and linguistically diverse students are concerned.

Those working within the system view it as effective and well honed. They do not see a need for closer examination of systematic processes reflecting bias and prejudice. In order to engage in such examination, school personnel would have to engage in some soul searching and self-reflection about their contribution to such discriminatory processes.

Addressing the Needs of Culturally and Linguistically Diverse Special Education Students

By the year 2020, approximately one in every two children will be ethnic minority (Valencia, 1991), with Hispanics representing the largest mi-nority population in the United States. Additionally, Baca and Cervantes (1989) estimated that there were approximately one million children in the United States who were both from non-English-speaking back-grounds and also had a disability (cited in Hoover & Collier, 1991).

Over the past twenty years, a large body of legislation has ad-dressed the need for the provision of appropriate services to culturally and linguistically diverse exceptional students (Salend & Fradd, 1986). This legislation has established the need for special education services that are delivered in a different way for students whose backgrounds are different from the mainstream. Without a difference in service deliv-ery these students would not receive an appropriate education. In a na-tionwide survey conducted by Salend and Fradd (1986) in which fifty states and the District of Columbia were surveyed, a clear need for pro-gram development for PEP (Potentially English Proficient) exceptional students was established. Of the states surveyed, only fourteen reported that they had a position in the state educational agency that was respon-sible for addressing the needs of PEP exceptional students, with only two states providing a specific funding category for this group. None of the states reported the adoption of curricula or tests to assist in the edu-cation of these students. Sixteen states indicated that they had a pro-gram for training educators to work with PEP exceptional students. Only one state had a formal certification program for teachers trained in this unique area of special education. These data indicate that although the need has been established at the legislative level, programs and teachers educated in bilingual special education are not widely available to deal with the large segments of students from culturally and linguistically diverse backgrounds.

Special Education programs sensitive to cultural and linguistic differences are needed because only in these settings can appropriate instruction for culturally and linguistically diverse/PEP exceptional children be provided. The literature suggests that a lack of understanding by the teacher about the students' linguistic and cultural backgrounds can create discontinuities between home and school, which detrimentally effect learning. A lack of understanding of how students' social, linguistic, and cultural backgrounds impact and interact with learning ensures that student needs will not be met in the classroom (Cummins, 1984).

Research in special education has identified key features of effective instructional practices with culturally and linguistically diverse education (CLDE) students, however, many of the ideas are not specific to the needs of young exceptional learners from culturally and linguistically diverse backgrounds. Furthermore, the limited literature that exists in early childhood special education and diverse learners makes recommendations that are important for educators to fulfill, yet none of the literature addresses the issue of whether teachers are equipped to fulfill them. We conducted a study to examine the instructional practices in early childhood special education teachers working with culturally and linguistically diverse children. The study was conducted to provide insight into the current state of early childhood educational experiences for CLDE students. Of particular concern was that early intervention includes ages 0–8 years. In most states the youngest children being served in a classroom setting are three years of age. The quality of those first experiences relative to linguistic and cultural aspects are critical for young culturally and linguistically diverse children in that they imprint messages that impact future educational experiences. Excerpts from our comprehensive study are shared with the reader in responding to issues of effective instructional practices and teacher preparedness in working with young exceptional learners from culturally and linguistically diverse backgrounds.

Teachers from five early childhood special education classrooms volunteered to participate in the study. Special attention was paid to the manner in which language and culture were addressed in instruction. Observations were conducted three days a week for approximately three hours each visit for five months. All five programs had at least a 73 percent Hispanic student population with varying degrees of linguistic abilities. Three of the programs were taught by bilingual Mexican American teachers who used some measure of native language instruction. Figure 9.1 depicts the outstanding features of each classroom. In addition to the

Classroom A	Classroom B	Classroom C	Classroom D	Classroom E
Integrated Preschool	Traditional Self-contained DD* Preschool	Traditional DD Preschool	Transitional Pre-kindergarten	Rural DD Pre-school and Paid Daycare
3–5 year olds	3–4 year olds	2–5 year olds	5–6 year olds	15 mo.–5 yr. olds
1 English-Only Regular Education Teacher 1 Bilingual Special Education Teacher	1 English-Only Teacher	1 English-Only Teacher	1 English-Only Teacher	1 Bilingual Teacher
1 Bilingual Educational Assistant	1 Bilingual Educational Assistant 1 English-Only Educational Assistant	1 Bilingual Educational Assistant 1 English-Only Educational Assistant	1 Bilingual Educational Assistant	N/A

*DD—Developmentally Disabled

FIGURE 9.1. Descriptions of Each Classroom, Ages Served, and Staff

observational data, parents of Mexican American children in the classroom participated in one interview lasting approximately ninety minutes. Teachers were also asked to participate in one interview lasting approximately ninety minutes. There was one interviewer for the parents and another interviewer for the six teachers. The parent interviews took place in the homes of the parents and the teacher interviews took place in the teachers' classrooms. Parents and teachers were asked open-ended questions that dealt with their philosophy of education and their attitudes toward native language usage in the classroom, second language learning, and multicultural education.

Importance of Home Language and Culture to Hispanic Families

In an attempt to evaluate the expectations of the family and its match with the practices of the school, parents were interviewed concerning their child's educational program and their expectations of the school. Home language use was also an important factor to be considered in determining program effectiveness. The Home Bilingual Usage Estimate was administered during parent interviews to determine the language usage by the child and family. Eighty-three percent of the students ($N = 45$) were exposed to English and Spanish in the home.

All of the parents interviewed stated their desire for their children to be taught and maintain both languages. While they felt it important for their children to learn English, none of them wanted their children to lose their primary form of communication in the home—Spanish. They saw the mastery of both languages as important in their children's future opportunity and success inside and outside the community.

Parents also made statements about their attitudes concerning the value of their culture. One parent summed up the general consensus of the majority of the parents by stating that "The biggest fear for me about my son's school is that he won't be taught our ways of life." When he was asked to elaborate, he identified culture as an extremely important factor in the process of educational development for his son. All but two interviewees made similar statements. Parent expectations were important elements of the study, especially as it related to teacher attitudes and practices toward bilingual and multicultural education.

Teacher Views

The views that teachers shared were largely influenced and limited by training and experience. None of the teachers had been trained in bilingual special education. The bilingual teachers were bilingual through their upbringing or had become bilingual later in life. Some had experienced native language loss and while they were Hispanic, spoke little or no Spanish. They had little or no training in bilingual or multicultural education, yet they were expected to be experts in working with the Hispanic students in their classrooms. This is a common error experienced by those who have little or no training in the area of bilingual or multicultural education. It is often assumed that if one can speak the language of linguistically diverse students then one is an expert.

The monolingual teachers, on the other hand, had adopted "folk" ideas about the use of native language instruction. While they might have bought into the idea of multicultural education and bilingual education, they had difficulty with implementation due to their lack of Spanish language fluency. They did not know how to make the English language understandable or meaningful for children acquiring English as a second language.

Maria
Uncertainty and Conflict in Teaching Practices

Maria, the bilingual special education teacher in Classroom A, indicated a conflict with the use of native language instruction with the Spanish-speaking children in the class. She stated:

> I don't have any classes in bilingual education. I feel like I am always going back and forth between Spanish and English. Children with Spanish don't try as hard because they know Spanish is coming. . . . I don't mind them using Spanish, I just don't know what is best. . . . I am always assessing myself. Is this the right way to deal with this situation?

Comments expressed by Maria reflect the attitudes of many teachers working with non-English-speaking students. She expressed not only a lack of preparation in teaching second language learners, but more importantly, a pervasive belief that monolingual Spanish-speaking students are unmotivated to learn the dominant language and are thereby passive learners. Her comments indicate that she sees her role as one where she needs to "spoonfeed" language and understanding to the students (e.g., "Children with Spanish don't try as hard because they know English is coming"). This type of student disempowerment sets the stage for later educational experiences. We will begin to understand that differential teaching methodology is not incidental but pervasive and rooted in dominance and power.

Sally
A Sense of Awareness but Inability to Effect Change

Sally, the monolingual regular education teacher in Classroom A, indicated that she believed children should be taught in their native language until they are ready to learn English. She felt strongly about the acquisition of both English and Spanish for those children from Spanish-speaking homes as well as those from monolingual English homes. While both teachers in Classroom A believed in multicultural education, the regular education teacher understood the hegemony of a traditional curriculum. She stated, "Multicultural education is a myth. . . . any [traditional] curriculum is heavily biased by the dominant culture because members of that culture created it." Both teachers stated that they give a tourist version of multicultural education by only introducing food, clothing, language, and the like, into the curriculum. Their comments are interesting because they realize that they provide a tourist version of multicultural education and that the traditional curriculum is heavily biased by the dominant culture, yet they still make little effort to change existing practices. This may signify their own feelings of disempowerment and a belief that they have to maintain the status quo. This type of cognitive dissonance creates an underlying tension that may further complicate the differential treatment of CLDE children.

Lorraine
Attempting to Make a Difference
but Hindered by Lack of Training

The teacher in Classroom B demonstrated positive dialogue about her beliefs relative to working with Spanish-speaking children. She appeared to be highly aware of integrating native language in a manner that reflected the subtleties and sensitivities inherent in the Mexican American culture. Lorraine appeared to recognize the importance of using terms of endearment in Spanish with young children. She stated: "I use a lot of Spanish. I think everyone ought to speak more than one language. The children respond to it. I like to use endearments in Spanish with all the kids (e.g., *mija, mi vida*). The educational assistant interprets a lot in the classroom. A lot of the snacks that we serve, we tell the kids what they are in Spanish. It adds to their self-esteem. We speak in Spanish and bring things from their culture to the classroom." Lorraine demonstrated a novice understanding of second language learners and multicultural education. If only superficially she was able to recognize the importance of bringing the language of the child's home and community into the classroom and also reported an awareness of the importance of bilingual education. She stated:

> Every child comes in with a dominant language, and basic concepts are formulated in that language. They learn through modeling and interaction with their language. A child who has a solid first language will acquire the second language more so than the child who doesn't have a good basis in his/her mother tongue. . . . I want to treat the kid's spirit.

Her views of multicultural education were more in keeping with global education. She wanted to give her students a "world mentality." Lorraine had ideas in keeping with the theoretical framework for working with culturally and linguistically diverse exceptional students, however, her lack of preparation hindered her ability to implement her ideas to their utmost effectiveness.

Anne
Children in American Schools
Should Be Taught in English

Although Anne, the teacher in Classroom C stated her belief that native language usage was necessary for Spanish-speaking children in her

preschool program, she reflected an attitude of English language preference for non-English-speaking children. Her views indicated that, by
using Spanish, children were actually being damaged. She stated:

> I believe it is necessary for native Spanish speakers to speak in Span-
> ish. When we don't use it (Spanish), the kids are lost. It is also very im-
> portant to teach English. . . . [but] if we are only teaching in Spanish,
> we haven't helped them [Spanish-speaking children]. They continue
> the cycle [of underachievement]. We need to evaluate this problem and
> see why this is happening. . . . I'm frustrated because the children rattle
> off Spanish and I don't know what they are saying. My educational as-
> sistants can't be available all the time. I think schools should provide
> Spanish training. I see this as a problem for myself and the school.

Anne's responses indicate some real misconceptions about how she
could best help her students. They also indicate a classist and racist attitude about Hispanic children. Her comments characterize her as the
"great savior" who can save the children from a cycle of underachieve-
ment and probably poverty by making sure she uses English with them.
Her attitudes also demonstrate a certain self-righteousness in that she
has convinced herself that she knows what is best for the children—in
her opinion, it was obvious that Hispanic students were better off not
speaking Spanish. Detected in her comments are feelings of anger and
frustration about having to deal with children who "rattle off Spanish"
when she does not understand what they are saying. Her feelings of inadequacy foster negative feelings and probably also make her resentful
toward the children that place her in such a position. Evident in the following example is the negligible treatment of Hispanic children relative
to social and educational interaction. In this example, the lack of understanding on the student's part is met with a reprimand. Anne is unaware
that José was able to process the information, although not in the immediate manner she expected. Teachers must be able to make accurate interpretations of behaviors and verbal responses from students who are
culturally and linguistically diverse. Below is an example of José's attempt to read his environment in two languages.

> ANNE: What is this (holds up a picture of an elephant)?
> MARY: An elephant
> ANNE: An elephant, yes!
> JOSÉ: Elephant (repeats what Mary has said after several seconds).
> ANNE: José, it's not your turn, be quiet.

While José responded accurately, he was punished for talking out of turn and was met with impatience. Anne did not allow the child to respond and, in fact, diminished that child's sense of self by reprimanding his attempts to participate. The Spanish-speaking child who speaks out of turn should not be automatically considered a discipline problem, but rather the teacher needs to be able to differentiate how linguistic differences impact behavior.

Embedded in Anne's comments is the issue of responsibility and who ultimately is responsible for what happens to culturally and linguistically diverse children in the schools. The teacher is feeling inadequate and blames her inadequacy on the schools who have not properly prepared her to deal with Spanish-speaking students. She passes off any ineffectiveness on the school administrators. The question of responsibility belongs to both those administrators who have selected a teacher who not only does not have the education to work with the Hispanic children in her class, but also the teacher who has not taken action to evaluate and improve her own skills. However, Anne appears not to be cognizant of the fact that she needs to do anything different.

Anne also demonstrated a lack of understanding about multicultural education. She indicated that multicultural education in her classroom centered around (a) having the educational assistants speak to non-English-speaking students in Spanish, (b) being aware of the children's culture in how she approached learning the classroom, and (c) being sensitive to family needs. In clarifying her sensitivity toward the family she demonstrated her biases and stereotypical attitudes. She stated: "If a child comes to school with a cold, they [Mexican American parents] don't bathe them. I try to be sensitive to the family needs. I try not to be critical and to be real careful in how I talk to parents about helping children."

Her comments reflect an attitude of knowing what is best for the children, rather than attempting to understand the parents' view of what is best. Again, superiority and classism are critical issues here. If one approaches education for the culturally and linguistically diverse student from a deficit model then one assumes all the power and control in interactions with students and parents. Anne was a prime example of someone operating from this perspective.

Susan
Integrating Exceptionality, Culture, and Language

Susan, the teacher in Classroom D, had a positive attitude toward using native language instruction in the classroom, however, she indicated that she used Spanish to reinforce what had been said in English. Despite her positive attitude, she did not realize that by using Spanish as the secondary language to reinforce English, she was giving English priority status. Her views about multicultural education indicated an attitude of taking the child "from where he is coming from and working from there." She felt that exceptionality, culture, and language couldn't be separated out. Susan's comment about the interactive qualities of exceptionality, culture, and language with preschool exceptional children from diverse backgrounds merits further discussion. While it is true that each quality should not be examined in isolation, often language and cultural variables are misperceived in the evaluation of a disability, especially with very young children.

Consequently, the special education teacher who has been educated to work with specific disabilities often ignores language and culture as integral aspects of the child's education.

Herlinda
Implementation of Appropriate
Attitudes and Pedagogical Principles

Herlinda, the teacher in Classroom E, stated that she believed bilingual education was not only important in an academic sense but also in the development of affective attributes, such as self-concept. Her belief toward dual-language instruction was rooted in her own personal experience toward loss of native language.

> I believe you should use Spanish in the classroom. Their [children from Spanish-speaking backgrounds] understanding should grow and maybe it should be in Spanish. I'm not an expert in bilingual special education. I teach in both English and Spanish. I think children should speak their native tongue. I grew up with not a word of Spanish. I have had to learn Spanish. I feel part of my own heritage is missing. . . . I think you should respect the heritage of your class.

In examining this teacher's attitudes and practices in her classroom it was obvious that her own personal experiences drove her philosophical stance. She had a heightened awareness of the need to integrate language and culture in the classroom. All classroom activities were child centered and directed to overlapping the experiences of the home with school. Her teaching and interactions were based on the background and knowledge that students brought into the classroom. She had high expectations of the children in the classroom and appeared to transfer her "you can do it" attitude. The children were not seen as starting out at a disadvantage due to their disability or cultural or linguistic background.

The most important insight gained from observations of this teacher relate to teacher education. Teacher education programs cannot expect to educate teachers to be effective with culturally and linguistically diverse students by merely providing pedagogical content and strategies. It is imperative that teacher education programs examine the theoretical and philosophical underpinnings behind teacher's desires to work with children in general and culturally and linguistically diverse children in particular.

Conclusion

It is evident that the United States educational system has a history of discriminatory practices toward culturally and linguistically diverse students and that these students continue to be overrepresented in special education classrooms. CLDE students have traditionally been measured by standardized tests of cognitive ability that do not take culture and language into consideration. In addition, CLDE students' behavior, attitudes toward schooling, and reasons for nonengagement have also been viewed through very narrow lenses and have not been analyzed from a systems perspective or a contextual base. From the student and teacher interviews reflected in this chapter, it is evident that in most cases the power structure in the schools and classrooms continue to be stratified, with CLDE students being at an obvious disadvantage. Students from culturally and linguistically diverse backgrounds were often seen from a deficit model or from a monocultural perspective by their teachers and student nonengagement was often viewed as a "child" problem as opposed to a "system" problem. From the findings in this study, it appears that if students fail to assimilate to the dominant standards early in their education by learning English quickly and by understanding the hidden curriculum of the classroom that educational setbacks are inevitable. Rarely, does the teacher or school take responsibility for the nonengagement of students. The authors have highlighted major findings in this chapter that demonstrate how early educational experiences may set the stage for school failure and substandard educational opportunities for CLDE learners.

The pervasive finding in the examination of all teachers was their lack of culturally and linguistically relevant knowledge and instructional knowledge about how to teach and learn with students from culturally and linguistically diverse backgrounds. This lack of education is even more critical when we consider that the teachers included in this study dealt with very young children for whom an educational experience that was closely tied to their previous home experience was imperative in making learning effective. Teachers expressed being torn about what language to use with the children. An age-old myth was evident, that by using the native language the student would be educationally damaged. Since many of the children in this study had a language-related disability, teacher conflict over the use of one language, English or Spanish, or the use of two languages, was also an issue. A lack of understanding of how students' social, linguistic, and cultural background impacts and interacts with learning ensures that students' educational needs will not be met. In fact, most of the teachers interviewed were conflicted about the use of Spanish in the classroom, with all teachers stating that they had little or no academic preparation in teaching culturally and linguistically diverse exceptional students.

Lack of teacher preparation in working with diverse exceptional learners placed the children in our study at an obvious disadvantage. Not only were the majority of teachers ambivalent about language usage in the classroom, they were also insecure about their own ability to teach these children. Even for the bilingual teachers in this study, it appeared that school personnel assumed that if one could speak the language of the children that one was an expert in bilingual education.

Teachers who utilized native language instruction were observed not utilizing reciprocal-interactive strategies. Questioning was the primary mode of interaction across all classrooms. In addition, the building of language skills was often lacking. When Spanish was used, it primarily consisted of social Spanish and did not build on academic skills in the home language. Thus, the lack of academic skills taught in a student's native language caused students to experience unequal schooling when compared to children of the dominant culture. Nearly all of the Spanish-speaking students in this study were not instructed in their native language nor provided multiple opportunities to expand their native language. Children of the dominant culture enter school knowing that their language will be the dominant language used in the total school environment and that their teachers will know and understand their backgrounds and culture. This overall lack of teacher preparation sets the stage for early academic failure where linguistic and cultural differences are seen by school personnel as barriers to education as opposed to attributes.

School personnel must also include the family when making educational decisions about culturally and linguistically diverse exceptional children. The barriers between culturally and linguistically diverse families and school personnel might only widen if reciprocal communication is not maintained. It is not known whether teachers were aware of the parent expectations that home language and culture be included in their child's education. The parents felt strongly about the maintenance of language and culture as well as the acquisition of English. In early childhood education, the communication with parents and the close ties between home and school are critical. Parent involvement in the child's education is evidenced by the requirement by law of an Individual Family Service Plan (IFSP), which outlines services and educational goals. If parents had been active participants in the development of the IFSPs of the children involved in the study, then educational goals would have been met in the students' native language as the parents desired. Yet, teachers were left to wonder what language to use and when to use it without specific guidance from the IFSP.

One of the main concerns generated from this study is that young children with disabilities from culturally and linguistically diverse backgrounds are being left out of the instructional loop in most instances. Instruction is not always made understandable to them, largely due to teacher conflict over language use or lack of training in appropriate methodologies. Instruction is not culturally relevant and is lacking in multicultural content. Children are disengaged from the educational process early in their educational experience. In a comparative analysis of the five classrooms, the needs of the children were not being met in four of the five classrooms. When one considers that all six of the teachers included in the study volunteered their participation, one can only wonder what the state of education is for young children with disabilities from culturally and linguistically diverse backgrounds in the educational system at large.

While early intervention appears to be a noble intent, the authors would like readers to ponder whether such intervention can have the same positive results for CLDE children as for mainstream children. The end result can very well be that young CLDE children are being plucked from their families earlier than ever. Families are the milieu in which much cultural, linguistic, and social learning takes place. Being placed in educational environments that are not responsive to cultural, linguistic, and other home experiences leads children to learn that they have no place in the school. In addition, beginning early intervention outside the home without total family involvement and inclusion leads to children being without their families as well. Not only are the children without a school, but they are also without family. Ultimately, this impacts on children, minimizing their culture, limiting their language, and stifling their identity, all under the banner of an equitable education.

10

Kip Téllez
Sharon O'Malley

Exploring the Use of History in Multicultural/Multilingual Teacher Education

Allowing them to be stupid as you say, to whom is that stupidity owing? Without question it lies altogether at the door of their inhuman masters, who give them no means, no opportunity of improving their understanding. . . . The inhabitants of Africa where they have equal motives and equal means of improvement, are not inferior to the inhabitants of Europe. . . . Their stupidity therefore in our plantations is not natural; otherwise than it is the natural effect of their condition. Consequently, it is not their fault, but yours; you must answer for it, before God and man. —*John Wesley*, Thoughts on Slavery, *1774*

David Remnick (1994), in *The New Yorker*, recalls Newt Gingrich's speech at the 1992 Republican National Convention. In his convention address, Gingrich claimed that his political rivals had engaged in a "multicultural nihilistic hedonism that is inherently destructive of a healthy society." Gingrich's speech was just one among many on that platform that sought to stir up resentment and anger by encouraging an attack on programs such as affirmative action and promoting the so-called common culture over multiculturalism. Remnick goes on to outline who and what Gingrich is against: counterculturalists, liberals, government, and multiculturalists. For Gingrich and like-minded neoconservatives, promoting a multicultural United States is tantamount to treason. Implicit in the rhetoric is the belief that the United States was once a strong country, unified by a set of common and fundamental beliefs. Today, they argue, those beliefs are in jeopardy.

Our purpose in this chapter is not to argue with Gingrich's primary point: that the so-called growth in multiculturalism, if left unchecked, will obliterate the American way of life. Gingrich, of course, is free to express his views on the state of the culture. Our own opinion of multiculturalism is simply the obverse of Gingrich's. For this chapter, however, our chief goal is to open a discussion designed to expose historical examples and strategies when working with preservice or inservice teachers, who often share Gingrich's and others' assumption of a golden age of a unified America. We believe that such a treatment may serve as an antidote to the arguments of the new political right and others, including, and especially, educators who believe that multicultural education is a "fad," something that was never a part of our collective educational history. Therefore, our central argument is that the denial of our multicultural past is but another road to teacher nonengagement in multicultural education.

The rhetoric of the neoconservatives is nostalgic but ahistorical. By arguing that America was once a unified civilization, neoconservatives claim that the so-called liberal bias of the sixties and seventies, and now the nineties, derailed a strong country, now limping with the weight of the multiculturalists. Educators, many of whom lack a pedagogical theoretical base as well as a grasp of history, are influenced more by the political debate over multiculturalism than their own professional organizations (e.g., Bishop, 1994; National Council of Teachers of English, 1942; Wirszup & Streit, 1987), which explicitly advance a multicultural education. Moreover, we find that teachers are often more familiar with the treatment multicultural education receives at the hands of canon historians such as Schlesinger (1992) than with the reasoned work of Takaki (1993).

In discussing the use of history in multicultural teacher education, we follow a trail of nonengagement unlike the balance of this book; that is, we examine the political and historical dimension of nonengagement by the teachers in whose hands a multicultural education lies. Thus, we will examine both our own attempts to introduce teachers to the benefits of an education sensitive to students' cultural and linguistic heritage and suggest strategies that may be effective for other multicultural teacher educators.

This chapter does not address the role of history in a multicultural education. That discussion is larger than the scope of this paper and must be considered by those with more knowledge of history. We do not consider ourselves historians and do not claim to present a comprehensive historical document but, instead, hope to meet the less comprehensive objective of examining a part of the history relevant to creating a successful multicultural teacher education. In addition, we hope to demonstrate the critical role of history in multicultural teacher education in our context. Our focus on the use of history in multicultural and multilingual teacher education is not meant to imply that history could not also be used to challenge teacher bias with respect to gender, class, or sexual orientation.

At this point, it is important to clarify our meaning of several terms. First, and most important, our version of multicultural education is similar to what Sleeter and Grant (1994) call an education that promotes both cultural diversity and the political element of social reconstructionism. This valuable definition suggests that any education that claims to be multicultural must establish a curriculum with an empowering, political dimension. In contrast to a multicultural education that examines only the "holidays and heroes," Sleeter and Grant's definition encourages both knowledge and social action. As strong proponents of linguistic diversity, our only addition to this definition is a stronger focus on multilingual proficiency within a multicultural education.

Regarding our use of the term *teacher*, a multicultural teacher educator can be either a university faculty member, a school district-employed "trainer" responsible for sensitizing inservice teachers, or an independent consultant whose services are used by many schools. Inservice teachers are those who have completed their certification and who are currently teaching independently. Preservice distinguishes those who are seeking the certification or license. We use the general term *teachers* when referring to both inservice and preservice teachers.

Categories of Nonengagement

Like most multicultural teacher educators, we have found ourselves in many awkward and often impossible instructional positions. Well-intentioned principals or district administrators have expected us to transform the views of teachers, some of whom are racist to begin with, in a one-hour, after-school inservice. In such settings, our arduous task appears all the more daunting when teachers begin to peruse magazines, grade papers, or just talk, avoiding any engagement with us or the topic. The admixture of their disinterest and our steadfast and at times emotional pleas to include diversity in schooling results in a comic sort of tragedy and an awkward teaching/learning situation, to say the least. Even the teachers who are listening and hoping for change may not fully understand how multicultural education fits into their own teaching, nor will they be provided any additional means to explore their pedagogy in order to make it culturally sensitive. Interested teachers seem disgusted by the behavior of the nonengaged, but are also powerless to alter the situation. And this predicament says nothing of the deep racial divisions and resentment among diverse teachers we often unearth. Like the fuse of a bomb, we see how slowly we can burn before the session explodes.

In one particular program, we were asked to work with schools that had been cited by the Texas Education Agency for too great a disparity between the minority population standardized test scores and those of the white population. The agency invited consultants to provide an introduction to multicultural education, hoping that the schools (represented by a mix of rural, suburban, and urban settings) would improve instruction and achieve subsequent gains on standardized test scores for its minority students. Of course, just one inservice, even one designed specifically to raise standardized test scores, is very unlikely to result in higher scores. It was no surprise to us when the scores did not improve dramatically in following years.

In these inservices, the majority of the teachers held firmly to the belief that the problem was not that they had failed to teach in a culturally sensitive manner, but that the students had failed to learn the "canon" curriculum they had presented. When asked to name the cause of low test scores, we were provided with the common villains: parents who do not care, kids who are unmotivated, and administrators who do not understand. In a review of the program, many invoked the mantra of the uninvolved teacher: "it was a total waste of time." This example represents our most common dilemma: too great expectations, too much pedagogical and cultural baggage to unload, too many dramatic new views to assimilate, and too little time and resources to scratch more than the veneer.

In other inservices, we were asked to provide workshops on language diverse students, most of whom are native Spanish speakers. In these cases, the schools had recently undergone dramatic year-to-year growth in the number of students for whom English is a second language. Such schools struggled with few bilingual staff and a faculty who were unaccustomed to teaching their content using English as a Second Language strategies. In these settings, we are often asked to develop teachers' initial Spanish language skills, in spite of the research demonstrating that it takes at least three years to become proficient in simply the day-to-day oral language, a skill much easier than knowing high-level academic content in a second language. Many teachers and administrators believe that Spanish can be learned in an afternoon or two; if the kids can speak it, how difficult can it be? They quickly learn that learning a second language is body- and mind-wrenching work. Unfortunately, most do not internalize this fact but instead become more convinced that their students must not be allowed to speak Spanish in order to "make room" for more English, a commonsensical view of language learning that has no basis in fact. We wonder if our inservices have done more harm than good.

Our workshops typically last one-half to one day, with perhaps a follow-up a few months later. Like Fullan (1991), we admit that this context is largely ineffective, but our attempts to engage in long-term staff development in most schools and school districts is not well received. Schools often lack the resources for a truly expansive program. Any sustained attention to multicultural education requires substitutes for participating teachers, stipends, or student-free days—all very costly initiatives. Despite the limitations of this context, and our pleas with schools to extend their program, we find the one-shot inservice the most common context for inservice multicultural teacher education. Inservice teachers, for their part, even those who resonate with a multicultural education, recognize the limits of this format.

Both of us have since stopped doing such short-term inservices. O'Malley is now director of bilingual and ESL programs in a large school district in Texas, offering her the opportunity to sustain long-term collaboaration with many teachers. Téllez has since developed models of professional teacher growth that require a longer committment from schools. Although we came to recognize fully the limitations of one-day inservices, we stand by our experiences and what we learned from the teachers who attended. Many of the schools who had in the past invited us to conduct one-shot inservices have turned to others who do not feel limited by this format. More common, however, are schools now firmly governed by site-based management, where teachers on the site-based decision team vote to avoid inservices altogether and instead provide "working" days when teachers can finish grades, meet with parents, or, in some cases, simply leave school early. Of course, many of the tasks teachers perform on work days are important, but we believe that there may be serious consequences when the school fails to develop a professional development strategy. It could be argued that eliminating professional growth altogether may be the ultimate form of nonengagement.

In another setting, we faced large sections of preservice teachers who have conducted enough in-school observations and talked with enough veteran teachers to know that multicultural education is not a focus in the schools. They believe that an 90 education course focused on multicultural education was something to "get through," a "waste of time" that fails to explore the "real world" of teaching. Like many preservice teachers, they often manage self-doubts about their ability to teach by retreating into a world of practice, about which most knew little, but which allows them to divest from their education courses. Education courses, they argue, especially multicultural education, do nothing to prepare one for the "realities" of teaching. In saying this, we are not implying that courses in education are uniformly of high quality and valuable in the preparation of teachers. Teacher education in too many places, including our own institution to some degree, fails to examine critically the full range of concepts and issues related to preparing teachers for diversity. Our experiences compel us to corroborate the views of others who maintain that teaching from an antiracist perspective generates resistance (Brandt, 1986; Banks, 1986). Our displeasure with both the one-shot inservice and the standard three-credit-hour class caused us to explore alternatives. We save a discussion of other strategies for the conclusion.

For our discussion in this chapter, we begin each section with quotes from reviews of or unsolicited comments about our courses or inservices. All of the comments were made by teachers. While the quotations, in some cases, represent the extreme view, we found that such comments served our goal of providing themes for the relevant historical information that runs counter to the particular view expressed. Although these categories were not derived using a particular research method, they are similar to categories of nonengagement found by other multicultural teacher educators (e.g., Koppelman & Richardson, 1995). Following the quotations, we examine each view and provide a sample of the relevant history helpful in enhancing multicultural teacher education.

Denial

All the talk about multiculturalism and revising history from different cultural perspectives is merely ethnic cheerleading. My people made it and so can yours. It's an even playing field and everybody has the same opportunities, so let's get on with the game and quit complaining. We've heard enough of your victims.

We don't need to talk about it. It's always been there. The more
we talk about it, the more hostile people get.

We are all alike, what does it matter?

Perhaps the easiest way to nonengage from the discussion on multicultural education is to deny there is a problem with the way schools work or to argue that no group is currently privileged or oppressed and therefore no need for a multicultural education. Of course, as veteran observers of schools, the readers of this chapter can collectively point to thousands of specific instances in which students of color have been miseducated, misdirected, and even mistreated.

The comments that begin this section suggest two forms of denial. The first we call "aggressive denial," that form of denial that seeks to silence the conversation not by arguing that "we are all the same," but rather by a hostile attack on the so-called complaints of people of color. Those who make aggressive denials are also likely to deny the need for affirmative action, for example, noting that any injustices done to minority groups have been accounted for. The "field," they argue, is even. Such aggressive denials are unlikely supporters of multicultural education. While an antidote to such views seems impossible to find, it is worth exploring a response if only as an exercise.

Altering the views of aggressive denials, who might be called "angry white males," poses an obvious challenge. Because aggressive denials generally consider themselves as well informed and capable of advanced argumentation, asking sincere questions about their views is often the only strategy. For instance, invite them to respond to a question such as, "What data do you use as evidence that the playing field is indeed level?" Wherever possible, encourage them to discuss history. "Was the playing field ever uneven? If so, what happened to make it more level?" Although aggressive denials often inspire anger among proponents of multicultural education, it is crucial that the discussion focus on their own beliefs, with a sincere desire to understand.

The historical data that can be brought to bear on the arguments of aggressive denials are limited. However, one strategy might include an exposure of the "playing field" metaphor. For instance, some aggressive denials argue that 1965 was a crucial year in American politics and, hence, education. Prior to that time, Americans were initiative oriented, goal directed, and personally responsible. Post-1965 America slid into a crisis of morality, a period in which people began to expect something for nothing. The public schools softened their expectations and the government grew uncontrolled. The mid-sixties also saw the first infusion of cultural group history into the college curriculum as African Americans pressed for black studies programs.

Invite aggressive denials to explore 1965. Do they agree that 1965 was a watershed year for American politics? What about education? What was happening with respect to a multicultural education? For instance, some U.S. historians argue that 1965 ushered in the wave of affirmative action, programs directed at the war on poverty, and other social initiatives now being attacked by legislators as wasteful and unfair. Education was also undergoing rapid change. The war in Vietnam was rapidly becoming the central issue for youth in both high schools and colleges. Gender roles were being questioned as women began to take on new responsibilities outside the home. Indeed, 1965 could be considered a microcosm of the entire decade of the 1960s, a time when aggressive denials may agree the country began its slide. By putting a focus on the year 1965, multicultural teacher educators can invite aggressive denials to consider this and other dates as watershed years in the history of education.

The value of exploring such dates can be enlightening. For instance, before 1965, the United States had, in a very real sense, the equivalent of legal racial apartheid. In the south particularly, Jim Crow laws provided for legal discrimination. It was only after the 1964 Civil Rights Act that such laws were struck down. Only after 1965 did the federal government outlaw, with the passage of the Voting Rights Act, unconstitutional voting qualifications. And it was only after 1968 that fair housing laws were enacted. Together, these laws formed the now famous liberal accord of 1964–1968, authored in large part, ironically, by one of the nation's few southern presidents, Lyndon Johnson. Ask aggressive denials if these laws began the decline they are referring to. An additional question: "How could the nation go back to a time when decentralization of discrimination laws made it legal to prevent people of color from voting?"

A primary goal when working with all teachers is for them to understand what historian Hugh Davis Graham calls the "irony of history" (Graham, 1994). In his excellent history of the post-civil-rights era, Graham suggests that our knowledge of the past with respect to civil liberties has been working in two contradictory directions. First, he sees our history as advancing in the direction of the realization of the "American" Creed of equal rights and opportunities. Popular opinion has generally shown wide agreement in the enactment American Creed (the legal victories of 1965–1968). When considered in this way, history is liberating. It shows us that we can be unified by a set of beliefs and that we are set on course to view our racist past as an ugly blemish on the face of an adolescent democracy.

The second way to use history is to argue that the prejudices and other discriminatory practices have become so entrenched that we need additional legislation to clean the future. History, from this perspective, is not at all liberating, but instead must be consistently unearthed to provide more evidence that the American Creed cannot be realized unless we forge legislation. Graham (1994) notes that those who benefit from additional remedies such as affirmative action must never allow our racist past to fade. In other words, in order to install programs designed to purge our racist past, one can never allow that history to fade. Perhaps we will know when to let go; perhaps our collective wisdom will inform us when to allow our racist history to be viewed as blemish. In the final years of the twentieth century, all evidence points to the fact that severe economic, social, and educational gaps between ethnic groups persist. How can each of us, multicultural teacher educators and aggressive denials alike, reconcile this double-edged sword of history? More importantly, what role do schools play in this irony?

The second category of denial responses centers on what a great many teachers believe is the organic flaw of multicultural education: *that it emphasizes unimportant or nonexistent differences and that, by focusing on group differences, multicultural education actually exacerbates tension among ethnic groups.* Of course, encouraging group identity at the expense of empathy for the "other" can indeed encourage group-on-group aggression. However, no rational proponents of multicultural education would suggest such a strategy.

The "soft denials" are those teachers who report that they are "color blind" in their classrooms. They proclaim, often with great pride, that culture plays no part in their teaching. They argue that they treat all children equally. This response is surprising for two reasons. First, it presents an intriguing paradox. If a teacher says that he or she treats all children equally, it implies that all children are the same. Yet, it is obvious that all children are not the same; therefore, treating them all equally is tantamount to an unethical education. If a child has a particular cognitive weakness or strength, most teachers would agree that modifications should be made to that child's instruction. If a child has a medical manifestation that requires him to use the restroom during class, only a teacher lacking all human compassion would demand that he must follow the same bathroom policy as the rest of the class. If a child demonstrates exceptional skill in mathematics, only the unprofessional (and perhaps unprincipled) teacher would discourage her, in the name of "equality," from reaching for higher levels of understanding. If teachers can get beyond the view that an ethical education may, in fact, imply that not all children are treated equally, but that each child must be treated as a individual and socially constructed human being, then the next step (the crucial step for a multicultural education) is the acknowledgment that different ethnic groups might be well served with an education that is, at times, consistent with their cultural identity. In other words, students who share a common cultural identity might benefit from an education that differs in some ways from other students who also share a common culture. This move from viewing students as diverse individuals to viewing students as members of diverse groups is often very difficult for many teachers, especially if they do not agree with the initial notion that an ethical education is one in which all children are treated as individuals. This strategy, if effective, can help teachers overcome the view that one curriculum works for all students.

Another striking feature of the soft denial argument is how commonplace it is. A great many teachers find it convenient to argue that all children should be treated equally, therefore there is no need for a multicultural education. Paraphrasing their words, "I treat all children the same, so it is impossible for me to teach to a particular ethnic group."

One useful response to soft denials is the examination of a few basic facts from recent history regarding the real differences in the life experiences of ethnic groups in the United States. We suggest that these data come from the U.S. Department of Commerce, Bureau of the Census. One particularly effective activity is for teachers to connect to the Bureau of the Census' World Wide Web site (htmp//:www.census.gov) and find documents that support the view that ethnic groups in the United States do not share similar life events. We have found that the discovery of data on the Internet gives all learners a sense of discovery, a feeling of ownership of the information found. Of course, all the reports cited can be found in the normal repositories of government documents.

The string of data reported below are taken from files maintained on the census web site. For instance, the Census report, *Blacks in America—1992*, shows that in 1979, black males earned a median income of $23,260, adjusted for inflation. In 1991, black males' median income decreased to $22,080, again adjusted for inflation. During the same period, white males' earnings went from $32,030 (1979) to $30,270 (1991). The fascinating point here is that both black and white earning power has decreased. Equally important is the persistent gap between white and black income. Teachers can suggest reasons why both ethnic groups might be concerned that real buying power has fallen. Could such a decline be used to advance some policies over others? Combine these data with those from another report, *Our Scholastic Society*, which demonstrates that black high school graduation and college participation rates are reaching rates similar to whites, and teachers can use "hard" data to begin these discussions. The obvious question here is why blacks are not realizing the economic benefits of additional schooling. Other census reports on the web are equally intriguing. For example, a report called *Housing in Metropolitan Areas—Hispanic Origin Households* shows that only four of ten Hispanic heads of household owned their own homes, compared with seven of ten for whites.

Whereas examining census data alone may not be enough to inspire a shift in thinking among the soft denials, they may provide the substance for a discussion about the real ethnic differences in the United States. Confronting these differences helps soft denials to overcome the view that U.S. society is "equal."

Misplaced Ethnic Pride

> *Why isn't there an organization for the advancement of whites, since there is an NAACP?*

This comment, or one very similar to it, surfaces at many inservices. Unfortunately, its popularity seems to be growing. Perhaps more frightening, it is often made without a sincere sense of wonder, but rather with open hostility. We find that the general hostility toward multiculturalism in the larger culture has spawned an increase in so-called white pride among educators, a view that may translate into pedagogical hostility. According to Howard (1993) general hostile reactions to diversity, once covert, have become more common and less veiled. An increase of racial slurs and hostile incidents has emerged alongside more dramatic and violent events, such as the Aryan nations organizing in Idaho, the killing of Vincent Chen in Detroit, the black boycott of a Korean grocery store in Flatbush, the murder of an African American man by skinheads in Idaho, and the killing of a Jewish talk show host by Neo-Nazis in Denver. Perhaps the 1992 Rodney King decision and the violent aftermath in Los Angeles served to ignite many of these events. Although Howard points out that hostility toward racial and cultural differences has always been a part of American life, he suggests that the recent upturn is related to several national and international events. First, the economic downturn and the lack of real wage increases for all ethnic groups has caused a prevailing sense of desperation among many middle-class families. They realize that they will fail to improve on the quality of life their parents enjoyed. Second, a fear of job competition from world markets has caused an increase in international hostility and has encouraged greater fear and anger toward foreigners. As multicultural teacher educators, we believe that these incidents should inspire new curricula and increased professional development in multicultural education. Many educators today see these incidents as isolated and that the best course of action is a return to the past when the schools "just taught" the content.

Within the context of multicultural teacher education, we find some educators unwilling to accept the view that U.S. schools have ever responded to racial incidents with much vigor. Some educators tend to believe that "thirty years ago" schools did not respond to racial problems. However, history demonstrates that a powerful intergroup education movement emerged as a response to the racial conflicts resulting in the

1943 incidents in Los Angeles, Detroit, and other cities. These riots, like many contemporary uprisings, had their roots in urban hopelessness and racism.

As a starting point for this discussion, multicultural teacher educators can recount the riots of 1943, perhaps focusing on the Pachuco uprising in Los Angeles (Rodriguez, 1980). The crises promoted schools of education to create instructional units, projects, and activities to counteract student prejudice (Cook, 1951; Taba, Brady & Robinson, 1952). Professional and civil rights organizations such as The American Council on Education, The National Council of Social Studies, The Progressive Education Association, and the Anti-Defamation League of B'Nai B'rith sponsored projects, programs, and publications teaching multicultural understanding and tolerance. Studies by Trager and Morrow (1952) and by Hayes and Conklin (1953) found that multicultural lessons and teaching materials helped teacher education students develop more democratic racial attitudes and values. These materials fostered intercultural interaction and sensitivity. When the crisis subsided, special funding for research and projects withered and support for intergroup education dissipated. Although some individual teachers and professors continued to incorporate these concepts into their own courses and programs, such programs were not institutionalized. Indeed, we wonder why such materials, which were proven effective, were lost. The primary point of the intergroup curricular efforts in multicultural education is to demonstrate that these successful efforts took place during the 1950s, the so-called watermark of unified American culture.

Responding directly to the comment on why there is not an NAACP equivalent for whites, we ask participants to recollect the organizations their family belonged to. For instance, we ask, "Has your family been deeply involved in a particular church?" Or, "Was your father in a fraternity in college? What function did these organizations serve?" Our intent with these queries is to point out first that very often one could add the words "for the advancement of white people" to the end of many organizations. For example, what if we renamed the Optimist Club of (the name of a town or city) for the Advancement of White People. The point we try to make is that even though "the advancement of white people" is not the name of the organization, the effect was very much the same. Most likely because there were no people of color in such organizations. It is also important to point out that the dominant culture does not require an ethnic identity. With power and privilege vested in one's ethnicity and race, it makes sense for the dominant group to downplay their privilege. As a concluding activity, we point out that LULAC and the NAACP encourages membership from all ethnic groups. And an examination of the history of the NAACP reveals great participation by whites.

Fear

ME threatens to destroy our national unity. I'm afraid to think
of what might happen. We may have another situation like Bosnia
on our hands.

For those of us who promote a multicultural education, the *failure*
to develop a culturally sensitive education is frightening. However, to
many teachers, multicultural education implies the further fragmentation of our so-called unified culture, and, with such fragmentation, additional societal disruption. In our view, fear is another method by which
people choose to avoid engagement in important discussions of race,
class, and gender. Teachers who express such views are, like all of us,
worried about the high violent crime rates among youth, the growing
number of youth who find gang life attractive, and school dropouts des-
tined for a street life of petty crimes and joblessness. Such a view, however, ignores entirely the complexities of what a multicultural education
hopes to achieve. However, addressing the concerns of teachers, no
matter how unreal they may seem, is the goal of this chapter; in that
spirit, how can multicultural teacher educators respond to teachers'
fears of multiculturalism and multicultural education? Specifically, how
might the thoughtful multicultural teacher educator respond to teachers
comparing U.S. diversity to that of another country or society in which
ethnic or religious groups are at war, such as the above comment on
Bosnia?

Recognizing that many teachers might have legitimate fears of a
multicultural society is critical. Although such fears appear almost silly
to proponents of multicultural education, it is important to take all fear
seriously. Of course, teachers who claim that they are fearful of increased ethnic divisions may be indirectly expressing the uneasiness
that their particular cultural group will lose privilege. By examining the
comments we quote here, we hope to assist multicultural teacher educators in responding to teachers' fear of multicultural education.

As idiosyncratic as the comment on Bosnia sounds, we have heard
it in one form or another in several courses and inservices. Although the
examination of this comment is specific, we offer this particular treatment as an example of the historical knowledge the multicultural
teacher educator must possess. Of course, no thoughtful, humane U.S.
citizen would hope for the kind of horrible atrocities the world has witnessed in Bosnia. And some teacher educators' first-blush response to
such a concern might be to dismiss it summarily. But as we have argued
before, leaving such a comment unteathered from human history can
lead to additional inaccuracies. Therefore, what historical data can be
brought to bear on the conflict in Bosnia and does it have any parallel to

ethnic differences in the United States? We would first point out that this chapter could not do justice to the full history of the conflict and invite readers to other, more complete sources (e.g., Malcolm, 1994; Mestrovic, 1993; Mestrovic, 1994). However, invoking history in response to such a comment is a crucial move.

Regarding Bosnia, the teacher educator must point out that it is difficult to compare the cultures of the Balkan peninsula to those in the United States. First, the simple bulk of history itself offers little in the way of comparison. The Bosnian conflict is an extension of a two thousand-year-old struggle for power and domination among many peoples. Our paltry two hundred-year-old history cannot compare with a region whose native people have experienced two millennia of nearly continuous invasion, domination, and revolution. Most recently, the Croats and the Serb, along with the Muslims, were subjected to suffocating control at the hands of the Soviets. Second, several observers have maintained that the war is the result of the failure of the Western nations, drunk with success over the fall of communism, to intercede on Croatia's behalf. Croatia held to the naive belief that the Western nations would come to their aid if the radical and warring Serbs attacked. Of course, recent history demonstrates that the United States and other United Nation allies severely underestimated Serb aggression. Third, as Mestrovic (1993) points out, the Serbians' use of ethnicity and religion as a motivating force in the war is merely a guise for their leaders' desire for total domination of the region. Not surprisingly, the conflict, by most accounts, has more to do with economic and political gains than ethnic pride or hatred, although the ethnic element exists, especially among the rank and file. In making this point, we argue that ethnic identity as a result of a multicultural education has as little to do with Bosnia as it did in Hitler's Germany, in which extreme nationalism and racism was used to obliterate six million Jews. Pride and knowledge in one's ethnic heritage seems to have never been a motivating factor in war or the disuniting of a country.

In short, concern that a multicultural education could lead to a U.S. "Bosnia" is unnecessary. What Bosnia has taught the world is that an oppressive and vicious element, when it wishes to justify an evil drive for power, often employs ethnic hatred to rally the front-line fighters. The lesson the world can learn from Bosnia is not that ethnic identity forms the basis for division, but that ethnic and religious boundaries are useful when the most evil among us seek economic and political power. Multicultural teacher educators would benefit from additional reading of the war in Bosnia, to learn more about how the Western media has portrayed ethnic hatred as a cause of the conflict and how the real root of the war goes back two thousand years.

Given the frequency with which teachers employ cross-national or cross-cultural comparisons of ethnic and religious group tension (such as the comment we cite on Bosnia), it is important that multicultural teacher educators are well versed in world politics, history, and cultures. Examples of so-called ethnic strife can be fruitfully employed to both allay fears that a multicultural education will divide a nation and provide examples of world conflicts which at first appear to be ethnic, but at a deeper level represent political and economic motives. For instance, teachers may find it illustrative to explore the history of the Arab-Israeli conflict, examining the foundations of Islam and Judaism, post-World War II Mediterranean, and the economic troubles of the region (e.g., Beilin, 1993; Cohen, 1987).

The historical treatment of our own nation's racial conflicts can also be used to provide a rich insight into multiculturalism and education. The U.S. government recently atoned (at least partially) for the internment of thousands of Japanese Americans during World War II. By providing monetary compensation to survivors and releasing documents reporting that the internments were not motivated by national security fears, the federal government has admitted that the basis for the camps was the result of simple racism and a desire to impound the considerable property and possessions of Japanese Americans.

We are also aware of teachers who argue that multicultural education is a form of a "giveaway" to minority groups. Teachers or others who make the giveaway argument argue that teaching concepts already familiar to students of color amounts to a dumbed-down curriculum and a subsequent lack of intellectual rigor. Other multicultural or multilingual initiatives that do carry a fixed price tag, such as bilingual education with its native language curricula, are also opposed by many educators. In response, we help teachers to explore the "Westward Movement" through the eyes of Native Americans. Almost half of what is now the United States was virtually stolen from native peoples and many Mexicans and given away to white settlers. Like the Bosnian example, the "ethnic" tension between whites and Native Americans was a direct result of economics. Clark (1994) reminds us that the U.S. land acquisition policies of the nineteenth and twentieth centuries began with violent wars and ended with U.S. Supreme Court rulings announcing that American Indians were "dependent wards" of the U.S. government. The final blow came with the 1903 Supreme Court decision, *Lone Wolf v. Hitchcock*, in which the U.S. government and its agents were found to be unbound by any previous agreements or contracts with any Native Americans. Imagine if we could calculate the costs of the land simply given to those white families willing to move to the so-called "untamed" West? The land acquisition and settlement process of the nineteenth century benefited an untold number of whites. We also invite teachers to consider the total cost of the labor provided to the nation by slaves. When examined in this way, thoughtful teachers find multicultural education a meager retribution for unpaid bills.

"Self/Culture"

I don't have a culture. I'm a Texan.

What about my own history of suffering from prejudice and discrimination? It has not been addressed.

Our first quote has an obvious element of humor, which we fully intend. Anyone who has lived in Texas understands how seriously a native Texan might take such a view. However, the primary point we wish to convey is the clear contradiction this teacher demonstrates. Texas culture may not represent the dominant tradition of a large number of people, even of those who live in Texas, but Texas, like all other states, does have the elements of an overarching culture. Therefore, to claim to be a Texan implies a culture nonetheless.

Whereas few teachers may define themselves primarily as cultural Texans, we find that many teachers do hold the view that they lack a culture. Teachers who hold such a view can make the easy jump from "I have no culture" to "Culture is not important in education" and "My teaching is culturally neutral." Teachers use this move to distance themselves from the need to learn more about multicultural education. Teachers who disavow any culture fail to recognize the cultural privileges in their own classrooms. Most important, teachers invest their own culture into pedagogy and curriculum, and when students of color do not respond, the blame is placed on the students. The challenge for multicultural teacher educators is to help teachers to distinguish (a) what is sound pedagogy for students of color and (b) what they believe is good teaching, but which is in fact a suitcase filled with their own cultural and ethnic heritage.

The most evident use of history for those teachers who fail to recognize their own "templates" for living and behaving is an examination of their own ethnic background. While we do not want teachers to equate culture with ethnicity, we point out that ethnicity, to some degree, determines an overall cultural pattern. For instance, a fourth-generation German immigrant may uncover traditions and rituals begun by distinctly foreign ancestors. These same traditions and rituals may now simply be perceived as "American," when they, in fact, represent clear German ancestry. To help teachers come to grips with the need for a multicultural education, we often recount our own family histories as a model. For instance, O'Malley recalls growing up with grandparents whose open racism toward blacks contradicted their own oppressing experiences as Irish immigrants in the 1920s. Tellez, a bicultural Mexican- and German American, describes his grandparents' schizophrenia, the result of working to fit the dominant culture while maintaining their Mexican values.

Although we believe we have had success in promoting multicultural education with many teacher groups, we recognize that our own appearance (we both look "white"), dialect (we are native speakers of so-called standard English), and general schooling experiences (advanced degrees) play a role in the reaction. In short, we believe our own histories play well to white teachers. Success, however, has wrought great self-doubt. What advantage do we hold as a result of our appearance and speech? Is our success owing to our roles as more or less white emissaries who have toured the land of multicultural America and can now bring that view to others? As we continue to explore the use of our own ethnic histories, we must keep one eye on the success of our methods and the other on the ethics of our approach.

As for the second comment, we must recognize that many "white" teachers' family histories are replete with prejudice and discrimination. On the other hand, some white teachers claim oppression when none existed. In either case, it is crucial to evaluate their views.

In response to such comments, we have used, with some success, a historical treatment of assimilationist ideology. We point out that for many years, the chief goal of the U.S. educational system was to replace immigrant languages and cultures with those of the dominant culture in the United States. In 1909 Ellwood Patterson Cubberly articulated the assimilationist goals.

> Everywhere these people (immigrants) tend to settle in groups or settlements, and to set up here their national manners, customs, and observances. Our task is to break up these groups or settlements, to assimilate or amalgamate these people as part of our American race, and to implant in their children, as far as can be done, the Anglo-Saxon conception of righteousness, law and order, and popular government, and to awaken in them a reverence for our democratic institutions and for those things in our national life which we as a people hold to be of abiding worth. (Cubberly, 1909, p. 14)

In response, we ask teachers to agree or disagree with Cubberly's views. Some, of course, disagree with his views. Others see nothing to argue about. Continuing the examination of history, we also explore historical figures who disagreed with Cubberly. Philosophers and writers such as Horace Kallen (1924), Randolph Bourne (1916), and Julius Drachsler

(1920) strongly defended the rights of immigrants living in the United States. They rejected the assimilationist argument made by leaders such as Cubberley. Diversity, said these pluralists, was a blessing. They argued that a political democracy must also be a cultural democracy and that the thousands of Southern, Eastern, and Central European immigrant groups had a right to maintain their linguistic and ethnic identity. What should the United States be, asked Horace Kallen, "a unison, singing the old Anglo-Saxon theme America, the America of the New England school, or a harmony, in which that theme shall be dominant, perhaps, among others, but one among many, not the only one?" They called their position "cultural pluralism" and believed it should be used to guide public and educational policies.

The arguments for cultural pluralism were not heard. Most of America's political, business, and educational leaders continued the push for assimilation of the immigrant and indigenous racial and ethnic groups. They felt that this was the only way they could make a unified nation out of so many ethnic groups.

Language

> *I don't like the idea of people speaking other languages.*
>
> *Speaking Spanish in class and hall with the use of Spanish profanity [is the biggest problem at our school].*

The examination of linguistic diversity cannot be mapped directly to the study of multiculturalism. However, we find teacher nonengagement to be of a similar nature. In particular, opposition to bilingual education is common. Teachers ask, "Why are we teaching Spanish to students in the United States? They've got to learn English!" As multicultural teacher educators, we must be well versed in the theoretical rationale for bilingual education and second language education (Cummins, 1986; Krashen, 1982).

The most common resistance response to bilingual education or even to modifying schools to accommodate "limited English proficient" students is itself historical. Resistant teachers argue that yesterday's immigrants prospered without special programs. These earlier waves of immigrants, they argue, were glad to leave their native language behind and learn English. They struggled to master the language of their adopted homeland, without the help of bilingual education. Teacher resistance to bilingual or ESL programs often relies on unchallenged historical narratives about their own family stories. For example, "My grandparents had to learn to speak English to be able to survive in this country. It was sink or swim." Teachers also seem quite certain that the schools operated in English only and the public schools were vehicles through which students were weaned from non-English tongues.

Fortunately, history is a superb ally against such views. We begin by pointing out that as early as 1664 wherever Europeans established schools in the new world, education in the vernacular was the rule, whether in English or another tongue. New arrivals worked to preserve their heritage, and language loyalties were strong. Indeed, we note that maintaining a distinct linguistic heritage was one of the core values of the Pilgrims. In Plymouth, they sought a climate where Puritanism and their culture could thrive (Crawford, 1991). Furthermore, they promoted the use of diverse dialects and languages.

In addition, German-speaking Americans were operating schools in their mother tongue as early as 1694 in Philadelphia, where they represented the largest linguistic minority. The 1790 census determined that persons of German descent represented 8.6 percent of the population of the original thirteen states. German-language schools were common until the early twentieth century. According to historian Heinz Kloss (1977), more than 600,000 American children were receiving instruction partly or exclusively in the German language. Nevertheless, there was always pressure to abolish it in favor of English instruction. In the 1750s Benjamin Franklin was impatient with the loyalty to the German language, hoping to abolish its use in the colonies. However, his views were in the minority and the Continental Congress accommodated politically significant groups of non-English speakers. Many official documents including the Articles of Confederation were published in German and French.

The Germans, in particular, felt very strongly about maintaining their heritage. German immigrants, in fact, implemented a system very similar to current bilingual education programs. The success of Germans in U.S. culture is testimony to the value of bilingual education. The story of German bilingual education, however, ends in tragedy in the late 1900s, when angry mobs raided schools and burned German textbooks. The descendants of the German bilingual students are now overwhelmingly monolingual English speakers, and most can only wish for full proficiency in German. We hope teachers will view the loss of German/English bilingualism as a failure of an oppressive educational system. Perhaps, we argue, contemporary bilingual education programs can right the wrong.

The incorporation of linguistic traditions was common for much of the nineteenth century according to Diego Castellanos (1983) in his book *The Best of Two Worlds*. Wherever immigrant groups possessed sufficient political power—be they Italian, Polish, French, Dutch German— foreign languages were introduced into elementary and secondary schools, either as separate subjects or as languages of instruction (Castellanos, 1983). Many immigrant groups supported, often at great sacrifice, their own private schools designed to perpetuate their religious and ethnic heritage. Norwegian Lutherans in Minnesota, Polish Catholics in Chicago, and Russian Jews in Boston created their own educational systems, sometimes to supplement the public schools and sometimes to compete with them, but always to preserve their own culture and language.

Conclusion

In documenting these historical strategies, we find ourselves endorsing the ideas presented here while at the same time realizing that "one-shot" inservices or even the familiar three-credit-hour university course holds little hope of convincing those not otherwise convinced to engage in a multicultural education. The decision to promote a multicultural education is, we believe, rarely purely cognitive and nonexperiential. Rather, such a decision is most often based on one's own experience of a disenfranchising schooling or first-hand experience with students who provide testimony (in many forms) that the current educational system is based on the dominant culture ideology, which may serve to disempower students of color. Developing advocates and proponents of multicultural education will take additional strategies and better information (both modern and historical).

With respect to improved practices, we suggest that in spite of the convincing historical arguments, multicultural teacher educators must recognize that encouraging teachers to see clearly the moral imperative of multicultural education, experiential strategies are required. At the University of Houston, we have experimented with a community-based field experience in culturally diverse settings (Tellez, Hlebowitsh, Norwood, & Cohen, 1995). Students are invited to volunteer in community agencies across the city where they interact directly with people. For instance, some choose to tutor in adult ESL settings, where they learn the challenges of negotiating U.S. society without English. They also learn the depth of concern such adults have for their children. This direct learning experience serves as an antidote to school settings in which teachers claim that language-minority parents show little interest in their children's education.

The success of our community-based field experience led us to propose an inservice teacher analog, knowing that experienced teachers are unlikely to engage in a community-based field experience. One possible strategy is to assist teachers in the exploration of their own teaching, in the form of teacher research as suggested by Díaz-Rico in this volume. We imagine that some inservice teachers might be willing to conduct action research into the direct educational experience of their students of color. Of course, teacher research takes a commitment of time and effort, but inservice teachers might be compelled to talk with their students about their experiences in the educational system. For instance, if schools were willing to provide teachers and students time to talk about sensitive cultural issues, with no requirements on teaching and learning, no tests, and a loosening of the traditional roles, teachers might come to know better the schooling experiences of their students of color.

In addition to experiential approaches, we also need better empirical evidence that a strong multicultural education works to improve academic skills. As university teacher educators, we extol the virtues of research in improving education but the scores of studies we rely upon to validate an educational innovation or practice (e.g., cooperative learning) are missing from the research on multicultural education. As a community of investigators, we must inform our work with research evidence.

Finally, our experiences in multicultural teacher education present many paradoxes. One of the most troubling is displayed by teachers whose parents were immigrants or whose families were once part of an ethnic underclass but who are now solidly situated in the middle class. We have found that these teachers are often the most unwilling to accept the value of multicultural education. How, we ask, could teachers whose own family histories are filled with discrimination stand so strongly against an education that might prevent other students from experiencing the discrimination of their parents, grandparents, or even themselves?

One insightful response comes from Freire's (1970) work. He writes that "at a certain point in their existential experience the oppressed feel an irresistible attraction towards the oppressor and his way of life. Sharing this way of life becomes an overpowering aspiration" (p. 49). This quote strikes teachers in different but often meaningful ways. We also connect it to the quote that begins the chapter.

As U.S. teachers, we must see ourselves as progressives, moving toward an education that is both sensitive to cultural ideas and lays the foundation for political engagement. As a concluding activity, we invite teachers to explore how our era might be viewed by future educators and historians. Most educators, for example, now agree that slavery was a vicious inhuman institution. Our role is to convince them that they are front-line workers in the progressive tradition of empowering those who have been oppressed. And that the failure to lift students of color out of the cellar of educational achievement will cause those who in-herit our schools to view the ethnic bias in our schools as we now view slavery. Some see clearly our point while others retain their narrow, ethnocentric, and assimilationist views. With our goals in mind, we have added history to the range of strategies we use in the challenging but rewarding pedagogy known as multicultural teacher education.

11

Susan M. Rumann

The Struggle for Cultural Self

"From Numb to Dumb"

n a social milieu of shock words such as *femi-nazi* (courtesy of Rush Limbaugh), *Democrat* (courtesy of all Republicans), *communist* (courtesy of conservative "hardball" players), the term *multicultural education* (MCE) falls prey to an elevated level of sensitivity as an "anti-American" genre. One only needs to turn on the radio or television to hear of the "invasion" of multiculturalism in America. One only needs to pick up a local newspaper to read of the "infiltration" of multiculturalism throughout America. Or, one only needs to speak with the average person on the street to be informed on the degradation of American society because of the multiculturalist. George Will (1994), columnist known for his traditional, mainstream support of the right, touts multiculturalism as being responsible for the decline in "America's moral status."

Granted with "voice" as a means of self-expression in which the

186

speaker transgresses from object to subject, the dominating voice of multicultural education arises out of an oppressive structure driven by an intent to silence. The "dumbing" of voice is enhanced through the practices of the "well-schooled mind" with a "numbing" of critical self-examination and self-actualization. In our Western society saturated with noise, there lies a conviction that "freedom of speech" is a guiding principal one would live and die for. Contradictorily, currently works by bell hooks, *Teaching to Transgress* (1994b), Donaldo Macedo, *Literacies of Power: What Americans Are Not Allowed To Know* (1994), and Henry Giroux, *Disturbing Pleasures* (1994) examine the manipulation of voice in a democratic society. In contrast to an influx of technology, expanding borders, and media influence affecting the everyday, there seems to be the nurturing of an anesthetized general population, "numb." When presented with the assignment of identifying self culturally, a group of upper-division college students were struck silent, "dumb."

In perceived acts of resistance, multiculturalism, or the notion of, continues to be examined by many educators (e.g., Giroux & McLaren, 1994; hooks, 1994a; Macedo, 1994; Nieto, 1992; and Sleeter, 1991, to name a few). Definitions of multicultural education range from token acceptance of ethnic/cultural differences through "miniworld" celebrations to critically examining the social injustices imbedded in the inequities of a system theoretically designed to nurture equal education for all (Lieber, Mikel & Pervil, 1994).

As a developing critical feminist educator working from a transformative pedagogy in my first year as a university instructor in the American Southwest, I facilitated a required multiculture education course (MCE 22). MCE 22 has been a required course of this university's teacher preparation program for seven years. Accordingly, the class began. The premise of MCE 22 was fixed in the definition of multicultural education as presented in Sonia Nieto's book *Affirming Diversity* (1992):

> Multicultural education is a process of comprehensive school reform and basic education for all students. It challenges and rejects racism and other forms of discrimination in schools and society and accepts and affirms the pluralism (ethnic, racial, linguistic, religious, economic, and gender, among others) that students, their communities, and teachers represent. Multicultural education permeates the curriculum and instructional strategies used strategies used in schools, as well as the interactions among teachers, students and parents, and the very way that schools conceptualize the nature of teaching and learning. Because it uses critical pedagogy as its underlying philosophy and focuses on knowledge, reflection, and action (praxis) as the basis for social change, multicultural education furthers the democratic principles of social justice. (p. 208)

The composition of the class paralleled the composition of many teacher-preparation courses in the southwestern/western United States. There were students of European American, Hispanic/Chicano, African American, Native American, and immigrant backgrounds; ranging in ages from approximately twenty to fifty years. The majority of the students were female with a third males. As well, there was a balance of elementary and secondary majors. (In all references to students pseudonyms have been used).

Praxis

I commenced the class with an assignment designed to facilitate the deconstruction of the various notions of multicultural education through an investigation of a cultural self. I centered my pedagogical focus on cultural self in an attempt to hearten the demolition of the us-versus-them framework rampant in MCE programs (Giroux, 1992). Multicultural education traditionally follows a undirectional vision of scrutinizing and validating the "other." This common practice is founded on the supposition that the students' "self" is at a critical level of awareness of her/his sociocultural and sociohistorical foundation.

The students entered MCE 22 eager and willing to be informed about what all the hoopla of multiculture education was, and what they could do to "deal" with it inside their future classrooms. To encourage the journey from the external, impersonal, simplistic toward the internal, personal, complex, I commenced MCE 22 with a writing exercise. I asked the students to describe themselves as cultural beings. The responses I received exceeded anything I could ever have imagined.

The students' initial responses were ones of confusion: *"What?" "Describe myself how?"* and so on. There were looks of bewilderment and frustration. There was murmuring among the students before attempting to address the question at hand. In addition, the written products reflected an uncertainty, with many scratch marks and jumbled thoughts. There was an aura of timid voice. Then, at our last meeting for a final writing assignment, I asked the students again to define themselves culturally and to contextualize themselves in our multicultural society. Initial student response this time was one of engagement with comments such as "I knew it." Immediately they attended to the task. The voices of the students had gained strength.

I Come From . . .

In the "quest for culture" many of the students began to view culture as a "commodity that some have more of than others. This "corridor talk," as Renato Rosaldo (1989) speaks of, is invalidated by the professions who study culture, yet is the talk of the classroom. My collected students examined self culture through the lens of having some or not—a commodity disassociated from self.

WHITE FEMALE: Aug. I don't know how culturally a caucasian female can be described, but having lived in areas that are "minority majority" I think I've been exposed to other cultures that have affected me.

WHITE FEMALE: Aug. I guess I'm cultured in more of a social sense, rather than in ethnicity.

WHITE FEMALE: Aug. Culturally I would characterize myself as Anglo American. I believe in strong family and personal values. . . . Growing up as an Anglo American I never considered myself as a part of culture. I misunderstood the meaning of "culture" and believed it only pertained to other people of other races. Now I understand culture to mean the backgrounds and experiences a person goes through in their life. My experiences make me believe I am culturally nonspecific.

The movement "from numb to dumb" is audible in the voices of the students. When confronted with the idea of a "cultural self," many students floundered, unsure of how *they* were of a cultural reality. A "mental revolution" (Ice Cube as cited in b. hooks, 1994a) must occur before anything positive can transpire. Nevertheless, the power of a colonized mind maintains one's ignorance. One student states, "At the beginning of the semester you asked us to describe ourselves culturally. It was difficult then and to be honest it hasn't gotten any easier." Yet, perhaps the beginning of a mental revolution can be heard in the voice of this white female as she states, "Who am I in a cultural sense? Many times I do not know. I feel that I don't have a definite culture like African Americans, Hispanics, and Asians have, but in this class I learned that I do have a culture and I am beginning to learn more about it every day. I am a white protestant female, lower middle class."

Mirror Mirror

As evidenced in the voices of many of the white students, there was an attempt at identifying self culturally through their association with the "other."

WHITE FEMALE: Aug. I have a strong background in music, but other than that I was raised in the typical way middle-class anglo's are raised. . . . I really can't explain my culture, because I know so little about others that I don't really feel mine is any different.

Dec. Even after all the discussion in class, I feel this is almost harder than before because now I know what culture is. I know I'm a female, white American, but I also feel like so many other people, I do what society tells me to do. . . . I believe I would have to see other cultures to realize mine, and the differences between mine and others.

WHITE MALE: Aug. Son of a Unitarian Minister . . . mid to lower middle class . . . descendants are from Ireland and Scotland. . . . I was raise in a predominantly white society . . . I guess I could use the old classification of (White Anglosaxon Protestant) as a description of my cultural background.

Dec. Culturally I am what I have developed to at this point in life. I started as a White Anglosaxon Protestant in an all-white environment learning nothing but European values and culture. I was unaware of diversity. I have developed over the years. . . . I began to appreciate that I was not a norm but rather a part of a whole. . . . Making friends with different cultures I began to lose the fears of my own culture. My culture? I am a student, but more than that, I am an equal student and appreciating fellow equal students.

This association presented itself unidirectionally from majority group members to minority group members. Cultural frames of reference provide a structure for reading one's world (Freire, 1968). Although Joel Spring (1995) states that ethnic identity does not play a dominant role in one's everyday life, it does act as a filter for comprehension and compassion. For example, a white female student stated: "As far as my ethnic background, I have a lot of European blood but don't consider myself culturally rich in that area." Others have suggested that maintaining identification with one's own culture and the mainstream culture has a positive effect on self (Phinney, 1992). Still, when one is systematically taught through the process of socialization in a white supremist ideological framework, it may come as no surprise that the mirroring of other is not evidenced in the reverse.

But, alas, what is culture viewed through a mirror of the politics of representation? It seems apparent on reading a multitude of informed sources that there are as many definitions of culture as there are researchers investigating the phenomenon (Apple, 1993; DeVillar, Faltis & Cummins, 1994; Langness, 1974; Martinez, 1994; Nieto, 1992; Phinney, 1992; Richard-Amato & Snow, 1992; and others). Awareness of this gave comfort to some of my students as they struggled throughout the semester to gain *a* definition of cultural self. In a critical, reflective state I wonder, At what point does one become disengaged with one's patterns of behavior, beliefs, values, and assumptions that define who one is?

Conceivably, culture can be viewed as an amoebic form that permits the penetration and expulsion of contextual forms, lending itself to a dialectical process, not one of a dichotomous relationship. The mirroring of self through others depresses the dialectical role of culture on the everyday, conceding to the dominant schooling practices of fragmentation and disenfranchisement. As bell hooks (1995) encourages, "To bear the burden of memory one must willingly journey to places long uninhabited, searching the debris of history for traces of the unforgettable, all knowledge of which has been suppressed" (p. 41). This journey passes through the notions of "official" versus "pragmatic" practices of teachers and students in the schooling environment (Kanpol, 1994). In relation to cultural self, "official" cultural becomes that which can fit into a box to be checked in completing official forms, and "pragmatic" culture acknowledges the amoebic engagement between self and society. Reengaging future teachers may secure "ways of knowing with habits of being" (hooks, 1994b, p. 43).

Culturelessness

An "absence" of culture could be head in a number of the students' voices. When asked to view themselves as a cultural entity some students were left wanting for a description. In essence, there was a vacuous sense of self.

WHITE FEMALE: Aug. In a way I feel like a mixture of cultures. . . . The only things I can say for real ethnic culture, I wasn't raised to be one way but my parents taught me about a lot of cultures including my white middle-class American culture.

Dec. Culturally I am a mixture. . . . My parents never

really pointed out what my culture should be, but let me expose myself to various cultures. . . . To try and describe myself specifically would be too hard because everything I have experienced is part of me. In our society sometimes I feel very average.

WHITE FEMALE: Aug. I was born in Arizona. . . . I do not know how to describe myself culturally.

Dec. At the beginning of this semester I had never thought of having of being involved in a culture, but now I realize that I am a part of some sort of culture. I am a part of a family.

WHITE FEMALE: Aug. The culture and values my parents raised me in is the normal culture I think everyone is used to.

Dec. My background is white, Anglosaxon just as my parents. . . . I am an American because I live in the United States, not because everyone has equal freedoms. I try to accept everyone, and I hope everyone tries to accept me.

WHITE MALE: Aug. It is hard for me to explain myself culturally because I don't quite know who I am yet.

Dec. I am culturally, by blood, of three descents; Irish, English and Dutch. I am, however, part of the New Mexican culture. . . . I am still not sure of my exact culture except that I am Anglo and an American.

WHITE FEMALE: Aug. I personally don't feel my family background is cultural.

Dec. Since the beginning of class when we had to first do this writing assignment I feel my viewpoints about my culture have changed a little. I feel my culture is my family and the strong bonds we carry and my personal view points about my morals and beliefs.

WHITE FEMALE: Aug. I have a "hillybilly" background. . . . I don't have much culture.

Dec. Culturally I am an upper middle-class Anglo female. I have no religion and my family is not close knit. Therefore, I still don't see myself as having a very definable culture.

The notion of the "dumbing" process illustrated in the previous descriptions of cultural self are grounded in the ideological practices of cultural homogeneity (Giroux, 1992). Many have spoken of the need to decolonize the minds of ethnic minorities (see Freire & Macedo, 1987; Giroux, 1992; hooks, 1995; and others). I propose the urgent need for the decolonization of the white person's mind. The idea that one is of the "normal culture" presents the possibility that to be an "American" means the same for all. Within the framework of white supremist ideology this may make sense.

Further, the simplification of tension between cultural self and society is reflected in a number of students' voices as they describe the external cultural self to the internal physiological self. As the facilitator of many discussions on culture/ethnicity, the dialogue often regresses to the notion that one may be different on the outside but we all have "two eyes, a heart, red blood, etc."

CHICANA FEMALE: Aug. I am a Hispanic/Mexican-American. . . . I see myself as a English- and Spanish-speaking, frybread-eating chicana.

Dec. I am an American.
I am a Chicana, I am Hispanic.
I am a Mestiza.
I am Indian.
I am Mexican, I am Spanish.
I am Anglo, I am Catholic.
I am Gomez/Ortiz and Ibarra/Pacheco.
I am who I am, nothing more, nothing less.
My blood still flows—no matter what I call myself, no matter what someone else calls me—it is still red.
And this is me, culturally.

WHITE FEMALE: Aug. I come from a balanced home; getting what I want when my parents decide to give it to me. I was raised in a Christian home. I'm white with a blend of Indian, Swedish, Irish, and English.

Dec. Culturally, I am an American. . . . I am free to say what I want and live the way God wants me to live. . . . But we are only different on the outside, inside we all have organs, blood, feelings, etc.

The desire to make connections through similarities among diverse peoples through the color of one's blood, must not be used as a means of ignoring differences due to the color of one's skin. A dialogue of similarities and differences must engage with the cultural codes of all (hooks, 1994b).

Fear: What Are You afraid of?

Fear, as an energy force, is traditionally not overtly validated in institutions or higher education, unless under the label of "psychology" and/or "counceling." Unfortunately, the absence of a dialectical engagement with fear does not make fear disappear. Fear could be heard in some voices, cultivating biases and prejudices. Fear, as a force unreckoned with, restricts the visionary ideals of multicultural education.

> HISPANIC FEMALE: Aug. To look at myself culturally I would have to say that I am a very well-rounded person. I am Hispanic with my last name being French bask [sic]. ... I consider myself a Hispanic with a hip last name.
>
> Dec. I feel that I am somewhat culturally deprived. I know what my culture is but I am in the dark when it comes to other people's culture. ... I think that I am deprived because I grew up in a *small* rural community away from many different races. I feel that if I had grown up with other races I wouldn't have the "fear" of them now.
>
> MEXICAN AMER-
> ICAN FEMALE: Aug. I come from a Hispanic background, my grandparents are from Mexico. ... I am of American-born Mexican decent. I was raised with the notion that as a woman we had very limited options.
>
> Dec. I come from a Mexican culture. ... We are told about our past relatives' experiences and taught to honor and be proud of our elders. I consider myself to be Mexican American. ... I am really trying to get along with others and learn about their cultures and not be afraid.

A Journey Begun

Culture became more personal as the class traveled through various constructs, a transformation from other to self was begun. Critical, educational praxis warrants the need to examine the historical, social, political, and cultural forces that silence—"dumb"—students and maintain the white supremist status quo of schools. A Hispanic female illustrated the beginning of her journey when she stated in August, "I'm Hispanic and am fluent in Spanish. . . . Growing up, my mother and father never shoved culture down my neck or tired themselves by drilling it into me. It's kind of hard to explain, but it's almost as if it sort of just happened to be learned naturally." In December her response was, "Since I have taken this class I've honestly thought about who I am culturally. This semester I even went as far as joining a Hispanic sorority, because at first I felt I needed to be among people of my own culture to really be a Hispanic person. I've grown very close to all of the girls, and I have learned a valuable lesson about myself as a result. As a person on the whole, culturally, I'm Hispanic and damn proud of it. . . . Being a young Hispanic lady is just part of me."

Nevertheless, there continues to be a lack of critical connectedness with cultural self and how one engages with the everyday. "Culture" seems to be a cloak one wears when necessary, rather than an amoebic life form. A structured way of learning from experience, bridging the gap between theory and practice, allows for critical pedagogy to take form in MCE 22. From the beginning there was an invitation to all, students and myself, to address notions of safety in the classroom. Safety in the classroom is traditionally focused on physical safety. I encouraged all of us to look at nurturing a learning environment of ideological safety. Ideological safety in the classroom is imperative if the goal of the learning experience is to go beyond rote response. Ideological safety was an ongoing issue of the critical dialogue in MCE 22. As well, further critical interaction between students and myself occurred through the use of dialogue journals. Often times I found that what one is apprehensive about presenting to the group as a whole only needs to be drawn out by the instructor, once informed. Dialogue journals foster trust between student and instructor—the backbone of critical reflection and interaction.

Higher education is not immune to the forces of alienation that permeate formal schooling, anesthetizing its population, fostering the movement from "numb" to "dumb." The purpose of formal schooling perpetuates an environment where an individual is stripped of her/his tribal association in order to facilitate integration into the larger nation-state. The students in MCE 22 engaged collaboratively in risk taking, knowledge building, questioning, and reflection in an attempt to problematize their real-life situations. Authenticity among and between myself and students was the guiding force of MCE 22. As bell hooks (1995) states, "Authentic help means that all who are involved help each other mutually, growing together in the common effort to understand the reality which they seek to transform" (p. 194).

Therefore, *if* the intent of courses such as MCE 22 is to nurture an awareness/respect of diversity/difference and then go beyond, there is a radical need to first recontextualize the self in a sociohistorical, cultural heritage. Multicultural education courses in teacher training programs must become agents for transforming consciousness as a first step in the process to a critically aware multicultural community. Multicultural education courses can be the canvas for constructing models for social change. As illustrated in a semester-long course, college students struggled with where, how, and/or why they could be viewed as cultural beings. Critical educators must not continue to take for granted that another is grounded in a cultural self. To ask them to enrich their awareness and acceptance of others prior to grounding themselves in a cultural context is presumptuous at best. Multicultural education and multicultural education educators must move toward a critical praxis of alliance between self and community.

12

Robert Smith

Challenging Privilege

White Male Middle-Class Opposition in the Multicultural Education Terrain

The increased diversity of public school students has resulted in greater attention to preparing teachers to work with students from diverse cultural backgrounds. Many teacher education programs now require coursework in multicultural education. Although students are introduced to multicultural education, teacher educators are having to face the challenge that students might not be supportive of multicultural education. Indeed, students might question the need to learn about other cultures and feel threatened when asked to examine their own cultural beliefs and assumptions. Some cultural groups are closed to examining their own beliefs, values, and stereotypes. The majority of those going into teaching are from privileged white and middle-class backgrounds, many of whom have had only limited experiences with people of a different race or social class. Such

197

students often oppose ideas taught on race, class, and gender stratification (Bohmer & Briggs, 1991).

This chapter examines white middle-class opposition to multicultural education focusing in particular on white male opposition and developing strategies for overcoming such opposition. The emphasis in the paper is on understanding and responding to male privilege. This is not to suggest that issues of gender and specifically masculinity are more signficant than race or even that the two can be considered separately. However, theoretical understanding of the development of masculinity in sustaining male privilege is less developed as compared to theorizing about white racial identity development. Ultimately, dealing with white male opposition requires being able to respond effectively to both racism and sexism.

My own teaching experience bears out the research by Sleeter (1992), Nel (1993), and Goodwin (1994), that white middle-class preservice and inservice teachers embrace a limited view of multicultural education. The context of my work is a medium-size university in one of the southeastern states. The students that I teach are overwhelmingly white (93%), middle class, and predominantly female (66%), and with a large number holding a fundamentalist view of religion. Many of my students are from small rural communities and describe having only limited experiences with people of a different racial or cultural background. The area has a history of racial tension. The university is located in a state with a minority population of about one-third African American, with Hispanic, Native American, and Asian Americans each accounting for approximately one percentage of the population. The counties in which most of our education students do their student teaching share a similar racial composition to that of the state. In the courses I teach—social foundations, secondary social studies methods, and a graduate course on multicultural education—I am constantly challenged in trying to respond to the racism, sexism, and classism of my students.

The students I teach will generally embrace a view of multicultural education that includes incorporating the contributions of different cultural groups and teaching about their foods, fashions, and folklores (the Contributions and Additive approach, of Banks's four levels of incorporation of ethnic content into the curriculum [Banks, 1994]). Furthermore, many preservice teachers will support teaching children tolerance and respect for those who are different than themselves. This approach to teaching about race, class, and gender differences, an approach identified by Sleeter and Grant as Human Relations (Sleeter & Grant, 1994), emphasises the positive aspects of cultural diversity but frequently fails to connect prejudice and stereotypes to structural inequalities in power and resources. In general, the white middle-class students I teach are accepting of multicultural education so long as it does not challenge their sense of fairness, of how power and opportunities are distributed in society.[1] Sleeter (1992) similarly concludes that "most of the white teachers [in her study] did not focus directly on the distribution of resources across groups or the ideology of equal opportunity" (p. 162). Both the research and my own teaching experience indicate that while the approaches of teaching tolerance and teaching about other cultures are important, unless students' beliefs about notions of equity and justice are challenged, multicultural education "becomes another approach that simply scratches the surface of educational failure" (Nieto, 1992, p. 1).

What do my students believe? Many of them believe in the ideology of individualism and hard work as the key to economic success. Therefore, they find it difficult to accept that "whites have benefitted economically, socially and psychologically from institutional and interactional racism and [that] males have benefitted from sexism" (Alquist, 1992, p. 89). Many white male students in particular are opposed to structural explanations of inequality as well as to the perspectives of women and racial minorities (Bennett, Niggle & Stage, 1990; Cooper Shaw, 1993; Cross, 1993; Dziech, 1995; Rakow, 1984). When asked as part of their social identity assignment to describe any incidents that they experienced or tension they observed that caused them to reflect on the beliefs they were taught about race, many of my white male students cite examples of what they see as "reverse discrimination"—for example, of having lost out on a scholarship to a person of color, or having been attacked or knowing a friend who was attacked by black males. While in most instances students add that they have not let this affect their judgment of all black people, it is the injustices done to whites that they identify, not insights about the system of white racial oppression.

In occupying two identities of privilege, it may be natural to expect males to feel threatened by discussions of racism and/or sexism. However, white males are not a uniform group. Considerable variation can exist among white males with some strongly opposed to ideas of white male privilege, and others more accepting of the view that women and people of color are unfairly treated. Occasionally I may even have a white male student in one of my classes who explores the concept of being an ally to women and to people of color. Identities are complex and overlapping, and white males can be at different points in their understanding of both racism and sexism. One student might deny that racism is a problem while agreeing that it is unfair that women receive less pay than men.

Part of the problem is not restricted to beliefs. Sleeter (1992) argues that too often our understanding of multicultural education is based on an inadequate theoretical perspective. In a review of perspectives on racism, she contends that too often racism is presented as a psychological problem involving misperception of individuals, rather than a structural arrangement involving the distribution of power and wealth across groups. Sleeter further states that far from racism being a result of individual misperception that can be corrected with information, it is fundamentally an unjust system by which whites maintain control of power and wealth. She concludes: "An educator must directly confront the vested interest white people have in maintaining the status quo, force them to grapple with the ethics of privilege, and refuse to allow them to rest comfortably in apolitical interpretations of race and multicultural teaching" (p. 189). What then are the challenges to teaching a course on multicultural education from a critical perspective in which inequalities in educational outcomes are related to inequalities in power in the larger political-economic system?

Challenges in Teaching Multicultural Education from a Critical Perspective

Teaching multicultural education from a critical perspective poses particular challenges. This includes dealing with student opposition to theories of oppression, maintaining an open environment in which students are able to discuss different views, and ensuring that all students are able to participate. Tatum (1992) identifies three sources of opposition to talking about race and racism: race is a taboo topic; many students have been socialized to believe that the United States is a just society; and finally, many white students deny any personal prejudice. Although Tatum writes specifically in relation to racism, the sources of opposition she identifies also apply, to varying degrees, to teaching about issues of sexism and classism.

One study that expands on Tatum's sources of opposition describes various forms or types of opposition. McCormick (1993) describes four broad areas of opposition in student responses to multicultural nonsexist education: denial, discounting, avoidance, and unreflectivity. Denial involves rejecting the existence of the problem of racism or sexism, while discounting denies the seriousness of the problem. Avoidance involves redefining the problem (for example, sexism is a communication problem), and unreflectivity refers to students who have not recognized or examined their own experiences with sexism.

While male student opposition to multicultural education will often include the four areas of denial, discounting, avoidance, and unreflectivity (McCormick, 1993), the research supports my own experience of male students who are disruptive, angry, and who will challenge not only the ideas presented but also the instructor's authority (Cross, 1993; Rakow, 1984). A particularly striking incident in one of my classes involved a vocal white male student who interrupted a female student. When told that he had to allow her to finish speaking, he left the room. This incident disrupted the class and created considerable uneasiness. It also clearly called attention to a behavior that he took for granted. As the instructor, it made me question whether I was going too far in "making" a student leave the room. In discussing the incident with the class, several students spoke out in support of my action, noting that I had not made him leave the room, while others expressed uneasiness about a member of the group feeling forced to leave under any circumstances.

The more frequent incidents of opposition relate to white male student anger, specifically challenges of why we need to be studying this topic, as well as rejection of the ideas presented by the instructor. In response to a video on civil rights in the 1950s, one white male student wrote: "I do not mind dredging the past if everyone's intentions are to move forward." Challenges to the instructor can intimidate other students and deter them from speaking out. In addition, the forcefulness with which the students present their ideas can be intimidating to other students. Such opposition makes it very difficult to provide a safe environment in which all students feel free to voice their opinions. Three options I employ are (1) establishing guidelines for participation, (2) asking students to self-monitor their own participation, and (3) conferencing with students.

Teaching white male students about racism and oppression is likely to be more difficult than teaching white females. In teaching white female students, connections can be made between racism and sexism, possibly making it easier for such students to acknowledge their privileged racial identity. Drawing out the similarities in the oppression females experience due to their gender and the oppression people of color experience due to their race may help females to grasp the structural nature of oppression. No easy connections can be made, however, for white male students. For white males of a working-class background, it may be possible to draw connections between the oppression working-class people experience and that experienced by people of color. However, because of the tendency of some oppressed groups to blame and attack other oppressed groups for their own lack of power, a lot of work may be required before such groups can recognize their common interests. Without such support white students can often feel attacked or feel guilty about who they are. Weis (1990) explores the changing predicament of white working-class males whose relative privilege, by virtue of being white and male, has been eroded by deindustrialization, weakening of labor unions, and by the struggles of white women and of men and women of color. White males may feel that their group and they personally are being cast into roles as victimizers and exploiters (Davis, 1992). How can we work with white middle- and upper-class male pre-service teachers to get them to examine their own privileged identities and to be more willing to accept a structural analysis of power and op-portunities? The next section of the chapter outlines difficulties encoun-tered in working with these preservice teachers and describes strategies for responding to student opposition.

Achieving a Clarified Cultural Identity
for White Males

In talking about white males it is important to acknowledge that white males are not a uniform group. Factors such as social class or religion can be of greater importance than the commonalities provided by race and gender. Similarly, in talking about male identity it is important to recognize that masculinity is not something given at birth. There is in-creased support for the view that male identity is socially constructed through interaction with the culture in which people both take on the prescribed roles and attempt to modify them. While there may be com-monalities in the experiences of masculinity of a white working-class male and a black middle-class male, their experiences of masculinity are going to be mediated by race and social class. Consequently, a fuller understanding of masculinity involves examining the interaction of mas-culinity with other aspects of culture.

For white males, awareness of one's own cultural identity is a major challenge (Bohmer & Briggs, 1991). In terms of race, many whites do not think of themselves as having a racial identity, or as Scheurich (1993) states, "we do not experience ourselves as defined by our skin color" (p. 6). Whites see themselves instead as being "normal" or as indi-viduals rather than members of a racial group. One of my white male students succinctly stated this as he reflected on his experience in the multicultural education course: "As a white man I hardly considered myself as an oppressor, possibly because I looked at the role from my personal point of view only, not from a gender or racial point of view." Another student wrote in response to the question, "What does it mean to you to be a white man?" that "I do not look at myself as white. I am a man who is too busy to worry about color."

In explaining the difference in awareness of black and white people in relation to race, Rutledge (1982) suggests that the victims of racism are much more aware of its presence than the victimizers. Moreover, one of the privileges of being white and middle class is that of being able to take for granted one's own subjectivity (Martin & Mohanty, 1986).

In relation to gender, white males often have difficulty seeing themselves as gendered beings. For one of their assignments, I require students to write a social identity paper in which they are to describe their experiences growing up—what they were told about their gender, race, and social class, and what they were told about people who were different from themselves. In writing this paper many male students will frequently exclude the category of gender. As with race, males often see themselves as "normal" or as individuals. Being able to take for granted one's own subjectivity is likewise one of the privileges of being male. This lack of awareness of a gendered identity is in part related to male socialization in which individual achievement and success are emphasized. In addition, responses to gender discrimination have focused on changing female socialization with the goal of expanding opportunities for females. Little attention, however, has been given to challenging male socialization.

Even though white males may see themselves as individuals rather than as members of a common gender or racial group, white male socialization often includes explicit and implicit beliefs about white male superiority. One white male described the messages he received from his family about his gender identity: "courage, strength, bravado, and female inferiority were unspoken but real value judgments that we were brought up to appreciate." Furthermore, the student stated this message was confirmed by other institutions: "White male Protestant superiority was the social norm in every institution I encountered as a child growing up." Another white male student provided a good example of the way in which sexism is unconsciously learned. In describing his upbringing he stated that, as far as he could remember, his dad "never said anything about women in a derogatory manner." In the next paragraph the student described how his parents have a black maid working for them. The student did not appear to see that having a black maid was a significant statement that he had learned about the position of women and particularly black women in society. Another white male student described how his father treated him differently than his sister. He stated: "He was a lot softer and approached her with more understanding, like she was slightly inferior." He also observed that his father "treated my mother in the same subconscious way." These excerpts from students' socialization reveal some of the common ways in which white males are socialized, including how they come to develop their view of the world and particularly their sense of prerogative, privilege, and power.

Understanding the process of male socialization is crucial to understanding white male opposition to multicultural education. One of the main pressures that males are subject to is that of competition and success. Morrison and Eardley (1988) state that

> Boys grow up to be wary of each other. We are taught to compete with one another at school, and to struggle to prove ourselves outside it, on the street, the playground and the sportsfield. Later we fight for status over sexual prowess, or money, or physical strength or technical know-how. (reprinted in Askew & Ross, 1988, pp. 14–15)

The emphasis on being tough or successful results in males fearing weakness, vulnerability, and displaying emotion. Such responses are dismissed and discounted as feminine. The fear of femininity limits men's behavior as well as their identification with other men. Restricted emotional expression, a fear of closeness between men, and few close personal relationships are all features of traditional male socialization that reinforce individualism (O'Neil, 1982). Consequently, male socialization acts to support the development of isolated and individualistic males who view themselves and the world from an individualistic perspective.

Responding to White Male Opposition

In addition to having to deal with students' cognitive responses to multicultural education, racism, sexism, and classism are topics in which students' identities are invested, and discussion often generates strong feelings. Being able to discuss issues and express feelings is an important part in the process of clarifying students' thinking. The importance of acknowledging and examining the beliefs and preconceptions held by preservice teachers has been recognized as a key factor in students' willingness to both accept new ideas and to change their practice (Lundberg & Fawer, 1994; McDiarmid & Price, 1993). Feelings of anger, guilt, and shame are common responses by white males to learning about oppression. Student anger can block opportunities to learn, be intimidating to other students, and be challenging for a teacher to deal with. Knowing how to respond to these emotions will reduce the likelihood that students' emotions will interfere with their cognitive development as well as be disruptive to the learning of others (Tatum, 1992).

Students' interactions are a microcosm of the larger society bringing together different races, social classes, and genders. Consequently, students' actions need to be monitored, and action has to be taken to prevent the power inequalities of the larger society from being reproduced in the classroom. For example, interactions between male and female students can exhibit some of the traditional power relationships of male dominance and female subordination (Maher, 1991). While male students are in the minority in most of the classes that I teach, they are often the most vocal. To avoid patterns of domination, I have students complete a self-assessment of their communication style and I ask them to monitor their own participation. They are reminded that multicultural education begins with ourselves and includes an analysis of who talks and who does not talk, who listens, and whose views are considered important. This self-monitoring is effective for some of the students but not for the more vocal male students. In such cases I use a number of approaches including not allowing any student to talk twice until every one has spoken once, and asking specific students to answer questions or to report back from their groups rather than allowing students to choose.

Several strategies are available for teaching about inequality that might also help in overcoming white male opposition. These include: simulation games, experiments in which students experience discrimination first hand, guided fantasy in which students imagine that they were born as the other sex, films, and guest speakers (Davis, 1992). Other strategies Davis suggests that can be effective in illustrating some of the injustices in society but in a more light-hearted manner include satire, political humor, and political music. While these different strategies can be used in working with white males, there are three key points that can help facilitate this process.

Understanding, Not Blaming

In examining racism and other forms of oppression, one of the goals is to understand the process by which people are socialized into oppressive behaviors. This process can be facilitated by providing students with a model of socialization that indicates how oppressive behaviors are learned. The goal of examining our own beliefs and prejudices, through such assignments as the social identity paper, is to uncover how these beliefs were acquired and not merely to blame individuals for these beliefs. This is particularly important for white males who may feel guilty or angry in discussing the oppression of females and people of color. It makes little sense to blame students for the beliefs they were taught, nor to blame the adults who taught these beliefs (e.g., parents and teachers). In most instances parents were trying to do what they thought was best for their children. However, the point is not to excuse people for the beliefs they hold: people must take responsibility for their beliefs and work to change them.

Examining Male Socialization

Given that the socialization for most males instills the belief in the individual and the importance of achievement and success, one of the starting points for males is to critically examine their own socialization. For those male students who have difficulty in describing the influences of gender on their socialization, a model of male socialization can be provided. Being taught to be physically tough, to avoid showing emotion, to prove oneself to one's peers, to avoid anything that might label one as feminine, to do well, and to have a girlfriend are all common elements of male socialization. Providing an opportunity for males to share their experiences with other males can allow individuals to see that what they took to be their own personal experience is part of a larger common identity related to being male. Men might feel a sense of relief in recognizing that there are some significant social-political reasons why they are or have been sexist (O'Neil, in press). Furthermore, men may be able to begin reclaiming that part of their identity in which their own development has been limited. By embracing a broader definition of masculinity, men are less likely to engage in the oppression of others in order to maintain a dominant male identity. Finally, in addition to having males and females meet in single-sex groups, both males and females can benefit from hearing how sexism and oppression limit people's lives.

Moreover, while it is important to identify the differences in power and opportunity that exists between social classes, races, and genders and to ask students to identify their membership in groups of privilege or targeted group, it is important for white males to realize that they can be allies to people of color and to women. For example, males can support females in their struggle for equal pay and more power. Similarly, white people can support people of color in their struggle for fairer treatment and more power.

Stages of Development

One of the most difficult challenges in teaching a course on multicultural education is the widely different levels of awareness of oppression that students bring to the course. Some students believe that the biggest problem of racism is reverse discrimination against whites, while others have a detailed knowledge of the history of racism and of their own responsibility as a white person in a society in which whites are privileged. In relation to gender, some male students recognize that it is unfair that males are paid more and have greater access to top positions in society than women while another male student might deny that sexism exists. Various models of levels or stages of development in students' awareness of racial identity (Hardiman, 1979; Helms, 1993; Tatum, 1992) and gender identity (O'Neil & Eagan, 1992) have been proposed. All of these models suggest that there is an identifiable pattern of stages that students move through with increased awareness of their racial and gender identity.

One of the earliest models of white racial identity development is provided by Hardiman (1979). Her model identifies four stages: *acceptance, resistance, redefinition,* and *internalization.* Acceptance is characterized by active or passive acceptance of white superiority, while resistance describes when a person becomes aware of their own racial identity for the first time. Redefinition involves attempts to redefine whiteness from a nonracist perspective, and internalization refers to the full acceptance of a nonracist white identity.

Developmental models for gender identity have also been identified (O'Neil & Eagan, 1992).[2] The "Gender Role Journey" describes five phases: (1) acceptance of traditional gender roles, (2) ambivalence, (3) anger, (4) activism, and (5) celebration and integration of gender roles. A transition from one phase may occur from situational events (e.g., divorce or illness), from normal developmental processes (e.g., puberty or ageing), and from increased awareness of how sexism negatively affects personal growth and development. Each phase includes specific cognitive, affective, and behavioral characteristics related to the gender role.

PHASE 1 *Acceptance of traditional gender roles* includes support for traditional notions of masculinity and femininity, with little awareness of the limitations imposed. This phase is characterized by feelings of being powerless and dependent.

PHASE 2 *Ambivalence* involves dissatisfaction with stereotypic notions of gender roles, with increased awareness of how gender roles and sexism violate people. In this phase there is confusion about one's masculine-feminine identity.

PHASE 3 Anger involves experiencing negative emotions about sexism with a recognition that sexism entails violence. The person may remain "stuck in the anger" or begin to make personal changes.

PHASE 4 Activism involves the person taking action to reduce sexism in personal and/or professional life. The activism may result in the person feeling confirmed or disconfirmed.

PHASE 5 *Celebration and Integration of Gender Roles* involves experiencing increased gender-role freedom in personal and professional relationships as well as continued efforts to educate the public about sexism (O'Neil & Eagan, 1992).

The original five-phase model for gender-identity development has been condensed into three stages. Empirical validation of the five-phase theory suggests a streamlining into a three-phase model with Phase 2 and 3 being collapsed into one factor and Phase 4 and 5 being collapsed into another factor (O'Neil, Eagan, Owen, & McBride Murry, 1993). However, further research is required to support this new three-phase model. Furthermore, while developmental models are useful in mapping out different phases or levels of understanding, the process of how individuals move through these phases—and particularly the assumed linearity in such models—requires further research.

Although there are some challenges to developmental models in their assumed linearity, such models can still be of use in dealing with ethnic- and gender-identity development. First, developmental models provide a framework for making sense of the range of different beliefs about racism or sexism. They also enable students to think about their own growth: where I am now, how I have changed, and what lies ahead. In presenting the racial-identity development model to the class, I ask students to identify where they think they are on the model, including that they may be spread out over a number of stages, and to share their findings with another member in the class. This assignment provides students with an opportunity to reflect on their own beliefs and actions.

Next, developmental models can provide reassurance to students in enabling them to situate their views, as well as those of their peers, within a broader theory. Students can therefore view their own anger or another student's anger as related to their position on the developmental model. While such action does not remove the anger or conflict between people at different stages, it does allow others to view the disagreement within a broader framework. In this way the racial-identity model can offer reassurance to students that conflicts are the result of students being at different stages and not a problem of individuals.

Recognizing the wide range of levels of awareness of racism or sexism may lend support to the provision of differential course experiences in which the individual's level of readiness for multicultural education would be matched to specific course experiences (Bennett, Niggle & Stage, 1990). Being able to tailor experiences to meet students' varying levels of awareness might increase the effectiveness of multicultural education courses.

Conclusion

White male students' responses to multicultural education vary considerably. One white male wrote in his course reflection: "I started the class feeling that I had little to learn. By the end of the course I had gained tremendous insight and was forced to acknowledge that I was not as socially conscious as I had thought." Less positive responses to multicultural education include, "I was expecting the course to be on how to implement lessons and curriculum and not a human relations course." The white male student stated, however, that he had learned "patience, tolerance, and self-control."

However, opposition to multicultural education is not confined to those of privileged identities. Students who are working class, female, or persons of color may also have internalized the ideology of individualism and therefore reject structural explanations. Students of subordinate groups may feel that their individual efficacy as well as their opportunities for success are threatened by theories supporting the institutional basis of discrimination.

Of course, not all students oppose multicultural education and some will enthusiastically embrace it. Many students in my own class will begin to see diversity in a positive light and become excited about incorporating literature and music of different cultural groups into the curriculum. A much smaller number, however, go beyond the Additive or Human Relations approach to locate schooling and the role of the teacher within a larger sociopolitical context.

The degree of success in responding to white male opposition is influenced by a number of other factors. First, the amount of change that can be accomplished in one course is limited. It is important not to have unrealistic expectations for change, given that students have acquired their beliefs and behaviors over a period of many years. It may be that some students leave the course at the same stage that they entered. For some white males this might mean they leave somewhat more aware but still feeling angry and discriminated against. Furthermore, even though I emphasize that the goal of examining oppression is not to blame groups but to understand oppression, some white males will state that they felt that they were being blamed.

Second, in courses in which issues of diversity are only a part of the curriculum, it is even more difficult to address issues of masculinity. Course objectives may make it impossible to devote much time to this topic. However, even though it may be difficult to specifically deal with issues of masculinity, there are still ways to include gender in the curriculum. For example, in the social foundations course that I teach I do not have the time to present a model of male socialization. Nonetheless, when students share their social identity papers one of the strategies I use is to divide the class into small groups based on gender. This allows the male students an opportunity to talk about their experiences and to identify common characteristics related to being male. Similarly, in a math methods course, issues of gender socialization could be explored in relation to students' prior experiences of learning math.

Third, the gender, race, and social class of the instructor may also be an influencing factor on white male student opposition. My own social identity as a white middle-class male may make it easier for me to work with white male students. Students may feel less threatened by someone who shares their identity. However, this may not be true for all male students as some may see another white male as a competitor rather than an ally, particularly when the unequal power relationship of teacher and student is included. Finally, for some students other factors, such as being working class, may be more significant to the person's identity than being male. Social class differences may make it difficult to reach agreement on a common experience of white male identity.

Responding to white male opposition to multicultural education requires an understanding of both issues of male dominance and racism. This chapter has focused on understanding and responding to male dominance. The model of gender-identity development provides a framework for describing the different levels of awareness that males have of sexism. Further research is required both to refine the model and to identify specific strategies appropriate to working with white males at different levels of awareness of sexism. Much work is still needed to bring together our understanding of issues of racism and sexism in being able to work successfully with white male opposition to multicultural education.

Notes

1. At a political level Van Dijk (1993) argues that expressing support for hospitality, understanding, and tolerance, as well as emphatic denials of racism, are all strategies used by white elites to maintain control.
2. The male responses on which the Gender Identity Developmental model is based are those of white males. Little research has been carried out on the interaction of gender and race. Several studies are currently examining the responses of African American men, Mexican American men, and Asian American men to see whether the model has any validity for other racial groups.

13

Carolyn R. O'Grady

Moving Off Center

Engaging White Education Students in Multicultural Field Experiences

Each student is unique and special for many reasons. Cultural background is only one characteristic that makes a student special. Sometimes we get so hung up on what is on the outside we forget to look inside.   —Senior

Physical appearance or cultural preferences are small elements in the entire makeup of any person. Deciding how to handle someone based on these elements is foolish.   —Senior

We must question [the validity of] the tests we are giving since an overwhelming majority in [upper level classes] are white students.
—Sophomore

The Vietnamese were not considered "special education," but they

were placed in the special education class. Tragically, they needed help—but not the help that the special ed class was designed to provide.   *—Sophomore*

Each of these comments was written by a White[1] teacher education student after completing a required multicultural field experience. Each comment contains a grain of truth. Yet where the first two comments reflect an emphasis on the uniqueness of each individual, regardless of cultural characteristics, the last two comments reveal a dawning awareness of racial inequity in education.

These examples of engagement with complicated issues of social power are the goal of multicultural educators who hope to enable students to question the status quo as it exists in schools today. Challenging students' assumptions about educational practice involves providing opportunities for students to be pushed out of their comfort zones and to decenter themselves as they analyze educational policies and practices. Field experiences offer one approach for engaging students in this process. However, not every type of field experience helps students go beyond the kind of one-dimensional assessment evident in the first two quotes above, to the deeper awareness of more complicated social issues found in the last two quotes. In what follows I will describe and compare two types of field experiences utilized in a liberal arts college in order to assess the value of field experiences in expanding students' understanding of multicultural issues in education. This chapter will also explore why one type of field experience may lead to greater student growth than the other.

The Context

I teach in an Education Department predominantly filled with White students. Our college is located just far enough from an urban area to be considered rural, and most of our students come to us from the midwest region, usually from rural or suburban areas. As a Lutheran college we draw a high percentage of students who have been raised in that religious tradition or who at least self-identify as Christian. The percentage of students of color in the college as a whole was less than 5.6 percent of the total population of about 2300 in 1994–95. In the Education Department the percentage barely surpasses 6 percent out of 250 students.

When asked to identify their ethnic background, the majority of students at this college name Scandinavian (particularly Swedish) and German. It is these White students who are the focus of this chapter. For some of them, coming to this college represents a great leap in their exposure to "difference." Many students encounter here for the first time someone who is African American, Asian American, Native American, openly gay or lesbian, Latina/o, or Jewish. Helping these White teacher education students understand issues of diversity presents special challenges.

In our department we attempt to develop multicultural literacy in our students through a multipronged approach. Curriculum content of all courses includes information about cultural diversity and students are expected to show multicultural competency in all assignments, from lesson plans to portfolios. Field experiences and practica are also important components of our program. In course work and practical experiences, students are asked to focus on many manifestations of diversity, including gender, physical and mental ability, religion, sexual orientation, race and ethnicity, and socioeconomic class. White students' responses to multicultural material varies widely, echoing the stages of racial identity development described by Banks (1988), Tatum (1992), Hardiman and Jackson (1992), and others. Although each of these models vary somewhat, they share a description of the learner at various stages on a voyage of self-discovery in regard to his or her own racial identity as White. When presented with curriculum content or experiences that challenge his or her preconceptions, the learner may choose to respond to new information with denial or may actively embrace a new paradigm, or rest somewhere in the middle.

This response continuum is a useful image to describe the engagement levels of education students in our program. At one end are those students who are actively working with the concepts they are learning. They are examining their own attitudes, exploring history from a variety of perspectives and struggling to integrate these new ideas into their world view. These are the students who are attempting to redefine their sense of self and of "others" (Tatum 1992). Hardiman and Jackson (1992) describe an individual at this stage as beginning to recognize and challenge the existence of oppression in society.

At the other end of the continuum are those students who are nonengaged. This response most closely resembles what Banks (1988) describes as "Ethnic Encapsulation" in which the individual may feel his or her own ethnic or racial identity is threatened by members of other ethnic or racial groups. Hardiman and Jackson (1992) describe this type of individual as one who might actively perpetuate stereotypes about members of other groups and who blames members of those groups for their subordinate position. This "blaming the victim" (Ryan, 1976) mentality might be expressed in class through overtly discriminatory comments about others who are different or through attacks on the instructor for presenting the material to begin with. These forms of active nonengagement are utilized by students who are unable to be open to new perspectives, perhaps because they are not yet ready for the information, or because it is too much in conflict with their own world view. These students often remain nonengaged regardless of the approach, and their readiness to engage must wait for further educational or life experience.

The bulk of students in our education classes fall somewhere in the middle of the continuum. These are the students who are "selectively" engaged (Frankenberg, 1993)—taking two steps forward in awareness but one step back out of discomfort—or who can cope with learning about one particular form of discrimination, say racism, but cannot handle another, perhaps gay and lesbian oppression. It is often difficult to teach these students about multicultural awareness because their responses are unpredictable and their growth in understanding is inconsistent or often one dimensional. Banks (1988) uses the terms *ethnic identity clarification* (Stage 3) and *biethnicity* (Stage 4) to describe individuals who begin to clarify personal feelings toward their own ethnic group and eventually learn to feel comfortable participating in another person's ethnic culture. Tatum (1992) describes White students who are moving through stages of awareness in which they begin to understand racism but deny their own racism or who attempt to confront the racist attitudes of those around them while continuing to accept the status quo. These students struggle to redefine themselves and others and are especially in need of educational experiences that will enhance their multicultural development. Multicultural field experiences can expand these students' awareness and help move them off center.

Multicultural Field Experiences as Change Opportunities

Research on the value of field experiences shows mixed results. McDiarmid (1992) notes that these field experiences usually fail to challenge prospective teachers' assumptions even though practicing teachers often cite classroom experience over methods classes as most educational. Other researchers have found field experiences to be the most valuable part of a preservice program. Multicultural field experiences in particular seem to positively influence prospective teachers' attitudes toward individuals of a different cultural group (Grant & Tate, 1995).

Because our college is in a predominantly White area and is attended by an overwhelmingly White student body, field experiences are crucial in helping our prospective teachers make concrete the multicultural theory they are learning in the classroom. The combination of classroom pedagogy with field experience appears to help students develop greater multicultural awareness (Grant & Tate, 1995), particularly when the field experience is extensive enough to require immersion (Witmer & Anderson, 1994). While classroom content is crucial in providing a foundation and a context for awareness, field experiences offer the possibility of moving students off center by critical reflection on their cultural identity and that of others. This process is important for all students, but especially for those who are selectively engaged with the course content.

A number of multicultural field experiences are required in our program. We have found that the most profound learning occurs when these encounters are contextualized. That is, when done as part of a class, or as a guided activity, field experiences can teach students not only about individual differences but also about the history of social inequality and the structural context of oppression. The two field experiences to be described here, one of which takes place in the context of a class and one of which does not, offer two different approaches to challenging students' perceptions.

The Human Relations Field Experience, described first, is one component of a Minnesota state requirement for preservice teachers that mandates training in human relations. At our college, this field experience takes the form of a fifteen-hour practicum during which education students "interact with individuals who are of a racial or cultural group different than their own." The Urban School Visit, the second field experience discussed, involves a one-day site visit to an innercity high school or elementary school, completed as part of the introductory course in our program, *Social Foundations of Education*. While all students in our program must complete each field requirement, they are not necessarily completed within the same academic year. The results described below are responses from two groups of White students who completed these experiences during 1994–95. Participants in the Human Relations experience (36 total) included sophomores, juniors, and seniors. Students completing the Urban School Visit (50 total) were predominantly sophomores.

Human Relations Field Experience

Students complete this requirement on an individual basis. They begin by approaching the Coordinator of Human Relations in the Education Department and requesting advice about "doing a multicultural experience." Often they are placed in an elementary school in a town nearby which has a growing Mexican American population and may need English language tutors. Students also may find their own placements and simply have these approved by the coordinator. Almost all requests are approved, as long as students meet the criterion of working with a member of a different racial or cultural group. These placements often involve working in some capacity with children, often in schools, but have also recently included working as a nanny for a Japanese family, doing child care in a women's shelter, becoming a member of the campus Asian Student Club, coaching multiracial teams, and working in a soup kitchen. Students have worked with racial or cultural groups that include immigrants from Mexico, China, Vietnam, Cambodia, and Zaire, as well as with Americans whose ethnicity is Japanese, African American, Native American, and Russian. During the experience students maintain a journal and after completing this experience students write a reflective essay describing their response to the experience.

There are several problems with the format of this field experience. First, students have been known to complete their fifteen required hours in as little as two days. This hardly leaves enough time for reflection on the experience. Second, students often look for a placement by going to the Coordinator of Human Relations, or to the Director of Community Service on campus, and asking for "a little person of color" to work with because they "have to do something multicultural." Not only is this condescending, but it reinforces the notion that multicultural experiences are something removed from real life. Third, students often leave this requirement to the last minute, trying to squeeze it in before student teaching, revealing their belief that this is just another hoop to jump through. Fourth, and most important, students' reflective essays reveal great variation in the students' abilities to learn from this exposure to diversity.

Because this field experience is done on an individual basis, there is no opportunity for students to discuss with others what they observe or how they feel about what they see. They usually have no preparation before the experience that will help them understand the cultural background of the people they work with. There is no postexperience debriefing that helps students explore both the larger social issues that may be reflected in their particular field setting and their own issues as White observers. Although each student has a nominal "supervisor" in the field (usually the person at the site who helps set up the placement) this person rarely has the time to provide college students with a broader perspective, or may not see these issues themselves.

This lack of context in which to understand the multicultural field experience often means that students simply cannot "see" any cultural or racial difference. For example, after tutoring Latino children Chuck[2] says, "To me, those kids were just like any other 7- or 8-year-old children. . . . This experience has once again reinforced my notion that people are people and that race should not be a deciding factor." Worse, students may have their stereotypes reinforced by the experience. Gene worked for more than fifteen hours in a high school near an Indian reservation. His attitude after this experience reflects deep-seated prejudice: "In a diverse environment, many problems exist, even more than in an all-White environment. There is a lot more drinking that goes on, as well as more drugs and divorce. . . . When a lot of minority students get to high school, they do not enjoy being in school and learning. They get pregnant and drop out of school."

Many students wrote similar thoughts to Elaine's, that "each child is an individual and should be treated as one." Students often respond that what they learned was that all children should be treated the same, "regardless of color." The desire of most of these preservice teachers to see all students as the same indicates their belief that treating students "the same" is synonymous with "being equal" (Nieto, 1992). Clearly students are not all the same, given racial and cultural differences, learning style and communication style differences, and differences in access to social status. A commonly expressed attitude is reflected by Jackie, who worked with Native American teenagers in a social service agency: "The one thing I have always found to be the connecting factor is that we are all human and beneath our layers of skin each one of us is exactly the same. What seems to create the boundaries between different cultures is our thoughts and views of being different." Jackie and Elaine fail to understand the impact historic discrimination has had on people of color, or the institutional racism that affects the lives of people of color. Both students can affirm the importance of honoring similarities among individuals, but not the equally important need to recognize differences. Jackie, for instance, does not have the tools to analyze the forces of social inequity that positions her, a White middle-class woman, as a privileged person (MacIntosh, 1990) and the field experience format provides no context in which to challenge her thinking. Greg has a similar response to his experience. He feels students should all be treated the same "regardless of color. We are all human beings and we all should be treated with respect." Like many students, Jackie, Elaine, and Greg have been socialized to see only a half truth, that children are individuals deserving respect. By understanding how others are systemically denied respect, often because of race, they would understand a more complex truth.

These students believe that by ignoring skin color they are being more fair to children of color on the assumption that "not seeing" color means they are treating all students equally (Valli, 1995). Unfortunately, this color evasion reinforces Whiteness as the norm (Frankenberg, 1993). These White students do not see themselves as White, and so are able to deny responsibility for perpetuating a racist system (Katz, 1978). These prospective teachers have not learned in this field experience to critique their own belief that the United States is a just society for all regardless of color, or their belief that racism is an individual phenomenon rather than a system of advantage and privilege based on race (McIntosh, 1990; Tatum, 1992).

Occasionally there are students, however, who are able to decenter themselves through this field experience and gain some insight into deeper issues. For instance, Gloria completed her field experience in an urban setting with Mexican American and White youth in a Catholic parish while simultaneously student teaching in a very small rural town. As she describes her student teaching placement, "there are no people of color in the school. This has led to a great ignorance of people of different colors. Many times in my class we have discussed the issue of migrant workers. During these discussions I have heard students use terms like 'spic' or 'wetback' and even 'dirty Mexicans.'" Although Gloria does not report how she handled these racist comments in her own class, she does describe her feelings about similar comments hurled by Anglo teenagers toward the Mexican American teenagers in the church program. She felt "more resentment" toward the White kids than toward the Latinos. "The bottom line is that I didn't like being White when I saw the very snob-like actions of the kids from the suburbs." She has begun the process of repositioning her identity as a White person by distancing herself from other Whites who appear to be overtly racist.

In evaluating her own future teaching approach, Gloria feels that "you should always keep the diverse learner in mind even if there is no diverse group to teach to." While her cooperating teacher felt it was "acceptable to minimize the importance of diversity because there are no minorities present," Gloria herself finds this "far from logical."

> In an area where people have little or no contact with culture other than their own, it is important for them to be daily reminded that there is a world that is very different than the one they live in. If children are not taught to develop compassion toward others, they will develop misunderstanding and soon they could develop some sick and wrong ideas about another culture.

Maureen worked in a summer program for urban children and developed an understanding of the importance of exploring one's own attitudes. She feels that "in order to accept each person in my class as an individual I must first examine and reexamine myself." When asked how teachers from one cultural background can encourage children to be proud of a culture different from that of the teacher, Maureen says "this is a question that haunts me, because it's disturbing to me that I am only contributing to the 'problem.' In too many diverse classrooms, the students are peering up at a white face." In realizing her inability to serve as a mirror (Style, 1988) in which all students of color in her class might see themselves, Maureen is also moved off center and is better prepared to see "otherness" in a clearer light.

It is not always clear why some prospective teachers were able to experience a shift in perspective during their Human Relations Field Experience and others were not. As educators we can never be certain which experiences will have the most effect on which students. And certainly, given the limitations of the experiences described, lack of student progress toward deeper multicultural awareness is understandable. What is evident here is that while some students experienced an increase in personal awareness, an important goal in multicultural education, they are clearly at the Contact Stage in which they lack awareness of cultural and institutional racism and of their own privileges as Whites (Tatum, 1992). They do not yet understand the social dimensions of racism and discrimination and, indeed, seem to have few clues that structural inequality even exists. Unfortunately, the construction of this Human Relations Field Experience offers no context for understanding the broader social implications of what they see.

Contextualizing the World
The Urban Field Experience

In contrast, education students enrolled in *Social Foundations of Education* have the opportunity to look beyond individual behaviors and beliefs to the larger social structure. During this class, students spend one day observing in an innercity, multiracial school. This one day cannot offer the kind of indepth experience that even fifteen hours has the potential to do, but it does allow students to apply what they learn in the classroom to what they see and hear in a real school.

Before students visit the urban school, the class has already discussed a wide range of issues in education, including the history and philosophy of education, legal and governance issues, and education in a multicultural society. Students have discussed such issues as bilingual education, tracking, private versus public education, class stratification in schools, stereotypes in textbooks and curriculum materials, gender equity, gay and lesbian issues, and mainstreaming. Students in the class explore their own backgrounds as a way to understand that who we are as members of multiple social groups has an impact on who we might be as teachers. In this process, the class discusses how stereotypes occur, the interconnectedness of various forms of oppression, the use of education to reinforce pressures to assimilate, and the ethnic and socioeconomic class differences among ourselves. In this way, students begin to learn that we are all products of our socialization and need to relearn some of our assumptions about others if we wish to practice equity in our classrooms.

Not all students are receptive to this kind of information. A few students in each class actively nonengage with the material. But for those students who are elsewhere on the continuum of engagement, the visit to an innercity school has the potential to expand their understanding of multicultural issues.

During the urban visit, students have the choice of observing in either an elementary or a high school. In either case, they are given an orientation by a member of the administration at the beginning of the day, which provides them with information on demographics and school issues. They are then matched with a teacher (in the elementary school) or a student (in the high school) and spend the day shadowing that person. Their task during this visit is to act as participant observers, coming away with a wealth of information about the environment of the school, teaching styles, the curriculum, and student interactions. Their purpose here is to observe rather than to judge, but their strong reactions to this experience are evident in the postvisit debriefing that occurs in class the next day and in the response essays they write afterward. Let us look at what the visit to Cityside High School reveals about how providing an in-class context for examining multicultural field experiences can yield rich insights into what is observed.

Cityside High School

Sixty percent of the student body at Cityside are students of color, particularly African American, Latino, and Hmong. There are two types of programs at the school, the Comprehensive Program, in which students are grouped by ability, and the International Baccalaureate (IB) Program, an advanced academic program. Through shadowing a high school student for the entire day the college students were able to encounter a wide variety of experiences in the school. As became evident during later debriefing, those college students who were paired with students of color felt they saw a very different kind of school than the one their classmates saw while shadowing White high school students.

Those students who attended classes in the Comprehensive Program were often dismayed by the kind of teaching they observed and by the behaviors of the students. Patrick was paired with an African

American student named Tanya and was appalled to learn that she was placed in special education classes because, as a teacher told him, Tanya is from a group home for teenagers.

> As explained by the teacher, this class was intended for students with social or behavioral problems, and included foreign students, an alcoholic, a medicated and institutionalized girl, two autistic children, a mother of an asthmatic baby, a freshman who was old enough to graduate, and a student who seems to be virtually deprived of academic discipline. In my day in Tanya's classes, with her friends, in her discussions, and in one-on-one personal conversations I found no indications of similar characteristics—or problems—with Tanya, nor did I find *any* social or behavioral problems with her at all.

Patrick was able to link earlier class discussions about mislabeling and tracking in schools to his observations of Tanya and her classes.

One high school teacher in the Comprehensive Program talked to Daniel about education in an innercity school and touched on the particular needs of students in such a setting.

> He mentioned the different learning styles of innercity kids and the adjustments that teachers had to make. He said that these kids do not learn in the traditional manner, but that does not mean they do not want to learn. Instead, they have to experience things and learn by practical means. With that in mind, the students' behavior was still shocking to me. . . . What bothered me most was the lack of effort and the lack of caring that was displayed by the students.

Daniel left with negative feelings toward learning in this school. "The overall impression that I got was that the students were unmotivated and had little respect for the teachers. The teachers attribute the students' lack of motivation to a different lifestyle. Therefore, the teachers abandon traditional techniques and do not push the students to challenge themselves." While Daniel struggles to see student differences and is convinced traditional techniques are best for all, his observations show greater insight and an ability to grasp complexity than did the kind of "all children are the same" comments made by some participants in the Human Relations Field Experience.

Several students made notes about how students grouped themselves. Tom observed that "for the most part they stick with their own race." He noticed in Physical Education class that "all the African American males played 5 on 5 full court. All the other males went to the side and shot around. The females did nothing but sit in the bleachers and talk. They were not encouraged to play by the teacher, an African American male. Instead, he joined in the full-court game." Tom got involved in the game and, in the process, facilitated a full-court game that included both White and African American males and some of the females.

A different section of this Physical Education class had a different feeling for Rita, who struggled to relax during her day in the school. She says, " [Physical Education class] was the only place I felt totally comfortable. It felt 'normal' to me. The teacher, a white male, had total control of the class and they seemed to really like him. The class had about thirty students and there seemed to be mainly white students." Although both Tom and Rita are White and both are Physical Education majors, their reflections indicate they are at different stages in their ability to feel comfortable with a diverse student population. Rita's racial identity remains at the center of her perspective, as she indicates more comfort with a predominantly White class (it seems more "normal" to her) than with an earlier experience in a predominantly African American class. ("These kids just did not seem to care at all.")

Sharon was one of the college students who revealed the most willingness to be engaged by this experience and allow herself to be pushed off center. She is able to monitor her feelings before, during, and after this, with resultant new insights and growth.

> I remember what I thought about [the idea of visiting] an innercity school—that it might be a good idea for some of my peers that grew up in rural areas where there was not a lot of ethnic diversity. I never thought I would have any problem at Cityside. I read a lot of books and had been unlearning the prejudices that had been taught to me as a child. I honestly thought that I was on the right track and knew a lot about diversity in America's schools.

But this was not how things turned out. "Early Monday morning as I walked through the halls, the feelings of confidence left me, and were replaced with fear and intimidation." She is paired with Juanita, an African American student.

> The more time I spent with Juanita I found that I began to hate it at Cityside more and more. I felt that I had lost all the control I had gained in the last semester. I felt that all the gains I made through all my reading and all my relearning was minimal compared to what I felt like being with the Cityside students. What made me the most upset were the students' attitudes. I felt frustrated by the way the students acted, like they did not care, like they were mad at the world, even mad at me.

These feelings of frustration finally erupted during a confrontation with Juanita and several of her friends. One of the friends, learning that Sharon had been raised in an affluent suburb of the city, remarked that where Sharon came from all people worried about was that some Black person would steal their "precious items" and didn't have to even think about paying the rent or putting food on the table. But Sharon was an exception to this assumption. Although she had been raised middle class, her family had lost all its money and was forced to declare bankruptcy. This experience of losing everything gave Sharon a different perspective on the world and enabled her in this encounter with Juanita and her friends to find empathy for their situation.

> I understood this attitude that some students had that was making me so angry. It was the exact same attitude that I carried around after losing my house. Even though I'll never be able to relate to this student as being African American, I can know what it feels like to feel that the world is sometimes against you, and understand that attitude of toughness, of distantness, because you feel alone and mad at how unfair opportunities are. After that realization I got down from my pedestal which I had been walking around on all morning. . . . I began to really talk with the students, and more importantly got a chance to open my ears and listen to what they were saying. When I left Cityside I no longer hated it here, I loved it.

Sharon comes to see her own Whiteness differently when she says that she cannot understand what it is like to be African American, but she also indicates an ability to connect with others over a shared understanding of injustice. By having her comfort zone challenged, Sharon finds the ability to empathize with Juanita's world view, thus moving herself off center.

These college students' abilities to make connections between their class content and their field experience is most evident in their analysis of social stratification at Cityside. Before the field experience the class had discussed whether education is truly the great equalizer or whether, as Bowles and Gintis (1976) claimed twenty years ago, it perpetuates social class inequities. At Cityside, students had the chance to explore this question in a real-life situation. Students who shadowed a teenager in the International Baccalaureate program had a very different experience than those who did not. The IB classes were in the east wing, while the comprehensive classes were held in the west wing. Several students were uncomfortable with what they considered physical segregation. Andy, who shadowed an IB student, noted, "I saw a great deal of diversity when going from one class to another, but all of my classes were predominantly white with the only exception being a black student in the calculus class. I attributed this segregation to a bias in admissions for the IB program. Nearly all the minorities were in the lower track and, once there, could not be promoted to the IB program."

Jim had an especially strong reaction to this situation. "It was in [Spanish class at 9:30 A.M.] that I remembered that the objective of the day was to witness firsthand a diverse, innercity school. Besides the few blacks that were on the student council, I had seen not even a handful of minorities in the classes that I had been in. Why was this happening? Was it because the classes were all upper-level classes?" Jim is unwilling to believe this is the reason, but by noon he has seen nothing different. When he mentions to one student in a class that "we were there to observe diversity in school systems she piped up 'good luck finding it here!' The sad part was that this was completely true from what I had been observing all day. Where were all the minority students? Are we dealing with modern-day segregation?" By the end of the day Jim feels he has an answer:

> Why were there only a few minorities in the classes I was in in spite of the 60 percent minority population in the school? I think the answer is simple: Discrimination. I would like to think this IB program is doing its job and helping all students that want to continue their education do so but, apparently, it is not doing its job. No one can tell me that it is just a matter of minority students not wanting to go to college because I find that very hard to believe. From what I can observe, the IB program is merely a branding program. All students, no matter what their race, are branded and kept in a program that will ultimately decide their fate. Sure, the students that are in the comprehensive program could still go on to college, but why is there a label being put on the students? . . . The IB program is just a way to separate the Haves and the Have-Nots.

By recognizing the existence of tracking and its relationship to systemic, institutional racism in schools, Jim is engaging with multicultural issues in a way that participants in the Human Relations Field Experience did not yet have the context to do.

Moving beyond Selective Engagement
Field Experience Outcomes

Certainly not all students were able to see things through a new lens, question their White identity, or assess social inequities during the

Urban School Visit even with the help of class context. Steve is representative of these students in noting a simple observation without questioning its deeper meaning when he says, "I realized that I had been with a girl that was in the IB program, and in that school non-whites in the IB program are like boys participating in the girls' dance line. . . . I just did not luck out that day, concerning finding cultural diversity." He never questions why this was so. He is unwilling or unable to look at this experience through a new lens and chooses to remain nonengaged.

However, reports from the majority of students indicate that multicultural field experiences may yield specific outcomes desirable for prospective teachers. These field experiences demonstrated the potential to nudge many students out of their comfort zones toward gaining new insights. A prerequisite of critical thinking for students is the process of identifying contradictions between what they have been taught about the world and the way the world is. Thus, Sharon, a White female, is able to connect with Juanita, an African American female, over a shared sense of injustice while recognizing they can never fully connect over racial identity. She is able to empathize with the feelings of a person of color while gaining a new awareness of her own Whiteness. Gloria is also able to gain a new awareness of herself as White when she finds herself feeling more resentment toward the White teenagers than the Latino teenagers in her field experience.

Some students in both field experiences began to understand for the first time that not all students of color will "see" themselves in, and be able to relate to, a White teacher. Others identified the importance of teaching about difference in their own classroom. As Gloria notes, all students, including Whites, need to learn about diversity. Other prospective teachers learn that they themselves might be part of the problem, as Maureen reflects on being yet another White face at the front of the classroom, or that they have prejudices they were not aware of, as Melanie finds while tutoring a Mexican American boy.

Both types of field experiences described here offer valuable opportunities for students to gain important practical experience.[3] However, multicultural field experiences that are completed as part of a class seem to offer the most promise for helping students move from limited half truths about diversity ("Each child is an individual and should be treated as one.") to broader complex truths ("Where were all the minority students? Are we dealing with modern day discrimination?"). Students in the urban high school visit were able to observe contradictions between their own educational experiences and those of many of the students of color they shadowed. In the process, they began to identify differences in learning styles, classroom management techniques, and the inequities of tracking and labeling. Discussing these concepts in an education class before and after the site visit helped White students go beyond merely an intellectual understanding of institutional inequities to their manifestation in an actual school and required that they actively engage with the material.

While the experiences of the few students reported here cannot be generalized to all settings or all students, several recommendations are evident from contrasting these two types of field experiences. As Witmer and Anderson (1994) note, the field experience cannot be expected to work by itself. "Students must receive preparation and support in learning from their experiences" (p. 74).

Recommendations

Successful multicultural field experiences must provide students with a context for evaluating their learnings before, during, and after their placement in the field. Before the experience, students need some understanding of the history of social inequality (as suggested by Téllez and O'Malley in this volume). This provides a context for understanding patterns of institutional oppression, such as tracking, labeling, language discrimination, and class inequity. If they will be working with a specific racial or cultural group students need background on the history of that group in the United States and issues that may affect that group's access to educational equity.

During and after a multicultural field experience it is crucial that students have the opportunity to reflect on what they are witnessing. Journaling and reflective essays are two methods for achieving this form of reflection, and both of these were used in each field experience described here. But the multicultural field experience that is experienced as part of a class has the additional benefit of offering the opportunity for a postexperience debriefing in which students can discuss and compare their experiences with their peers. This allows students to analyze an environment from a variety of perspectives and also provides a space for individuals to work through emotions that may arise in response to the experience. When Sven admits that during his Human Relations Field Experience he felt "always worried about being called a racist or having one of the African American students not like me" there is no one to help him sort through these emotions. In comparison, Bob is able to discuss with his peers that visiting Cityside inspired "feelings of uneasiness, apprehension and excitement" in him. Helping students understand the affective side of developing multicultural competency is as important as helping them develop cognitive skills in multicultural issues.

It is also important that students as well as the instructor have an awareness that we are all at different stages in our awareness of our own and others' ethnic identities (Banks, 1988). When Virginia writes "To be honest I did not think of Teng as a Chinese American. I thought of him as a preschooler who had difficulty with English," she is unable to differentiate between Teng's identity as a Chinese immigrant and her own identity as a White American. She demonstates her inability to engage with race as a factor in her relationship with the child. On the other hand, Nancy's report from a first-grade classroom of "one incident where an African American girl was making derogatory remarks to a group of Hmong students" reveals her willingness to name racial conflict between ethnic groups and she goes on to cite the important role of the teacher in intervening in such conflict. As McDiarmid (1992) notes, "the only reliable test of changes in belief is what these students will do in their own classrooms" (p. 51). As instructors we can begin by assuming different levels of awareness in our students and provide opportunities for them to move from there.

A particularly promising approach to field experiences is service learning, a teaching method that integrates community service into the school curriculum. In a service learning program, individuals engage in community activities in a context of rigorous academic experience. Service learning allows teachers to employ a variety of teaching strategies that emphasize student-centered, interactive, experiential education. As the Alliance for Service Learning in Education Reform states, "Service learning places curricular concepts in the context of real-life situations and empowers students to analyze, evaluate, and synthesize these concepts through practical problem solving, often in service to the community" ("Standards of Quality," n.d., p. 3).

The benefits of combining service and learning are powerful. This integration enables participants to learn how to critically reflect on their experience and learn how to work collaboratively with others. It can also increase motivation for learning and strengthen social and civic responsibility (Kendall, 1990). In addition, service learning has the potential to help students understand and address the underlying problems behind social issues.

The best service learning programs build on reciprocity between the school and the community in which it is embedded. Densmore (1995) emphasizes that our social and intellectual objectives as educators require that we go outside the classroom with our students. She warns that when there is little or no working relationship between the school and community, students find it difficult to apply what they learn in the classroom to their life outside of the classroom. When college teachers and community members work together, we can achieve the goals of a "curriculum for diversity" that confronts and addresses all students' life experiences and the connection of those experiences to underlying social and economic realities (Densmore, 1995).[4]

Providing a context for a multicultural field experience helps to ensure that the field experience will challenge rather than increase stereotypic attitudes about other cultural groups (Valli, 1995). Through this process White preservice teachers may find that moving off center offers greater engagement with a diverse world. As Sharon reminds us, "I learned that I can talk about multiculturalism all I want, I can read every book I can get my hands on, but if I do not do anything, it means nothing."

Notes

1. In this chapter, the word *white* is capitalized as are all names that refer to racial or ethnic groups (unless within a quote). Language expresses social attitudes, and as these have shifted over the years, so has publishing convention. Overt racial supremacy was reinforced in the segregationist South when *white* was capitalized in the press and *negro* was not (Allport, 1954). In the last twenty years, *white* has commonly been published lowercase while *Negro, African American,* and even *Black* have not. This most recent convention assumes what Frankenberg (1993) calls whiteness as "an unmarked marker of others' differentness" (p. 198) and reinforces often unconscious racial supremacy. Convention seems to be shifting again, as the latest (4th) edition of the American Psychological Association Publication Manual (1995) recommends capitalization of Black, White, and other racial and ethnic group names.
2. All names are pseudonyms.
3. Because of the kinds of dilemmas described here, the format of the Human Relations Field Experience is currently being revised to offer students more opportunity to place their learnings in context. A long-range goal is to incorporate this field experience into an existing class.
4. An analysis of this promising approach to field experiences is beyond the scope of this article. See O'Grady (forthcoming) for a discussion of school-community partnerships in a multicultural context.

14

Betsy J. Cahill
Eve M. Adams

Identity and Engagement
in Multicultural Education

This chapter represents an exploration of issues influencing
student engagement and nonengagement in university classrooms. Our purpose is to raise a number of issues and questions regarding student engagement in classrooms where multicultural themes are addressed by the participants—students and teachers.
Included in this discussion is an inquiry into the values and world-
views that all the participants might bring to the teaching-learning
relationship.

To investigate these issues we will use an interdisciplinary approach, drawing from the fields of education, psychology, and women's
studies. We will share stories from our teaching, counseling, research,
and antioppression experiences. It is through our collaborative relationship that we have attempted to understand our roles educators who

value the continuous process of self-awareness related to issues and assumptions about diversity, "difference," and classroom practices.

Betsy is an assistant professor in early childhood education, with fifteen years' teaching experience in preschool through primary. She has been active in the antibias movement and social policy issues in early childhood, and conducts research on gender identity and oppression. Eve's background is in counseling psychology and she has provided numerous presentations and workshops on "appreciating diversity" for a broad range of students, staff, and faculty. Eve is part of the multicultural group of women who conceptualized the Optimal Theory Applied to Identity Development model that is discussed further in this chapter.

We begin the next section of this chapter with a brief look at the questions that emerge from an exploration of the terms *student engagement* and *nonengagement*. We will then share one model of identity development that has informed our understanding of these issues, as well as our responses in the classroom. We have chosen to focus primarily on how a student's self-identity as a member of a majority or minority group, and their developmental stage of identity development, influences their engagement with education that is multicultural (Tatum, 1992). The last section of this chapter is a dialogue that reflects our work and collaboration as friends and colleagues. The dialogue is drawn from our ongoing discussions on the joys and challenges of antioppression work. We have chosen the dialogue format to emphasize the importance of the relational as educators.

Emerging Questions

I'm not sure how to feel about this article. Confused. Annoyed. Confronted. What Now? So What? . . . How can I adjust myself and my attitude to understand this article? That is the hard part for me. I never want to be the kind of person that denies reality or even refuses to analyze what is going on. That is my goal for now.
—Angel, *responding to* White Privilege *(McIntosh, 1992)*

This vignette was written by a student who *appeared to* be engaged in classroom materials that challenge and confront the existence of institutionalized oppression. We emphasize "appeared" because it is with a limited perspective that her engagement is perceived. As teachers we can hope that students are actively involved in the readings, class dialogues, and experiences in and out of the classroom. However, this may be an idealized vision of multicultural education where students, as critical thinkers within a collaborative environment, become aware of the pervasiveness of oppression and actively pursue challenging the status quo.

Our position as teachers does not truly allow us to know any student's lived experiences, construction of personal identities, and acceptance or rejection of dominant ideology. There is a growing body of feminist and critical literature that is questioning and perhaps redefining praxis in multicultural education and emancipatory awareness (Ellsworth, 1989; Gore, 1990; McLaren, 1994; Orner, 1992). For example, issues concerning the teacher/student hierarchy of power and control may overshadow any real possibility of student "empowerment" and voice within a classroom setting. Teachers have assumptions regarding the best way to educate students toward multicultural dispositions and knowledge, yet even the most liberating classroom experience is oppressive if it is dictated. In our efforts to guide the students across the "multicultural terrain," how are we imposing or replicating the very power relations we are questioning?

Lather (1991) suggests that educators continue to problematize and advance emancipatory pedagogy. With this challenge more questions emerge related to the topic of student nonengagement with multicultural issues in education. The foremost question is, "What is student nonengagement?" In their introduction, Chávez Chávez and O'Donnell, suggest that nonengagement describes those students who reject or challenge the notion that there are systemic forms of oppression. With this description more questions emerge. Who is defining engagement and nonengagement? How do we recognize student engagement and nonengagement, or what are the markers of engagement? For example, a student who is Native American may be actively involved in his community, including tribal events, yet choose not to self-disclose about his life experiences, nor participate, in class. Is this student nonengaged? Is there ever a time nonengagement serves a vital function for a student? While we do not propose to answer all these questions, we pose them because within these questions and their possible answers lie our own biases and assumptions related to student engagement and nonengagement.

The Optimal Theory Applied to Identity Development Model

We have chosen to explore these questions using an identity development model that informs our practice as educators. It is from this framework that we attempt to understand student nonengagement and resistance to multicultural themes and issues. The Optimal Theory Applied to Identity Development (OTAID) model is grounded in the psychological literature of minority identity development and Afracentric psychology, and is an attempt to understand self-identity pluralistically (Myers, et al., 1991). We use the term *Afracentric* with intention. The African world view was based on a matriarchal culture, therefore the term *Afracentric* is more accurate than the generic masculine form *"Afrocentric."* Theoretically the OTAID model is considered multicultural because its tenets are found within Afracentric, Eastern, and Indigenous Peoples traditions. This model of personal development assumes a holistic view of life where self-worth is inherent in one's being, because each person is viewed as a unique manifestation of spiritual energy. Whereas, self-worth within the Eurocentric conceptual system is often measured by external criteria such as appearance, income, and education so that the individual is in a perpetual state of achieving. This extrinsic orientation prompts a need to "be better than" and contributes to the "isms" within society by developing and maintaining hierarchies (e.g., racism, sexism, classism, heterosexism; Myers et al., 1991).

The OTAID model describes the process by which a person dismantles this internalized hierarchical system that he or she has learned as a result of growing up in the United States. Thus this model, when applied to multicultural education, describes how a person moves from nonengagement to self-knowledge and self-discovery in the classroom. Next, we will describe the assumptions and stages of the model in order to inform the reader as to our references to OTAID in our dialogue.

OTAID Assumptions

The OTAID model describes a specific developmental process by which some people raised in the United States move from an identification with the dominant cultural values of material wealth, competition, individuality, and an external definition of self toward a greater identification with the Afracentric principles of communalism, holism, and self-knowledge as the basis of all knowledge. This model makes the assumption that our purpose as human beings is to gain self-knowledge, and from this, a greater sense of self-acceptance.

The identity development process is a dynamic process, and one's world view is modified due to time and various events, as we interact with our environment. Therefore our world view influences the way we view ourself, particularly how much of our identity is wrapped up in identifying with a particular group and focusing on the relations between various groups.

"World view" can be defined as how one perceives the world and interprets one's interactions with the environment. It is one's sense of truth or reality. It is the basis on which people make all their judgments and decisions. Ultimately it determines what is noticed and what a person is unable or refuses to see. Some things may be hard to see because when enough people share the same values and world view, we start using the words *truth* or *reality*.

Each stage or phase of the model describes a different world view. There is no given time frame for how long one stays in a stage. It is very possible for a person to perceive life from one stage for the majority of their lifetime. Whether or not a person makes much movement is influenced heavily by their interaction with their environment. Thus the classroom experience is one environmental influence that can be transformative.

OTAID Stages

When we are born, our world view is that all life is inherently good. This stage is called *Absence of Conscious Awareness* because there is no awareness that there is any other way to view one's experience. This stage is associated with infancy but, rather than the traditional view that the baby has no sense of self, it is instead perceived as having a sense of self that encompasses all that the child knows. There are no boundaries and all of life is connected. For example, a baby doesn't know where its arm ends and its mother begins. This world view fades as the child grows and there is a physical and cognitive understanding of the self as an individual. Self-identity is influenced by the family's world view.

Then in the next stage, *Individuation*, one begins to psychologically separate from the family world view, and incorporates the values of the community one has immediate access to and the cultural values presented in the media. At this point there is a belief that, "If I follow the rules, beliefs, and values of the dominant culture, I can be accepted as part of society." This is the endpoint in identity development for many people. Thus if some characteristic of a person (such as race) isn't valued by society, then the person isn't consciously aware of this, or denies this. A gender example might be that a teacher has lower expectations of a female student than of a male student due to the teacher's sexist beliefs. The female student is either unaware of, or denies, the preferential treatment, or she attributes the teacher's favoritism to some difference in the students' personalities (such as she isn't as funny or smart as the male student). A person at this stage would agree with the statement: "I have not been oppressed or discriminated against" (Sevig, 1993).

The next worldview shift into *Dissonance* happens when some act of discrimination occurs such that the person recognizes that she or he is not valued by society because of some external criterion such as ethnicity, age, class, or sexual orientation. The person recognizes that they don't fit into society to the degree they hoped. An example of this discrimination would be a African American student being mistaken for the janitor at the college when he is walking to class. Depending on a person's self-worth and support network they may respond with anger, depression, or shame. The more one internalizes the oppression, the more likely one will feel shame or depression, perhaps feeling that such treatment is inevitable.

If instead, one focuses on how unfair society is, then anger is the predominant emotion in the Dissonance stage. With anger there is generally faster movement into the next stage. An example of a statement at this stage is "I recently realized for the first time that I am a target of discrimination" (Sevig, 1993).

In *Immersion* the person rejects the dominant culture and begins to explore the culture of the group with which they currently identify. This is done in order to feel less isolation and to feel more positively about oneself. There is little interest or less emotional connection to those outside one's culture, often as a result of distrusting people outside one's group. Many special interest groups or civil rights organizations are filled with people at this stage. There may also be a judgment against members of one's own group who still adhere to the dominant cultural values (i.e., stay-at-home mothers, Latinos in the corporate world, gays who are in the closet). A sample statement at this stage is "I primarily focus my political awareness and activity on issues facing the Islamic community."

The next stage is *Internalization* where there is a sifting process so that self-knowledge of one's own unique value system is heightened. The oppressed part of self is seen as one of many components to self-identity, and valued for its place in the larger picture. As one becomes more accepting of many parts of self, and less influenced by others, the more similarities can be found with others outside one's own group. For example, after Malcolm X made his pilgrimage to Mecca he stated a recognition that people of all colors could live in harmony. There is less judging of others in one's own group and less distrust of the oppressor group. A person at this stage might use the following statement: "I recently realized I don't have to like every gay man just because I'm gay."

This broadened sense of community continues in the *Integration* stage. The person feels a sense of connection or understanding with not only those who are similarly oppressed, but also with those who may have very different experiences with oppression. This shift includes recognizing that there is no clearly identified oppressor and oppressed, as each of us fits into both categories. At this point all people are viewed as oppressed by the dominant cultural values of competition and external criteria of self-worth. While people who oppress others are viewed as attempting to gain more external power, they are not perceived as threatening to one's self-identity. There is a conscious recognition that power comes from true self-knowledge, and oppression is having been socialized into a world view that leads to a fragmented sense of self. The expansion of community creates a climate for greater integration of oneself. For example, a Jewish woman is able to see the common elements of oppression as she recognizes with equal clarity the sexist beliefs of her Jewish friends and racism and antisemitism in her white, Christian friends. In the process she comes to more fully understand how all of these issues impact her as a whole, and to some degree, everyone. A statement at this stage might be: "Personally knowing people in other oppressed groups, I see how much we have in common" (Sevig, 1993).

The last stage is *Transformation,*which is an emotional, cognitive, and behavioral manifestation of the Afracentric world view. The last of the hierarchical thinking is removed as there is no longer a distinction between human and nonhuman life (i.e., animals and the environment). Issues of the environment, peace, and human rights are all viewed as important. Self-identity expands so that self is no longer viewed as a member of just a group, but rather a part of the larger Earth community. Thus one's sense of self is a connection to all of life.

Here the model has come full circle, as a person in the first stage—*Absence of Conscious Awareness*—also viewed all of life as interconnected. At this point acts of oppression are viewed as an opportunity to learn, and oppressors are seen as disconnected and unaware of their inner power. All negativity is view as an opportunity to grow and understand oneself better.

This position, however, does not preclude feelings of anger or acts of confrontation. For example, a Latina woman has resolved her anger toward Anglos who are prejudiced by seeing them as lacking in self-acceptance and therefore doing the best they can given their level of insight and understanding. Yet within the classroom context she will determinedly challenge a teacher's stereotypic assumptions. At this stage a person might state: "Oppression exists because we aren't in touch with what connects us to each other" (Sevig, 1993).

Finally, an essential assumption of the OTAID model is valuing each person exactly where they are, yet realizing that the exploration and naming of one's world view causes it to continuously expand. The last stage merely closes the circle and the process begins again. Therefore, no one ever arrives, they just bring more of themselves through each time.

A Dialogue

In this section we share a reflective dialogue that describes our research, counseling and classroom experiences, and personal musings as related to the OTAID model.

B: Let's begin by talking about people who are taking a course in mul-
    ticultural education or counseling because it is required. They don't
    want to be there, and see no value in being there. According to the
    OTAID model they are in the Individuation stage and it is working
    for them. The students appear to be nonengaged in the course. This
    is reflected in journal writing, passive resistance to class discus-
    sions, or lack of interest in participating in activities.

E: In Individuation I am assuming that these students do not recog-
    nize themselves as being a member of an oppressed or oppressor
    group. They instead, very much believe in the cultural values of the
    dominant society. They are likely to experience anger at having to
    focus on oppression (a concept they don't even buy into) or,
    through more open-minded exploration, they might be willing to
    take a look at these issues as if it were an abstract concept such as
    learning about the law of gravity.

    In class, I facilitate discussion that allows students to talk
    about their experiences around oppression, although often they
    focus on generalities about other people and other groups. Their
    opinions are based primarily on information from the media and I
    need to keep bringing the discussion back to personal experiences
    with members of these groups, and their own experiences with
    prejudice or discrimination. I think, if nothing else, this focus
    makes the student aware that they have limited knowledge of dis-
    crimination and oppression. Hopefully this ignorance will prompt
    them to become more involved in the class. However, this engage-
    ment may either be cooperative or resistant depending on how
    threatening this exploration may be to their current world view.

    It is important to get them to be aware of their world view,
    because this is what gets the students focused on themselves,
    rather than general cultural issues. Often after presenting a
    description of Afracentric and Eurocentric world views I ask them
    to write an essay describing their values, beliefs, and assumptions
    using the different categories or variables such as communality
    versus individuality. This is a very difficult task, but it helps me un-
    derstand them, and it helps the students to realize their biases.
    Sometimes I have them write an autobiography. Later in the course
    I have them write a cultural autobiography so that they can see
    how cultural issues have shaped who they are.

B: Tatum (1992) suggests there are three sources of student resistance
    to discussing oppression. One, oppression is a taboo topic and is
    therefore not appropriate to discuss in class. Two, the United States
    is a just society where individual efforts are rewarded through up-
    ward mobility. And three, although oppression may still exist, the

students themselves are not to blame because they are not prejudiced.

Many students I work with have been trained in, or raised with, the human relations approach toward diversity where they believe that they are colorblind. Antioppression work seems irrelevant because they truly believe themselves capable of getting along with all people regardless of differences. These students feel more comfortable living without the knowledge of how issues such as class or race may affect a person's life.

E: These students don't feel they need a class that addresses cultural issues because they believe they already have the skills they need to work with diverse populations. They may perceive themselves as having good people skills, a strong knowledge base from which to teach, or well-trained in the "universal" learning or psychological theories they have been taught. And this can create a form of nonengagement when the students become educators. They want to treat all of their future students the same and ignore the differences. Yet they may need, for example, to make more efforts to engage the female students in their math classes when they are teachers. In order to do this, students have to be comfortable with and even value differences. This flies in the face of the "melting pot" ideology in which most of us have been raised.

B: So, a person in the Individuation state may be experiencing, perhaps for the first time, challenges to the dominant ideology. Yet a personal challenge for me is how can I support, rather than just understand, the transformative process for a member of dominant society. I struggle with defining my role in helping a white, Christian, heterosexual man become aware of the existence of oppression when they have not, at an awareness level, experienced oppression.

E: It's been my experience that this student could be challenged to recognize that as a male there are certain standards that he has to measure up to, to be a good male. And although he fits that criteria right now, he will constantly be measured by those standards. And eventually he will age and will have to deal with ageism, if nothing else.

B: But it is much more difficult for him to move beyond the Individuation stage because he is being rewarded by society for having met the criteria valued in our culture. It may take a lot of time and self-awareness for him to move toward an understanding of the pervasiveness of oppression.

E: I also think that his empathy for specific people in his life who are oppressed may help make oppression more real for him. This will

help the student make connections with how oppression affects
those he is close to—mother, girlfriend, grandfather.

B: I've also found that a good novel may help a student begin to do
some perspective taking. Julie, in her journal, reflected on institutionalized racism and classism in the book *I Know Why the Caged
Bird Sings* (Angelou, 1969) with this response:

> I always thought of racism or discrimination as being mean or some
> kind of cruel act. I know how I feel when I feel out of place or
> unwanted. I can't imagine facing this every day. These are some of the
> many things we take for granted or just never think of. I know I didn't.

E: Another strategy I've used to engage students is panel presentations. Facilitating direct experience with people—they become real
individuals, not some object that is discussed in a book. I also try
to engage the nonengaged student by having them become more
knowledgeable about a certain cultural group of their choosing for
a classroom presentation. The presentation also makes them own
their statements and forces them to be more thoughtful about what
they are saying.

B: Although some students in the Individuation stage may be behaviorally passive and uninvolved in the classroom community, I am
hopeful and tentatively confident that the introduction to multicultural issues will be just that—an introduction leading to further
exploration. This is possible, particularly when colleagues make
the issue of oppression and diversity an integral part of classroom
discourse, regardless of the course title.

E: I agree, we have to see the big picture. This is where the model is
helpful in providing more patience in recognizing that this may be a
long process for a person who is just initially becoming aware of
oppression issues. I become less frustrated when realizing that I
may be laying groundwork. So we may not see engagement in the
time we have with them and yet we have made them more open to
engaging in the topic later on. This approach does assume that
these issues will continue to be addressed in later courses.

B: I think it might be harder for the educator who is teaching the required Multicultural Class because this may be the first time that
many students are experiencing such challenges to their world view
and the teacher may have more nonengaged students in the Individuation stage; whereas, I mostly teach courses that sequentially follow the Multicultural course. Therefore I work with students who
have, at a minimum, a beginning awareness of these issues.

Interestingly, I've had students tell me that when they took
the Multicultural Class, they felt uncomfortable with the way in

which the professor approached the topics; one student used the term *in my face.* The power of the message can lead to blaming the messenger.

E: I really try to be cognizant of the environment in the classroom. I want students to leave my classroom willing to engage in this dialogue even if we don't agree. If I can foster a certain level of openness for further discussion, I feel successful. However, I also think that students leave more guarded regardless of how we teach because of their fear of the subject, or the shock of recognizing the enormity and pervasiveness of oppression. In this situation I turn the responsibility back on the student and ask, "What do you think would be a better way to get you to understand or learn about something that you've had so little exposure to either in your personal life or educational experiences?" It's a difficult task, especially when students have such different emotional reactions. I also like to ask whether their appraisal of the class has changed over time.

B: There are times that I feel disappointed and angry at a student who refuses to look at oppression, even at a personal perspective. Yet I hesitate to take on the role of the confronter toward the student because I don't want to alienate him or her. I fear I will lose him.

E: I agree, there needs to be the element of support. I had an experience this semester with a student who was of Mormon background and very much adhered to all the principles of the Mormon Church. When we addressed the issue of counseling lesbians and gays, she felt homosexuality was morally wrong and she could not counsel someone who did not want to change that "lifestyle." Which is fine. . . . That is her value system. As long as she is aware of that limitation and knows she should not engage in a therapeutic relationship with a gay person. But this student showed a greater intolerance and lack of knowledge about the gay community when compared to her growing awareness and knowledge level about other oppressed groups.

I confronted her on her nonengagement, which was allowing her to feel comfortable with this lack of knowledge about gay experiences (i.e., the issues facing a person in the "coming out" process). I did not state that she should accept homosexuality, but I was directly challenging that I felt she needed to become more educated about this population. I recommended that she do more reading and discussion in this area, particularly because she has such a strong and clearly defined value system. I supported her for her intelligence and thoughtfulness throughout the class, and basically affirmed that I would like to see that in all topics of the class.

While I don't believe I came across as angry, I did feel angry and disappointed that her beliefs in certain areas could be so inflexible.

B: I believe I have a tendency to focus less on the cognitive and more on the feelings of the students. I don't think I do enough challenging of someone in the Individuation stage. I think I do a lot of supporting so that they feel safe in the process of change. A safe environment facilitates risk-taking behavior where students will try to grapple openly with hard issues. But the work of Keeley, Shemberg, Cowell, and Zinnbauer (1995) has also helped me learn to confront resistance because, regardless of my preparing a safe environment, resistance does have its place in the classroom. My role is to avoid personalizing student resistance and adopt a problem-solving attitude: How can I understand this resistance and move toward learning? I need to invite the class to explore and generate reasons for student nonengagement.

E: I feel a particular need to be confrontative with people who are claiming that they are the victims of "reverse discrimination" or "reverse racism." This is a complicated concept because these students perceive themselves to be in Dissonance (feeling discriminated against), yet they believe in the mainstream cultural values and still feel they can be a part of the larger society (Individuation). If they don't feel they are valued it is because a minority of people, such as "liberals" or special interest groups, are making life more intolerable for them right now. I think they are using the words *oppression* or *discrimination* in place of something that may be more accurately defined as suffering or inconvenience. And that's why it is important for me to have a discussion in class on the difference between oppression and suffering. I like to use Marilyn Frye's (1983) article on oppression, which makes a clear distinction between the two terms.

B: When a student talks about "white" oppression I have to work hard not to be judgmental of this person's reality. For example, a student who had not received a graduate assistantship told the class that she had been discriminated against because she was not a person of color. Yes, whites can suffer and be terribly inconvenienced, but there are not systematic barriers placed around them and they have bought into, and been rewarded by, the cultural values of mainstream U.S. culture. And that is very different from someone who, even if they play by all the rules, will always be outside that system and will always have to be dealing with systemic barriers such as discrimination in hiring or not having proper representation in the government. I truly believe there is no such thing as reverse racism, even if an Anglo is not treated fairly by a member of a minority group.

E: I'd like to talk about the person who truly is in dissonance. This is someone who feels very marginalized by the system, and that gets played out in the classroom very frequently. When a person is in the Dissonance stage I have seen two different types of reactions. For some students, they are doing a lot of inner work and, hopefully, we can see them engaged through a journal. I think we might have no idea about the level of engagement of some students in the Dissonance stage without a method to privately share feelings.

B: This is particularly true for a person who internally processes the material. These students may be strongly relating to the course because they recognize themselves as victims of oppression. It can be very painful and we may see nonengagement behaviorally in the class discussions or activities.

E: Yet for other students who are more externally focused, they may feel angry at society. These students can be quite engaged with the material, yet often their focus is on all the suffering due to oppression. So, what I try to respond with is a look at the contributions of that cultural group. I try to find a balance between images of strength, as well as limitations, due to the oppressive state.

For example, when we deal with the oppression of women, I show a short video called *One Fine Day* (Weaver, 1984), which is a series of photographs of women in the United States from the 1700s to the present. Most people respond feeling sad and angry that they knew so few of the women in the video, which tells how little they learned about women's history. At the same time they feel a great deal of pride in women's accomplishments and lives. This sort of activity helps to engage the person who is nonengaged because active involvement in exploring only oppression is too painful.

That's why it's important for me to be aware that students' perceptions of the classroom environment can differ greatly from mine. I'm at a place where my recognition of some new element of oppression is not surprising or scary to examine. But for some students such an act of recognition carries tremendous loss. For example, one of my students stated in her journal:

> I am aware of the fact that women are discriminated against and I feel angry about that, however, I'm still willing to play the role of the quiet, submissive, dutiful and cooperative female because I don't want to make waves and I don't want to make men feel threatened.... I'm afraid that if I stand up for my rights as a woman then I'll be labelled a bitch or a radical feminist.

I think that the fear isn't so much about labels, but what interpersonal ramifications there are in confronting the system. Old friends may reject them. They don't identify or really know people who are comfortable with those labels. In addition, I try to help them see that even having seen oppression, you can't make it go away. This is why the level of awareness that is required for a course addressing multiculturalism is so threatening. I often have a hard time letting go of the students who are in Dissonance, because when the class is over they may have no other place to work through all these feelings. The outside world does not encourage people to examine oppressive experiences and the effects oppression has on one's psyche.

B: The barriers to moving through Dissonance can be just as great inside the classroom as outside. Students may not feel ready to share their beginning awareness of their own oppression with the class community, because it is too risky. This is particularly true for a student who fears any type of self-disclosure as a member of an oppressed group. An illustration of this point occurred in class when we were reading Valerie Polakow's (1992) critical work on motherhood, poverty, and "children at risk." A divorced mother with three young children had been silent through the entire semester, until a class member said that no one should ever have to seek public assistance because there are so many jobs available. This student, ever so quietly, began to tell her personal story of a secure, middle-class lifestyle, then divorce and resulting poverty. She discussed her shame around accepting public assistance in housing and food and her discouragement in finding a job that paid enough so she could afford child care. By the end of the story this woman was crying and yelling at her classmate's ignorance to the fact that many women are a divorce away from poverty. This was real risk taking on the part of this woman.

E: This fear of self-disclosure doesn't just occur for members of oppressed groups. Although students are encouraged to be aware of their prejudices, very few are willing to disclose their biases in front of their peers. I did a fishbowl exercise where I had Anglo students who had lived in the Southwest discuss their perceptions of Hispanics (as the Hispanic students sat around them). Many observations were made, but much was left unsaid. One student who hadn't said much, started her next journal entry with, "Okay, I admit it, I'm prejudiced against Hispanics." She wasn't apologetic, she was just stating a fact. Two weeks later she shared how she had worked through some of her prejudices, and had gone out on a date with a Hispanic friend. However, I don't think it was the classroom experiences that changed her perceptions. She had told her brother about the class discussions and he challenged her stereotypes. I don't think she would have heard this challenge by a classmate or myself.

B: I want the students to know that I care about them and appreciate their reactions to class materials, including rejection and hostility. I recognize that hostility is a form of student engagement and an honest part of student involvement with uncomfortable topics. Unfortunately, I occasionally have difficulty finding a balance in the classroom so that students who are uncomfortable with anger can also feel a part of the dialogue. This is particularly problematic with the nonengaged students because I wonder if one reason they are nonengaged is because of peer hostility.

One suggestion I want to try comes from the work of Davis (1992). She uses anonymous essay writing with her students. They write whatever they cannot say easily in class, and with student permission these essays are shared in class. Personalized accounts of victimization such as sexual assault or gay bashing can release some anger for the student author and gives these students a sense of naming their own experiences while educating others.

E: I see a lot of hostility with students in the Immersion stage, where they are highly engaged in the classroom—maybe even "turning off" other students because they are confrontive. They can easily see oppression and can even recognize how it plays out in the classroom context. As a teacher, I need to decide how I want to clarify what they are saying so other class participants can hear them, which could be seen as oppressive on my part.

On the other side is someone in the Immersion stage who is so immersed in their own cultural group that they are nonengaged in the classroom because the class is such a part of the dominant culture and mainstream values. They are not going to waste their time and energy trying to educate a bunch of people who don't want to be educated anyway and are members of the oppressor group. So, they might be silent in class. And they often do not perceive the teacher as an ally in antioppression work.

B: I can fully appreciate this stance. An analogy might be my role as a faculty member where during some committee work I perceive the agenda as antithetical to my value system. Usually I speak up and express my feelings, but occasionally I just get tired of fighting the accepted ideology and instead nonengage. I find it helpful to do perspective taking, such as this discussion, to better relate my life in academia with the students' lives.

E: Another way I've seen nonengagement in students who are in Immersion is that they are nonengaged when the focus is on other cultural groups' experiences, and they are only engaged when it comes to their own cultural group.

B: It is at these opportunities that I attempt to make conceptual linkages between a person's experience with oppression and other groups' experiences. Together we explore parallel oppressions and the connections between all the "isms."

E: This ability to see the similarities within different forms of oppression becomes more developed in the Internalization stage. At the Internalization stage, where a student is not so identified with one group, you just don't tend to see nonengagement. These are people who are really exploring their own identity and the class is often a perfect fit for them. Where I do see some resistance at this stage is when students engage in rank ordering regarding which group has experienced worse, greater, or more pervasive oppression than other groups. As they move into Integration they become even more interested in learning more about other groups, as well as the multiplicity of their own self-identity. Alex's last journal entry is a good example of this:

> I would like to thank you for the opportunity to learn more about myself. My Latino self. My male self. My queer self. My feminine self. My Anglicized self. My oppressed self. My biased self. My Belizean self. My spiritual self. My single self. My youthful self. This journal provided such an opportunity. Thanks for letting me introspect. And for allowing me to peek into the world views of others that are culturally diverse.

B: As we talk about these different world views, I recognize that it is easier and more enjoyable for me to work with the students who self-identify with an oppressed group because they are more able to grasp the concepts of oppression.

E: I definitely enjoy having the students who are at Internalization, or even Integration, where they really start seeing the connections between all types of oppression. I don't know that I've met anyone in the Transformation stage. But I wouldn't want a class full of just those students at these latter stages.

As an instructor I am guided by the Afracentric belief that the basis of all knowledge is self-knowledge, so my goal is to develop students who recognize their lack of knowledge, and feel motivated to learn more about the group and individual experiences of the diverse people with whom they work. Ultimately, I hope they ask many questions of their own students and colleagues, rather than judging or analyzing others whom they barely know. I believe the best teachers and therapists are those who ask thought-provoking questions.

Ending Reflections

We have discussed how the OTAID model helps us to understand the function of student nonengagement in the classroom, and to inform our practice. Our approach provides an integration between literature on the engagement of resistant learners and theories of identity development. Thus we ask the question, "What helps facilitate engagement for a given student at a given developmental stage?" Our integration of these two areas have yielded the following guidelines.

1. Recognize the seduction toward labeling a student as "engaged" when the student's behavior is compatible with your own world view, and "nonengaged" or "resistant" when the student's world view is in conflict with your own (Lindquist, 1994).

2. Establish a classroom of inclusion, support, and safety (Keeley et al., 1995; Tatum, 1992; Wlodkowski & Ginsberg, 1995).

3. Focus on self-generated knowledge (Adams, 1991; Tatum, 1992).

4. Identify the types of student nonengagement and explain the developmental process people often go through when examining issues of oppression so students know what to expect (Tatum, 1992).

5. Speak to the resistance when it occurs by asking students to explain their own attitudes and behaviors in the classroom (Keeley et al., 1995).

6. Recognize that student resistance toward critically analyzing society may be a function of students' learned passivity in educational settings in general.

7. Examine how you collude with student resistance as a result of your own socialization or the identity stage you are at. Have you been socialized to avoid conflict? Are you looking for resistance because you are in the Immersion stage?

8. Listen for students' antioppression attitudes and then make those beliefs and actions the social norms of your classroom. Do not let the search for student resistance blind you to each student's already developing capacity for change (Lindquist, 1994).

9. Be aware of power relationships in the classroom and consciously use strategies that support student empowerment (Ahlquist, 1991; Lather, 1991).

10. Facilitate students' antioppression work outside the classroom, as well as inside (Davis, 1992; Tatum, 1992).

It is through an Afracentric world view that we perceive our responsibility as multicultural educators to demonstrate to the students that they are more important than the material we are teaching. By applying this framework we can encourage the development of the students' emotional skills, promote community and diversity within the classroom

context, and support and value the process of self-knowledge and communal responsibility to the larger pluralistic community (Adams, 1991).
Thus, when viewed through Afracentric lens, even the most unpleasant
or uncomfortable parts of the multicultural education terrain become
an essential part of the transformative process for both students and
teachers.

15

Diane J. Goodman

Lowering the Shields

Reducing Defensiveness in
Multicultural Education

R ecently I co-taught a graduate class on educational and cultural diversity for preservice teachers that covered issues of race, sex, and disability. We began with an overview of multicultural education and racism and racial issues. One of the first assignments was an informal reaction paper to the readings on different racial groups in a mainstream multicultural education textbook and an article on white privilege (McIntosh, 1988). Jack, a white male student in his late twenties, struggling to work and go to school, handed in a paper vehemently critical of the book and the article. He said he felt the book was white- and male-bashing. He claimed he never received any privileges as a white male and worked hard for everything he ever got. He completely denied any notion of institutionalized or systematic disadvantage for people of color, attributing achievement to personal effort.

I first wondered if we were reading the same textbook. I puzzled at how he could have found the book so offensive, when I considered it so benign, and insufficiently political. I was also disturbed at his lack of thought, reflection, or understanding of the material. I saw no meaningful consideration of the content, even if he did not agree with the perspective taken.

A few weeks later, when we discussed sexism and gender equity, Jack was quite interested and supportive. He could relate to the limitations of gender roles for males and females and agreed that gender inequality existed in schools and society. After class he told me that it would have been better to have begun with gender issues and sexism because the race material made him too defensive. While he still felt the book was biased against whites, he could also acknowledge that he might have overreacted to the material since he felt attacked as a white male. He had a point.

Jack's comments revealed several important issues for teaching about multicultural issues. When I immediately began with material that felt too threatening and challenging to his current world view and self-perception, Jack quickly became defensive, which prevented constructive engagement. It was after discussing gender equity, material that was more consistent with his beliefs and sense of himself, that he felt more ready to look at issues of race and racism. Not only did he not feel attacked, but it reinforced and broadened what he already accepted and experienced. His views were affirmed and then deepened. Once he could experience this kind of connection, he could then consider topics that were more challenging or dissonant in a more open way.

Jack's response also demonstrated that the nonengagement we experienced often occurs when students feel their needs and concerns are ignored in favor of someone else's. Until they have their experiences and feelings acknowledged and taken seriously, students are more likely to compete for attention and resist exploring issues about others that they see as unrelated to themselves. The class discussion of gender inequities and sexism began with attention to the negative effects for both males and females, and students were encouraged to share their own experiences, which Jack did. Ultimately, the particular barriers that girls and women face were explored.

Understanding Students' Defensiveness

My experience with Jack reminded me that we need to begin where students are ready to begin, and often this means dealing with the feelings and defensiveness that result in their nonengagement, the unwillingness to acknowledge or confront structural and systemic inequalities. While nonengagement has many sources and expressions (Roman, 1993; Sleeter, 1992; Tatum, 1992), I will focus on this one aspect, defensiveness, and discuss ways to reduce the defensiveness of students when learning about multicultural and social justice issues. First, I will address how to initially engage students, creating a context that allows them to be more open to the class material and experience. Then I will suggest how, by re-framing the way students conceptualize social change, we might de-crease their defensiveness and enhance their commitment to equity.

When I refer to defensiveness, I am referring to an emotional reac-tion, not a reasoned intellectual response. People become defensive when they feel threatened or fearful. When people feel defensive they don't learn. They shut down, turn off, and resist new information or ways of viewing the world. When they feel attacked and blamed they are likely to try to defend their position rather than question it. My goal as a teacher is not to have everyone think as I do, but to help them engage with the material in a critical and self-reflective way, allowing them to develop a more informed and thoughtful understanding of themselves and their world.

Moreover, when a student is nonengaged, we tend to locate "the problem" solely within the psyche or brain of the student. Yet, I think it is also useful to look at the teacher-student relationship and at ourselves as teachers. We need to consider, as well, what is happening between the teacher and the student that is either facilitating or impeding the stu-dent's openness.

Social-Political Context

I doubt that anyone who deals with multicultural issues will find Jack's responses unique. Since beginning to do social justice education in 1984, I have encountered similar reactions among the undergraduate and graduate students I have taught, and from the staffs and administra-tors I have done training with in university and workplace settings. However, I do feel that the defensiveness and nonengagement has in-creased and intensified in recent years.

The Reagan years began a conservative trend that has been hostile to social justice efforts and has sought to dismantle existing programs and laws that attempt to address inequalities and discrimination. As the popularity of multiculturalism has grown, so has the corresponding backlash. Criticism and ridicule of such efforts is widespread, particu-larly judging by the proliferation of conservative talk show hosts who use it as fodder. It is now socially sanctioned to devalue and dismiss mul-ticultural education as "political correctness" and to be openly hostile to social justice agendas. It is out of this social and political climate that most of our students come.

The popular presses have made much of late of the "angry white male." Recent elections of conservative politicians and attacks on affirmative action provide evidence of this trend. Cose (1995) found that men are feeling increasingly uncared about and victimized. They feel that equality has essentially been achieved and that the playing field has been sufficiently leveled. They believe that white women and people of color are now getting special benefits, at the expense of white men. In response to these perceptions, they feel angry, frustrated, resentful, confused, and afraid, and tired of feeling blamed and guilty.

These sentiments and perspectives have been echoed by many students in my classes, not solely by white men. As people see shrinking opportunities, a contracting economy, and cuts in aid and services, they are less willing to accept efforts that they perceive benefit others or to have sympathy for the plight of oppressed groups. Even if they do recognize inequalities, it is more difficult to imagine or support remedies that will not impact on their privileges. These real and imagined social realities shape how students enter our classrooms.

Psychological and Educational Perspectives

Effective multicultural education needs to deal with the emotional and psychological, as well as intellectual dimensions of learning and change (Fried, 1993; King, 1991; Lewis, 1990; Romney, et al. 1992; Tatum, 1992). Nonengagement is evidence that it is not simply a cognitive process. We provide enlightening facts and theories, yet students still are unmoved and uninvolved. As Britzman and colleagues (1993) so aptly point out:

> The commitment to rationality—and to rational persuasion—is antithetical to teaching multiculture. It actively erases the complex, contested, and emotionally charged investments students and teachers confront when their subject positions are called into question. (p. 196)

Critical, transformative multicultural education threatens students' self-concepts and identities, ideologies and world views. When we talk about power and privilege, and systematic and structural changes, there are good reasons why people, especially from advantaged groups, would resist these changes and become defensive. Social change threatens the privileges (often invisible) that have been taken for granted and changes the rules of the game. It raises the fear of the unknown and the concern for one's well being.

Robert Kegan (1982), in his theory of human development and the changing ways people make meaning of themselves, others, and the world, helps shed light on Jack's and other similar reactions. He maintains that growth unfolds through alternating periods of dynamic stability, instability, and temporary rebalance. Individuals need a sense of "confirmation," an environment of support, before moving on to situations of "contradiction," conditions that challenge current meaning-making systems. They then need context for "continuity," which allows for the transformation and reequilibration.

This framework is applicable and instructive for dealing with the defensiveness of nonengaged students. Students enter our classes with a whole range of feelings, attitudes, and beliefs. From those students whose perspectives are similar to those being discussed and advocated in the class, or from those who are already predisposed to positively engage with the material, we tend to encounter little resistance. For them, there more readily exists a context of support or confirmation, and they are able to engage with the challenges or contradictions the class presents.

However, for students who are entering with the fear, anger, frustration, resentment, and pain alluded to earlier, we are likely to confront nonengagement. This is exacerbated by students' expectations that teachers will be spouting "p.c." rhetoric and requiring the "party line" in order to do well in the class. If they do not feel their feelings, views, and experiences are welcome or validated, the context for growth is diminished. Without some sense of confirmation, before posing the challenge or contradiction, these students are likely to maintain or increase their defensiveness.

This notion and importance of confirmation is echoed by other psychological and educational theorists. In counseling and family therapy, psychologists refer to this as "joining." The therapist must be able to form a partnership with the client or family, creating a bond of trust and common purpose.

> Joining a family is more an attitude than a technique and it is the umbrella under which all therapeutic transactions occur. Joining is letting the family know that the therapist understands them and is working with and for them. Only under his [sic] protection can the family have the security to explore alternatives, try the unusual, and change (Minuchen & Fishman, 1981).

As this brief quote highlights, it is the stance and expression of acceptance that is central, not the particular behaviors or techniques an individual teacher uses. Furthermore, as Kegan (1982) suggests, this context of safety and support can allow students to entertain and explore alternative ways of being and thinking. It supports a critical and liberatory educational process.

According to Rogers (1980), acceptance (or unconditional positive regard) along with genuineness and empathic understanding are critical conditions of any growth promoting relationship, including those in the classroom. The need for the students to experience being heard, understood, and cared about is paramount. Students must initially feel accepted for who and where they are.

I have also found that the greater the rapport and trust established with a student, the easier it is to address nonengagement. When I am in touch with my caring for the student, and I know that the student believes that I care and have her/his interests at heart, it provides a greater range of educational options. I feel freer to use (appropriate) humor and physical contact and to be more direct. I can more easily trust that the student will take my actions as intended and will in turn be more responsive.

Addressing Defensiveness in the Classroom

Safety and acceptance needs to come from not only the teacher but also from the larger classroom community. Class ground rules are a central part of developing this confirming climate. While these guidelines can be suggested by the teacher (Tatum, 1992; Disch & Thompson, 1990; Cannon, 1990), I prefer to let the class develop them. Given the content and structure of the class, I ask students to identify the things that would make this a safe and productive educational environment for them. Invariably students include items such as really listening, respect, being nonjudgmental, no put-downs, and confidentiality. I will make suggestions to the list, as necessary and agreed to by the students, often including the importance of speaking from one's own experience. Trust is built in the process of constructing the list, and students subsequently feel greater ownership and investment in the rules they have created.

Personal Stories and Feelings

The opportunity for students to voice their feelings, experiences, and viewpoints and have them acknowledged is central to the process of confirmation and to the practice of feminist and critical pedagogy (Freire, 1970; Giroux & McLaren, 1986; Weiler, 1988). It validates their concerns and communicates that divergent perspectives are welcome in the class. Not only does this help students feel heard and respected but it provides teachers with information about the needs and concerns of students, which can inform the class content and process. In addition, it allows students to hear themselves, helping them to sort out and work through some of their experiences and reactions, and provides a point from which to compare their views later in the course. (See Tatum, 1992, for a good illustration of using student self-interviews at the beginning and end of the course.)

Another reason students need the opportunity to voice their feelings and concerns in a confirming environment is that when people are focused on their own pain and needs, they are frequently unable to attend to or care about the misfortune of others. Preoccupation with self and self-concern can reduce one's attention to or caring about others (Staub, 1978). Dealing with one's own pain and experience of discrimination and prejudice is often a prerequisite for engaging in the exploration of the mistreatment and oppression of other people. Therefore, students may need to have the opportunity to explore some of their own feelings about their experiences before moving on to consider the feelings of others.

People from one oppressed group often need to express and have their experiences with oppression validated before they can allow other oppressed groups to be the focus of discussion. If not, they may feel that the others' oppression is seen as more important than their oppression. For example, Jews can be reluctant to fully engage in a discussion of racism if they feel their experiences with anti-Semitism have not been recognized as another legitimate form of oppression. Similarly, men of color may resist discussions of sexism, and owning their own involvement in it, until they feel racism, especially as targeted at men, has been adequately acknowledged.

In talking about experiences, people from privileged groups may need to have recognized the ways in which their lives have not been full of benefits and the ways they have suffered at the hands of social inequity. Few people from dominant groups feel powerful or greatly advantaged. Even though they are the so-called benefactors of oppression, they may feel victimized as well, as discussed earlier. They often have personal stories about how they were discriminated against, excluded, or stereotyped. They often feel angry and hurt by those experiences. White students have recalled how they were snubbed by people of color and assumed to be racist. Some students recount aspects of their socialization that have had negative or painful consequences. People from wealthy families have discussed how they have felt isolated from other people and received material goods in place of love and family connection. Men talk about how they were taught to hide and ignore their feelings and pretend to be someone they weren't.

Students from dominant groups may also perceive that it is they who are really at a disadvantage in many cases. Some white students may feel that is it unfair that people of color get special financial support or programs. White men may feel that they are unfairly losing jobs to white women and people of color due to affirmative action and that they are cast as the scapegoats in society and blamed for all social ills.

Regardless of the accuracy of their beliefs, their emotions and experiences are real. These affect their openness and ability to participate in a self-reflective and critical educational process. While it is important to acknowledge different experiences and perspectives, this does not mean they need to be accepted as reality. Students as well as teachers need to develop the skills to actively listen and the capacity for intersubjectivity, without having to accept all views as equally legitimate. Listening empathically and understanding does not necessarily mean agreement.

Sharing Experiences Appropriately

As teachers we need to make careful choices about the best way to allow students from dominant groups to give voice to their feelings of pain and mistreatment, without alienating other students or derailing the class. There have been a variety of ways I have attempted to allow students to express their experiences and perspectives. These choices depend on the dynamics and makeup of the class, time available, personalities of the students, and my state of being, among other factors. Students should be reminded of the class ground rules as necessary.

Time can be created in the class for people to share their feelings and experiences as part of the regular whole class discussion. Another option is to have paired or small-group discussions. In homogeneous groups, students initially could talk with others who share their background. Or, students could participate in self-selected heterogeneous groups of people with whom they have a personal relationship. In these contexts, students could have greater time and freedom to discuss their experiences with people likely to be supportive. Subsequently, there could be a more limited sharing with the whole class.

Students can also do free writing during class, in response to the readings, discussion topics or focus question, which could then in part be shared with the whole class. Journal writing is another effective way for students to express and reflect on their own experiences, without the concern for other students' reactions and judgments. Teacher responses (not evaluation) to their journal entries, enable teachers to recognize the student's feelings and can allow a dialogue between student and teacher. Students who require more attention than is available or warranted in the whole class or in these assignments, can be invited to speak with the teacher after class or during office hours.

While it can be one of the more challenging tasks to listen to people from privileged groups talk about their concerns and mistreatment, especially when it may seem relatively insignificant or distorted, I have seen important growth and openness occur as a result, for the students themselves, and often for their classmates and myself. Even students from marginalized groups have reported that hearing experiences and feelings have helped them to humanize and better understand people from privileged groups. We can also help all students make links between their feelings and experiences and those of other people, promoting empathy and a broader understanding of the dynamics of oppression.

Offering Challenge and Contradiction

The follow-up to confirmation or joining is challenge or contradiction. The intent is not to allow students to remain in their often limited world view but to help them construct new and more complex understandings of themselves and society. Once they feel a sense of confirmation, challenges to their current world view and self-constructions are more likely to be received.

> Teachers ultimately need to help students understand and make sense of their experiences in a larger social, political, historical context. While acknowledging the validity of the student's emotional reaction, the professor can help the student understand the cognitions that shape it. Invisible constructs become visible. . . . The teacher points out the effect of a student's frame of reference on his or her understanding of information and ultimately the role that culture plays in shaping everyone's frame of reference. (Fried, 1993, pp. 125–26)

Students also need sufficient accurate information to correct misperceptions and faulty assumptions, and fill in gaps in knowledge. They need a basis from which to question the myth of meritocracy and recognize that the playing field is still unequally sloped and rocky.

People from dominant groups might use their own personal experiences to generalize or incorrectly assume that there is pervasive discrimination of people from their group, while minimizing the discrimination faced by people from oppressed groups. They more commonly have the tendency to want to see everything on an individual basis and to ignore the treatment of groups of people and institutionalized practices. It is necessary to help students make the distinction between behavior directed at an individual in a specific situation and actions taken systematically against groups of people over time.

Students need to understand the differences in access to social power, as well as the degrees and extent to which people may face discrimination or unfair treatment. In systems of oppression, the dominant groups still have greater opportunities, choices, access to resources, and ability to define normalcy than the dominated groups. They are not faced with the systematic limitations and diminishment of their power, dignity, self-esteem, safety, and opportunities for advancement. A range of information, including statistics, historical perspective, and data about institutional and cultural oppression, can help students broaden their understanding of their own and others' experiences and gain a clearer picture of social reality.

The purpose of sharing this information is not to negate or discount students' feelings or experiences but to help them examine and reflect on them in more critical and informed ways. Returning to the earlier example, some white males might express their anger at "reverse discrimination" and their fear of not being able to find reasonable employment. We can recognize, in a genuine and empathic way, the feelings they have about apparent unfairness, and their insecurity and fear about the future. Once this has occurred, we can then correct inaccuracies in their understanding of affirmative action and the awarding of jobs.

A definition and some background on the development of affirmative action probably would be useful, as well as a discussion of how the economy has changed and contracted. For example, it could be explained that affirmative action began when the government acknowledged that there was systematic and pervasive discrimination against people of color (especially African Americans) in hiring and promotion that could not be remedied by leaving it up to the employers. According to the law, anyone benefiting from affirmative action must have relevant and valid job or educational qualifications, thus the intent is not to hire unqualified people simply because of their race or sex. Facts and research about current sex and race discrimination in the workplace could be provided that might challenge their assumptions that women and people of color have "made it" and that white men are now the ones being discriminated against. Instead of blaming white women and people of color, students can be encouraged to think about the larger economic system and direct their attention to why various groups need to be competing against each other for jobs in the first place. The point is not to convince students to adopt a particular point of view or political position, but to engage them; to have them meaningfully and critically consider and grapple with social justice issues.

Feelings arise from how people perceive situations and make sense of what they experience; new information and interpretations can lead to a change in perspective. If white students perceive African American students' desire for a black-only meeting or political event as a rejection of them personally or hatred of white people, they are likely to have different reactions than if they see it as a need for African Americans to affirm their own culture and connections, and share experiences without the influence of white people or racism.

Identifying the Benefits of Eliminating Oppression

In my experience, helping students to reconceptualize social change can reduce the defensiveness that often occurs when challenges to the status quo are proposed. Students are likely to resist perspectives or strategies that they deem detrimental to their current status or well being. While people from marginalized groups tend to be more able to see how changing the status quo can be positive for them, often people from dominant groups see efforts at progressive social change as a win-lose situation (in which they will lose). From this vantage point, it is not surprising that we encounter defensivenss to multicultural issues.

One approach is to help reframe the discussion from a win-lose model to a view that everyone could benefit from the elimination of oppression. As students from advantaged groups see how they have been limited by oppression and why it is in their self-interest to foster social change, it can help reduce defensiveness and increase their investment in social justice. Students have shared a range of stories that reflect their understanding of some of the costs of oppression. White students have told of being ostracized from their families for dating a person of a different race, and their fear of engaging with people of different races or cultures. Heterosexuals have acknowledged how their homophobia has led to the loss of friendships and family relationships with gays and lesbians. Men have expressed feeling pressure to assume certain "masculine" roles and behaviors that do not accurately reflect who they are and limit who they can be. People from wealthy families have told of feeling isolated, deprived of love and emotional connection, and the inability to relate to those from other class backgrounds. Many students can see that the social decay is directly related to unfair social and economic systems. This is not to pretend that there are not real advantages to their privileged status. Nonetheless, we can help students from dominant groups understand what they have to gain, not just what they have to lose, by creating greater social equity.

There is a complex interrelationship between the oppressor and the oppressed (Freire, 1970; Memmi, 1965; Miller, 1976). Living in a society where there are systematic, institutionalized inequalities affects everyone, whether in the advantaged or disadvantaged roles. These conditions have profound personal psychological, spiritual, and social ramifications. They affect and limit how we think about ourselves and others, how and with whom we interact and the opportunities and choices we have about how to lead our lives. While oppression provides benefits for those in dominant groups, for all of us in some ways, there are negative consequences.

The Negative Effects of Oppression
for People from Privileged Groups

The costs and limitations of oppression to those in privileged groups have been discussed in general (Freire, 1970) and in relation to specific oppressions: classism (Mogul & Slepian, 1992); heterosexism (Blumenfeld, 1992); sexism (Kivel, 1992; Thompson, 1988); and racism (Bowser & Hunt, 1981; Terry, 1981). Even though each form of oppression has its own particular effects on those in the dominant group, numerous similarities can be found across these experiences.

Drawing on the works by the authors cited above, in addition to my own experiences working with individuals on these issues, I will briefly discuss some of these common and interrelated themes on how people from privileged groups are negatively impacted by oppression. Some of these themes are very personal in nature and focus more on the individual and her/his interpersonal relationships. Others look at the societal ramifications, which impact the individual as a member of society. Many of these factors also impact people in dominated groups, though the focus here will be on people from privileged groups.

One negative effect of oppression on people from dominant groups is the loss of knowing one's real self and potential. Limitations on intellectual, moral, and emotional growth are one aspect of this loss. People are socialized into roles, with corresponding expectations of how to be and behave. Even accomplishments may be doubted as people wonder if they were attained fairly or because of a favored status (McIntosh, 1985). Some may develop a distorted sense of superiority to justify their advancements or advantages. In order to deal with apparent social inequities and to assume one's place as a dominant group member, people may also need to deny their own emotional capacities and feelings of empathy and mutuality.

A second effect is moral ambivalence, guilt, and shame. Many people prefer to see themselves as decent, caring people and hold principles of fairness and justice. However, they live in a society where there are pervasive inequities, reflected in homelessness, poverty, violence, and job discrimination, to name a few. Many people need to grapple with the discrepancy between the reality in which they live and their moral/spiritual beliefs. They need to reconcile the fact that some people have so much, while others have so little. They may feel embarrassed or guilty for having more than others and for not doing more to change inhumane or unjust conditions.

A third consequence of social inequality for people from privileged groups is fear. People express many types of fears including doing or saying the wrong thing and being offensive or seen as oppressive; of revealing aspects of themselves for fear of judgment; and of retaliation from oppressed groups if social power relations change. In particular, people report a variety of fears of different people and experiences, resulting in a more narrow existence.

This, in part, accounts for another negative effect of oppression for people in privileged groups, the loss and diminishment of relationships. As the above examples suggest, due to fears, avoidance of different people, lack of self-knowledge and expression, and limited experiences and knowledge of others, human connection and intimacy are lessened while isolation is increased. Due to social segregation, there are relatively few opportunities for positive interaction and many barriers to deeper and more authentic relationships across groups. Prejudices and assumptions work in both directions. People from dominant groups often complain that they are not seen for who they feel they really are but viewed by people from marginalized groups through a distorted, stereotypic lens.

Due to the lack of relationships and absence of sufficient information, people from dominant groups are often ignorant of or misinformed about much of the human race, and the cultures, contributions, and achievements of many other kinds of people. This results in a distorted view of reality and reinforces the sense of superiority. It further diminishes people's ability to consider more productive and effective ways to structure social systems, live their lives, and understand the lives of others.

Oppression and inequality also breed social unrest. As violence increases, the world is less safe for everyone. There is restricted ability to move about freely and fewer desirable places to live, work, go to school, and recreate. People have increased fears about their safety and that of their family and loved ones.

Keeping an unjust system in place is also expensive. A significant amount of taxes and economic resources go to supporting law enforcement, the judicial and penal systems, and providing social support services, among many others. Good and reasonably safe housing and schooling become increasingly expensive. Economic and human resources are directed at addressing the effects of social inequalities.

Lastly, there is the loss of knowledge to foster social progress and well being. When groups of people are disenfranchised, given limited opportunities, or have their cultures ignored or obliterated, the society as a whole loses. We lose the potential for new ways to think about old and new concerns and the contributions to the arts and sciences that enrich and advance our country and the world.

Each of these costs also has corresponding benefits that would accrue to people from privileged groups if social inequality were eliminated. These include a fuller, more authentic sense of self; more meaningful relationships and human connections; greater moral consistency and integrity; freedom from many fears; improved work and living conditions; access to other cultures and wisdom; more resources to address common concerns; and greater opportunity for real democracy and justice.

Most broadly, oppression undermines our humanity and authenticity. According to Paulo Freire (1970), "As oppressors dehumanize and violate their [the oppressed's] rights, they themselves also become dehumanized" (p. 42). "Dehumanization, which marks not only those whose humanity has been stolen, but also (though in a different way) those who have stolen it, is a distortion of becoming more fully human" (p. 28). Therefore, as we participate in the dehumanization of others, which we inevitably do by participating in institutions, policies, practices, and social relations that reflect and support societal inequality, our own humanity is diminished.

The notion of authenticity has been addressed in the writing of Robert Terry (1981). Although he focuses on racism, his points are apt for other oppressions as well. He maintains that authenticity is the process in all of our lives to make sense out of our world and act purposefully in it. Racism distorts authenticity since it distorts our ability to be true to self and to the world.

Building on the notions of dehumanization and inauthenticity, Wineman (1984) proposes why someone would seek to change a system in which they are advantaged. He suggests that superiority and domination are self-limiting experiences.

Exercising power over others, does not oppress the oppressor, it is simply a less attractive, less gratifying, less human way of life than treating people as equals and respecting their full humanity. Negative consciousness or rejecting access to the privilege and power of the oppressor is based on the notion that equal relations can be experienced as more rewarding than top-down relations.

Helping Privileged Students Identify
Their Self-Interest in Social Justice

I have engaged students in thinking from this perspective by asking them to identify the ways they feel they have been negatively affected by some form of oppression in which they are part of the dominant group. This makes most sense once they have already done some exploration of oppression and multicultural issues. After considering this question individually, they then listen to the responses of peers, provoking further reflection and discussion. This may be one of the few times when the pain of people in privileged groups has been acknowledged and validated. For people who have never named or discussed it, it can be a powerful experience and provide great relief to let go of the secrets or the feeling that they were the only ones. When I have conducted this exercise with groups, simply viewing the list of costs generated by the group has had a significant impact.

Some of the experiences and feelings discussed in this exercise may be similar to those students recount earlier in the class, as referred to in the discussion on confirming and joining. An awareness of how oppression hurts people from advantaged groups may help people better understand some of the pain and anger expressed in those stories. Yet, there can be an important distinction between those who are speaking to the limitations of privilege and those who are responding to the perceived erosion of their privilege.

Students may suggest situations in which they see themselves as the victim of "reverse racism" or another form of oppression. They often mention the denial of financial aid or scholarships because they were not a minority as an example of how they are negatively affected by racism. It is important to help them reframe and understand this situation not as a victim of racism but as a result of racism in our society. If there were no racism, there would be no need for special scholarships based on race, and therefore more money would be available to anyone who might need it. It's not the fault of students of color, but of a system of racial discrimination and bias that has motivated the establishment of these kinds of programs and supports.

Students can be encouraged to imagine what it would be like if there were no oppression and how that would be beneficial to them. What would it feel like to be rid of the limitations, pressures, guilt, moral ambivalence, and ignorance? What would it be like if the list of costs were obliterated? Visualizations, drawing and writing, as well as discussion and list making, can help make these imaginings feel more concrete.

We can also help students to identify and experience more equal and satisfying relations in everyday life. Imagining a total transformation of society can seem too unrealistic or abstract to be useful. Yet, in most of our daily lives we have the kinds of experiences that would be more available in a just and caring society. Encourage people to notice how they feel when they do have emotionally honest and mutually satisfying relationships with others; when they are behaving in accordance with their values; when they feel that they are acting out of their deeper sense of humanity and love; when they have positive, enriching relationships with people who are different than themselves; when they feel a sense of personal integrity and moral consistency. Help them verbalize these situations and positively reinforce these kinds of connections and ways of being.

We also need to acknowledge the losses and realities of giving up power and privilege. There are good reasons why people in dominant groups do not want change. There are strong incentives to maintain the current system, and negative repercussions for those to challenge it. Because hierarchy and dominant/subordinate relations are firmly entrenched in our society, people can see this as normal and base their sense of self on feeling superior to someone else. It can also be easy to avoid being conscious of the limiting effects of oppression, especially if one is cut off from one's own feelings and those of others. Despite the costs, there are real benefits of being part of a dominant group and legitimate fears that they will lose some of the advantages they now take for granted. Discuss how greater equity can be achieved by finding ways to spread what are now unearned advantages to those who are disadvantaged without eliminating those basic conditions for people who are currently privileged.

Helping students think about social change in these terms can allow an openness to considering new information about multicultural issues. Obviously, there will be some people who, despite these efforts, will not find their self-interest in eliminating oppression sufficiently compelling to contemplate change. I believe that for others, this can offer new ways of viewing themselves and the world, and act as a catalyst for taking personal and social action. Regardless of whether or not some students identify many costs or potential benefits to themselves, it can help them move away from a paradigm in which they feel guilty, blamed, and vilified. It can afford them a sense of freedom to examine different ways of thinking without having to be as defensive and therefore closed.

It is important that these exercises not degenerate into "poor me" or how everyone is oppressed. Views and experiences must be kept in a greater societal perspective with the focus of creating change toward justice and equity. Furthermore, while it may be necessary for some to begin with a very narrow sense of self-interest, ultimately we need to help students consider not only the potential benefits to themselves, but also to others. We need to move toward what others have called enlightened self-interest, recognizing that our well being and that of others are interdependent and intertwined. Students need to be encouraged to understand the common interest in creating a society that is just and humane.

The concept of and examples of allies can be useful to students as they consider how to put into action their desire to create greater equity (Tatum, 1994). This can also help students construct a different sense of identity—from oppressor or victim to ally. For those who are ready, engaging in some type of social change action can be an opportunity for continuity, for integrating their new systems of meaning and sense of identity, and creating a new base of support.

Conclusion

Given the larger social culture, the worsening economy, and the vested interests people have in the status quo, students' defensiveness is unlikely to be easily or quickly eliminated. Nevertheless, we owe it to our students, and to ourselves and others, to attempt to reach those who are antagonistic or hesitant to join our commitment to multiculturalism. Providing a climate for confirmation and ways to envision their self-interest in challenges to the status quo can help reduce the defensiveness undermining their engagement with multicultural issues.

Depending on the group, the process of confirmation and challenge can take time, both in and outside of class. I often face the ongoing dilemma of feeling the need to cover the material (which is of great importance) and to work with the issues the class raises and at a pace that respects the time needed for change. In part, the difficulty with Jack occurred because the course addressed such a wide range of material and we felt pressured to move through too many things too quickly (this class no longer will be taught). While I continue to struggle with this balance, I become convinced that if we are serious about creating sensitive, knowledgeable, and effective multicultural educators (and human beings), we need the opportunity to work with students in ways that respect the realities of this endeavor.

Underlying good teaching, I believe, is respect and compassion for our students. It is the commitment to help them grow and develop into the best person they can be. Remembering, feeling, and expressing this can be most difficult with nonengaged students in multicultural education. It can be helpful to reflect on our own process of unlearning oppression, including our past and present fears, avoidance, and defensiveness. While ultimately a very liberating process, it is also a very challenging one, which requires real courage. Most people can relate to the anxiety of having one's assumptions and world view shaken, the disappointment and estrangement from family and friends, the guilt and embarrassment for one's ignorance or hidden prejudices, and to being attacked for one's insensitive behavior (however unintentional).

The more we can stay in touch with our own feelings and experiences as we try to unlearn oppression, the more we can empathize with those students we want to dismiss (or even strangle at times). The more we can stay connected to them in genuine and accepting ways, the greater the potential we have to reach them. There are reasons, often good ones, why students resist multicultural education and social change agendas. However, if the defenses against change can be lowered, we can open avenues toward growth and new possibilities.

Note

I want to thank Sue Books, Lee Bell, Jim O'Donnell and Rudolfo Chávez Chávez for their helpful comments on earlier drafts of this article. I also would like to acknowledge the influence of Cherie Brown and the National Coalition Building Institute on my thinking about working with people from privileged groups.

16

Nancy Lesko

(E)strange(d) Relations

Psychological Concepts in Multicultural Education

Disciplines *leak* in actual teaching. Sociology leaks into history, psychology into literature, cultural studies leak into the study of curriculum. This chapter is about the leaking of psychology and psychological concepts into class discussions in multicultural teacher education. I inquire into the effects of particular psychological leaks into multiculturalism. Is the importation of psychological concepts into multiculturalism a discursive tactic to change the subject from institutional racism or structured inequalities to psychological constructs with their underlying humanistic and individualistic bases? Is the use of psychological constructs a strategy that does not directly deny the importance of multicultural perspectives, but severely limits its scope and possibilities? Finally, what lessons can be drawn for multicultural teacher education from this leaking of psychological concepts?

This chapter concentrates on classroom discourse. This discursive analysis differs from much inquiry into nonengagement, which focuses on the motivations, perspectives, and social contexts of individuals or members of groups. "Resistance" often examines an individual subject who thinks and acts, has intentions, and makes decisions accepting or screening out social factors. An individual student or teacher "learns," "resists learning," or "is motivated." This chapter shifts the focus to the structure of class discussion and possible positions that students can take when multicultural ideas are put forth as a structuring element. For example, once issues of institutional racism and structural inequalities are articulated, what positions of response are available in classrooms? If students disagree with the course readings that point to structured inequalities in schools, what positions are open to them to disagree?

In my classes at Indiana University–Bloomington over the past several years, students regularly turn to psychological concepts (among others) in their responses to class readings. In this chapter I explore the advent of psychological discourse in three ways: First, I examine how the students' introduction of cognitive developmental stages and self-esteem can be viewed as a discursive position in response to the facts of structural inequalities. Second, I consider the effects of psychological concepts as an expert—that is—professional, response to issues of institutional racism and inequality. Finally, I appraise possible responses to the psychologization of issues of discrimination and inequality.

Over the past seven semesters of teaching multicultural education* to undergraduates preparing to become secondary teachers of math, science, social studies, English, physical education, math, art, and music, I have attempted to observe, analyze, and revise my teaching in relation to their responses to the readings, issues, and strategies. I have been attentive to students' responses, attitudes, and perspectives across the spectrum of social and political viewpoints. This chapter is part of the process of reflecting on and revising my multicultural teaching.

Two psychological concepts that enter my classroom each semester are: *cognitive developmental stages* and *self-esteem*. I have watched and listened to the ways these concepts get introduced, taken up, and their effects. I was intrigued that they arrived so regularly in a course that focuses on structural inequalities of race, gender, class, and sexuality in

---

*My students are primarily white, heterosexual, middle-class midwesterners from small towns. My classes are approximately half male and half female. Most of my secondary teacher education students are in their early twenties and entered college directly on completion of high school. Each semester I have between two and ten students who differ from that general portrait in age, ethnicity/race, class, or sexuality. The multicultural class is usually taken within the first two semesters of professional coursework.

schools. This chapter is an attempt to understand their presence, their effects, and meanings.

Cognitive Developmental Stages

One emphasis in my course, stemming undoubtedly from my own background as a social studies teacher, is the responsibility of teachers to develop curricula that are intellectually challenging and to help young people to think critically about their worlds. I use several examples of curricula to illustrate: Bill Bigelow's (1991) description of how he teaches students to "rethink Columbus's discovery" and Liz Lindsay's summary of the antiracist science unit she teaches on nutrition and hunger (1989). Each teacher narrates the scope of the units of study, aims, major activities, and the ways students respond to both the different kinds of activities and the substance of the lessons.

Bigelow begins his teaching by stealing a girl's purse and claiming that he discovered it, thereby launching a heated discussion of language and point of view in history. His high school students subsequently read eyewitness accounts of Columbus's exploits, role play Columbus exhorting the Indians to bring him more gold, and analyze elementary history textbooks' portraits of Columbus's "discovery." In helping students to see the arrival of Columbus through Native Americans' eyes, Bigelow aims to get students to read "the word and the world" critically (Freire & Macedo, 1987).

Lindsay's antiracist approach to nutrition and hunger integrates geography, history, economics, and politics into the science classroom. Lindsay has students study the nutrition of various kinds of foods in the British diet, the kinds of foods imported from Third World countries, and the history and economics of the Irish potato famine. Later, students see the resemblances between Ireland and the Third World as they study conflicting interpretations of the causes and solutions to world hunger. Students learn how cash crops occupy the best land. Lindsay reflects:

> Students frequently express surprise at the alternative viewpoints and conflicting interpretations. I think that the experience helps students to become more critical in reading about science and less willing to accept explanations separated from the broader social and political context. (1989, p. 105)

Invariably in my education class discussions on these approaches to teaching, some students protest. In general, students do not denounce

the idea of teaching secondary students to think in a critical multicultural way, because critical thinking has achieved a degree of acceptance
among teachers and teachers-to-be, at least rhetorically. A handful of
students in each class chastise Bigelow for "going too far," for teaching
only his interpretation of history. However, many students state that although these goals and approaches are valuable and they believe in
them, middle school students, for example, cannot be taught following
these examples. They explain that middle school students do not have
the cognitive competence. They are not at a sufficiently advanced cognitive stage to think abstractly and critically in the ways Bigelow and
Lindsay demonstrate.

Kerry argued the developmental stage perspective in my class in the
spring 1995 semester. Although she grew up in a conservative, religious
town in the midwest, her Spanish major and study in Mexico as a high
school student provided her with additional perspectives from which to
view U.S. society and culture. Generally unsympathetic to multicultural
issues, she was in favor of bilingualism. She saw this position as anom-
alous to her other views that multiculturalism built barriers between
people and tore the people of the United States apart. When the class
was involved in a discussion of Bigelow's and Lindsay's approaches, she
argued that kids in middle schools could not think in the ways that the
authors were advocating because they were not at an advanced enough
stage of cognitive development.

Other students who advocated teaching for critical thinking stopped
in their tracks at Kerry's argument. Eventually someone retorted, "Well,
maybe middle school aged students cannot be taught to think critically,
but certainly upper high school aged students can be." There was a mur-
mur of agreement on that and the discussion continued.

What occurred was one of many sequences of disagreement, then
compromise and agreement in a class discussion. Yet its discursive
structure is important to examine for it illustrates the use of powerful,
professionalized, psychologized discourse in arguing for the impracti-
cality, even impossibility, of critical multicultural teaching.

Kerry and other students used the ground of expert psychological
knowledge to limit the claim of multiculturalism on their attitudes and
practices. Although many students in my classes are unsympathetic to
policies and programs designed to support the achievement of youth of
color or girls in schools and to create different teaching and curricular
practices, students usually avoid explicit support for racism, sexism, or
classism. While some students will outrightly state that affirmative action and other similar programs that are targeted to give "special treatment" to historically marginalized groups of youth are unfair, others
will not be so direct. Nevertheless, their opposition to rethinking their

expectations for themselves as teachers and the school systems in which they expect to work can take various forms. One such form is the use of psychological stage theories to say that teaching for critical thinking is implausible because students are not mature enough to accomplish it.

Numerous scholars of the history and sociology of psychology argue that the discipline has been constructed and wielded in ways that maintain class, race, and gender hierarchies (e.g., Rose, 1990; Henriques et al., 1984). However, there have been few analyses of the relationships between contemporary developmental stage theories and thinking about children and youth, teaching, and multiculturalism. In one exception to this general silence, Bev Clark (1994) argues that developmental stage theories contribute to an adult-centered discourse of juvenile immaturity. When people want to avoid using explicit class or race markers to establish mental or emotional deficiencies, they use age markers, or age-based markers. Developmental stage theories are such age-based markers that confirm the fact of inferiority on the basis of a lower stage of cognitive development that has been empirically validated. Such hierarchical rankings are legitimate, since age discrimination is widely accepted.

Part of Kerry's strategy was to shift the discussion terrain to one that is not contested: age and scientific, chronological stages of cognitive abilities. It is a masterful discursive position: it is professional knowledge, it is scientific knowledge, and it appears to be on neutral factual terrain of real age differences between adults and children. Part of its unassailability is the conception of youth as inferior that dominates in and out of educational thought and schools. Alanen (1988) characterized the Western, adult-centered view of children and youth as "elitist." When students speak of middle school and high school students as less cognitively able, as immature, as unable to think independently, a hierarchy of adult (even college-aged) over youth is reaffirmed. This hierarchy is typically supported, even reified, in courses in teacher education. It is an assumed inequality of authority, knowledge, and experience that is accepted and built upon. It is a discursive position that is unassailable unless the class shifts to examine the history and sociology of psychology and the process of age structuring.

Additionally, Kerry's protest assumed a particular definition of thinking. In their recent attempt to suggest a conception of "postformal" thinking, Kincheloe and Steinberg argue that "the way we define thinking exerts a profound impact on the nature of our schools, the role that teachers play in the world, and the shape that society will ultimately take" (1993, p. 301).

Kerry's use of conventional stage theories of thinking and the positioning of youth at a lower level of ability is a powerful illustration of

Kincheloe and Steinberg's position: Kerry's assertion that youth cannot do critical, multicultural thinking defines the nature of curriculum (as conventional), the nature of classroom activities (as primarily comprehension and application activities), and the role of teachers as managers of knowledge. Kerry's acceptance of conventional thinking on thinking is limited by its unpoliticized nature, its reductionism, its uniformity, and its location as innate qualities of particular individuals (Kincheloe & Steinberg, 1993). And each of those characteristics matters for what her own classroom, assignments, aims, and interactions with students will be like. Without a critical interrogation of psychological knowledge and of conceptions of children and youth in the multicultural classroom (or elsewhere in the teacher education program), Kerry's challenge to critical multiculturalism stands.

Self-Esteem

The second psychological concept that appears unannounced and with substantial commonsense baggage is the idea of *self-esteem* and the role that it plays in learning and in school achievement. In a recent review of the empirical literature on self-esteem, Kohn (1994) concludes that the beliefs about the importance of self-esteem's contribution to school achievement are unsupported. Nevertheless, many teachers and researchers assume that self-esteem is a vital component for youth to be successful and that youth from historically marginalized groups are especially likely to have inadequate self-esteem. Critics of multiculturalism, in turn, charge that educators want to use history to teach self-esteem, rather than to teach history. Schlesinger (1992) derides the proposition that history (or other curricular areas) can or should be self-esteem enhancers.

The presence of self-esteem in my multicultural classes is slippery; it arrives early each semester without a major fanfare or argument. In spring 1995, Suzanne introduced it the third or fourth class session, after we saw a video about public hearings in California on history textbook selections. Suzanne was an articulate, active white student, from a strongly Catholic family that she portrayed as "perfect" in that her parents supported her but gave her lots of freedom and talked openly with her and her siblings on all topics. We had read an introductory article by Perry and Fraser (1993) on the necessity of recreating schools as multicultural and democratic organizations. The reading and video had both stressed the relationship between schooling practices and social democratic processes.

Suddenly, Suzanne skipped to the importance of a multicultural history curriculum and textbook for the self-esteem of youth of color. Numerous students' heads bobbed in agreement. Although Suzanne became more supportive of multicultural approaches to teaching as she learned more about them, her conceptualization relied on an individualized psychological construct of self-esteem to understand the value and significance of multicultural school materials to students.

How can we understand this shift from the terminology of white dominance and economic and social inequality to that of self-esteem, even for a student in support of multiculturalism (McIntosh, 1988; Baldwin, [1963] 1988)? Several explanations are plausible. First, according to some sociologists and historians, middle-class Americans are radical individualists, without concepts or language for a social self, for a self that is part of a community. Radical individualism is also a privilege of whites and the affluent while denied to people of color and the poor. From this line of thinking, we could hypothesize that Suzanne and other students cannot conceptualize a social dimension to themselves; their conception of a human being is an individual, autonomous, unique peerson. The idea of socially constituted human beings, who cannot exist in full potential apart from an active social membership, is unknown. Thus, one understanding of the presence and role of self-esteem is that it is a "default" understanding of human beings (and how negative social relations affect an individual child), when no concept of a socially-constituted individual is possible (Henriques et al., 1984).

A second, more pernicious, analysis is that self-esteem is a code word, or euphemism, for motivation, initiative, and the willingness to follow rules and norms. When educators advocate that middle school youth, for example, need self-esteem, the term is sometimes translated into the conventional ideas that young adolescents with self-esteem follow rules, value school, learning, and grades, are able to think and act like white middle-class kids, and believe that doing one's homework and avoiding drugs and sex will lead to college attendance and a good job. So, self-esteem can be a back door to standard expectations that youth will become engaged in school, follow rules, and achieve up to their potential. In this interpretation, self-esteem functions as a "soft," therapeutized language for control and conformity expectations.

A third explanation echoes the previous analysis of developmental stage theories, that the language of human subjectivity is largely provided by psychology. We psychologize human beings, and that means we also largely behavioralize them, viewing them as sets of inputs and outputs. For example, in my interviews with four undergraduate education majors about their conceptions of youth, they viewed adolescents as mechanized beings, as responding to outside stimuli but without independent or autonomous aspects. This is a socialized view, but social in its belief in conformity of individuals to group parameters. The reduction of issues of democratic schools and multicultural curricula and texts to self-esteem shrinks both the problem and the solutions.

In my classes, the use of self-esteem in relation to critical multiculturalism flattens and diminishes the ideas of thinking and knowledge to a psychological sense of oneself. I am not denying that some sense of self-worth plays a role in learning. However, the commonsense uses of self-esteem locate the problem that it signifies in individual students and, implicitly, in their deficient family backgrounds, rather than in (among other things) the emptiness of the formal school curriculum and relationships with teachers (Wexler, 1992).

Despite its significant limitations, Suzanne used self-esteem in a way that also empathized with historically oppressed groups and attempted to side with them and to see conventional school practices from their perspectives. So, the term may also indicate a striving to connect with Others, but the psychological concept of self-esteem is inadequate to the task of creating multicultural curricula and teaching practices.

Reflection and Self-Reflection

Susan Buck-Morss (1979) provides a sociohistorical critique of Piagetian concepts of cognitive development. She argues that Piaget's developmental trajectory toward abstract formal thinking is linked with the emergence of Western capitalism with its commodity structure (exchange principle, reification, and fetishism). What Piaget considers to be the first significant cognitive development (beyond the sensorimotor stage), Buck-Morss equates with "the prototypical experience of alienation": "It is the ability of the child to divorce subject from object . . . separate the mental image or concept of an object from its actual empirical existence . . . 'bracket out' the empirical object" (1979, pp. 353–54). Such cognitive development values the split between thinking and doing: "For Piaget, the culmination of learning is when the child can 'do' everything in his head, that is, when he can divorce theory from practice" (p. 354).

Buck-Morss's critiques of Piaget's theory of cognitive developmental stages is one powerful response to Kerry's use of cognitive stage theory to undermine the necessity of curricular and teaching reforms. Sociological and historical analyses such as that provided by Buck-Morss are necessary in teacher education if students are not to use psychological concepts to bolster nonengagement with multicultural issues. Buck-Morss concludes that in order for children of lower social classes to think in formal abstract ways, they must consciously participate in abstract, mediated levels of society. Thus, her analysis leads back to the necessity of political and economic change, as well as school curriculum reform. Similar historical and sociological critiques can be used to interrogate the psychological concept of self-esteem (e.g., Murrell, 1993).

While Buck-Morss's critique helps in teaching about Piagetian theory in a sociohistorical way, it also clarifies the difficulty of undoing the abstract formalist thinking of middle-class teacher education students so that they can apprehend, in a nonpejorative way, the connections between lifeworlds and ways of thinking. My two examples indicate that psychological theories and concepts have a thorny presence in teacher education and a very difficult coexistence in a multicultural education that emphasizes structural inequalities such as institutionalized racism. Kieran Egan (1983) proposes that psychological research and theories are of no value in education because psychology's aims are to describe (and predict) rather than to educate. Even without formal coursework in psychology, however, students will continue to interpret topics in multicultural courses in psychologized terms. These psychologized interpretations must, in turn, be incorporated into more structural analyses. Buck-Morss's critique presents one approach to doing that.

I am now convinced that students' psychologized assumptions and interpretations must be critically examined. In a course already packed with content, I have not taken students' ideas regarding cognitive developmental stages and self-esteem as texts to be interrogated for their histories, social positionings, and effects. However, the process of narrating these discussions and analyzing them as politics of nonengagement has changed my mind. Having their own interpretive frameworks scrutinized is likely to be a compelling exercise for many students.

As I continue to teach multicultural education, experiences such as those chronicled in this chapter push me toward believing in a larger role for epistemology and considerations of knowledge and knowing in multicultural education. As Britzman and colleagues (1993) conclude, the problem of multiculture is a problem of interpretation and interpretive practices. At the same time, interpretive practices in education connect with actual pedagogical practices, so the interpretations and the concrete practices must be scrutinized together.

In my teacher education program, the issues of multiculturalism are the explicit focus of only one course. The kinds of interrogation of psychological and other interpretive constructs that I suggest here are hard to pursue when the demands to cover other materials regarding history, specific group studies, and curriculum transformation are also great. Nevertheless, the interrogation of the interpretive practices drawing on psychological constructs will be prioritized in my future multicultural teacher education classes.

17

Gary L. Anderson
Mary Bentley
Bernardo Gallegos
Kathryn Herr
Elizabeth Saavedra

Teaching Within/
Against the Backlash

A Group Dialogue about
Power and Pedagogy in the 1990s

ell hooks (1994), in her book, *Teaching to Transgress*, distinguished critical and feminist pedagogies from what she called "engaged pedagogy." According to her account, engaged pedagogy maintains the emancipatory goals of critical and feminist pedagogies, but she argues that only when teachers are engaged in their own process of self-actualization can authentic engagement occur among students and teachers in classrooms. While critical and feminist pedagogues might justifiably argue that there is nothing in their stance that precludes the self-actualization of teachers, hooks's shift of focus from students to teachers provides an opportunity to address the daily dilemmas that critical teachers face as they attempt to make sense of their own work. Nonengagement in classrooms, according to hooks, occurs when either teachers or students are not engaged in an authentic process of self-actualization, which for us presupposes continuous dialogue and introspection that results in transformative learning.

In engaged classrooms both teachers and students must be willing to push themselves to uncover and examine authoritative discourses and how certain knowledges become "subjugated knowledges." Engaged classrooms are sites of resistance as students and teachers are engaged in a critique of power. hooks (1994) cites Chandra Mohanty on this point: "Resistance lies in self-conscious engagement with dominant, normative discourses and representations and in the active creation of oppositional analytic and cultural spaces" (p. 22).

While the authors embrace this definition of engaged pedagogy, we have found its implementation to be enormously complex. We have found that authentic engagement in critical classrooms is difficult to foster because it tends to interrupt the privilege of those who are used to wielding power in social interactions in all social arenas, including classrooms. The result is often a test of wills between those professors who attempt to interrupt authoritative discourses and those who seek to reassert them from a position of privilege related to positions occupied outside of classroom contexts.

Through our ongoing reflection, we have discovered that power is drawn from many arenas and takes various forms depending on the context. The particular dynamics of a context and the players within it will determine who has power. As professors, there is an inherent power (what most theorists would call "authority") that comes with the position one occupies in the institutional hierarchy; however, the form of that power and the potential for drawing on the resources of that power will be limited depending on the other members occupying the same context. For instance, a professor that is a nontenured Chicana in a class that is predominantly minority will elicit different power relations than if the class has a large number of members of privileged groups.

It is this complexity that we wish to capture by providing a dialogue among five engaged teachers seeking to create "oppositional analytic and cultural spaces" in university classrooms. While the following dialogue represents a single segment from a four-hour taped session, this session is typical of ongoing discussions we have about our pedagogy. It is, in fact, through these discussions that we seek self-actualization and professional renewal on an ongoing basis.

In this chapter a diverse group of five university professors, who have met together regularly around a common interest in exploring how our politics and our teaching intersect, will present a segment from a collective dialogue. The topic of this segment is how we confront the apparent contradiction of becoming "players" in the power system of classrooms, and how we attempt to interrupt and interrogate authoritative discourses without simply replacing them with new, more "progressive" ones. As we encounter resistances to this process of interruption from students who are used to occupying privileged positions in the classroom, we must develop a repertoire of strategies to open up and foster the kind of "oppositional analytical and cultural space" that we seek for all of our students.

Resistances occur in engaged classrooms in part because students and teachers are socialized to view teaching and learning as neutral, nonpolitical activity. In this chapter we develop a view of the classroom as a dynamic, micropolitical space in which power is negotiated continuously. Delpit (1988) has argued that classrooms represent "cultures of power." A classroom contains a culture of power to the extent that social relations in the classroom reproduce social relations in the wider society. For example, the curriculum tends to reflect the dominant culture (middle class, male, European-American, heterosexual, able bodied, etc.)—that is, men tend to demand their privileged position in the public sphere and dominate discussions; a hierarchical system is reproduced through the student-teacher relationship, evaluation procedures, and so on. Power, in this view, is a human accomplishment, situated in everyday interaction and drawing on both interactional activities and structural forces.

Teachers who attempt to interrupt and interrogate power relations that favor dominant groups are often viewed as "political," and in the ideological atmosphere of the 1990s, as "politically correct." The attempt by many teachers to engage in a critical pedagogy, along with policies that interrupt privilege in the wider society, has produced what Faludi (1991) terms a "backlash." While mostly those who belong to dominant groups engage in this backlash, increasingly those from nondominant groups are identifying with the interests of dominant groups. While critical pedagogues are used to teaching "on the defensive," there is in the 1990s an increasing sense of intolerance for the expression of nondominant views in the classroom (Jacoby, 1994).

Focusing on the role of education in the reproduction of classed, raced, and gendered social relations, writers on critical pedagogy tend to have a well-elaborated theory of power in society, but a poorly developed theory of power grounded in the classroom. This is because too often those who write about critical pedagogy are what Jacoby (1994) calls "professors who are radical" rather than "radicals who are professors." This means that for radicals the university is too often an ivory tower from which to theorize rather than a place in which to live out one's theories through relationships in the classroom and the larger institution.

Some work, primarily by feminist pedagogues, does a better job of focusing attention on the micropolitics of social relations in the classroom

(Kramer-Dahl, 1996; Lewis and Simon, 1986; Ng, 1995; Rosenberg, 1997; Weiler, 1988). hooks (1994) argues that classrooms cannot be neutral or even safe spaces for most students and teachers since they reflect oppressive conditions that exist outside the classroom. Ellsworth (1989) has added the notion that students cannot be "emancipated" through what are ultimately impositional forms of pedagogy informed by their own authoritative discourses.

According to Britzman (1991), the dilemma of critical and feminist pedagogies is that, unlike traditional pedagogies that avoid controversy (McNeil, 1986), they of necessity bring "unpopular things" (i.e., racism, classism, sexism, homophobia) into the classroom. Once these "unpopular things" are unleashed in the classroom, teachers must figure out what to do with them. This is a dilemma the traditional teacher rarely has to cope with, but which becomes an everyday part of a critical teacher's professional life. This is particularly true when a critical teacher is female, openly gay or lesbian, or a person of color. Britzman asks,

> Can pedagogy decenter authoritative discourses without unleashing unpopular things? The answer is no. The social categories of race, class, and sex are what Stuart Hall calls, "combustible materials" (Hall, 1981, p. 59). They incite so easily because everyone embodies these categories and through these categories identity, investments, and desires are made. (Britzman, 1991, p. 172)

If the work of critical teachers requires the daily handling of "combustible materials," then we are in urgent need of strategies that can either defuse them or otherwise deepen analyses into why these materials are so combustible. As we move away from moralizing postures on the part of teachers, and toward a more engaged and authentic pedagogy, what exactly do we do with the unpopular things we unleash in the classroom?

How We Construct Students and How They Construct Us

Early on in our group dialogue, it became apparent that while we had common experiences in the classroom as critical educators, these experiences played out differently depending on our own positionality. We are, collectively, European American and Native American (Chicano and Chicana); lesbian and heterosexual; male and female. All of us are from working- and lower-middle-class origins. We each can be viewed as privileged in certain settings—that is, female but also white, Chicano but also male. We also have life histories, political ideologies, and personal idiosyncracies that make each of us unique in many ways.

Our encounters with students, as we engage in critical work, intersect with the meanings they construct of us: What is it they are experiencing as they realize a lesbian is teaching their course on human sexuality? What do they do when they encounter a Chicano or Chicana professor for the first time in a position of authority in the classroom? What meaning do they make of a white male professor critiquing and working to dismantle the privilege that he has enjoyed through his ascribed status? And for all of us, how do students respond to critical professors who teach from a transformative perspective?

Because we are each uniquely positioned in terms of the meaning students make of our lives and what we present to their classroom experience, each strategy of our pedagogy has to be filtered through our own positionality. We can tease at common themes and dilemmas while also clearly stating that classroom dynamics often play out in unique ways, dependent on the meanings students give each of our uniquenesses along race, sexual preference, and gender lines. Our strategies of what may "work" as we teach toward social justice and equity vary depending on our own cultural capital and how it is perceived in our classrooms.

While theoretical insights abound in the literature on critical pedagogy, few struggle openly with the ways they cope with the "unpopular things" that are unleashed in critical classrooms. (For exceptions see Britzman, 1991; Ellsworth, 1989; and Ng, 1995.) The intention of presenting this dialogue is less to provide "tips" or "coping strategies" to other critical teachers than to allow the reader to eavesdrop on a diverse group of critical teachers attempting to make sense of their work.

Some who read the following dialogue will be struck by the extent to which the authors talk of "neutralizing" or "silencing" those who attempt to reassert a culture of privilege in the classroom, and will wonder whether this is not antithetical to an engaged pedagogy that seeks to open up dialogue rather than stifle it. All of us have passed through different understandings of how power works in classrooms and how one should respond to power; all of us continue to ask ourselves: as we use power to interrupt privilege, are we using it to liberate or subjugate? All of us have struggled with various forms of Rogerian, Freirian, and feminist pedagogy. While all of us have taught for many years now and have consistently been generally rated highly by our students in our class evaluations, we continue to actively struggle with our teaching.

Understanding our experiences through the examination of the micropolitics of social relations in our classes, we realize that we have to make explicit the ways that power relations are socially constructed. We also need to understand how some individuals' vulnerabilities are greater depending on how many categories of oppression they embody. In the dialogue that follows, we will share the ways that we have come to understand how power works and is shaped in various contexts. While the reader can't observe us in our respective classrooms, we offer examples of the questions and dilemmas we face in our teaching. In doing so we run a high risk in terms of the meanings that can be made of such struggles when seen only in print rather than interacting with us in relationship; we move away from being "experts," offering teaching tips, to including the reader in what it is we "know" so far with the full realization that we are still in process.

Envisioning Transformative Teaching
The Group Dialogue

KATHRYN: Who are we teaching for?

BERNARDO: I had a woman in my class one quarter who from the beginning didn't like the readings. She thought they were too political. I felt I knew where she was coming from. She was a working-class white woman from one of the few European American communities left in the section of Los Angeles where I teach. It's kind of a working-class community that is surrounded by Mexicans. She asked the question, "What about us?" when we discussed privilege—which was a legitimate question, as clearly poor and working-class European Americans are often invisible in discourses of power. I could see her point, but she was uncritically procapitalist, America right or wrong, and more importantly, unwilling to examine her beliefs or engage in a discourse that looked at power relations and that may have helped her to make sense of the space that poor and working-class whites occupy. She often made comments like, "The problems in schools have nothing to do with critical pedagogy or constructivism. Some people are just plain lazy and that's all there is to it." At the very end of the class her comments were, "Too bad we had to read all these 'socialists' trying to promote their propaganda."

KATHRYN: Did you think about how to "engage" her? I often have that debate with myself: How much am I willing to swoop back and pick them up; how much energy do I give?

BERNARDO: I did. In the past, in similar situations, students like her took up most of my attention. They became the center, the focus of the class. They also occupied my consciousness after the class was over. But I kept thinking about the other thirty-nine people in the class. At some point I had to move on because the other students were just sitting there basically unattended.

MARY: Watching the debate.

BERNARDO: Yeah, Exactly.

MARY: And not active.

KATHRYN: And is it your sense that the others could take the material and they could be going with it meanwhile?

BERNARDO: Yes, because when I read their weekly reflection papers, they were really engaging the material, but in class many of them were silent and not participating.

MARY: This last summer I did an experiment that I was sharing with Kathryn the whole time I was doing it, and she was actually helping me muddle through some of it—really more like giving me permission to try it.

KATHRYN: I was used as the sounding board at the end of every day.

MARY: Right. So what I realized was that for the thirteen years that I have been teaching human sexuality, I have been teaching to that group of powerful white men in the class who are vocal. So I've made it my task, I discovered, to move them. I felt that if I could move them a couple of inches, I was doing a good job. I finally realized that by doing that, I was in effect ignoring the other twenty people in the class.

So this past summer I said, okay, I'm not going to do that anymore. I'm going to teach to the whole class for a change. So this time when, for example, homophobic remarks would come up like "They should put all the fags on a boat and blow it up" or "if two women are parenting they should have to undergo intensive psychological screening," I refused to engage it. So instead of taking up all the air time to unwind that for them, and therefore even justify that point of view by giving over class time to it, I just ran over them. I mean literally, Bump! Bump! just ran right over them. I'd say, "We're not going to spend time on that," and then I would continue, and they became more and more aggressive in their attempts to occupy class time. And so when they did that, when they pulled power, I pulled power.

Then I found other interesting things emerging, like the women trying to rescue the men. "This class seems a little hostile to me." I got comments like that and comments like "Why don't you teach us about normal sex? Why are you always talking about these weird things." And of course the interesting thing is, three or four men in the back would go out huffing, just so angry, and all the minority students and the women would be gathering around me after class saying, "When you said this . . . " But they wouldn't engage during the public discourse so they would have to engage with me after class was over. So I found myself talking to a larger percentage of the class after the class about what had just happened.

I've really—I mean Kathryn can tell you—I've bent over backwards. I've talked about air time; I've talked about the work by Sadker and Sadker (1994), about how they talked about women never speaking up and men occupying all the air time. I unwound it every way I could think of and finally I just said . . .

KATHRYN: You were giving them enough information for them to make meaning out of their own behavior. You were giving them this information, but I think that for those men in your class, it was such a natural position to be so privileged. Here's what I'm beginning to think: that it's hard for them to "get it" until you help them experience not being privileged—which usually means they get incredibly pissed off at you.

MARY: That's true. I gave them every opportunity I could think of to understand their own behavior and when they didn't, what I did was refuse to engage them in the privilege. I talked to the *numbers* instead of the *power*, and that was the difference, and that was really hard. I came out of there every day feeling like I was going to get beat up, raped, or something was going to happen to me. I got slammed on class evaluations both by those three guys and by anyone who was interested in those three guys.

BERNARDO: I've had similar classes in which I felt I had to do some things that would appear very traditional and almost authoritarian. For example, I've sometimes had to establish a rule that students must raise their hands in order to speak. I've also given everyone a name tag and I pass around a magic marker; they have to put their name on it and set it in front of their desks, so I can call on people. I tell them at the beginning of the quarter that I do this because I don't want a few people occupying all the class time, that they have to raise their hands and keep their comments to no more than three or four minutes. And I tell them that I will be calling on people who don't raise their hands.

I feel uncomfortable with the authoritarianism implied
in this structure, but I can't have an ocean of people just
speaking out when they feel like it because so many of the
students get silenced. Another problem that occasionally
occurs is students making unsolicited rude remarks while
another student is speaking, often delegitimizing that student's discourse. This can demoralize and intimidate students and keep them from speaking.

GARY: This raises another issue. Bernardo and a local Indian historian spent an hour in my class the other night talking about
New Mexico history and the Genizaros (Detribalized Plains
Indians from whom many New Mexicans are descended).
This white guy tried to delegitimate the whole thing by basically saying "Can't we be more forward looking? This is all
in the past and this is all pretty negative."

Now normally I welcome remarks like that, because
often they are legitimate questions that others are also
thinking about but may feel are inappropriate or impolite.
In fact, I often try to anticipate these questions and raise
them myself so that students don't have to raise them. In
this case, however, this student's body language and intona-
tion patterns were such that it was not asked as a question,
but tossed out as a challenge to two Native American scholars who were describing a relatively recent history of colonization in the state—a state, I might add, in which so-
called minorities are the majority population. Then this
student, as he often did in class, wanted to elaborate on
how white people are also oppressed. Bernardo interrupted
him and said that while the notion that many white people
are also oppressed had merit, he had been invited to talk
about Native Americans in New Mexico.

Now I have another student who raises these kinds of
questions, but in an authentic way, almost as if she's thinking out loud. In a discussion on race, class, and gender, she
raised the question of whether these categories aren't often
used as excuses by people who want special consideration.
Then we had a very productive discussion on this topic.
Other students then see that raising issues like this is important and welcomed as long as the questions are authentic and not attempts to silence other discourses.

KATHRYN: I think that's a common theme; that some students are
going to be critical: "How come we have to spend our time
on weird stuff or negative stuff or down beat stuff?" What

I'm curious about though, Bernardo, is how does this white guy respond to you as a Chicano?

BERNARDO: There are different responses. I can tell you about one guy in particular, who happened to be the only white male in my class, and who would attempt to monopolize air time in class. One evening he approached me during the break and said, "Some of the students have been talking about the literature in here being real negative." So in class I raised the issue and asked if the class had appointed him as their spokesperson and if so why? The class responded that nobody had appointed him and that they could speak for themselves. After that exchange he became very respectful of other people's air time. As a former football player myself, I was able to connect with him. He was a football coach in a school that was majority Mexican and I felt a sense of respect for him. I also connected with his working-class origins so I worked on our common ground to develop a relationship with him.

I think we have to work to neutralize some of these students because our classrooms, or at least mine in East Los Angeles, are often like ideological and discursive battlegrounds. And then there are always a few students who will stonewall you all through the course.

MARY: I think I used to make it my job to try to change them. Like I asked before: do you teach to the power or do you teach to the class? I think I tried to make it my job to move that power a little bit. I needed to move those four or five students a little bit.

BERNARDO: How do you actually do it? Do you limit their speaking time? Do you counter their arguments? Or do you just ignore them?

MARY: Well, it would depend on what's brought up. I can remember from my undergraduate summer course a kid saying something like "I read some research that said that women really secretly want to be raped." Okay, so here you are with this dilemma, knowing first of all that there is no such research, and, second, that he really stepped over a line with that one, and that it's very personal. So I countered the power with power. What I ended up saying to him was: "There is no such research. You shouldn't go quoting research that you don't know and by misquoting research you've just stepped on every woman in the room." But then what happened was that he got angrier and angrier.

In the sex education class, when I was doing it to men—as a woman—it was even more difficult because I think the men were getting angrier and angrier and the women were actually secretly liking it more and more. But everybody was watching it. It was kind of interesting because the class became watching the interaction as much as the content, process, or pedagogy. It became watching the interaction of power, as well as how I was going to deal with the power. What happened finally in my sex education class was that a kid got so frustrated that he got up and wrote on the board.

ELIZABETH: What did he write on the board?

MARY: What he wanted to say.

BERNARDO: Because other people were talking

MARY: And he couldn't stand it. I would call on him twice and that was it. Or he would be saying something and I would say "Wait, we're going to hear from someone over here" and he would start fidgeting and running around and getting really upset. Finally he just went to the side board and wrote on the board. And I let him write on the board and that was fine. I called on two or three more people, and then I said, "Oh, and this guy wrote on the board, so there's another comment on the board."

ELIZABETH: I don't think I would have even acknowledged him writing on the board.

MARY: Well, it seemed kind of silly not to acknowledge that he was over there writing. That would give him a lot of power by not acknowledging it. But it's true that this set of young men were so accustomed to occupying the whole class that when they had somebody that not only recognized that, but didn't go there with them, they could not stand it. They would not stand it. They would not be silenced, period. And there were still people in that class that didn't say a word the whole class period—I mean the whole summer they did not say a word. And I think there were some people that were really distraught by the interaction even though I would say, "Remember that we're trying to have equal time here." I would talk about power. I did everything I could think of. Kathryn's comment was right; I gave them the opportunity to understand their behavior, but they've never had to, so why should they? For some white girl telling them to be quiet and not calling on them?

KATHRYN: It's like that Kathy Ferguson (1984) statement: "Men don't listen to women because they don't have to."

ELIZABETH: Somewhere else I was reading that people in power don't have anything to lose; they have the power so they don't have to listen. They're not about to start either.

MARY: I think the biggest thing was that I realized that I was teaching to the power and that for me was a huge discovery in my own professional development—that I wasn't teaching a class, I was teaching to the power.

ELIZABETH: But sometimes these students aren't the students in power. Very rarely do I have white men in my classes. The majority of students in my classes are minorities themselves, so rolling over the students isn't an appropriate strategy for me. Many of my students have differing perspectives. So we have to uncover the ideologies behind their statements.

I had a Vietnamese woman—who was clearly not a student of power; but she was just very conservative and seemed very racist. This was a class in bilingual education/ESL that I was teaching. In the first class, the Vietnamese woman was very upset and all we did was cover the syllabus and some basic content of the class. She dropped the class after the first day because she said I was a feminist and too radical. She just was not interested in the class because I introduced the class as discussing issues of bilingualism, issues of linguistic minority students. She didn't want to deal with it. She wanted to take an English-only class and methods class that would help her teach linguistic minority students English.

I think that if you're not teaching to the power, you have two choices. One is to decide who you are teaching to and who are you? And then, what stance are you going to take? I have seen it, and I have tried it where you actually take someone's comment, unpack it, and in the process of unpacking it you really create a strong demonstration about the difference between what you're talking about and what you're trying to construct and what is. I think the process of deconstructing is a very valuable strategy. It's just that you've got to find the right times. if you're teaching to the power, it may not work. At other times, it may work because you can help them to see the stance that they have taken.

I think I'm a little uncomfortable with just saying we silence, we reverse, turn the tables on them or whatever it is we're doing. We have to find the right opportunities and really study that particular context and the interactions and the dynamics in the people who are involved. Do I use this as a strategy to help people realize what I am trying to say? Even if you're not going to change that one person, it's a demonstration for the rest of the people in the group.

MARY: What does that look like?

KATHRYN: Yeah, say more about it.

GARY: So you use them as a teachable moment?

ELIZABETH: For example, in the cultural studies class this semester, in the very first class, I wrote down the comments people were making. Some of them were very harsh, racist, sexist comments, very negative toward minorities; you know, the typical stuff that comes up. And I would specifically record their discourse; I would write it down.

KATHRYN: So you're taking notes there in class?

ELIZABETH: Yes, of the things that they said. And then I said "Let's go back. One individual said this; let's go back and take a look at what that might mean and how that could be interpreted by different people in this group." And we critiqued it. First of all, people became very conscious of what they did and how they were interpreted by people. Second, the people who experience it learn how to listen, to become a student of human nature; they learn to listen to what they're saying and strategize to do something, to voice an opposing opinion.

GARY: So you can have an immediate discourse analysis of the discourse of your classroom and turn it into an object that they can then talk about.

ELIZABETH: Right. There was an incident when I was a doctoral student. We were in a class and a student made the comment that the reason that the United States was so technologically, economically, politically, and socially advanced was because of the English language. . . . So the professor said, "Is this your opinion or have you read something?" And the student said, "This is what research says." So the professor said, "What research?" The student said "You know, they've done it." Well, who is they? And the professor questioned this person to get to the very bottom of where it was coming from. It was pretty tense, but we were loving every minute of it; it was sort of what you were talking about, Mary, where those of us who didn't say anything were loving seeing him grilled. Finally it got down to the student saying, "Well, that's what I think is the reason." The professor just finished it off saying, "Then it's your opinion. Has it ever occurred to you that your opinion is racist?" And then the guy said "Well, I guess

it could be considered racist." Then we got into a discussion
of what is racism and what is not. So it's like interrogating.
The professor used a questioning strategy. He just moved
right into it. He held people accountable to what they were
saying and where it was coming from, unpacking and critiquing it. I think in the process of critiquing and giving information—this is what we've been reading in bell hooks
(1994) and James C. Scott (1990)—that instead of just reading about it, they are experiencing it; they're living it.

BERNARDO: You know, I think that what you're saying is still problematic in that we still devote a whole bunch of time to issues
that this particular person raised. I've started to question
doing exactly that because I realize that at the end of the
eleven weeks, there are thirty people in there whom I don't
even know because they haven't said anything. Nobody
knows them. What possible avenues could the discourse
have taken had they spoken, had they said something? . . .
when, in fact, to deconstruct someone's statement, in terms
of just time, is twenty, maybe thirty minutes.

ELIZABETH: But that's where you have to study the context, because
like in the cultural studies class it was appropriate—that's
what cultural studies is. I think we have to ask ourselves,
Are we teaching the content or are we teaching the people?
For example, there's another person, a minority women, in
the same class who has taken the victim role; if she doesn't
like certain things that are going on, if she thinks that she's
not getting enough floor time, she uses lots of gestures and
behaviors to get attention. I just ignore it because I'm thinking "you either jump in there like the rest of us or we'll
move without you," and because we're trying to cover
something, we're on a roll.

So I think it's a matter of making choices about when
do we push content, when do we leave content on the shelf
because there are some dynamics here we have to explore.
Those thirty-nine people are going to be silenced if we
allow racist or sexist comments. People take power in another way. If they come up with a strong statement, like
that student stating his particular belief, it silences people
and they say, "I'm not going to speak up. Look at this guy.
I'm not even going to waste my time in this class if this is
the kind of thinking that occurs here."

KATHRYN: But it sounds like the other important thing in the cultural studies example that you gave was that it was the first night and you were setting the climate of the course. So it sounds like it was really a message for people to reflect on their discourse. And that you might have made a different choice eight weeks into the class, sort of "If you're not on board by now, what am I going to do with you?" But it sounds like it was setting the culture of the class.

ELIZABETH: See I don't think you do it every time; I think you find the right moment to set a stage. You know what I'm saying—it could be used as a strategy. . . . In my bilingual ESL class, the class had divided and there were the pro-bilinguals and then there were the ESL people; I had described it the last time we met as "the class from hell." I could always count on the probilingual people to reiterate what I would say in class; they'd talk about their experiences and there was this sense of real camaraderie.

In one of the classes, a Latino—I think he was feeling pretty secure, thinking that, whatever he said, I was going to back him up, that he was in the "in crowd" with me—he was talking about a particular situation in the school district and he made a comment about women; it was very negative, very sexist. I turned to him and really confronted him. I said "Listen to what you just said. How is it different? Why are these issues relevant for bilingual linguistic minorities but then when it comes to women we don't see how we situate them?" And he sort of got bent out of shape with me; it's like "you and I hang together; we're on each other's side." So when I confronted him, it was kind of shocking to everybody because it was like "What has he done? You're supposed to be on each other's side."

GARY: Well that returns us to the insight that people size us up in a certain way and make a certain set of assumptions about us. You know, "I'm Chicano; you're Chicana. Obviously you're going to be on my side." Or they may assume that because I'm a white male, they can make a bunch of assumptions about me. They may assume that we're going to be on the same wave length, and then, when they realize that we're not, they may be even more upset.

MARY: You know, it's not that I haven't tried that discourse analysis. I do that in my classes up one side and down the other. But still, it falls on deaf ears very often, and it ends up being a challenge for power rather than a discourse analysis. I'm doing it as a discourse analysis, and it ends up being a challenge for power because of who I am, not because of the content of what I'm saying but because *I* am challenging *them*.

ELIZABETH: It's not that power is handed to you; sometimes we make our own power. I think we situate ourselves: I'm the person who is facilitating this group. I am the person who is responsible for the dynamics and interactions.

KATHRYN: But I think there's something where because I'm a woman I up the ante. I notice that some students, for lack of a better word, "fight back" in a different way. I'll give an example. When I was giving that secondary education workshop on gender, it was really interesting to me; I mean I worked for an hour and a half, working the line on gender and the issues gender raises in education. Afterward people stood in line to talk to me and the first guy who came through in line said "Well, all I really wanted to say was how much I like your hair and the way it flows and looks so good." And I thought "I just worked for an hour and a half on gender and you stand in line to tell me you like my hair?" But what it did to me was I just shut up; I thought, "how did we get here, where this is your comment?"

   The next person in line, a man, explained to me that he could understand how men end up raping women because some women don't respect men like they're supposed to. What I was registering was real threat. He went on to say that no wonder women end up alone, without a relationship with a man. So then I thought "Oh, okay, these are your tactics of fighting back because for an hour and a half I got to run the show about gender." The strategy was to wait until after the class and to give these comments in a one-on-one, private way. I thought this is fighting in a way that I could feel right to my bones; this is a threat. We're talking about rape here and ending up alone. I could feel it. So part of my anger was feeling like that wouldn't happen to you, Bernardo or to you, Gary. As a woman, I have to keep thinking "Okay, here are my vulnerable edges and this is where I'm vulnerable to getting skewered. You know, talk about raping me and that's one of them, one of my vulnerabilities because I'm a woman." So there's a certain uniqueness because of who we are that seems to elicit different things from students that we then each have to figure out how to deal with. So, let's say maybe you, Gary, as a white man—I don't know what the comparable vulnerable thing is for you.

GARY: Well, there are much fewer vulnerable things. My left-wing political orientation, perhaps, makes me vulnerable in the academy, in spite of right-wing characterizations of universities as hotbeds of radicalism. I think radical white males have a lot of work to do in terms of figuring out how to use their privileged position in the classroom. I know, for instance, that I can get away with presenting radical feminist positions in the classroom, whereas a women would get clobbered, unless maybe it was a women's studies class. And then some people have multiple vulnerabilities. For Elizabeth, being female is a vulnerability on top of being Chicana. How many mainstream, dominant-culture students have taken a course from a Chicana? In other words, she doesn't fit the professional profile. "Oh they just hired her because she's minority"—all that stuff, or they just never encountered someone like her in this position. In fact bell hooks (1994) writes about one of her white students who had a terrible time with the very idea of a black woman grading her papers and giving her a course grade. A black women with authority over them was totally unheard of and several students said as much and dropped the course because they couldn't deal with the thought of a black woman giving them a grade.

KATHRYN: Right, that's the point. In this group I would be interested in hearing how do things spin out differently? We face some things in common, maybe just around the kinds of approaches to the material we teach, but then I think there's a different spin probably for each of us. For you, Mary, as a lesbian woman and for me as a heterosexual white woman, a Chicana, whatever.

BERNARDO: I think that the race, class, and gender of the professor does play a very large part in who's going to oppose you and who's not. I've had students tell me that they felt a great deal of the opposition in class had more to do with me as an "Indian" in front of the class than with the content of the readings.

KATHRYN: Right! Sometimes we disrupt privilege just by who we are.

ELIZABETH: That's right. In any given class you have to weigh "who you are" and "who they are" and then you have to decide how to best handle the situation. You decide what strategy you will use based on what your vulnerabilities are, and the power or privilege your students are relying on. Then you figure out the best way to handle this while maintaining your strength and integrity.

Reflections on the Group Dialogue

Embedded in our dialogue are a number of strategies that we employ in our attempts to create classrooms that allow for multiple discourses: we cite the research that could shed a different perspective on issues and we include them in our class readings; we confront students with their own behaviors and their own language in the hope that a process of self-reflection and self-monitoring can begin; we lay out to students our hope that a variety of voices could be heard in class and give structure to the classroom in a way that allows for this; we share our observations of what's going on in the classroom with students to see what kinds of shifts we can manage together. The list could go on, a list that many of us could create under a category of working to be a good teacher and, through the years, continuing to expand our repertoire of teaching skills; there's nothing particularly controversial or even novel in our attempts to create classrooms where multiple discourses could be evident.

But there's another level of our language that leaps out that introduces our use of overt power in our classrooms: counter power with power, silence them, refuse to engage, run over them, neutralize them. Each of these reflect the recognition that there are students who will not allow multiple voices in the classroom and who will interrupt such efforts; these are the students who, despite all the strategies listed in the previous paragraph, persist in dominating behaviors and discourses, apparently unresponsive to gentler measures that might lead to self-reflective shifts and discoveries.

Then there are words that we use to describe ourselves, in at least parts of our roles as teachers: manipulative and authoritarian. These terms were uttered by a few of us in our dialogue but could have been laid on the table by any of us; what happens if we begin to deconstruct our own discourse? This introduces the queasiness we feel in recognizing the apparent necessity of countering power with power. We couple this with the way this makes us feel as teachers; uncomfortable with ourselves but without, ultimately, alternative "strategies" when we've exhausted the repertoire developed over years of self-reflective practice.

Often the level of backlash in a classroom is the result of our own successes at moving students out of their current comfort zones. When the dominant discourse is challenged, a threat is perceived by some students, and these students take measures to preserve the status quo. Our militaristic terminology reflects that sense of warfare, that something very important is at stake: whose truths get named and who gets to decide? So we as teachers feel threatened and sometimes threatening; we are not trained to think of ourselves in these ways. Yet our teaching is about the unraveling of master narratives that subjugate many of us and therefore, evoke strong, powerful responses by those who feel their privilege threatened; it is pretense to think that this can all be "nicely" done when all involved feel they are fighting for their lives.

So we grapple with issues of power and are embarrassed by our use of "power over" techniques as we envision worlds of "power with" and "empowerment." Yet in saying that, we need to name where it is we currently locate ourselves on our continuum of teaching strategies, so we can continue to be self-reflective with our own discomfort and continue to understand the multiple dynamics involved in the micropolitics of our classrooms.

A Micropolitical View of the Engaged Classroom

Once we shift from a functionalist (whether conservative or radical) view of the classroom to a micropolitical view, we must shift our theory of power. The outcomes of classroom encounters are not based on teacher plans and intentions as more rational, functionalist models would have us believe, but rather the outcomes of classroom encounters are the result of conflict and bargaining. Power is not simply negotiated between teachers and a monolithic category "students," but rather it is negotiated between teachers and students and *among students*. This negotiation also has much to do with how students construct teachers (lesbian, leftist, "neutral," "Chicana," "Hispanic," etc.) and thus how they position themselves vis-à-vis the instructor. Students who feel their privilege being interrupted may "strike back" in class by usurping class time (a scarce classroom resource) or might make racist or sexist comments to the teacher after class in private that reassert their power over the teacher. They may also attempt to "bond" with teachers who they feel share their own attitudes or categories of privilege/oppression. The occurence of these things depends not only on who we are, but also the extent to which we bring "combustible materials" into the classroom. Viewing classrooms as a shifting force field of power relations acknowledges that teachers cannot escape the power struggles that occur therein. It also provides an understanding that we can all be both oppressed and oppressor at once.

Because classrooms are force fields of power, those who wish to engage in critical pedagogy need to reject the notion that the right teaching strategies will make the backlash go away. A pedagogy is more than a set of instructional strategies. In our dialogue we discussed the pros and cons of strategies such as small-group discussions and the desconstruction of racist, classist, sexis, or homophobic remarks made by students. We have found that these strategies work in some cases but backfire in others as discussed above.

By refusing to find easy answers in progressive teaching strategies, we are not supporting the currently popular argument that politically progressive teachers should be instructionally conservative (Delpit, 1986; Hirsch, 1996). In fact, we all consider ourselves political and educational "progressives," incorporating many student-centered, holistic, and relational techniques into our teaching. Two strategies that we have found particularly successful, for example, are the use of "quick writes," a technique borrowed from writing process teachers, and inquiry projects. By having students take ten minutes in class to write down their ideas, quieter students often feel more confidence in reading or summarizing their ideas and teachers can "call on" students to speak knowing they have had time to collect their thoughts about the topic. Some of us have collected the student comments and with students' permission read them anonymously to the group. In this way more diversity of views are expressed and the few empowered or more verbal members of the class are less likely to dominate.

An inquiry model involves students in doing mini-investigations (i.e. interviews, observations, self-study, etc.) about topics dealt with in class. In this way students bring the world into the classroom and often raise critical issues themselves. For example, a group of preservice students, preparing to become teachers, were convinced that their professor had staged a graphic example of gender discrimination in a local middle school during the week they were specifically to observe hall and classroom interactions to see what they "said" about gender. During the week a teacher in the school cheerfully announced a "unique opportunity" for the midschoolers in her class: the boys could work with a local engineer and construction company, exploring the possibilities of working with heavy construction equipment while the girls would "do makeovers" in the classroom. Convinced that nothing so blatant was a part of schooling in the nineties, the preservice students collecting the data gleefully brought their data to class, convinced that they had "found out" their university professor who must have staged the whole thing. Reassured that they were just observing a typical week in the life of a school rather than a staged event, the students quickly moved into the reality of observing discrimination rather than needing to be "convinced" by the professor that there are still inequities being perpetuated in schools. The data gathered by the students provided the framework to describe issues of gender in schools from which they eventually worked on problem solving. The data also shed light on the assigned readings, bringing to life their own observations and experiences as compared to that raised in the literature.

In classrooms that eschew an engaged and critical pedagogy for one in which expert knowledge is shared with students and in which innocuous small-group activities and discussions take place, it is unlikely that power struggles will become visible. This is because there are no "combustible materials" in the classroom that might produce any disequilibrium within students or power struggles among students and the teacher. Students in these classrooms who are from dominant groups or nondominant students who share the dominant ideology, are comfortable in these classes because the status quo is being reinforced. A particular world view is being presented that assumes a basic consensus of values in society, where conflicts of interest may exist, but where they are dealt with through fair and neutral social systems set up for that purpose.

Such classrooms are the norm in most colleges of education. They are viewed as neutral spaces in which knowledge is co-constructed with students. Unfortunately, more often than not, knowledge is only being co-constructed with some of the students, those who reflect the social values of the instructor and have the cultural capital to demand a real voice in the classroom. Here silencing and neutralizing go on in hundreds of subtle forms from the instructors' syllabus in which female and minority authors and their perspectives are often underrepresented to the subtle forms of silencing that occur when a classroom reproduces the dominant culture of power.

Conclusion

Noncritical teachers are generally unaware that they are teaching to the power in their classrooms. For example, Sadker and Sadker (1994) discuss how invisible sexist teaching is. *Dateline*'s Jane Pauley wanted to air a show on television about sexism in the classroom, but the female staffers could not discern any sexism in the classroom they taped. Sadker and Sadker had to point out what to them was obvious sexism in what on the surface appeared to be excellent teaching. They describe a lively discussion in the school library:

> With both girls' hands and boys' hands waving for attention, the librarian chose boy after boy to speak. In one interaction she peered through the forest of girls' hands waving directly in front of her to acknowledge the raised hand of a boy in the back of the room. Startled by the teacher's attention, the boy muttered, "I was just stretching." (Sadker & Sadker, 1994, p. 3)

When these patterns of bias are intentionally interrupted in the classroom, those who are used to privilege often feel angry without knowing why. They also begin to reassert what they view as their right to privilege, and often see the teacher as the culprit. Meanwhile, those students who are made to feel powerless or invisible in classrooms that reflect broader power relations in society often respond with silence. Assertiveness is always risky for the powerless. It is this level of risk that we ultimately seek to reduce through an engaged pedagogy in our classrooms.

References

Preface

Moraga, C. (1991). La güera. In *Race, class and gender*, 2d ed. Margaret L. Anderson & Patricia Hill Collins. Wadsworth, 1995.

Omi, M., & Winant, H. (1986). *Racial formation in the U.S.* New York: Routledge.

Sleeter, C. E. (1996). *Multicultural education as social activism*. Albany: State University of New York Press.

Introduction

Bartolomé, L. (1994). Beyond the methods fetish: Toward a humanizing pedagogy. *Harvard Educational Review* 62(2): 173–94.

Chávez, R. Chávez, O'Donnell, J., & Gallagos, R. L. (1995). Dilemmas of a multicultural education. In Alfonzo Nava (ed.), *Educating Americans in a multiethnic society* (3d edition). San Francisco: McGraw-Hill.

Davis, N. M. (1992). Teaching about inequality: Student resistance, paralysis, and rage. *Teaching Sociology* 20: 232–38.

Giroux, H. A. (1983). *Theory and resistance in education*. South Hadley, Mass.: Bergin & Garvey.

Grant, C. A., & Secada, W. G. (1990). Preparing teachers for diversity. In W. R. Houston (ed.), *Handbook of research on teacher education* (pp. 403–22). New York: Macmillan.

Hardiman, R. (1979). *White identity development theory*. Amherst, Mass.: New Perspectives.

hooks, b. (1994). *Teaching to transgress: Education as the practice of freedom*. New York: Routledge.

———. *Talking back*. Boston: South End Press, 1989.

Jackson, B. W., III (1976). The function of a black identity development theory in achieving relevance in education for black students. Unpublished Doctoral Dissertation, University of Massachusetts at Amherst.

Jackson, B., & Hardiman, R. (1986). Oppression: Conceptual and development analysis. Unpublished manuscript. University of Massachusetts at Amherst.

King, J. E. (1991). Dysconscious racism: Ideology, identity, and the miseducation of teachers. *Journal of Negro Education*, 60(2): 133–46.

Reyes, M. de la luz (1992). Challenging venerable assumptions: Literacy instruction for linguistically different students. *Harvard Educational Review* 62(4): 427–46.

Rodríguez, L. J. (1993). *Always running La vida loca: Gang days in L.A.* New York: Simon & Schuster.

Roman, L. G. (1993). White is a color! White defensiveness, postmodernism and antiracist pedagogy. In C. McCarthy & W. Crichlow (eds.), *Race, identity and representation in education* (pp. 71–88). New York: Routledge.

Ross, D. D., & Smith, W. (1992). Understanding preservice teachers' perspectives on diversity. *Journal of Teacher Education* 43(2): 94–103.

Sleeter, C. E. (1993). How white teachers construct race. In C. McCarthy & W. Crichlow (eds.), *Race, identity and representation in education* (pp. 157–71). New York: Routledge.

Tatum, B. D. (1992). Talking about race, learning about racism: The application of racial identity development theory. *Harvard Educational Review* 62(1): 1–24.

West, C. (1994). *Race Matters*. New York: Vintage Books.

1. Engaging the Multicultural Education Terrain

Apple, M. (1992). *Ideology and curriculum* (2d ed.). New York: Routledge.

———. (1989). *Teachers and texts: A political economy of class and gender relations in education*. New York: Routledge.

———. (1982). *Education and power*. Boston: Routledge and Kegan Paul.

Banks, J. A., & Banks, C. A. (ed.) (1996). *Handbook of research on multicultural education*. New York: Macmillan.

Berger, P. L., & Luckman, T. (1966). *The social construction of reality: A treatise in the sociology of knowledge*. New York: Anchor Books.

Bourdieu, P., & Passeron, J-C. (1992). *Reproduction in education, society, and culture* (2d ed.), translated by Lois Wacquant. London and Newbury Park, Calif.: Sage.

Chávez Chávez, R. (1997). *A Curricular Discourse constructs in achieving equity: Implications for teachers when engaged with Latino and Latina students*. A Commissioned Paper for the Hispanic Dropout Project, Department of Education, Office of Bilingual Education and Language Minority Affairs [http://www.ncbe.gwu.edu/miscpubs/used/hdp/hdp-3.html].

———. (1995). *Multicultural education in the everyday: A renaissance for the recommitted*. Washington, D.C.: AACTE.

Cuban, L. (1993). *How teachers taught: Constancy and change in American classrooms, 1880–1990*, (2d ed.). New York: Teachers College Press.

Davis, N. J. (1992). Teaching about inequality: Student resistance, paralysis and rage. *Teaching Sociology* 20: 232–38.

Estrada, K., & McLaren, P. (1993). A dialogue on multiculturalism and democratic culture. *Educational Researcher* 22 (7): 27–33.

Fernandez-Balboa, J. M., & Marshall, J. P. (1994). Dialogical pedagogy in teacher education: Toward an education for democracy. *Journal of Teacher Education* 45(3): 172–82.

Foucault, M. (1979). *Discipline and punish: The birth of the prison*, trans. Alan Sheridan. New York: Vintage Books.

Freire, P. (1970). *Pedagogy of the oppressed*. Trans. Myra Bergman Ramos. New York: Continuum.

———. (1994). Foreword. In D. Macedo, *Literacies of power: What Americans are not allowed to know* (pp. xi–xii). Boulder, Colo.: Westview Press.

Fuller, M. L. (1994). The monocultural graduate in the multicultural environment: A challenge for teacher educators. *Journal of Teacher Educators* 45(4): 269–77.

Giroux, H. A. (1988a). *Schooling and the struggle for public life: Critical pedagogy in the modern age*. Minneapolis: University of Minnesota Press.

———. (1988b). *Teachers as intellectuals: Toward a critical pedagogy of learning*. Granby, Mass.: Bergin and Garvey.

———. (1991). *Postmodernism, feminism, and cultural politics: Redrawing educational boundaries*. Albany: State University of New York Press.

———. (1993). *Living dangerously: Multiculturalism and the politics of difference*. New York: Peter Lang.

Giroux, H. A., & Purpel, D. (eds.) (1983). *The hidden curriculum and moral education: Deception or discovery?* Berkeley, Calif.: McCutchen.

Goodwin, A. L. (1994). Making the transition form self to other: What do preservice teachers really think about multicultural education? *Journal of Teacher Education* 45(3): 119–31.

Guba, E. G. (1990). *The paradigm dialog*. Newbury Park: Sage.

———. (1993). Relativism. *Curriculum Inquiry*. 22(1): 17–23.

Hidalgo, F., Chávez Chávez, R., & Ramage, J. (1996). Multicultural education: Landscape for reform in the twenty-first century. *Handbook of teacher education*, John Sikula (senior ed.). New York: Macmillan.

Kincheloe, J. L., & Steinberg, S. R. (1993). A tentative description of post-formal thinking: The critical confrontation with cognitive theory. *Harvard Educational Review* 63(3): 296–320.

King, J. E. (1991). Dysconscious racism: Ideology, identity, and the miseducation of teachers. *Journal of Negro Education* 60(2): 133–46.

Kliebard, H. M. (1995). *The struggle for the American curriculum*. New York: Routledge.

Larkin, J., & Sleeter, C. E. (1995). *Developing multicultural teacher education curricula*. Albany: State University of New York Press.

Lightfoot, S. L. (1983). *The good high school: Portraits of character and culture*. New York: Basic Books.

Lincoln, Y. S., & Guba, E. G. (1985). *Naturalistic inquiry*. Newbury Park, Calif.: Sage.

Macedo, D. P. (1993). Literacy for stupidification: The pedagogy of big lies. *Harvard Educational Review* 63(2): 183–206.

Maxcy, S. J. (1992). *Educational leadership: A critical pragmatic perspective.* New York: Bergin & Garvey.

McLaren, P. (1989). *Life in schools.* New York: Longman.

Meier, D. (1987). Central Park East: An alternative story. *Phi Delta Kappen* 88(10): 753–57.

O'Loughlin, M. (1992). Appropriate for whom? A critique of the culture and class bias underlying developmentally appropriate practice in early childhood education. Paper presented to Conference on Reconceptualizing Early Childhood Education: Research, Theory, and Practice, Chicago, September 1992.

Pang, V. O. (1994). Why do we need this class? Multicultural education for teachers. *Phi Delta Kappan* 76(4): 289–92.

Romo H., & Falbo, T. (1996). *Latino high school graduation: Defying the odds.* Austin: University of Texas Press.

Rosaldo, R. (1993). *Culture and truth: The remaking of social analysis.* Boston: Beacon.

Schwartz, P., & Oglivy, J. (1979). *The emergent paradigm: Changing patterns of thought and belief.* Analytical Report 7, Values and Lifestyles Program. Menlo Park, Calif.: SRI International. In Lincoln, Y. S., & Guba, E. G. (1985). *Naturalistic inquiry.* Newbury Park, Calif.: Sage.

Sizer, T. R. (1992). *Horace's school: Redesigning the American high school.* Boston: Houghton Mifflin.

———. (1984). *Horace's compromise: The dilemma of the American high school.* Boston: Houghton Mifflin.

Sleeter, C. E. (1992). *Keepers of the American dream: A study of staff development and multicultural education.* Bristol, Pa.: Falmer Press.

Sleeter, C. E., & McLaren, P. L. (1995). *Multicultural education, critical pedagogy, and the politics of difference.* Albany: State University of New York Press.

2. From Claiming Hegemony to Sharing Space

Aaronsohn, E., Carter, C. J., & Howell, M. (1995). Preparing monocultural teachers for a multicultural world: Attitudes toward inner-city schools. *Equity and Excellence in Education* 28 (1): 5–9.

Arends, I., Clemson, S., & Henkelman, J. (1992). Tapping nontraditional sources of minority teaching talent. In M. E. Dilworth (ed.), *Diversity in teacher education: New expectations* (pp. 160–80). San Francisco: Jossey-Bass.

Bollin, G. G., & Finkel, J. (1995).White racial identity as a barrier to understanding diversity: A study of preservice teachers. *Equity and Excellence* 28 (1): 25–30.

Brown, C. E. (1992). Restructuring for a new America. In M. E. Dilworth (ed.), *Diversity in teacher education: New expectations,* pp. 1–22. San Francisco: Jossey-Bass.

Cochran-Smith, M. (1991). Learning to teach against the grain. *Harvard Educational Review* 61(3): 279–310.

Cummins, J. (1994). From coercive to collaborative relations of power in the teaching of literacy. In Ferdman, B. M., Weber, R., and Ramirez, A. (eds.), *Literacy across languages and cultures.* Albany: State University of New York Press.

Garibaldi, A. M. (1992). Preparing teachers for culturally diverse classrooms. In M. E. Dilworth (ed.). *Diversity in teacher education: New expectations* (pp. 23–39). San Francisco: Jossey-Bass.

Hodgkinson, H. (1991). Reform versus reality. *Phi Delta Kappan* 73(1): 9–16.

Howard, G. (1993). Whites in multicultural education: Rethinking our role. *Phi Delta Kappan* 75(1): 36–41.

Irvine, J. J. (1992). Making teacher education culturally responsive. In M. E. Dilworth (ed.), *Diversity in teacher education: New expectations*, pp. 79–92. San Francisco: Jossey-Bass.

James, J. R. (1993). *Recruiting people of color for teacher education.* Bloomington, Ind.: Phi Delta Kappa, Hot Topics Series.

King, J. E. (1991). Dysconscious racism: Ideology, identity, and the miseducation of teachers. *Journal of Negro Education* 60(2): 133–46.

Ladson-Billings, G. (1994). *The dreamkeepers: Successful teachers of African American children.* San Francisco: Jossey-Bass.

McDiarmid, W. W. (1990). *What to do about differences? A study of multicultural education for teacher trainees in the Los Angeles Unified School District.* East Lansing, Mich.: National Center for Research on Teacher Education.

McIntosh, P. (1988). *White privilege and male pivilege: A personal account of coming to see correspondences through work in women's studies.* Working paper no. 189. Wellesley, Mass.: Wellesley College Center for Research on Women.

Nieto, S. (1996). *Affirming diversity: The sociopolitical context of multicultural education*, 2d ed. White Plains, N.Y.: Longman.

Pang, V. O. (1994). Why do we need this class? Multicultural education for teachers. *Phi Delta Kappan* 76(4): 289–92.

Schoem, D., Frankel, L., Zúñiga, X., & Lewis, E. A. (1993.) *Multicultural teaching at the university.* Westport, Conn.: Praeger.

Sleeter, C. E. (1992). *Keepers of the American dream: A study of staff development and multicultural education.* London: Falmer Press.

———. (1994). White racism. *Multicultural Education* 1 (4): 5–8, 39.

Tatum, B. D. (1992). Talking about race, learning about racism: The application of racial identity development theory in the classroom. *Harvard Educational Review* 62(1): 1–24.

Trueba, H. T., & Wright, P. G. (1992). On ethnographic studies and multicultural education. In Saravia-Shore, M., and Arvizu, S. F. (eds.). *Cross-cultural literacy: Ethnographies of communication in multiethnic classrooms*, pp. 299–337. New York: Garland.

United States Bureau of the Census (1993). *Monthly News* (July).

Weinberg, M. (1990). *Racism in the United States: A comprehensive classified bibliography.* Westport, Conn.: Greenwood.

3. Mediating Curriculum

Delpit, L. (1995). *Other people's children.* New York: New Press.

Doll, W. (1993). *A post-modern perspective on curriculum.* New York: Teachers College Press.

Eisner, E. W. (1985). *The educational imagination: On the design and evaluation of school programs.* New York: Macmillan.

Freire, P. (1970). *Pedagogy of the oppressed.* New York: Continuum.

hooks, b. (1994). *Teaching to transgress: Education as the practice of freedom.* New York: Routledge.

McCutcheon, G. (1995). *Developing the curriculum: Solo and group deliberation.* New York: Longman.

McLaren, P. (1989). *Life in schools: An introduction to critical pedagogy in the foundations of education.* New York: Longman.

Ross, E. W., Cornett, J. W., & McCutcheon, G. (1992). *Teacher personal theorizing: Connecting curriculum practice, theory, and research.* Albany: State University of New York Press.

Wheatley, M. J. (1992). *Leadership and the new science.* San Francisco: Berrett-Koehler.

Wingspread Group on Higher Education. (1993). *An American imperative: Higher expectations for higher education* [on-line]. Available: pub/wingspread/report.txt.

4. Engaging Students' Re-Cognition of Racial Identity

American Association of Colleges for Teacher Education (AACTE). (1973). No one model American. *Journal of Teacher Education* 24(4): 264–65. Washington: AACTE.

Baldwin, J. (1963/1988). A talk to teachers. In R. Simonson, and S. Walker (ed.), *The Graywolf annual five: Multicultural literacy* (pp. 3–12). St. Paul, Minn.: Graywolf Press.

Balenger, V. J., Hoffman, M. A., & Sedlacek, W. E. (1992). Racial attitudes among incoming white students: A study of ten-year trends. *Journal of College Student Development* 33: 245–52.

Berger, P., & Luckmann, T. (1967). *The social construction of reality.* Garden City, N.Y.: Doubleday.

Bigelow, W. (1990). Inside the classroom: Social vision and critical pedagogy. *Teachers College Record* 91(3): 437–48.

Bloom, A. (1987). *The closing of the American mind.* New York: Simon.

Boggs, C. (1984). *The two revolutions: Gramsci and the dilemmas of western Marxism.* Boston: South End Press.

Brown, D. D. (1994). Discursive moments of identification. *Current perspectives in social theory* 14: 269–92.

Bruner, J. (1990). *Acts of meaning.* Cambridge, Mass.: Harvard University Press.

Bury, J. B. (1932). *The idea of progress.* New York: Dover.

Chávez Chávez, R., O'Donnell, J., & Gallegos, R. (1995). Multiculturalism in the pedagogy of the "Everyday": Students' perspectives to "dilemmas" in a multicultural course. A paper presented at the annual meeting of the American Educational Research Association, San Francisco, April 1995.

Davis, N. J. (1992). Teaching about inequality: Student resistance, paralysis and rage. *Teaching sociology* 20: 232–38.

D'Souza, D. (1991). *Illiberal education: The politics of race and sex on campus.* New York: Free Press.

Frankenberg, R. (1993). *White women, race matters: The social construction of whiteness.* Minneapolis: University of Minnesota Press.

Golding, S. (1992). *Gramsci's democratic theory.* Toronto: University of Toronto Press.

Gould, S. J. (1981). *The Mismeasure of Man.* New York: W. W. Norton.

Hall, S. (1986). Gramsci's relevance for the study of race and ethnicity. *Journal of Communication Inquiry,* 10(2): 5–27.

Henriques, J. (1984). Social psychology and the politics of racism. In J. Henriques, C. Urwin, C. Venn, and V. Walkerdine (eds.), *Changing the subject: Psychology, social regulation and subjectivity* (pp. 60–89). London: Macmillan.

Hirsch, E. D. (1987). *Cultural Literacy: What every American needs to know.* Boston: Houghton Mifflin.

Jones, J. M. (1972). *Prejudice and racism.* Reading, Mass.: Addison-Wesley.

Macedo, D. (1994). *Literacies of power.* Boulder, Colo.: Westview Press.

Nieto, S. (1992). *Affirming diversity.* New York: Longman.

———. (1996). *Affirming diversity.* (2d ed.). New York: Longman.

O'Donnell, J. (1995). Toward an anti-racist pedagogy: A theoretical instructional paradigm. In A. Nava (ed.), *Educating Americans in a multiethnic society* (pp. 34–48). New York: McGraw-Hill.

O'Donnell, J., & Gallegos, R. (1993). *Learning and unlearning racism: Multicultural education revisited.* Boulder University of Colorado, BUENO Center for Multicultural Education. Monograph Series 9(1): 17–58.

Omi, M., & Winant, H. (1994). *Racial formation in the United States.* (2d ed.). New York & London: Routledge.

Rizvi, F. (1993). Children and the grammar of popular racism. In C. McCarthy & W. Crichlow (eds.), *Race, identity and representation in education* (pp. 126–39). New York & London: Routledge.

Roman, L. G. (1993). White is a color! White defensiveness, postmodernism and anti-racist pedagogy. In C. McCarthy & W. Crichlow (eds.), *Race, identity and representation in education* (pp. 71–88). New York & London: Routledge.

Sáenz, B. A. (1992). I want to write an American poem. In R. Gonzalez (ed.), *Without discovery* (pp. 127–43). Seattle, Wash.: Broken Moon Press.

Said, E. (1993). *Culture and imperialism.* New York: Knopf.

Seidman, I. E. (1991). *Interviewing as qualitative research.* New York: Teachers College Press.

Shor, I. (1992). *Empowering education: Critical teaching for social change.* Chicago & London: University of Chicago Press.

Sleeter, C. E., & Grant, C. A. (1991). Race, class, gender and disability in current textbooks. In M. W. Apple & L. K. Christian-Smith (eds.), *The politics of the textbook*. New York: Routledge & Chapman Hall.

Sleeter, C. E., & McLaren, P. L. (1995). Introduction: Exploring connections to build a critical multiculturalism. In C. E. Sleeter & P. L. McLaren (eds.), *Multicultural education, critical pedagogy and the politics of difference* (pp. 5–28). Albany: State University of New York Press.

Tatum, B. D. (1992). Talking about race, learning about racism: The application of racial identity development theory. *Harvard Educational Review* 62(1): 1–24.

Troyna, B., & Hatcher, R. (1992). *Racism in children's lives*. London: Routledge.

Vygotsky, L. (1987). *Thought and language*. Ed. A. Kozulin. Cambridge, Mass.: MIT Press.

Zinn, H. (1980). *A people's history of the United States*. New York: Harper & Row.

5. Toward a Just Society

Baldwin, J. (1961). In search of a majority. In *Nobody knows my name: More notes of a native son*. New York: Dial Press.

Balenger, V., Hoffman, M., & Sedlacek, W. (1992). Racial attitudes among incoming white students: A study of ten-year trends. *Journal of College Student Development* 33: 245–52.

Banks, J., & McGee, C. (eds.) (1989). *Multicultural education: Issues and perspectives*. Boston: Allyn and Bacon.

Bennett, C. (1986). *Comprehensive multicultural education: Theory and practice*. Boston: Allyn and Bacon.

———. (1995). *Comprehensive multicultural education: Theory and practice*, 3d. ed. Boston: Allyn and Bacon.

Bennett, M. J., & Bennett J. (1996). A developmental model of intercultural sensitivity: Language classroom applications. Presentation, annual meeting, Teachers of English to Speakers of Other Languages, Chicago.

Bernauer, J. (1987). Michel Foucault's ecstatic thinking. In J. Bernauer & D. Rasmussen (eds.), *The final Foucault*. Cambridge, Mass.: MIT Press.

Bodinger-deUriarte, C. (1991). Hate crime: The rise of hate crime on school campuses. *Research Bulletin, Phi Delta Kappa* 10: 1–6.

Bourdieu, P. (1973). Cultural reproduction and social reproduction. In R. Brown (ed.), *Knowledge, education, and cultural change*. London: Tavistock.

Chávez Chávez, R., O'Donnell, J., & Gallegos, R. (1995). Multiculturalism in the pedagogy of the "everyday": Students perspective on dilemmas in a multicultural education course. Presentation, Annual meeting of the American Educational Research Association, San Francisco.

Delgado-Gaitan, C., & Trueba, H. (1991). *Crossing cultural borders*. Basingstoke, U.K.: Falmer Press.

Díaz-Rico, L. T. (1992). *Constructing metacognition for learning to teach*. Poster session, Third International Conference on Cognitive Instruction, International Association for Cognitive Education (Riverside, Calif.)

————. (1993). From monocultural to multicultural teaching in an inner-city middle school. In A. Woolfolk (ed.), *Readings and cases in educational psychology*. Boston: Allyn and Bacon.

————. (1996a). *Multicultural education: From surface to substance*. Videotape for Educational Forum. Scottsdale, Ariz.: Educational Management Group.

————. (1996b). *Multicultural education: Culturally compatible teaching*. Videotape for Educational Forum. Scottsdale, Ariz: Educational Management Group.

Díaz-Rico, L., & Smith, J. (1994). Recruiting and retaining bilingual teachers: A cooperative school-community-university model. *The Journal of Educational Issues of Language Minority Students* 14 (Winter): 255–68.

Díaz-Rico, L., & Weed, K. (1995). *The crosscultural, language, and academic development handbook*. Boston: Allyn and Bacon.

Dreyfus, H. L., & Rabinow, P. (1982). *Michel Foucault: Beyond structuralism and hermeneutics*. Chicago: University of Chicago Press.

Erickson, F. (1977). Some approaches to inquiry in school-community ethnography. *Anthropology and Education Quarterly*, 8(2): 58–69.

Fairclough, N. (1988). *Power and language*. New York: Longman.

————. (1995). *Critical discourse analysis*. New York: Longman.

Foucault, M. (1979). *Discipline and punish: The birth of the prison*. New York: Vintage.

————. (1982). On the genealogy of ethics: An overview of work in progress. In H. Dreyfus & P. Rabinow (eds.), *Beyond structuralism and hermeneutics*. Chicago: University of Chicago Press.

————. (1988). Technologies of the self. In L. H. Martin, H. Gutman, & P. H. Hutton (eds.), *Technologies of the self*. Amherst: University of Massachusetts Press.

Giroux, H., & McLaren, P. (1987). Teacher education as a counter-public sphere: Notes towards a redefinition. In T. Popkewitz (ed.), *Critical studies in teacher education*. London: Falmer Press.

Goetz, J., & Lecompte, M. (1984). *Ethnography and qualitative design in educational research*. Orlando, Fla.: Academic Press.

Gold, Y., & Roth, R. (1993). *Teachers managing stress and preventing burnout*. London: Falmer Press.

Gore, Jennifer. (1994). Power and pedagogy: An empirical investigation of four sites. Presentation, Annual meeting of the American Educational Research Association, New Orleans.

Grant, C. A., & Secada, W. G. (1990). Preparing teachers for diversity. In W. R. Houston (ed.), *Handbook of research on teacher education* (pp. 403–22). New York: Macmillan.

Hamilton, D. (1994). Combating hate. *Los Angeles Times*, May 17, B1, B4.

Heath, S. B. (1983). *Ways with words*. New York: Cambridge University Press.

Henry, W. (1994). In defense of elitism. Book excerpt, *Time*, August 29, 63–65.

Hsu, L. K. (1986). A blueprint for "United States Culture." In C. Bennett, *Multicultural education* (pp. 17–20). Boston: Allyn and Bacon.

Into the Circle. Video. Tulsa, Okla.: Full Circle Communications.

La Vida de Maria. Video. Santa Cruz, Calif.: Golden Mountain Productions.

Lewis. B. (1991). *Kids' guide to social action.* Minneapolis, Minn.: Free Spirit.

Li, J., & Bennett, M. (1994). *Young children in poverty: A statistical update.* New York: National Center for the Study of Children in Poverty.

Martin, J. (1995). Political correctness has a good side. *The Sun,* July 5, D2.

Martin, L., Gutman, H., & Hutton, P. (1988). *Technologies of the self: A seminar with Michel Foucault.* Amherst University of Massachusetts Press.

McIntosh, P. (1988). White privilege and male privilege. Wellesley College.

Moll, L. (1993). Bilingual classroom studies and community analysis: Some recent trends. *Educational Researcher* 21(2): 20–24.

Reid, D. (1992). Linguistic diversity and equal. In P. Pinsent (ed.), *Language, culture and young children: Developing English in the multi-ethnic nursery and infant school.* London: David Fulton.

Scheurich, J. (1993). Toward a white discourse on white racism. *Educational Researcher* 22(8): 5–10.

Spindler, G., & Spindler, L. (1990). *The American cultural dialogue and its transmission.* Basingstoke, U.K.: Falmer Press.

Vobejda, B. (1990). Census: Hispanics more likely to live in poverty. *Washington Post,* June 8, A10.

Wright, R. (1977). The stranger mentality and the culture of poverty. In E. Leacock (ed.), *The culture of poverty.* New York: Simon and Schuster.

6. Fostering Engagement

Agger, B. (1989). *Socio(onto)logy.* Urbana, Ill.: University of Chicago Press.

Banks, J. (1994). *Multiethnic education: Theory and practice.* (3d ed.) Boston: Allyn & Bacon.

Cannella, G. S. (1995). *Deconstructing early childhood education.* Paper presented at the annual meeting of the American Educational Research Association, San Francisco, Calif., April 1995.

Collins, P. H. (1991). *Black feminist thought: Knowledge, consciousness, and the politics of empowerment.* New York: Routledge.

Comer, J. (1988). *Maggie's American dream.* New York: Plume.

Delpit, L. (1993). The silenced dialogue: Power and pedagogy in educating other people's children. In L. Weis & M. Fine (eds.), *Beyond silenced voices: Class, race, and gender in United States schools* (pp. 119–39). Albany: State University of New York Press.

Dewey, J. (1959). *Moral principles of education.* New York: Philosophical Library.

Estrada, K., & McLaren, P. (1993). A dialogue on multiculturalism and democratic culture. *Educational Researcher* 22(3): 27–33.

Freire, P. (1985). *The politics of education.* South Hadley, Mass.: Bergin & Garvey.

———. (1978). *Pedagogy-in-process.* New York: Continuum.

———. (1973). *Education for critical consciousness.* New York: Continuum.

————. (1970). *Pedagogy of the oppressed.* New York: Continuum.

Giroux, H. A., & McLaren, P. (1986). Teacher education and the politics of engagement: The case for democratic schooling. *Harvard Educational Review* 56(3): 213–38.

Greene, M. (1986). In search of a critical pedagogy. *Harvard Educational Review* 56(4): 427–41.

Halpin, Z. T. (1989). Scientific objectivity and the concept of "the other." *Women's Studies International Forum,* 12(3): 285–94.

Heath, S. B. (1983). *Ways with words: Language, life, and work in communities and classrooms.* New York: Cambridge University Press.

hooks, b. (1994). *Teaching to transgress: Education as the practice of freedom.* New York: Routledge.

Hurtado, A. (1989). Relating to privilege: Seduction and rejection in the subordination of white women and women of color. *Journal of Women in Culture and Society* 14(4): 833–55.

Kessler, S. A. (1991). Alternative perspectives on early childhood education. *Early Childhood Research Quarterly* 6: 183–97.

Kincheloe, J. (1993). *Toward a critical politics of teacher thinking: Mapping the postmodern.* Westport, Conn.: Bergin & Garvey.

Kliebard, H. M. (1986). *The struggle for the American curriculum.* Boston: Routledge & Kegan Paul.

Kozol, J. (1991). *Savage Inequalities: Children in America's Schools.* New York: Crown.

————. (1989). *Rachel and her children.* New York: Crown.

————. (1985). *Illiterate America.* Garden City, N.Y.: Doubleday.

Lerner, G. (ed.). (1972). *Black women in white America: A documentary history.* New York: Vintage.

McLaren, P., & Tadeu da Silva, T. (1993). Decentering pedagogy: Critical literacy, resistance and the politics of memory. In P. McLaren & P. Leonard (eds.), *Paulo Freire: A critical encounter* (pp. 47–89). New York: Routledge.

Macedo, D. (1994). *Literacies of power: What Americans are not allowed to know.* Boulde, Colo.: Westview Press.

Nieto, S. (1992). *Affirming diversity: The sociopolitical context of multicultural education.* New York: Longman.

Oakes, J. (1985). *Keeping track: How schools structure inequality.* New Haven, Conn.: Yale University Press.

Ogbu, J. (1978). *Minority education and caste.* New York: Academic Press.

O'Loughlin, M. (1992). Appropriate for whom? A critique of the culture and class bias underlying developmentally appropriate practice in early childhood education. Paper presented at the conference on Reconceptualizing Early Childhood Education, Chicago, Ill. (September).

Paley, V. (1995). *Kwanzaa and me: A teacher's story.* Cambridge, Mass.: Harvard University Press.

————. (1992). *You can't say you can't play.* Cambridge, Mass.: Harvard University Press.

————. (1981). *Wally's stories.* Cambridge, Mass.: Harvard University Press.

————. (1979). *White teacher.* Cambridge, Mass.: Harvard University Press.

Pinar, W. F. (ed.). (1975). *Curriculum theorizing: The reconceptualists.* Berkeley, Calif.: McCutchan.

———. (ed.). (1988). *Contemporary curriculum discourses.* Scottsdale, Ariz.: Corsuch Scarisbrick.

Rawls, J. (1971). A *theory of justice.* Cambridge, Mass.: Harvard University Press.

Rogoff, B. (1990). *Apprenticeship in thinking: Cognitive development in social context.* New York: Oxford University Press.

Shor, I. (ed.). (1987). *Freire for the classroom: A sourcebook for liberatory teaching.* Portsmouth, N.H.: Heinemann.

Silin, J. G. (1995). *Sex, death, and the education of children: Our passion for ignorance in the age of AIDS.* New York: Teachers College Press.

Sleeter, C. E. (1989). Multicultural education as a form of resistance to oppression. *Journal of Education* 17(3): 51–71.

Sleeter, C. E., & Grant, C. A. (1993). (2d ed.). *Making choices for multicultural education: Five approaches to race, class, and gender.* New York: Macmillan.

Spodek, B. (1989). *What should we teach kindergarten children?* (Cassette Recording No. 612-89121). Alexandria, Va.: Association for Supervision and Curriculum.

———. (1982). The kindergarten: A retrospective and contemporary view. In L. Katz (Ed.), *Current topics in early childhood education,* vol. 4 (pp. 173–91). Norwood, N.J.: Ablex.

Spradley, J. R., & McCurdy, D. W. (1988). *The cultural experience.* Prospect Heights, Ill.: Waveland.

Weis, L., & Fine, M. (eds.). (1993). *Beyond silenced voices: Class, race, and gender in United States schools.* Albany: State University of New York Press.

Zeichner, K. M. (1993). *Educating teachers for cultural diversity.* Unpublished manuscript.

Zeichner, K. M., & Liston, D. P. (1990). Traditions of reform in U.S. teacher education. *Journal of Teacher Education* 41(2): 3–20.

Zeichner, K. M., & Melnick, S. (1993, April). *Studying the preparation of teachers for cultural diversity.* Paper presented at the annual meeting of the American Educational Research Association, Atlanta, Ga.

7. Confessions of a Methods Fetishist

Adler, M. (1984). *The paideia program.* New York: Macmillan.

Althusser, L. (1971). Ideology and ideological state apparatuses. In *Lenin and philosophy* (pp. 127–86). New York: Monthly Review Press.

Apple, M., & Christian-Smith, L. K. (eds.) (1991). *The politics of the textbook.* New York: Routledge.

Bartolomé, L. (1994). Beyond the methods fetish: Toward a humanizing pedagogy. *Harvard Educational Review* 64(2): 173–94.

Bloom, A. (1987). *The closing of the American mind.* New York: Simon & Schuster.

Bourdieu, P. (1990). *The logic of practice*, Trans. R. Nice. Palo Alto, Calif.: Stanford University Press.

Brodkey, L. (1987). Writing critical ethnographic narratives. *Anthropology and Education Quarterly* 18: 67–76.

Campbell, J. (1949.) *The hero with a thousand faces*. Reprint. Princeton, N.J.: Princeton University Press, 1972.

Cazden, C. (1988). *Classroom discourse*. Portsmouth, N.H.: Heinemann.

Dressman, M. (in press). Congruence, resistance, liminality: Reading and ideology in three school libraries. *Curriculum Inquiry* 27(3): 267–315.

Fiske, J. (1987). *Television culture*. New York: Routledge.

———. (1989). *Understanding popular culture*. Boston: Unwin Hyman.

Foley, D. (1990). *Learning capitalist culture: Deep in the heart of Tejas*. Philadelphia: University of Pennsylvania Press.

Foucault, M. (1977). *Discipline and punish*. New York: Vintage.

Freire, P. (1970). *Pedagogy of the oppressed*. New York: Continuum.

Heath, S. B. (1983). *Ways with words*. Cambridge: Cambridge University Press.

Kristeva, J. (1989). *Language the unknown: An initiation into linguistics*. Trans. A. M. Menke. New York: Columbia University Press.

MacLeod, J. (1987). *Ain't no makin' it: Leveled aspirations in a low-income neighborhood*. Boulder, Colo.: Westview Press.

Mamchur, C. (1994). Don't you dare say "fart." *Language Arts* 71: 95–100.

McLaren, P. (1993). *Schooling as a ritual performance*. (2d ed.). New York: Routledge.

Peirce, C. S. (1931). *Collected papers of Charles Sanders Peirce, Vol. II: Elements of Logic* (pp. 134–78). Cambridge, Mass.: Harvard University Press, 1958.

Roosevelt, D. (1995). *We can't use it in da ghetto. Doubts about responsible teaching in a writing workshop*. Paper presented at the meeting of the American Educational Research Association, San Francisco (April).

Rosen, H. (1985). The voices of communities and language in classrooms [review of the book *Ways with words*]. *Harvard Educational Review* 55: 448–56.

Sleeter, C. E., & Grant, C. A. (1991). Race, class, gender, and disability in current textbooks. In M. Apple & L. K. Christian-Smith (eds.), *The politics of the textbook* (pp. 78–110). New York: Routledge.

Toulmin, S. (1990). *Cosmopolis: The hidden agenda of modernity*. Chicago: University of Chicago Press.

Turner, V. (1969). *The ritual process: Structure and anti-structure*. Ithaca, N.Y.: Cornell University Press.

West, C. (1994). *Race matters*. New York: Vintage.

Willis, P. (1981). *Learning to labor: How working-class kids get working-class jobs*. New York: Teachers College Press.

8. Upstream in the Mainstream

Ada, A. F. (1990). *A magical encounter: Spanish language children's literature in the classroom*. Compton, Calif.: Santillana.

Anaya, R. (1995). *The Anaya reader*. New York: Warner Books.

Beyer, L. E., & Apple, M. W. (1988). Values and politics in the curriculum. In Landon E. Beyer and Michael W. Apple (eds.), *The curriculum: Problems, politics and possibilities* (pp. 3–16). Albany: State University of New York.

Borland, H. (1963). *When the legends die.* Philadelphia: J. B. Lippincott.

Boyer, E. (1987). *College: The undergraduate experience in America.* New York: Harper & Row.

Britton, J. (1989). Writing and reading in the classroom. In Anne Haas Dyson (ed.), *Collaboration through writing and reading: Exploring possibilities* (pp. 217–46). Urbana, Ill.: National Council of Teaching of English.

Brown, C. (1978). *Literacy in thirty hours: Paulo Freire's process in northeast Brazil.* Chicago: Alternate Schools Network.

Bruner, J. (1994). Life as narrative. In A. H. Dyson & C. Genishi (eds.), *The need for story: Cultural diversity in classroom and community* (pp. 28–37). Urbana, Ill.: National Council of Teaching of English.

Chávez Chávez, R., Belkin, L. D., Hornback, J. G., & Adams, K. (1991). Dropping out of school: Issues affecting culturally, ethnically, and linguistically distinct student groups. *The Journal of Educational Issues of Language Minority Students* 8: 1–21.

Chomsky, N. (1995). A dialogue with Noam Chomsky. *Harvard Educational Review* 65(2): 127–44.

Crichton, M. (1993). *Acceptance speech from the national press club.* New York: National Public Radio.

Dorfman, A. (1983). *The emperor's old clothes: What the Lone Ranger, Babar, and other innocent heroes do to our minds.* New York: Pantheon Books.

Dykstra, D. I. (1996). Teaching introductory physics to college students. In Catherine Fosnot (ed.), *Constructivism: Theory, perspectives, and practice* (pp. 182–204). New York: Teachers College Press.

——— (1995). Toward a scholarship of teaching: Against the dichotomy between research and teaching. Unpublished manuscript.

Eiseley, L. (1987). The sorcerer in the wood, 1947–1966. In Kenneth Heuer (ed.), *The lost notebooks of Loren Eiseley.* Boston: Little, Brown.

Fox, M. (1993). *Radical reflections: Passionate opinions on teaching learning and living.* New York: Harcourt Brace & Company.

Freire, P. (1970). *Pedagogy of the oppressed.* New York: Continuum.

———. (1973). *Education for critical consciousness.* New York: Continuum.

———. (1987). Letter to North-American teachers, Trans. Carman Hunter. In Ira Shor (ed.), *Freire for the classroom: A source book for liberatory teaching* (pp. 211–14). Portsmouth, N.H.: Heinemann.

———. (1991). Forward. In Eleanor Kutz & Hephzibah Roskelly, *An unquiet pedagogy: Transforming practice in the English classroom.* Portsmouth, N.H.: Boynton/Cook & Heinemann.

Freire, P., & Macedo, D. (1987). *Literacy: Reading the word and the world.* New York: Bergin and Garvey.

———. (1995). A dialogue: Culture, language, and race. *Harvard Educational Review* 65(3): 377–402.

Gabbard, D. A. (1993). *Silencing Ivan Illich: A Foucauldian analysis of intellectual exclusion.* San Francisco: Austin & Winfield.

Gadotti, M. (1994). *Reading Paulo Freire: His life and work.* Albany: State University of New York.

————. (1996). *Pedagogy of praxis: A dialectical philosophy of education.* Albany: State University of New York.

García, E. H. (1995). The Mexican Americans. In Carl Grant (ed.), *Educating for diversity: An anthology of multicultural voices* (pp. 159–68). Needham Heights, Mass.: Allyn & Bacon.

Giroux, H. (1983). *Theory and resistance in education: A pedagogy for the opposition.* South Hadley, Mass.: Bergin and Garvey.

————. (1988). *Teachers as intellectuals.* New York: Bergin & Garvey.

————. (1996). *Fugitive cultures: Race, violence and youth.* London: Routledge.

Giroux, H., & McLaren, P. (1986). Teacher education and the politics of engagement: The case for democratic schooling. *Harvard Educational Review* 56(3): 213–38.

Greene, M. (1994). Multiculturism, community, and the arts. In A. Haas Dyson & C. Genishi (eds.), *The need for story: Cultural diversity in classroom and community* (pp. 11–27). Urbana, Ill.: National Council of Teaching of English.

Gussin-Paley, V. (1994). *The boy who would be a helicopter: The use of storytelling in the classroom.* Cambridge, Mass.: Harvard University Press.

Hayes, C. W., & Bahruth, R. (1985). Querer es poder. In Jane Hansen, Tom Newkirk, & Donald Graves (eds.), *Breaking ground: Teachers relate reading and writing in the elementary school* (pp. 97–108). Portsmouth, N.H.: Heinemann.

Hayes, C. W., Bahruth, R., & Kessler, C. (1991). *Literacy con carino.* Portsmouth, N.H.: Heinemann.

Kozol, J. (1991). *Savage inequalities.* New York: Crown.

Krashen, S. (1983). The din in the head, input, and the language acquisition device. In John Oller & Patricia Richard-Amato (eds.), *Methods that work* (pp. 295–301). Rowley, Mass.: Newbury House.

Leistyna, P., Woodrum, A., & Sherblom, S. A. (eds.) (1996). *Breaking free: The transformation of critical pedagogy.* Cambridge, Mass.: *Harvard Education Review*, Reprint Series No. 27.

Lortie, D. C. (1975). *Schoolteacher: A sociological study.* Chicago: University of Chicago Press.

Macedo, D. (1994). *Literacies of power: What Americans are not allowed to know.* Boulder, Colo.: Westview Press.

McLaren, P. (1988). Forward: Critical theory and the meaning of hope. In Henry Giroux, *Teachers as intellectuals.* New York: Bergin & Garvey.

Moffett, J. (1989). Introduction. In Anne Haas Dyson (ed.), *Collaboration through writing and reading: Exploring possibilities* (pp. 21–24). Urbana, Ill.: National Council of Teaching of Education.

Montessori, M. (1964). *The Montessori method.* Cambridge, Mass.: Robert Bently.

Morton, D. (1992). On "hostile pedagogy," "supportive" pedagogy, and "political correctness": Letter to a student complaining of his grade. *Journal of Urban and Cultural Studies* 2(2): 79–94.

Paterson, K. (1977). *Bridge to Terabithia.* New York: Crowell Publishing.

Postman, N. (1985). *Amusing ourselves to death: Public discourse in the age of show business.* New York: Viking.

Robinson, B. (1972). *The best Christmas pageant ever.* New York: Harper Collins.

Schniedewind, N. (1987). Feminist values: Guidelines for teaching methodology in women's studies. In Ira Shor (ed.), *Freire for the classroom: A source book for liberatory teaching* (pp. 170–79). Portsmouth, N.H.: Heinemann.

Shor, I. (1990). Liberation education: An interview with Ira Shor. *Language Arts* 67(4): 342–53.

Shor, I., & Freire, P. (1987). *A pedagogy for liberation: Dialogues on transforming education.* New York: Bergin & Garvey.

Smith, F. (1981). Demonstrations, engagement and sensitivity. *Language Arts* 58(1): 103–12.

Steiner, S., & Bahruth, R. (1994). *In the spirit of collaboration: Experimental elementary teacher preparation* [film]. Boise, Idaho: Simplot-Micron Instructional Technology Center.

Storey, D. (1993). *Newboy.* Reprint from Rethinking our classroom workshops. Washington, D.C.: Network of Educators on the Americas.

Taylor, M. (1976). *Roll of thunder, hear my cry.* New York: Dial Books.

Trueba, H. (1991). *Dreams come in all languages.* Keynote address at the Wisconsin Conference on Bilingual ESL/Multicultural Education, Peewaukee, Wisc.

Villanueva, V. (1993). *Bootstraps: From an American academic of color.* Urbana, Ill.: National Council of Teaching of English.

9. Engaging Special Education Practitioners with Language and Culture

Baca, L. M., & Cervantes, H. P. (1989). *The bilingual special education interface.* Columbus, Ohio: Merrill.

Cummins, J. (1980). The role of primary language development in promoting educational success for language minority students. In *Schooling and language mminority students: A theoretical framework* (pp. 3–50). Los Angeles: California State University, Evaluation, Dissemination and Assessment Center.

———. (1984). *Bilingualism and special education: Issues in assessment and pedagogy.* San Diego, Calif.: College Hill Press.

De León, J. (1990). A model for an advocacy-oriented assessment process in the psychoeducational evaluation of culturally and linguistically different students. *Educational Issues of Language Minority Students* 7 (Summer): 53–67.

———. (1995). Intelligence testing of Hispanic students. In H. Kayser, *Bilingual speech language pathology: An Hispanic focus.* San Diego, Calif.: Singular Press.

Dunn, L. M. (1987). *Bilingual Hispanic children on the U.S. mainland: A re-*

view of research on their cognitive, linguistic, and scholastic development. Circle Pines, Minn.: American Guidance Service.

Figueroa, R. A. (1989). Psychological testing of linguistic minority students: Knowledge gaps and regulations. *Exceptional Children* 56(2): 145–52.

Grossman, H. (1995). *Special education in a diverse society.* Needham Heights, Mass.: Allyn & Bacon.

Hamayan, E. V., & Damico, J. S. (1991). *Limiting bias in the assessment of bilingual students.* Austin, Tex.: Pro-Ed.

Hoover, J. J., & Collier, C. (1991). Meeting the needs of culturally and linguistically diverse exceptional learners: Prereferral to mainstreaming. *Teacher Education and Special Education* 14 (1): 30–34.

Mercer, J. (1973). *Sociocultural factors in testing minority children.* Proceedings of the National Education Association Conference on Testing, 45–49.

Nieto, S. (1992). *Affirming diversity: The sociopolitical context of multicultural education.* White Plains, N.Y.: Longman.

Ogbu, J. (1987). Variability in minority school performance: A problem in search of an explanation. *Anthropology and Education Quarterly* 18: 312–14.

Ortiz, A. A., & Garcia, S. B. (1988). A prereferral process for preventing inappropriate referrals of Hispanic students to special education. In A. A. Ortiz & B. A. Ramirez (eds.), *Schools and the culturally diverse exceptional student: Promising practices and future directions* (pp. 6–18). Reston, Va.: Council for Exceptional Children.

Ortiz, A. A., & Yates, J. R. (1988). *Characteristics of learning disabled, mentally retarded, and speech-language handicapped Hispanic students at initial evaluation and reevaluation.* ERIC ED 298 705.

Rueda, R. (1991). Characteristics of literacy programs for language-minority students. In E. H. Hiebert (ed.), *Literacy for a diverse society: Perspectives, practices, and policies* (pp. 93–105). New York: Teachers College Press.

Salend, S. J., & Fradd, S. (1986). Nationwide availability of services for limited English proficient handicapped students. *The Journal of Special Education,* 20: 127–35.

Valencia, R. R. (1991). *Chicano school failure and success: Research and policy agendas for the 1990s.* London and New York: Falmer Press.

U.S. Department of Commerce, Bureau of the Census (1989). *The Hispanic population in the United States: March 1988.* Series P-20, No. 438.

Ysseldyke, J. E., & Algozzine, B. (1983). Diagnostic classification decisions as a function of referral information. *Journal of Special Education* 13: 429–35.

10. Exploring the Use of History in Multicultural/Multilingual Teacher Education

Banks, James A. (1986). Race, ethnicity and schooling in the United States: Past, present and future. In Banks, J. *Multicultural education in western societies* (pp. 30–50). London: Holt.

Beilin, Y. (1993). *Israel : A concise political history.* New York: St. Martin's Press.

Bishop, R. S. (1994). *Kaleidoscope: A multicultural booklist for grades K–8.* Urbana, Ill. : National Council of Teachers of English.

Brandt, G. (1986). *The realization of anti-racist teaching.* London: Falmer Press.

Bourne, R. S. (1916). Trans-National America. *The Atlantic Monthly* 118.

Castellanos, D. (1983). *The Best of two worlds; Bilingual-bicultural education in the U.S.* Trenton: New Jersey State Department of Education.

Clark, B. (1994). *Lone Wolf v. Hitchcock.* Lincoln: University of Nebraska Press.

Cohen, M. J. (1987). *The origins and evolution of the Arab-Zionist conflict.* Berkeley: University of California Press.

Cook, L. A. (1951). *Intergroup relations in teacher education: An analytical study of intergroup education in colleges and schools in the United States: Functions, current expressions, and improvements.* Washington, D.C.: American Council on Education.

Crawford, J. (1991). *Bilingual education: History, politics, theory and practice.* Los Angeles: Bilingual Education Services.

Cubberly, E. (1909). *Changing conceptions of education.* Boston: Houghton Mifflin.

Cummins, J. (1986). *Empowering minority students.* Sacramento: California Association for Bilingual education.

Drachsler, J. (1920). *Democracy and assimilation.* New York: Macmillan.

Freire, P. (1970). *Pedagogy of the oppressed.* New York: Continuum.

Fullan, M. G. (1991). *The new meaning of educational change.* New York: Teachers College Press.

Graham, H. D. (1994). Race, history, and policy: African-Americans and civil rights since 1964. In H. D. Graham (ed.), *Civil rights in the United States* (pp. 12–39). University Park: Pennsylvania State University Press.

Hayes, M. L., & Conklin, M. E. (1953). Intergroup attitudes and experimental change. *Journal of Experimental Education* 22: 19–36.

Howard, G. R. (1993). Rethinking Our Role: Whites in Multicultural Education. *Phi Delta Kappan* 1: 36–41.

Kallen, H. (1924). *Culture and democracy in the United States.* New York: Boni and Liveright.

Kloss, H. (1977). *American bilingual tradition.* Rowley, Mass.: Newbury House.

Koppelman, K., & Richardson, R. (1995). What's in it for me? Persuading nonminority teacher education students to become advocates for multicultural education. In R. J. Martin (ed.), *Practicing what we teach* (pp. 145–162). Albany: State University of New York Press.

Krashen, S. (1982). *Principles and practice in second language acquisition.* Oxford: Pergamon.

Malcolm, N. (1994). *Bosnia: A short history.* New York: New York University Press.

Mestrovic, S. G. (1993). *Habits of the Balkan heart.* College Station: Texas A & M.

———. (1994). *The balkinization of the West.* London: Routledge.

National Council of Teachers of English. (1942). *Americans all: Studies in intercultural education.* Washington, D.C.: National Education Association.

Remnick, D. (1994). *Lost in space. The New Yorker Magazine*, December 5, pp. 79–86.

Rodriguez, D. (1980). *Pachuco*. Los Angeles: Holloway House.

Schlesinger, A. M. (1992). *The disuniting of America*. New York: Norton.

Sleeter, C., & Grant, C. (1994). *Making choices for multicultural Education: Five approaches to race, class, and gender*. New York: Macmillan.

Taba, H., Brady, E. H., & Robinson, J. T. (1952). *Intergroup education in public schools*. Washington, D.C.: American Council on Education.

Takaki, R. T. (1993). *A different mirror: A history of multicultural America*. Boston: Little, Brown.

Téllez, K., Hlebowitsh, P.S., Norwood, P. & Cohen, M., (1995). Social service and teacher education at the University of Houston. In J. Larkin & C. Sleeter (eds.), *Developing multicultural teacher education curriculum*. Albany: State University of New York Press.

Trager, H. G., & Morrow, M. R. (1952). *They learn what they live: Prejudice in young children*. New York: Harper & Brothers.

United States Department of Commerce, Bureau of the Census. (1994). Web site: www.census.gov.

Wirszup, I., & Streit, R. (1987). *Developments in school mathematics education around the world: Applications-oriented curricula and technology-supported learning for all students*. Reston, Va.: National Council of Teachers of Mathematics.

11. The Struggle for Cultural Self

Apple, M. W. (1993). *Official knowledge*. New York: Routledge.

DeVillar, R. A., Faltis, C. J., & Cummins, J. P. (1994). *Cultural diversity in schools*. Albany: State University of New York Press.

Freire, P. (1968). *Pedagogy of the oppressed*. New York: Herder & Herder.

Freire, P., & Macedo, D. (1987). *Literacy: Reading the word and the world*. New York: Bergin & Garvey.

Giroux, H. A. (1992). *Border crossings*. New York: Routledge.

———— (1994). *Disturbing pleasures*. New York: Routledge.

Giroux, H. A., & McLaren, P. (1994). *Between Borders*. New York: Routledge.

hooks, b. (1994a). *Outlaw culture*. New York: Routledge.

————. (1994b). *Teaching to transgress*. New York: Routledge.

————. (1995). *Killing rage*. New York: Henry Holt.

Kanpol, B. (1994). *Critical pedagogy*. Westport, Conn.: Bergin & Garvey.

Langness, L. L. (1974). *The study of culture*. Novato, Calif.: Chandler & Sharp.

Lieber, C., Mikel, E., & Pervil, S. (1994). Radical change in assessment: A catalyst for democratic education. In J. M. Novak (ed.), *Democratic teacher education* (pp. 229–50). Albany: State University of New York Press.

Macedo, D. (1994). *Literacies of power*. Boulder, Colo.: Westview.

Martinez, O. J. (1994). *Border people*. Tucson: University of Arizona Press.

Nieto, S. (1992). *Affirming diversity*. White Plains, N.Y.: Longman.

Phinney, J. S. (March, 1992). Acculturation attitudes and self-esteem among high school and college students. *Youth and Society* 23(3): 299–312.

Richard-Amato, P. A., & Snow, M. A. (eds.) (1992). *The multicultural classroom.* White Plains, N.Y.: Longman.

Rosaldo, R. (1989). *Culture and Truth.* Boston: Beacon Press.

Spring, J. (1995). *The intersection of cultures.* New York: McGraw-Hill.

Sleeter, C. E. (1991). *Empowerment through multicultural education.* Albany: State University of New York Press.

Will, G. (1994). The restoration. *Newsweek* 124(22), November 28, p. 78.

12. Challenging Privilege

Ahlquist, R. (1992). Manifestations of inequality: Overcoming resistance in a multicultural foundations course. In C. Grant (ed.), *Research and Multicultural Education* (pp. 89–105). Bristol, Pa.: Taylor & Francis.

Askew, S., & Ross, C. (eds.), (1988). *Boys don't cry.* London: Open University Press.

Banks, J. (1994). *Multiethnic education: Theory and practice.* Needham Heights, Mass.: Allyn & Bacon.

Bennett, C., Niggle, T., & Stage, F. (1990). Preservice multicultural teacher education: Predictors of student readiness. *Teacher and Teacher Education* 6 (3): 243–54.

Bohmer, S., & Briggs, J. L. (1991). Teaching privileged students about gender, race and class oppression. *Teaching Sociology* 19: 154–63.

Cooper Shaw, C. (1993). Multicultural teacher education: A call for conceptual change. *Multicultural Education* 1 (3): 22–24.

Cross, B. E. (1993). How do we prepare teachers to improve race relations? *Educational Leadership* 50(8): 64–65.

Davis, N. J. (1992). Teaching about inequality: Student resistance, paralysis and rage. *Teaching Sociology* 20: 232–38.

Dziech, B. (1995, January 13). Coping with the alienation of white male students. *The Chronicle of Higher Education* 41(18): January 13, B1–B2.

García, J., & Pugh, S. (1992). Multicultural education in teacher preparation programs—A political or an educational concept? *Phi Delta Kappan* 74(3): 214–19.

Goodwin, A. L. (1994). Making the transition from self to other: What do preservice teachers really think about multicultural education? *Journal of Teacher Education* 45(2): 119–30.

Hardiman, R. (1979). White identity development theory. Unpublished manuscript.

Helms, J. (1993). Toward a model of white racial identity development. In J. Helms (ed.), *Black and white racial identity* (pp. 49–66). New York: Greenwood Press.

Lundberg, M., & Fawer, J. (1994). Thinking like a teacher: Encouraging cognitive growth in case analysis. *Journal of Teacher Education,* 45(4): 289–97.

McCormick, T. E. (1993, April). *Teaching a course on multicultural nonsexist education to a predominantly white female population of future teachers: Issues and problems.* Paper presented at the annual meeting of the American Educational Research Association, Atlanta, Ga.

McDiarmid, G. W., & Price, J. (1993). Preparing teachers for diversity: A study of student teachers in a multicultural program. In M. O'Hair & S. Odell (eds.), *Diversity and teaching* (pp. 31–59). Fort Worth, Tex.: Harcourt Brace Jovanovich.

Maher, F. (1991). Gender reflexivity and teacher education: The Wheaton program. In B. Tabachnick & K. Zeichner (eds.), *Issues and practices in inquiry oriented teacher education* (pp. 22–34). Philadelphia: Falmer Press.

Martin, B., & Mohanty, C. T. (1986). Feminist politics: What's home got to do with it? In T. De Lauretis (ed.), *Feminist studies, critical studies* (pp. 191–212). Bloomington: Indiana University Press.

Morrison, P., & Eardley, T. (1988). About men. In S. Askew & C. Ross (eds.), *Boys don't cry* (pp. 14–15). London: Open University Press.

Nel, J. (1993). Preservice teachers' perceptions of the goals of multicultural education: implications for the empowerment of minority students. *Educational Horizons* 71(3): 120–25.

Nieto, S. (1992). *Affirming diversity: The sociopolitical context of multicultural education.* New York: Longman.

O'Neil, J. M. (1982). Gender role conflict and strain in men's lives. In K. Solomon & N. Levy (eds.), *Men in transition: Theory and therapy* (pp. 5–44). New York: Plenum Press.

———. (1996). The Gender Role Journey Workshop (1985–1995): Exploring sexism and gender role conflict in a coeducational setting. In M. Andronico (ed.), *Men in groups: Realities and insights.* Washington, D.C.: APA Books.

O'Neil, J., & Eagan, J. (1992). Men's and women's gender-role journeys: A metaphor for healing, transition, and transformation. In B. R. Wainrib (ed.), *Gender issues across the life cycle* (pp. 107–23). New York: Springer.

O'Neil, J., Eagan, J., Owen, S., & McBride Murry, V. (1993). The gender role journey measure: Scale development and psychometric evaluation. *Sex Roles* 28(3/4): 167–85.

Rakow, L. F. (1984). Gender and race in the classroom: Teaching way out of line. *Feminist Teacher* 6: 10–13.

Rutledge, E. M. (1982). Students' perceptions of racism in higher education. *Integrated Education* 20(3–5): 106–12.

Scheurich, J. J. (1993). Toward a white discourse on white racism. *Educational Researcher* 22(8): 5–10.

Sleeter, C. (1992). *Keepers of the American dream: A study of staff development and multicultural education.* Bristol, Pa.: Taylor & Francis.

Sleeter, C., & Grant, C. (1994). *Making choices for multicultural education.* New York: Macmillan.

Tatum, B. D. (1992). Talking about race, learning about racism: The application of racial identity development theory in the classroom. *Harvard Educational Review* 62(1): 1–24.

Van Dijk, T. (1993). *Elite discourse and racism.* Newbury Park, Calif.: Sage.

Weis, L. (1990). *High school as a site for the encouragement of white domi-nance.* New York: Graduate School of Education Publications.

13. Moving Off Center

Alliance for Service-Learning in Education Reform (n.d.). *Standards of quality for school-based service-learning.* Pamphlet.

Allport, G. W. (1954). *The nature of prejudice.* South Hadley, Mass.: Addison-Wesley.

Banks, J. A. (1988). *Multiethnic education: Theory and practice,* 2d ed. New York: Allyn & Bacon.

Bowles, S. & H. Gintis. (1976). *Schooling in capitalist America.* New York: Basic Books.

Densmore, K. (1995). An interpretation of multicultural education and its impli-cations for school-community relationships. In C. A. Grant (ed.), *Education for diversity: An anthology of multicultural voices.* Boston: Allyn & Bacon, pp. 405–18.

Frankenberg, R. (1993). *White women, race matters: The social construction of whiteness.* Minneapolis: University of Minnesota Press.

Grant, C. A., & W. F. Tate. (1995). Multicultural education through the lens of the multicultural education research literature. In J. A. Banks and C. A. McGee Banks (eds.), *Handbook of research on multicultural education* (pp. 145–66). New York: Macmillan.

Hardiman, R., & B. W. Jackson. (1992). Racial identity development: Under-standing racial dynamics in college classrooms and on campus. In M. Adams (ed.), *Promoting diversity in college classrooms: Innovative re-sponses for the curriculum, faculty, and institutions* 52 (pp. 21–37). San Francisco: Jossey-Bass.

Katz, J. H. (1978). *White awareness: Handbook for anti-racism training.* Nor-man: University of Oklahoma Press.

Kendall, J. C., et al., (eds.) (1990). *Combining service and learning: A resource book for community and public service,* vols. 1 and 2. Raleigh, N.C.: Na-tional Society for Internships and Experiential Education.

McDiarmid, G. W. (1992). Tilting at webs of belief: Field experiences as a means of breaking with experience. In S. Feiman-Nemser and H. Featherstone (eds.), *Exploring teaching: Reinventing an introductory course* (pp. 34–58). New York: Teachers College Press.

McIntosh, P. (1990, Winter). White privilege: Unpacking the invisible knapsack. *Independent School* 31–36.

Nieto, S. (1992). *Affirming diversity: The sociopolitical context of multicul-tural education.* New York: Longman.

O'Grady, C. R. (forthcoming). *Transforming the world: Service learning and multicultural education.*

Ryan, W. (1976). *Blaming the victim.* New York: Vintage Books.

Style, E. (1988). Curriculum as window and mirror. *Listening for all voices: Proceedings of the Oak Knoll School Conference.*

Tatum, B. D. (1992, Spring). Talking about race, learning about racism: The application of racial identity development theory in the classroom. *Harvard Educational Review* 62(1): 1–24.

Valli, Linda. (1995, April). The dilemma of race: Learning to be color blind and color conscious. *Journal of Teacher Education* 46(2): 120–29.

Witmer, J. T., & C. S. Anderson. (1994). *How to establish a high school service learning program.* Alexandria, Va.: Association for Supervision and Curriculum Development.

14. Identity and Engagement in Multicultural Education

Adams, A. J. (1991). Afracentric pedagogy: A holistic response to teacher and student passivity. Unpublished manuscript.

Ahlquist, R. (1991). Position and imposition: Power relations in a multicultural foundations class. *Journal of Negro Education* 60(2): 158–69.

Angelou, M. (1969). *I know why the caged bird sings.* New York: Bantam.

Davis, N. J. (1992). Teaching about inequality: Student resistance, paralysis, and rage. *Teaching Sociology* 20: 232–38.

Ellsworth, E. (1989). Why doesn't this feel empowering? Working through the repressive myths of critical pedagogy. *Harvard Educational Review* 59(3): 297–324.

Frye, M. (1983). *The politics of reality: Essays in feminist theory.* Freedom, Calif.: Crossing Press.

Gore, J. (1990). What *can* we do for you! What *can* "we" do for "you?" Struggling over empowerment in critical and feminist pedagogy. *Educational Foundations* 4(3): 5–26.

Keeley, S. M., Shemberg, K. M., Cowell, B. S., & Zinnbauer, B. J. (1995). Coping with student resistance to critical thinking: What the psychotherapy literature can tell us. *Journal of College Teaching* 43(4): 140–45.

Lather, P. (1991). Post-critical pedagogies: A feminist reading. *Education and Society* 9(1–2): 100–11.

Lindquist, B. (1994). Beyond student resistance: A pedagogy of possibility. *Teaching Education* 6(2): 1–8.

McIntosh, P. (1992). White privilege. *Creation Spirituality* (January/February), 33–35.

McLaren, P. (1994). *Life in schools: An introduction to critical pedagogy in the foundation of education.* White Plains, N.Y.: Longman.

Myers, L. J., Speight, S. L., Highlen, P. S., Cox, C. I., Reynolds, A. L., Adams, E. M., & Hanley, C. P. (1991). Individual development and world view: Toward an optimal conceptualization. *Journal of Counseling and Development* 70: 54–63.

Orner, M. (1992). Interrupting the calls for student voice in "liberatory" education: A feminist poststructuralist perspective. In C. Luke & J. Gore (eds.), *Feminisms and critical pedagogy.* New York: Routledge.

Polakow, V. (1992). Deconstructing the discourse of care: Young children in the shadows of democracy. In S. Kessler & B. Swadener (eds.), *Reconceptualizing the early childhood curriculum*. New York: Teachers College Press.

Sevig, T. D. (1993). Development and validation of the self-identity inventory: A pancultural instrument. *Dissertation Abstracts International*, 54, 54408A (University Microfilms No. 94-01353).

Tatum, B. D. (1992). Talking about race, learning about racism: The application of racial identity development theory in the classroom. *Harvard Educational Review* 62(1): 1–24.

Weaver, K. (1984). *One fine day* [film]. Patterson, N.Y.: Ishtar Films.

Wlodkowski, R. J., & Ginsberg, M. B. (1995). A framework for culturally responsive teaching. *Educational Leadership* 53(1): 17–21.

15. Lowering the Shields

Blumenfeld, W. (1992). *Homophobia: How we all pay the price*. Boston: Beacon Press.

Bowser, B. and R. Hunt (1981). *Impacts of racism on white Americans*. Beverly Hills, Calif.: Sage.

Britzman, D. P., Santiago-Válles, K., Jiménez-Múñoz, G., & Lamash, L. M. (1993). Slips that show and tell: Fashioning multiculture as problem of representation. In C. Cameron & W. Crichlow (eds.), *Race, identity and representation in education* (pp. 188–200). New York: Routledge.

Cannon, L. W. (1990). Fostering positive race, gender, and class dynamics in the classroom. *Women's Studies Quarterly* 27: 126–34.

Cose, E. (1995). *A man's world*. New York: Harper Collins.

Disch, E., & Thompson, B. (1990). Teaching and learning from the heart. *NWSA Journal* 2: 68–78.

Freire, P. (1970). *Pedagogy of the oppressed*. New York: Herder & Herder.

Fried, J. (1993). Bridging emotion and intellect: Classroom diversity in process. *College Teaching* 41(4): pp. 123–28.

Giroux, H., & McLaren, P. (1986). Teacher education and the politics of engagement: The case for democratic schooling. *Harvard Educational Review* 56(3): 213–38.

Kegan, R. (1982). *The evolving self: Problems and process in human development*. Cambridge, Mass.: Harvard University Press.

King, J. (1991). Dysconscious racism: Ideology, identity and the miseducation of teachers. *The Journal of Negro Education* 60(2): 133–46.

Kivel, Paul. (1992). *Men's work*. Center City, Minn.: Hazelton.

Lewis, M. (1990). Interrupting patriarchy: Politics, resistance and transformation in the feminist classroom. *Harvard Educational Review* 60:(4): 467–88.

McIntosh, P. (1985). Feeling like a fraud. *Stone Center work in progress*, Paper no. 18. Wellesley College, Wellesley, Mass.

———. (1988). White privilege and male privilege: A personal account of coming to see correspondences through work in women's studies. *The Stone Center work in progress paper*. Wellesley College, Wellesley, Mass.

Memmi, A. (1965). *The colonizer and the colonized.* Boston: Beacon Press.

Miller, J. B. (1976). *Toward a new psychology of women.* Boston: Beacon Press.

Minuchin, S., & Fishman, C. H. (1981). *Family therapy techniques.* Cambridge, Mass.: Harvard University Press.

Mogil, C., & Slepian, A. (1992). *We gave away a fortune.* Philadelphia: New Society Press.

Rogers, C. (1980). *A way of being.* Boston: Houghton Mifflin.

Roman, L. (1993). White is a color! White defensiveness, postmodernism and antiracist pedagogy. In C. Cameron & W. Crichlow (eds.), *Race, identity and representation in education* (pp. 71–88). New York: Routledge.

Romney, P., B. Tatum, & J. Jones. (1992). Feminist strategies for teaching about oppression: The importance of process. *Women's Studies Quarterly* 1 and 2: 95–110.

Sleeter, C. (1992). Resisting racial awareness: How teachers understand the social order from their racial, gender, and social class locations. *Educational Foundations* 6(2): 7–32.

Staub, E. (1978). *Positive social behavior and morality: Social and personal influences.* New York: Academic Press.

Tatum, B. T. (1992). Talking about race, learning about racism: The application of racial identity development theory in the classroom. *Harvard Educational Review* 62: 1–24.

———. (1994). Teaching white students about racism: The search for white allies and the restoration of hope. *Teachers College Record* 95(1): 462–76.

Terry, R. (1981). The negative impact on white values. In R. Bowser & R. Hunt (eds.), *Impacts of racism on white Americans* (pp. 119–52). Beverly Hills, Calif.: Sage.

Thompson, C. (1988). *As boys become men.* New York: Irvington.

———. (1992). On being heterosexual in a homophobic world. In W. Blumenfeld (ed.), *Homophobia: How we all pay the price.* Boston: Beacon Press.

Weiler, K. (1988). *Women teaching for change: Gender, class and power.* South Hadley, Mass.: Bergin & Garvey.

Wineman, S. (1984). *The politics of human services.* Boston: South End Press.

16. (E)strange(d) Relations

Alanen, L. (1988). Rethinking childhood. *Acta Sociologica* 31(1): 53–67.

Baldwin, J. [1963] (1988). A talk to teachers. In R. Simonson & S. Walker (eds.), *The graywolf annual five: Multicultural literacy* (pp. 3–12). Saint Paul, Minn.: Graywolf Press.

Bigelow, B. (1991). Discovering Columbus: Re-reading the past. In B. Bigelow, B. Niner, & B. Peterson (eds.), *Rethinking Columbus* (pp. 6–9). Milwaukee, Wisc.: Rethinking Schools.

Britzman, D. P., Santiago-Valles, K., Jimenez-Munoz, G., & Lamash, L. M. (1993). Slips that show and tell: Fashioning multiculture as a problem of representation. In C. McCarthy & W. Crichlow (eds.), *Race, identity, and representation in education* (pp. 188–200). New York: Routledge.

Buck-Morss, S. (1979). Socioeconomic bias in Piaget's theory. In A. R. Buss (ed.), *Psychology in social context* (pp. 349–64). New York: Irvington.

Clark, B. V. (1994). On ignoring the hidden laughter in the rose garden; or how our anxiety of immaturity enables us to belittle students. *Feminist Teacher* 8(1): 32–37.

Egan, K. (1983). *Education and psychology: Plato, Piaget and scientific psychology*. New York: Teachers College Press.

Freire, P., & Macedo, D. (1987). *Literacy: Reading the word and the world*. Boston, Mass.: Bergin & Garvey.

Henriques, J., Hollway, W., Urwin, C., Venn, C., & Walkerdine, V. (1984). *Changing the subject: Psychology, social regulation, and subjectivity*. London: Methuen.

Kincheloe, J. L., & Steinberg, S. R. (1993). A tentative description of post-formal thinking: The critical confrontation with cognitive theory. *Harvard Educational Review* 63(3): 296–320.

Kohn, A. (1994). The truth about self-esteem. *Phi Delta Kappan* 76(4): 272–83.

Lindsay, L. (1989). Nutrition and hunger: Two classroom approaches. In D. Gill and L. Levidow (eds.), *Anti-racist science teaching* (2d ed.) (pp. 94–106). London: Free Association Books.

McIntosh, P. (1988). White privilege and male privilege: A personal account of coming to see correspondences through work in women's studies. Wellesley, Mass.: Center for Research on Women.

Murrell, P. (1993). Afrocentric immersion: Academic and personal development of African American males in public schools. In T. Perry & J. W. Fraser (eds.), *Freedom's plow: Teaching in the multicultural classroom* (pp. 215–30). New York: Routledge.

Perry, T., & Fraser, J. W. (1993). Reconstructing schools as multiracial/multicultural democracies. In T. Perry & J. W. Fraser (eds.), *Freedom's plow: Teaching in the multicultural classroom* (pp. 3–26). New York: Routledge.

Rose, N. (1990). *Governing the soul: The shaping of the private self*. London: Routledge.

Schlesinger, Jr., A. M. (1992). *The disuniting of America: Reflections on a multicultural society*. New York: W. W. Norton.

Wexler, P. (1992). *Becoming somebody*. London: Falmer Press.

17. Teaching Within/Against the Backlash

Britzman, D. (1991). Decentering discourses in teacher education: Or, the unleashing of unpopular things. In K. Weiler & C. Mitchell (eds.), *What schools can do: Critical pedagogy and practice* (pp. 151–76). Albany: State University of New York Press.

Delpit, L. (1986). Skills and other dilemmas of a progressive black educator. *Harvard Educational Review* 56(4): 379–85.

———. (1988). The silenced dialogue: Power and pedagogy in educating other people's children. In L. Weis & M. Fine (eds.), *Beyond silenced voices:*

Class, race, and gender in United States schools (pp. 119–39). Albany: State University of New York Press.

Ellsworth, E. (1989). Why doesn't this feel empowering? Working through the repressive myths of critical pedagogy. *Harvard Educational Review* 59(3): 297–324.

Faludi, S. (1991). *Backlash: The undeclared war against American women.* New York: Doubleday.

Ferguson, K. (1984). *The feminist case against bureaucracy.* Philadelphia: Temple University Press.

Hall, S. (1981). Teaching race. In A. James & R. Jeffcoate (eds.), *The school in the multicultural society* (pp. 58–69). London: Harper & Row.

Hirsch, E. D. (1996). *The schools we need and why we don't have them.* New York: Doubleday.

hooks, b. (1994). *Teaching to transgress: Education as the practice of freedom.* New York: Routledge.

Jacoby, R. (1994). *Dogmatic wisdom: How the culture wars divert education and distract America.* New York: Anchor Books.

Kramer-Dahl, A. (1996) Reconsidering the notions of voice and experience in critical pedagogy. In C. Luke (ed.), *Feminisms and pedagogies of everyday life.* Albany: State University of New York Press.

Lewis, M., & Simon, R. (1986). A discourse not intended for her: Learning and teaching within patriarchy. *Harvard Educational Review* 56(4): 457–72.

McNeil, L. (1986). *Contradictions of control: School structure and school knowledge.* New York: Routledge.

Ng, R. (1995). Teaching against the grain: Contradictions and possibilities. In R. Ng, P. Staton, & J. Scane (eds.), *Anti-racism, feminism, and critical approaches to education* (pp. 129–52). Westport, Conn.: Bergin & Garvey.

Rosenberg, P. (1997). Underground discourses: Exploring whiteness in teacher education. In M. Fine, L. Weis, L. Powell, & L. Mun Wong (eds.) *Off white: Readings on race, power, and society* (79–89). New York: Routledge.

Sadker, M., & Sadker, D. (1994). *Failing at fairness: How America's schools cheat girls.* New York: Charles Scribner's Sons.

Scott, J. C. (1990). *Domination and the arts of resistance: Hidden transcripts.* New Haven, Conn.: Yale University Press.

Weiler, K. (1988). *Women teaching for change: Gender, class and power.* South Hadley, Mass.: Bergin & Garvey.

About the Contributors

Eve M. Adams is coordinator of services at the Center for Learning Assistance and adjunct assistant professor in the Department of Counseling and Educational Psychology from Ohio State University. Her professional interests include identity development of oppressed groups, the psychology of oppression, multicultural counseling, and outreach and consultation strategies to increase the appreciation of diversity.

Gary L. Anderson is a faculty member at the University of New Mexico and teaches in educational administration. His interests include educational administration, critical ethnography, and Latin American education.

Robert Bahruth has worked in multicultural classrooms since 1974. His book *Literacy con Cariño* tells the success story of migrant students he taught in Texas. He holds a Ph.D. in Bilingual Education from the University of Texas–Austin, where he also received the George I. Sanchez Endowed Presidential Scholarship for significant contributions to the field of minority education. He is professor of teacher education at Boise State University.

Mary Bentley is a faculty member at Ithaca College. At the time this chapter was written she was on faculty at the University of New Mexico. Her interests include health education, women's education, and cultural studies. She is the founder and creator of the Abiquiu Series on Women, a collaborative educational project for women in northern New Mexico.

Betsy J. Cahill is assistant professor and coordinator of early childhood education in the Department of Curriculum and Instruction at New Mexico State University. She received her M.S. in early childhood education with a focus in social policy and her Ph.D. in curriculum and instruction from Kent State University. Her interests include teacher education, early childhood education, and feminist scholarship.

GAILE S. CANNELLA, a faculty member at Texas A&M University, is a former elementary/early childhood teacher. Currently, she is focusing on critical theory, feminism, and postmodern perspectives as applied to teacher education. Her book, *Deconstructing Early Childhood Education*, offers critique of the field and the social construction of the "child."

RUDOLFO CHÁVEZ CHÁVEZ is a professor in the Department of Curriculum and Instruction at New Mexico State University. He teaches curriculum and multicultural education courses. His research interests include issues of why Chicano/Latino students are placed "at-risk," discovering the "isms" in preservice teacher education students, and multicultural teacher education curriculum.

BEVERLY E. CROSS is associate professor of curriculum theory at the University of Wisconsin–Milwaukee. Her specializations include curriculum planning and development, postmoderm curriculum theory, and urban school curriculum. Her research centers on curriculum development and decision making in urban schools through critical theory perspectives. The research primarily explores the relationship of curriculum decision making to what urban children have an opportunity to learn or not learn. She has authored several articles and book chapters that investigate issues of power, voice, and representation on the curriculum and teaching practices in urban schools.

JOZI DE LEÓN is associate professor in bilingual special education and bilingual education diagnostics at New Mexico State University. She has more than twenty-one years experience in language minority student education and twelve years in bilingual special education and assessment of language minority students. She is the director of a bilingual preschool for Mexican American children with special needs. Her research focuses on early childhood special education and culturally and linguistically diverse children.

LYNNE T. DÍAZ-RICO, associate professor of education at California State University, San Bernadino, teaches multicultural education and second language acquisition theory. She is co-author of the *Crosscultural, Language, and Academic Development Handbook* (Allyn & Bacon, 1995) and of articles on culturally compatible teaching and teacher induction. She is currently writing a book on the teaching of reading to English language learners.

MARK DRESSMAN is assistant professor of curriculum and instruction at

New Mexico State University, where he teaches a broad range of courses in literacy education and curriculum studies. He has recently published articles in *Curriculum Inquiry* and *Journal of Literacy Research*, as well as critical ethnographic study of the politics of literacy in three school libraries, *Ordered by Desire* (Bergin & Garvey, 1997). His current interests focus on the construction of adolescent identity in ethnographic texts, teacher-practice journals, and in the talk of English teachers and adolescents.

BERNARDO GALLEGOS is a faculty member at California State University, Los Angeles, where he teaches social foundations of education in the School of Education. He is a native of Albuquerque.

DIANE J. GOODMAN is a faculty member in the Educational Studies Department at the State University of New York at New Paltz. She has extensive experience teaching and consulting in diversity and human relations with a variety of organizations and universities. Her particular areas of interest include intergroup relations, experiental social justice education, and engaging people from privileged groups in multiculturalism.

KATHRYN HERR is a faculty member at the University of New Mexico. Her interests include middle level education, equity issues, school and community relations, and cultural studies. She is the editor of the interdisciplinary journal *Youth and Society*.

NANCY LESKO is associate professor of curriculum and instruction and women's studies at Indiana University, Bloomington. She teaches courses in multicultural education, feminist and poststructuralist educational theory, and curriculum studies. She has recently completed the books *Masculinities at school* (Sage, forthcoming), and *Act your age! Developing the modern scientific adolescent* (under review).

CATHERINE MEDINA is assistant professor of special education at Northern Arizona University. Her research has focused on issues related to bilingual/multicultural special education and the students identified as severely emotionally disturbed.

SONIA NIETO's scholarly work has focused on multicultural and bilingual education, the education of Latinos, curriculum reform, and Puerto Rican children's literature. She has written numerous articles and book chapters on these issues, as well as a book, *Affirming Diversity: The Sociopolitical Context of Multicultural Education* (Longman, 1996, 2d ed.). She has also edited a number of volumes and journals, the most recent being a co-edited volume with Ralph Rivera, *The Education of Latinos in Massachusetts: Research and Policy Consideration* (Boston: Gastón Institute, 1993). She has written articles in such journals as *The Harvard Educational Review*, *Multicultural Education*, and *Theory into Practice*.

JAMES O'DONNELL teaches in the Department of Curriculum and Instruction in the College of Education at New Mexico State University. His areas of interest are multicultural education, antiracist pedagogy, critical theory, curriculum theory and qualitative research.

CAROLYN R. O'GRADY is assistant professor of education and co-director of the Women's Studies Program at Gustavus Adolphus College in Minnesota.

SHARON O'MALLEY received her doctorate from the University of Houston. She is currently the director of bilingual and ESL programs in the Galveston Independent School District in Texas. Her research and policy interests include bilingual education and teacher development.

ROBERT ORTIZ is assistant professor of bilingual special education at New Mexico State University. He has a background in social work and special education. Dr. Ortiz's research interests have focused on parents of culturally and linguistically diverse children with special needs. His research has predominately focused on fathers' involvement in their children's literacy development.

SUSAN M. RUMANN is an assistant professor in bilingual education at the University of Houston–Downtown. Her professional experience, nationally and internationally, has been working with diverse populations from the fourth grade through the university level. Her major professional interests are in critical feminist pedagogy, literacy, and bilingual education.

ELIZABETH SAAVEDRA is a faculty member at the University of New Mexico and teaches courses in biliteracy development, cultural studies, and discourse analysis. Her interests include teacher transformation through study groups, biliteracy development, and critical literacy.

ROBERT W. SMITH is associate professor in the School of Education at the University of North Carolina at Wilmington, where he teaches courses in the foundations of education, multicultural education, and secondary social studies methods. His specialty is preparing preservice and inservice teachers to develop learning environments that support students from culturally diverse backgrounds. His particular area of interest is in working with white males to change stereotypical racist and sexist discrimination.

STANLEY STEINER is associate professor of teacher education at Boise State University. He teaches multicultural children's and young adult literature courses along with other literacy classes. He holds a Ph.D in curriculum and instruction from the University of Wyoming.

KIP TÉLLEZ received his Ph.D. from the Claremont Graduate School, and is now an assistant professor in the College of Education at the University of Houston. His research interests are multicultural teacher education, second language learning, and Latino youth issues in education, including the study of youth gangs.

Index